# Designing Distributed Applications

## With XML ASP IE5 LDAP and MSMQ

### Stephen T Mohr

Wrox Press Ltd. ®

# Designing Distributed Applications

Published by Wrox Press Ltd. Arden House,1102 Warwick Road,
Acocks Green, Birmingham, B27 6BH
Printed in USA
ISBN 1-861002-2-70

# Trademark Acknowledgements

# Credits

**Author**
Stephen T Mohr

**Additional Appendix Material**
Alex Homer

**Managing Editors**
Anthea Elston
Dominic Shakeshaft

**Editors**
Jon Duckett
Soheb Siddiqi
Karli Watson

**Index**
Catherine Alexander

**Technical Reviewers**
Michael Boerner
Robert Chang
Michael Corning
Jeff Dunham
Craig McQueen
Mark Oswald
Simon Robinson

**Design/Layout**
Mark Burdett
Noel Donnelly

**Cover**
Andrew Guillaume
Concept by Third Wave
Photo by Steve Sharp

To my wife, Denise, who kept the wheels turning while I was absorbed in this book, and for my sons, James and Matthew, for whom this book will be legacy code

# Table of Contents

# Table of Contents

# Introduction

The open standards and protocols of the Internet allow us to rapidly develop networked applications. These applications cannot exist without a network, because the tasks needed to realize an application's goals are distributed across numerous computers on the network. Each individual task is hosted by the machine best suited to accomplishing it. Since networked applications use Web protocols, they are accessible to almost anyone on the network. Indeed, most organizations are fielding intranet applications because they bring the benefits of the business to the most people at the least cost. As thoughtful programmers and administrators, we might begin wondering how to make sense of all the new applications on our networks. Widely accessible servers seem to be natural candidates for reuse. Ordinarily, however, servers are matched closely with a single client, usually developed concurrently with the server. When this happens, we repeat all the database logic and all the validation and business logic over and over again. As we move to deploy a new kind of application, we wonder if there isn't a better way.

What does it take to make a network application flexible enough that we can go on using it with new clients? We'll find in the course of this book that the application needs to be cooperative, promoting itself on the network and sharing data with clients of varying levels of sophistication. Processing should be distributed, with each task being accomplished on the network node best able to handle it. We'll want to define a set of principles for developing cooperative networked applications in terms of what can be accomplished with current Internet software.

Before we begin, however, we'll look at several initiatives for future distributed systems. While this trip through the crystal ball is exciting, most of us need to deliver applications that run on today's system, and deliver them sooner rather than later. Our look at the future is intended to help us identify techniques and practices we can use today in the hopes of building toward the benefits of the future. We'll look for common features in futuristic initiatives in the hopes of identifying goals for our own, present-day applications. The systems we'll examine are Microsoft Windows DNA, Microsoft Millenium, and Sun Jini. Although we'll have to learn enough about each technology to be able to make intelligent assessments, the object of this exercise is to extract the important enabling concepts rather than to become experts on any of these systems. We're looking for inspiration and guidance, not entertainment. By the end of the first chapter we'll have analyzed these futuristic projects, and will take what we have learnt from these prototypes to articulate 5 principles, which will form the foundation of how we think about developing our cooperative networked applications.

This book is about building distributed applications using open Internet protocols. While there is nothing to prevent you from using the techniques presented in this book over the public Internet, you will most likely find they are most useful on intranets and extranets between trusted partners. Although this is a technology book with lots of code samples, it is mainly about putting five simple principles to work in practical, real world applications. When you finish, you will have an informal philosophy of Web application development and an introduction to the new technologies that power it. You will also have some new utilities to provoke thought and jumpstart your own work.

# Definitions

Before tackling a topic as broad as internetworking and networked applications, we need to put some order and shape on the discussion. The best way to do that is by establishing some definitions right from the start. We need to know what we mean by **network application** and what we mean by **distributed computing**. This book is about **cooperative applications**, so we should also be clear on what that means. Our networks will play host to common **services**, so we'll define what *we* mean by that term. Of course, the meaning of these terms will only come into focus as we make our way through this book, but we need to have a sense of the journey we're embarking upon. In the course of building such software, we'll use **intranets** and the **Internet**, as well as **component software**.

# Network Applications

A simple definition of this term is any application that requires a network for its correct operation. Traditional client-server applications fit this definition, but what we have in mind is something closer to multi-tier applications. An application should *live* on the network, not just be resident on it. A server application in a networked system has an organic quality. It has a life cycle of enhancements and revisions (it will not necessarily require a complete re-build when our aims change). The number of distinct client applications that use it waxes and wanes depending on its utility and relevance to the practices of the business. While it runs, it fields dynamic requests and feeds clients with the data that drives their work. Such an application should make vital use of network resources in the implementation of its goals. A network application doesn't degrade when denied access to a network – it ceases to function. The logic of the application is partitioned into multiple tiers, each implementing a service such as data retrieval, business logic, or end user presentation and formatting. The communications and access to resources on other computers are at the heart of a network application.

# Distributed Computing

Where there are network applications, someone has thought about distributed computing. There are often many reasons to distribute computing tasks between two or more networked machines. To do this there must be an infrastructure to address the problems introduced by this distribution. A common set of basic services must also be provided to facilitate the construction of distributed applications. This is the environment in which network applications perform.

More than just networking protocols, distributed computing involves the segmentation of a job into subtasks across a network and the facilities offered by the network that enable a network application to integrate subtasks into a complete solution. Compare this to a craftsman's workshop. The workshop performs a variety of closely tied tasks with common tools in a common area. Now consider a modern assembly line. Each task is given its own area and tools with workers who specialize in that well-defined task. They become experts who are highly efficient and productive. If the overall process changes, we simply route the work through the task areas in a different sequence. We cannot easily do this in a craftsman's workshop because the overall work assumes certain relationships between the tools, the tasks, and the workspace. A traditional monolithic application is like that workshop. If we want to quickly develop effective applications and systems, we need to build well-defined and reusable task-oriented services. Security, resource identification, data exchange formats, and more are the tasks and services of a distributed computing environment. So, distributed computing spreads a single logical process over two or more physical machines joined by some communications protocol.

# Cooperative Applications

The history of computing is full of magnificent applications that were dead the day they were introduced. The programmers did a fine job crafting clever solutions to difficult problems, but the solutions were purpose-built for a single set of requirements. If someone else had a slightly different set of requirements, or the original application needed small enhancements, the whole edifice crumbled. This is a tragic waste of the talents of good programmers. Programmers would like their code to live on, helping those who come after them with new problems. Our clients, customers, and employers want code that works, code that can be maintained without heroic effort, and code that can accept change without self-destructing. I call applications that work in harmony with other applications and services on a network **cooperative applications**. They are robust, and the tasks they perform have a certain generality to them. They are designed with evolution in mind. They are accessed through clean interfaces and easily exchanged data formats and structures. This term is at the heart of this book. Some smart programmers are already writing network applications; the question for them is how a network application can be built so that the entire distributed computing environment is improved? How can a cooperative application be built in the face of real world concerns such as limited budgets, aggressive schedules, and incompatible legacy systems? Unlike applications developed in the classroom, real network applications are built by programming teams separated by time, space, and organizational boundaries. Real applications deal with issues of legacy servers and interfaces that cannot be changed without breaking other applications. We will see that the process of developing network applications is improved when the applications are cooperative.

As we might suspect from the term, cooperative applications share their data and logic. This is more than the simple exchange that must occur whenever two applications communicate across a network. We want to define the exchange in such a way that applications not yet written can easily negotiate an exchange format, even in the face of minor programming errors or evolving data definitions. Humans can tolerate small discrepancies when data is presented to them. If we are successful, our formats should give applications enough information to allow them to similarly tolerate small changes in the order of data fields or the loss of some items of information. The introduction of new and unknown data elements should not break older clients. For their part, client applications must defer to the network to obtain a connection with the servers they need. This will allow the distributed computing environment to remain robust and secure while users and resources are in flux. In short, then, a cooperative application is one that is a good citizen of the network, cooperating with the network infrastructure and other applications in an often ad hoc fashion to accomplish its goals.

Cooperative applications minimize the coordination needed between programming teams. With open standards and data exchange formats, teams may work independently on specialized tasks, secure in the knowledge that whole applications can be stitched together from their individual contributions. We cannot completely eliminate the need for some core commonality, of course. A shared philosophy of development is at the heart of cooperative network applications. It is a simple philosophy, as anything must be if it is to be widely adopted. This philosophy, combined with a few well-known resources, results in cooperative applications in a healthy networking environment.

# Services

We're accustomed to thinking of server-side code in terms of a single application. Generally, though, such code is intended to perform a specific task when approached via a well-defined interface. One of the great benefits of server-side code, whether in the client-server or multi-tier models, is the ability to have many clients or client applications use the same set of logic in the performance of a common task. This logic is centrally developed, configured, and managed, leading to a high degree of confidence in the quality and accuracy of the results served to client applications. If this task is generally useful and captures some helpful abstraction about the business or process at hand, then we have a black box that provides a **service** to any consumer who can understand the server code's interface.

In this book, we'll take 'service' to denote a generalized implementation of some widely useful task. Services are hosted on servers and accessed via an interface over Web protocols. Specifically, in this book we will implement services as **Active Server Pages** (**ASP**) running on a Web server and accessed using defined structures exchanged via HTTP. These data structures form two **vocabularies**: one for specifying the nature and parameters of a request for service, and one for returning the response to a request. We call these **query** and **response vocabularies**, respectively. As we will see in Chapters 3 and 4, the vocabularies used by our services will be in an implementation independent format that is widely accessible from all common computing platforms.

Services are named for the purpose of locating them by using the name of the vocabulary rather than the name of the implementation. For example, if I have an ASP that offers a service in terms of a `Customer` vocabulary in response to a `CustomerQuery` request vocabulary, a client would ask the network for the location of any or all services speaking either `Customer` or `CustomerQuery`. That way, we focus on the nature of the service rather than a particular implementation. Service implementations change more frequently than the processes they represent. After all, the service represents some task or function in the real world. We want to tie our services to what they model, not who is doing the modeling.

We use ASP for service implementation because it is a good balance between performance and convenience of implementation. Our definition of service does not require ASP, however. We are free to use any technology that is accessible via HTTP and fits the requirements of the system. Non-Microsoft environments might use Java servlets or NSAPI. The point is not the implementing technology but the abstraction of generally useful application logic in terms of Web-accessible, server-hosted resources.

# Intranets versus the Internet

Anyone writing about open standards internetworking must draw a line and say where intranets end and the Internet begins. An intranet, for our purposes, is a controlled environment. When designing a network application for an intranet we can make certain assumptions about available resources and supported technologies. The owner of the network controls the choice and selection of these resources. The network itself consists of one or more low-latency local area networks. An internet formed by joining smaller networks, or the *public* Internet, by contrast, affords the application designer fewer assumptions. We are then restricted to open internetworking standards like HTML and HTTP. One or more wide area network segments generally separate clients and servers; this will usually be the public Internet. Clearly, there will be times when the distinction is blurred. When designing an application that is to be used, not only by our employer, but also by our employer's suppliers, we might well use the public Internet for its communications but require agreed-upon security measures and even specified, proprietary technologies. This is the case for **extranets**. An extranet uses the Internet for transport, but uses some form of secure identification and authentication to allow trusted partners to work more closely than they would in the anonymity of the Internet. They would use security measures such as digital certificates and certifying authorities for identification. Public key encryption would secure their data from outside parties despite the fact that the data is travelling outside the secure confines of the partners' internal networks. The key is control. Intranets are networks using open standards, but within these networks the administrator controls logical definitions, formats, and protocols as well as guaranteeing access to some set of resources.

# Component Software

Strictly speaking, neither our vision of cooperative network applications, nor the more commonly accepted concept of distributed computing, requires component software. Components, however, have become an important, practical tool for the implementation of complex applications, and our examples will be no exception. Component software is based on the idea of building programs from smaller blocks of code that are called by the application at runtime. COM on Microsoft Windows (sometimes called ActiveX) and JavaBeans are two well-known component software technologies in common use. Components are generally object-oriented, and are always intended to be installed on the host system for dynamic use by any number of applications.

Many Web developers will be unfamiliar with component software. Much of the enabling framework is new, difficult, and sometimes arcane. Improvements to the enabling framework technology, the use of 4GL (fourth generation languages) for building components, and experience are all simplifying the task of developing COM, CORBA, and JavaBean components. The Web developer, however, need not understand how to build components using these frameworks. For our purposes, component software technologies accessible from Web scripting languages are ideal. We'll be able to drop chunks of features into Web pages with little effort. We'll gain the benefits of discrete chunks of code without having to be familiar with the internal workings of the code. We can always buy useful components from third parties as we need them. Best of all, once a component is thoroughly tested, we know any application that uses the component will perform the same task in the same way using the same rules. We'll be able to quickly prototype systems and build finished applications simply by integrating pre-built blocks of functionality.

Components are, at present, built on top of proprietary technologies. No component technology has yet been endorsed by an international standards body chiefly involved with internetworking. As such, we can't use components to communicate directly between clients and servers without degrading the cooperative nature of the network. Such use would assume the presence of specific enabling technology and language features. It doesn't violate the cooperative spirit, however, to use component technology within one part of a network application. This is precisely what we shall do, using component technology to simplify the task of rapidly developing one service or task within a larger, distributed application that executes on the network.

We've established a common understanding of some terms we'll use throughout this book. We've also set some high expectations and hopes for the applications we shall build. This is an exciting time to be involved with distributed, Web-based application development. The technology is changing daily, and the business opportunities expand almost exponentially as traditional businesses seek to expand into e-commerce and intranet applications. If this field is to be more than a passing fad we, as professional and dedicated programmers, will have to strive to realize the promise of networking through the implementation of cooperative applications. It's time to get to work and build the tools we need.

## What Does This Book Cover?

The majority of this book is given over to introducing programmers to some of the technologies required for building distributed applications for Web environments. There are lots of code samples, and we'll cover a lot of products and techniques. This is not a book about teaching the use of specific tools, however. You'll learn a lot about such things as directories, messaging, and the Extensible Markup Language (XML), but we cannot hope to explore so much ground in fine detail. The technology surveys are designed to show why a particular technology or technique is important to distributed applications. You will have a better idea about when and where to use the technologies presented. You'll learn techniques that help promote the principles of cooperative applications. You should be challenged to learn more. Any one of the base technologies covered in these chapters can be, and in most cases has been, expanded into a book of its own.

We'll start by learning how to explore a network's resources through the use of **directories**, data stores that guide users and applications to the resources they need in response to runtime queries. We'll use XML to implement our own techniques for handling common data exchange problems in real world networks. We introduce an older technology, messaging middleware, which helps Web applications remain responsive while scaling to very high levels of service. We'll even turn our use of XML on its head by using a database-oriented technology to manipulate the data we exchange between services.

The last three chapters of the book are devoted to case studies in a fictional business. We use the tools and techniques presented in the earlier chapters to show how programmers can cope with practical challenges. We build simple applications that should be recognizable as the sort of systems that real world businesses need to develop in a Web-based world. We even cause our fictional programmers to commit errors that are typical of those that occur every day in order to show how later programming teams can use our principles and techniques to overcome the problems stemming from those errors.

The focus throughout is on giving working programmers the tools they need to develop advanced Web applications for the new world of intranets, extranets, and e-commerce. While the specific technology introductions we offer will help working programmers, the real benefit and goal of this book is in the principles and philosophy you will learn as you work through the examples.

# Who Is This Book For?

This book assumes you have a basic understanding of Web development. In particular, you should have a good understanding of HTML and Javascript. VBScript is used in Chapter 2 for some tasks, but the remainder of our examples will be in JavaScript. We are using Active Server Pages (ASP) and Microsoft Internet Information Server for our Web server technology, so you should know how to put together a typical ASP.

One open standard that is fundamental to our approach is the Extensible Markup Language (XML). It is introduced in Chapter 3, but this book does not aim to teach you XML. Rather, we will use it as a tool to help us move forward. A good introductory book on XML is *XML Applications* (Wrox Press, ISBN 1-861001-5-25). The World Wide Web Consortium (W3C) is the key standards body for XML. At the time of writing, they had only recently issued recommendations for XML and its associated Document Object Model (DOM). We believe strongly in using the DOM. One of the first XML tools to implement this model is the MSXML parser, which is a COM component that is installed with Microsoft Internet Explorer. While MSXML first appeared with IE 4.0, its DOM implementation debuts with IE 5.0. All the examples in this book use that version of the component.

Some of the technologies needed for distributed development are not new, but come from outside the world of Web development. Two of these are network directory services and messaging systems. We have chosen to illustrate their use using the Active Directory implemented in Microsoft Windows 2000 and Microsoft Message Queue, available with the Windows NT 4.0 option pack. These implementations were chosen for two reasons. Firstly, they will be readily available to many readers of this book due to the huge installed base of the Windows operating system. Secondly, their APIs are exposed through COM components that may be readily programmed through Web-based script code. While COM development may sometimes be an advanced topic, any intermediate or advanced Web script programmer can use COM components. These components are the fastest way to get access to a new API from Web applications.

We will develop a few components of our own in this book. Rest assured, however, you will not have to become a COM programmer fluent in C++ or Java. We will be using Microsoft's scripting technology beta implementation. This involves two scripting technologies, called scriptlets and DHTML scriptlets. DHTML scriptlets appeared with IE 4.0 and let you expose script in HTML pages as components that can be embedded in other Web pages. That was refined in beta to introduce simple scriptlets. Scriptlets allow you to write COM components using script code and access them from any tool – browsers, Visual Basic, C++ – that permits you to use COM components. Although you wouldn't write high performance production COM components in JavaScript, scriptlets provide a fast and inexpensive way to prototype and test COM interfaces. You can use them in small-scale applications, too. We will use scriptlets because I want to make component development accessible to the average Web developer. When you see the advantages of deploying business logic in component form, you may be inspired to investigate COM programming with compiled languages. This book has an interest in using component software, but it is not intended to teach COM development itself.

Finally, this book is for any programmer who is enthusiastic about the potential for application development using Web tools and techniques.

# What You'll Need To Use This Book

Internet Explorer 5.0 is almost essential to using this book. If you do not have IE 5.0 available to you for some reason (your company might use an earlier version for instance), you can use the parser (MSXML.DLL) from IE 5.0 with IE 4.0. MSXML has some dependencies on other DLLs, but these are installed with both IE 4.0 and 5.0. Most of the examples we develop, particularly in Chapters 3 and 4, will run on IE 4.0 with the newer MSXML version installed. Some examples in Chapter 6 require IE 5.0, as do the case studies in chapters 8 and 10.

You will need Windows NT running IIS for the majority of the examples. However, you will need access to Windows 2000 and its Active Directory in order to make full use of the component we develop in Chapter 2. Since this is in late beta as this book goes to press, we have included a stub version of the component that can be used by anyone running Windows NT, Windows 95/98, and the Windows scripting technology. If you use Active Directory, you will also need the Active Directory Service Interface components, version 2.0, which are freely available for download from Microsoft's site. The full source code for our components and examples can be downloaded from our Web site at `http://www.wrox.com/Store/Details.asp?Code=2270` or our UK site, which also features some working samples, `http://webdev.wrox.co.uk/books/2270`.

Chapter 7 requires an installation of Microsoft Message Queue. This is bundled with current shipments of Windows NT Server. It is also available for free download from Microsoft as part of the Windows NT 4.0 option pack. The messaging components we build are not used in the case studies, however, so you may work through those examples without Message Queue.

# Conventions Used

We use a number of different styles of text and layout in the book to help differentiate between different kinds of information. Here are some examples of the styles we use and an explanation of what they mean:

> **These boxes hold important, not-to-be forgotten, mission critical details that are directly relevant to the surrounding text.**

*Background information, asides and references to information located elsewhere appear in text like this.*

❑ **Important Words** are in a bold font
❑ Words that appear on the screen, such as menu options, are in a similar font to the one used on the screen – the File menu, for example
❑ All filenames are in this style: SvcCustomer.asp
❑ Functions and methods look like this: WriteSvcCustomerBody()

Code that's new, important or relevant to the current discussion will be presented like this:

```
function WriteSvcCustomerBody(rsSvcCustomers)
{
    Response.Write("<SvcCustomer>");
    WriteCustomerBody(rsSvcCustomers);
    Response.Write("<SvcPlan>" + rsSvcCustomers("cust_plan") + "</SvcPlan>");
    Response.Write("</SvcCustomer>");
}
```

However, code that you've seen before, or which has little to do with the matter at hand, looks like this:

```
function WriteSvcCustomerBody(rsSvcCustomers)
{
    Response.Write("<SvcCustomer>");
    WriteCustomerBody(rsSvcCustomers);
    Response.Write("<SvcPlan>" + rsSvcCustomers("cust_plan") + "</SvcPlan>");
    Response.Write("</SvcCustomer>");
}
```

# Tell Us What You Think

We've tried to make this book as accurate and enjoyable as possible, but what really matters is what the book actually does for you. Please let us know your views, either by returning the reply card in the back of the book, or by contacting us via e-mail at feedback@wrox.com

# Source Code

All the source code from the examples in this book is available for download from the Wrox Press web site:

```
http://www.wrox.com
http://webdev.wrox.co.uk
```

# Support

We've made every effort to make sure there are no errors in the text or the code. However, to err is human and as such we recognize the need to keep you, the reader, informed of any mistakes as they're spotted and corrected. The web site acts as a focus for providing the following information and support:

- ❑ Errata sheets
- ❑ Information about current and forthcoming titles
- ❑ Sample chapters
- ❑ Source code downloads
- ❑ An e-mail newsletter
- ❑ Articles and opinion on related topics

Errata sheets are available for all our books – please download them, or take part in the continuous improvement of our products and upload a 'fix' or a pointer to the solution.

# About the Author

Stephen Mohr is an experienced software architect working for an e-commerce and Web solutions consultancy. Having programmed and designed object-based applications in C++ and COM, he now designs architectures for systems and products using COM, Java, and Web development tools. He was responsible for the selection of XML for several ongoing Web-based projects. He has also developed numerous intranet applications using advanced Web programming techniques. A former Air Force officer with experience in ballistic missile operations, Stephen holds BS and MS degrees in computer science from Rensselaer Polytechnic Institute. His research interests include distributed systems and the practical application of artificial intelligence technology.

# Learning The 5 Principles of Cooperative Network Application Development

We often look back at events with the benefit of hindsight, wishing that we had known what was going to happen before we embarked on a task. The world of computing is evolving at such a rapid pace that, if we want to be developing applications that will survive in the workplace (perhaps so that we can build on them rather than re-building them – and hopefully get ourselves more business in the process), we can learn a lot by attempting to look into the future.

Of course, if I had a crystal ball that could really tell the future, I would have already earned my millions and could be sailing around the world. The next best thing is to look at current research efforts that are leading the field so we can learn how others see the future shaping up. In this first chapter we will be looking at three initiatives for future distributed systems. We'll look for common features in the hopes of identifying goals for our own, present-day applications. We'll examine 3 systems:

- ❑ Microsoft Windows DNA
- ❑ Microsoft Millenium
- ❑ Sun Jini

Although we'll have to learn enough about each technology to be able to make intelligent assessments, the object of this exercise is to extract the important enabling concepts rather than to become experts on any of these systems.

Having seen the enabling concepts that make each system so special, we will see how the principles on which they are based can be applied within current boundaries. Our findings will form the foundation for the rest of the book. By looking at the aims of distributed computing tomorrow, we can address the principles of building distributed applications today. So, what are these visions?

# Looking at Future Visions

Our desire is to direct our intranet development in such a way that the resulting network actually promotes further development. Each application should draw from existing resources while adding its own resources to the network. No substantial application should be a dead end. Enhancements to applications should be organic, adding something to what came before without destroying it. This is the principal benefit of cooperative network applications. However, we need some specific goals and principles to guide us.

We can look to some future systems for inspiration. They won't provide the complete solution as they are focused on operating system enhancements and are therefore proprietary. Two of the systems we will look at are research efforts. They do, however, aim to provide powerful support for distributed computing. First, we shall look at Microsoft Windows DNA. This is an emerging effort to integrate and improve a variety of component-based technologies on the Windows platform. Next, we will look deeply into the future with Microsoft's distributed computing research project Millennium. Finally, we will hit the middle ground as we look at Sun Microsystem's Jini, the prototype distributed computing environment for Java development.

Remember that this is not simply an excursion into the realm of technical prediction. All of the systems build on the existing state of the art in distributed computing. Each represents the best efforts of top-notch talent to drive the art toward a better future. Each, to some greater or lesser extent, will influence current and near-term practice. Windows DNA, for example, is rapidly coming to fruition. It is the future of the most widely deployed desktop operating system. Meanwhile, Jini is enjoying a high level of exposure for its promise to integrate disparate devices on a common network. Although we cannot realize the full potential of these efforts – which is why they are systems for a future day – we can glean useful insight into the best practices in distributed computing. We will learn concepts that we can apply in smaller measure today, improving our applications in the process. In adopting these practices, we will, by default, align our present-day systems with future platforms and allow our systems to grow. Once we finish our examination of the future, we will return to the problems of the practical world and see what we can distill from our trip.

## Windows DNA

Windows **DNA – Distributed interNet Applications** Architecture – draws on existing operating system technologies and adds enhancements designed to aid the development of professional-grade component-based applications. Many of the technologies embraced by the term pre-date the DNA program. The program is really an attempt to unify related efforts and better communicate Microsoft's vision for the Windows platform. DNA seeks to bring together the best features of Web-centric computing and personal computers. It aims to do this by building a platform for robust, PC-centric network computing. Of necessity, it extends the Windows platform in two directions:

- ❑ Toward the communications-based model of the Web, which we refer to as **Web Metaphor Computing**
- ❑ Deeper into network and operating system services

### *Pieces of DNA*

Some of the pieces of DNA are present in the current Windows platform. Others are due in Windows 2000 Server (the new name for Windows NT5) or later. All are part of, or closely related to, the Windows operating system. Some are evolutionary improvements to core operating system services – networking, security, file and print services, for example – while others are application-oriented services like encryption.

Application-oriented services are not essential to the core operating system, but dramatically improve the common features available to programs written for the platform. They provide a rich infrastructure on which developers can build large-scale, robust network applications.

| Web Metaphor Computing | Availability and Comments |
| --- | --- |
| Dynamic HTML | Available since IE 4.0 |
| Scripting | Currently available |
| Familiar Web-based user interface | Available since Windows 95/Windows NT 4.0 |
| HTTP servers and clients | Currently available |
| **Component Software** | |
| COM components, COM+ | Currently available; tool support for COM+ is forthcoming |
| **Network Services** | |
| Transactions | Available now; will be more closely tied to components when language enhancements for COM+ become available |
| Queued messaging communications | Available now; coming to components with COM+ |
| Security | Upgraded to Kerberos with Windows 2000 |
| Directory services | Coming with Windows 2000 |
| Universal data storage and database access | Currently available and evolving |
| Central network administration | Evolving |

## Web Metaphor Computing

Windows DNA envisions a Web-based interface as its dominant user interface and Web-style communications as a major link between application-level components. To this end, Microsoft continues to integrate its Web browser technology with the operating system. On the client, Internet Explorer is the core browsing and rendering engine. While on the server, Windows NT comes bundled with Internet Information Server (IIS). IIS provides some valuable extensions to the basic HTTP server model such as in-process scripted extensions and session state maintenance to facilitate the construction of Web-based applications that are implemented by drawing on the features provided by the Windows platform.

If Web-based techniques are to be a core paradigm for building applications, both browsers and servers must provide advanced features and robust performance. Microsoft's version of **dynamic HTML** (**DHTML**) adheres closely to the W3C document object model (DOM). Introduced with version 4.0 of their Web browser, DHTML provides powerful layout and presentation features. In addition, its event model allows Web pages to be highly interactive. DHTML permits a level of interactivity such as is seen in Java applets with performance typical of in-page scripts. Future versions of the Web browsing client will improve the performance of interface elements to achieve results closer to that experienced with applications written with compiled languages.

We will also make use of **scriptlets** in subsequent chapters as we develop some utilities for Web development. Scriptlets are reusable chunks of DHTML functionality formed by combining browser-based scripting with the COM component software technology provided by Windows.

The introduction of PCs led to a shift in power and control away from centralized mainframe applications. Each desktop computer hosted applications rich in features and interactivity. While this was satisfying to end users – who could now control the configuration and availability of the computing services available to them – it made central management and support of applications difficult and expensive. Web-based applications strive to combine the best features of the two models and strike a balance between them. The portion of the application residing on the user's local computer is comparatively thin, containing only that code needed to present results and an interactive interface to the user. Feature rich, fast HTML browsers permit applications to offer a thin client implementation of rich user interfaces tied to powerful server-based applications. The chief advantage of this is that programmers can rapidly produce new user interfaces to existing services using DHTML and script code. Windows DNA not only provides a rich client browser, but also integrates the browser into the core operating system to ensure the availability of these user interface services.

## Component Software

Windows' component software technology is the Component Object Model (COM). Available for several years, COM provides binary level reuse of object-based software components. COM is officially neutral with regard to the choice of a programming language for implementing COM components. Many languages have been used to build COM components, including C++, Java, Visual Basic, SmallTalk and COBOL. Microsoft is promoting COM by releasing new operating system services as COM components and building new applications, notably Internet Explorer, from COM components. Access to databases and the forthcoming directory service, for example, is through COM object frameworks. Beginning with Internet Explorer 4.0, Web page scripts may be exposed as COM components for reuse in other browser-based applications. The scripting technology supported by Windows is also evolving so that COM components may be written in script, and be available to any application on the same basis as traditional COM components. We will see – and build – examples of this later in this book.

Why should Web developers care about component software? Component software technologies, especially COM and CORBA, have a reputation for being the province of advanced C++ programmers. Sometimes they are regarded as being too hard and expensive for practical use. One of the benefits of Web applications is the ability to rapidly prototype (and sometimes even deploy) a new application. The techniques are extremely flexible. Scripting languages are relatively easy to learn, and script code is easily changed. There is no compiling, so, if it doesn't work, we can change it and try again. Browsers and HTML offer powerful user interface features; try changing a dialog box written in a compiled language, then change an HTML form and see if it isn't faster. Components supercharge Web page development. Regardless of how hard they are to develop, they are no harder to use from script than the elements of a browser's document object model. On the server, components offer pre-built chunks of functionality to script, and you can buy many useful components from a thriving market of third-party vendors. Most of these components are implemented in compiled languages, so you get the features *and* good runtime performance.

Equally important is the fact that the vendors of component technologies are working to simplify the task of building new components. COM was originally the exclusive domain of C++ developers. Many components are now written in Visual Basic, and Microsoft is even testing technology to allow script programmers to build COM components.

As already mentioned, you are going to see numerous examples of such components throughout this book, and all the components in our toolkit are written exclusively in JavaScript and VBScript. If you have a useful bit of code, you can easily and quickly package it as a component. This is an excellent way to rapidly prototype components!

Windows DNA continues the evolution of COM with a body of enhancements collectively known as COM+. The enhancements deal chiefly with performance, integration with operating system services, and simplified implementation through implementation language support.

### Performance Enhancements in COM+

The runtime environment provided by the Windows 2000 operating system has been modified to provide faster access to components, role-based security, and load balancing. The registry of COM components and their implementing software is also cached in memory, which greatly speeds the process of locating software and instantiating a component instance. For a long time programmers have asked for the ability to make asynchronous calls on COM components, contending that synchronous calls are not scalable. This is largely because a synchronous call on a COM component may time out if too many clients are making method invocations against a single remote component. The result is a failure from the point of view of the calling client. Applications relying on synchronous calls are unduly delayed when making calls against a heavily loaded server, so COM+ introduces the ability to make queued, asynchronous calls to COM components.

### Integration with Operating System Services

COM+ is well integrated with operating system services, such as data access and transaction processing. COM+ also introduces a new concept called **interception**. Interception permits the dynamic redirection of processing in response to events and method calls. A component programmer indicates that some particular operating system or custom service should be used by his application in conjunction with particular method calls or types of operations. At runtime, calls to that component are intercepted by the operating system and redirected to the appropriate service. For example, a component might use interceptors to provide transparent access to transaction services provided by the operating system. It might also intercept instance creation calls and implement a load-balancing scheme for scalability. Using interceptors, the properties of a component may even be dynamically bound to the fields of a database table. Windows NT has added several services to the basic operating system in the last few years, and COM+ allows component programmers easy access to them through interception.

### Simplified Implementation

While interceptors can be used to offer increased functionality, they can also simplify the basic task of programming COM components. Default implementations of basic COM tasks are provided by the COM+ runtime. A standard implementation for firing events is provided, for example. Prior to COM+, a programmer had to write this code himself, or make reference to some library implementation of these services. COM+ uses a declarative programming model for this. Keywords are added to component declarations as attributes, and compilers that understand COM+ provide stubs invoking the appropriate service for the attribute at runtime. Taking the example of firing an event, the programmer indicates that a COM+ component fires events from a particular interface through a keyword declaration in his code. The proper stubs to maintain lists of components wishing to receive those events are added by the compiler. When he wishes to fire a particular event in the body of the component implementation, the programmer simply invokes the method he wishes to fire. The runtime intercepts the call and walks the list, ensuring listeners receive the event.

*Next I'm going to present several code fragments in order to illustrate the benefits of COM+ as compared to current COM practice. I will alternate between COM+ and the equivalent COM code. These are necessarily code fragments and must not be taken for complete implementations. In particular, I will concentrate on the declarations, leaving the actual implementing code aside. My emphasis here is on showing Web developers – many of whom will not be COM and C++ programmers – the coming changes in Windows and COM+, and how component development is made easier as part of our look into the future.*

Consider a hypothetical plant manufacturing application. We have tanks holding some volume of fluid. During the manufacturing process, we charge the tank with some amount of fluid and later drain the tank of some amount of fluid. The charging process can incur faults due to leaks, overfilling, or a blocked transfer line. We can model this in COM and COM+ as a tank component that sources (fires) events to some component monitoring the process. Here is the COM+ declaration for the tank and fault event interfaces:

```
cointerface ITank
{
    float ChargeTank([in]int nSourceTankID, [in]float fVolume);
}

cointerface IChargingFaultEvent
{
    void Leak(String strFaultText);
    void OverCharge(String strFaultText);
    void LineBlockage(String strFaulttext);
}
```

The keyword `cointerface` specifies that these are COM interfaces.

Here's the C++ declaration for a COM+ component representing a tank full of hydrazine:

```
coclass HydrazineTank: implements ITank, fires IChargingFaultEvent
{
    // indicate transactions required, state model, source of data, thread model
    attributes:
        transaction = "required";
        state = "stateless";
        data_source = "DSN=FluidTankDatabase";
        threading = "single";
    public:
        Pump m_pTransferPump;
        DataSource m_dsTank;
        // indicates that the value of m_fVolume comes from a column in the
        // db referenced by the DSN named in m_dsTank
        [source=m_dsTank, column="cur_volume"] float m_fVolume;
        float ChargeTank(int nSourceSerial,
                         float fTransferAmount) throws SQLException;
};
```

The keyword `coclass` indicates that this class will be the implementation of a COM component. This causes the compiler to provide some basic code required by all COM/COM+ components. We've indicated that it implements the `ITank` interface and fires events from the `IChargingFaultEvent` interface.

The attributes section tells the operating system several important pieces of information. First, our component requires a transaction. In COM, this cannot be done in code; instead, we have to manually perform some configuration in Microsoft Transaction Server (MTS) and add lines of code delineating the boundaries of the transaction. Next, we've indicated this is a stateless object – it does not guarantee persistent state between method invocations. This should improve scalability because resources consumed by the component may be released between method calls, but it requires us to store the volume of the tank in the database rather than in a member variable. Following this, we've indicated the source of data for the volume of the tank represented by this component. The value of `m_dsTank` is a DSN that refers to the database in which the volume is stored. The runtime may fetch the value of the `cur_volume` column and cache it in memory in our COM+ implementation. This value can be selectively refreshed from the database. In COM, we would need to do this retrieval in code every time we needed to get the value. Finally, we've indicated the threading model. The features declared by these attributes are implemented through interception. The attribute keywords tell the compiler to attach the proper stubs to our component. At runtime, these stubs intercept method calls and property references and perform the necessary tasks.

Now contrast this with a similar component declaration using present-day COM. We will use C++ to fully contrast the COM+ implementation with a COM implementation in the same implementation language. Admittedly, a Visual Basic or Java implementation would be simpler. Using the ActiveX Template Library and Microsoft Visual Studio version 6.0, the work done by the first line of the COM+ declaration – declaring this to be a COM component and indicating the interfaces used – requires the following:

```
class ATL_NO_VTABLE CHydrazineTank :
   public CComObjectRootEx<CComSingleThreadModel>,
   public CComCoClass<CHydrazineTank, &CLSID_HydrazineTank>,
   public IDispatchImpl<ITank, &IID_ITank, &LIBID_SAMPLETANKLib>
{

   ...
   BEGIN_COM_MAP(CHydrazineTank)
      COM_INTERFACE_ENTRY(ITank)
      COM_INTERFACE_ENTRY(IDispatch)
      ...
   END_COM_MAP()
   ...
```

In addition to declaring this to be a COM object exposing the `ITank` interface, we also managed to squeeze in a declaration of the component's threading model. Clearly, though, the COM+ declaration is more readable and efficient from the programmer's standpoint.

Returning to the COM+ declaration, the member variable `m_TransferPump` is a pointer to a COM object representing the pump that transfers fluid in and out of our tank. When we wish to create an instance of this component for use with our tank component, we simply use the following lines in COM+:

```
m_pTransferPump = new Pump();
if (m_pTransferPump == NULL)
   ... // some error handling code
```

In COM, assuming the COM libraries are initialized, we require:

```
m_pTransferPump = NULL;
HRESULT hr = ::CoCreateInstance(CLSID_PUMP, NULL, CLSCTX_INPROC_SERVER,
                              IID_IPumpInterface, (void **)&m_pTransferPump);
```

```
if (SUCCEEDED(hr))
{
    ... // okay to use
}
```

When our tank object detects a fault, we want to fire an event. In COM+, that's as simple as:

```
OverCharge(strFaultText);
```

The COM+ runtime handles the task of alerting all the monitoring objects that have connected to our tank component for monitoring purposes. In COM, we have to do the work ourselves:

```
IEnumConnections    *pEnum;
CONNECTDATA         cd;

If (FAILED(m_rgpConnectionPt[0]->EnumConnections(&pEnum)))
    return FALSE;

While (NOERROR==pEnum->Next(1, &cd, NULL))
{
    IChargingFaultEvent *pEvt;

    if (SUCCEEDED(cd.pUnk->QueryInterface(IID_IChargingFault, (PPVOID)&pEvt)))
    {
        pEvt->OverCharge(strFaultText);
        pEvt->Release();
    }
    cd.pUnk->Release();
}
pEnum->Release();
```

COM+ offers features using the transaction and state attributes, which require much more work to achieve in COM. First, programming a stateless component is as much philosophy as declaration, whether we use COM or COM+. We have to be sure we don't rely on state between method calls. COM+ provides some default implementations for tasks that a COM programmer using MTS (Microsoft Transaction Server) must provide himself. MTS will assist the programmer by notifying the program when the runtime environment is going to take action that will disrupt state, provided the COM component supports the `IObjectControl` interface. This adds an entry to our interface map and three methods, declared as follows:

```
BEGIN_COM_MAP(CHydrazineTank)
    ...
    COM_INTERFACE_ENTRY(IObjectControl)
    ...
END_COM_MAP()

public:
    STDMETHOD(Activate)();
    STDMETHOD_(BOOL, CanBePooled)();
    STDMETHOD_(void, Deactivate)();

    CComPtr<IObjectContext> m_spObjectContext;
```

The member variable m_spObjectContext is a pointer to an interface supported by the MTS runtime environment that allows the object to signal when it is ready to release state. This allows the runtime to reclaim resources. When the component has finished some section of work and wishes to indicate that it no longer needs to hold state, it would make the following call:

```
m_spObjectContext->SetComplete();
```

If it could not complete and wished to give up state, it would call the SetAbort() method of the IObjectContext interface.

To ensure that the component always executes within a transaction, the administrator installing the component in a particular MTS environment must configure the component's transaction attribute in the MTS runtime for Requires a Transaction or Requires a New Transaction, thereby calling for automatic transaction control.

Hopefully, these comparisons of code fragments have convinced you that COM+ simplifies life for the component creator. By giving the compiler knowledge of many of the available system services, COM+ frees the programmer to concentrate on the semantics of his application. The programmer only has to declare what services should be involved with his component and the compiler becomes responsible for adding the integration stubs needed to make this happen. Additionally, COM+ allows enforcement of the programmer's transaction requirements, thereby ensuring consistency and reducing the system administrator's burden.

## Network Services

A modern operating system offers key services essential to computing, such as file and print services. Applications written to the platform tend to have some common requirements, and implementations answering these needs tend to be added to the operating system over time. These services, such as networking support and security features, are needed by many applications. Although arguably not part of the core operating system, they are so useful that programmers come to depend on them. The popularity of UNIX and Windows stem in part from the rich application services that are bundled with the core operating system. Any operating system that aspires to run mission critical applications in an inherently networked environment requires some key services which are not ordinarily found in a stand-alone environment. Windows DNA builds on existing services and adds new ones in an effort to prepare Windows NT for mission critical enterprise computing tasks. Let's take a look at some of these:

| Feature | Status in Windows NT 4.0 | Status in Windows 2000 Server |
| --- | --- | --- |
| Security | Proprietary method | Ability to use various methods; Kerberos is used by default |
| Network Administration | Microsoft Management Console offers a basic framework for adding management components | Features for replicating a standard configuration to networked machines from a server added and management generally improved |
| Directory services | Proprietary, local registry performs similar function | Active Directory introduces a true directory service oriented to the needs of this operating system |

*Table Continued on Following Page*

| Feature | Status in Windows NT 4.0 | Status in Windows 2000 Server |
|---|---|---|
| Transaction Processing | Microsoft Transaction Server (MTS) and Distributed Transaction Coordinator offer this to COM components | MTS features merged with COM+ |
| Messaging Middleware | Microsoft Message Queue (MSMQ), now bundled with NT Server, previously available with the NT4 Option Pack | MSMQ used by COM+ to offer asynchronous method invocations on components |
| Universal Data Access | COM object frameworks available; support varies by database vendor | Continues; designated as the core infrastructure for data access in Windows 2000 |

### Security

The security services built into versions of Windows NT prior to Windows 2000 Server were proprietary and faulted by many for weakness and a lack of scalability. Windows 2000 Server introduces an implementation of the Kerberos network security protocol as its default security service. Not only does this strengthen security, it also increases interoperability with other operating systems. Implementations of Kerberos, which originated at the Massachusetts Institute of Technology, are widely available for many common operating systems.

### Central Network Administration

The move to pervasive networking in commercial settings is behind the increasing demand for centralized administration of network resources. We won't go into too much detail here – one of the assumptions we make is that application developers will have little or no formal authority to make 'top-down' changes in the computing environment.

The Active Directory (covered next) will give Windows 2000 Server a central store for configuration, location, and access control information. Rather than having many local configuration files, applications and hardware should store their configuration information in the Active Directory. The Microsoft Management Console (MMC), currently available with Windows NT, will take advantage of this store to make it easier for an administrator to configure remote resources under Windows 2000. Application installation programs will be able to take advantage of the Installation service, which handles many tasks previously handled by the installation programs directly. The advantage of bringing the operating system into the installation process is that it can more easily track the status of shared libraries and configuration information, making upgrades and program removal more reliable. Plug and Play support for peripheral hardware, introduced with Windows 95, will also be included with Windows 2000. This will, among other things, help lower support costs as well as permit remote configuration of disk partitions (provided, of course, that the storage device is Plug and Play compatible). System instrumentation is improved so that compatible devices can offer the operating system more status information than is currently possible.

### Active Directory

One centralized aspect of Windows DNA is of great interest to us in our search for lessons in distributed computing. Windows 2000 Server introduces the Active Directory, a directory service native to Windows.

Simply stated, a directory service is a central, hierarchical store of information, intended to be read by network clients. A directory will typically contain information about the configuration and capabilities of networked machines. Generally speaking, a directory contains information that is frequently read, but seldom written. As a result, an effective directory is optimized for read access. Although the Active Directory is a proprietary implementation, it supports the Lightweight Directory Access Protocol (LDAP), an open standard protocol for querying directories. Active Directory supports both COM and C-language APIs for programmatic access.

An active directory instance is global to its domain, although any authorized directory server in the domain may take ownership for authoring purposes. The directory itself is replicated between the primary server and backups on the domain. Directories may forward requests to trusted directory servers in other domains. This helps the directory service scale to enterprise levels by distributing the load across multiple servers. Properly done, the majority of directory queries from clients will be satisfied by directory servers, close – in network segment terms – to the originating client. As we will see in Chapter 2, the Active Directory is a valuable means of describing the application services on our networks.

### Transaction Processing

Transaction Processing (TP) monitors are a familiar fixture in enterprise computing environments. Mission critical applications such as banking need the reliability of transactions and high-throughput computing. The Microsoft Transaction Server (MTS), which is bundled with current versions of Windows NT Server and also available for free download as part of the Windows NT 4.0 option pack, is an attempt to provide these services on PC networks using an object-based interface. TP monitors are well-known fixtures in mission-critical mainframe applications and MTS was developed to help programmers write such scalable, mission-critical applications for the Windows platform.

Applications are built as packages of components, and it is MTS that breaks down the tasks performed by these applications into functional blocks, which are implemented by these components. So, to deploy an application on MTS, the administrator registers the components with MTS and defines the security roles for users of the application. MTS is then able to stand between a client application and the COM runtime, and perform scalability enhancing services like resource pooling, as well as distributed transactions. Note the similarity between MTS and the description of interceptors in COM+. MTS is the means of implementing transaction services in COM. When language tools support transaction attributes in COM+, the functionality of MTS will be seamlessly tied to components.

The transaction services provided by MTS can be distributed across multiple databases. MTS uses the Distributed Transaction Coordinator (DTC) service for its transaction services. DTC was originally developed for Microsoft SQL Server to permit transactions across multiple databases. Each database engine implements the local functions of a distributed transaction; MTS (through DTC) merely orchestrates the semantics of coordinating the transaction across multiple databases. Transactions are one of the most useful tools in relational databases. When two or more database commands are enlisted in a transaction, should a single operation fail any commands that have completed are rolled back, the database is restored to its state prior to the transaction. If all operations succeed, however, the state is committed – the database permanently reflects the results of the transaction.

In a distributed system, we will often wish to use data from more than one database; indeed, we may wish to use databases from different vendors. A store, for example, might draw inventory from a regional warehouse. The program controlling this might update an Oracle database at the warehouse and a SQL Server database at the store. Obviously, we do not want to subtract inventory from the warehouse database if the addition to the store database fails.

That is where distributed transactions come in, allowing a programmer to declare a transaction in which operations take place on more than one database. It is the DTC that ensures the same data integrity across databases that conventional transactions offer within a single database.

*For more information about MTS check out Professional MTS MSMQ with VB and ASP from Wrox Press, ISBN 1-861001-46-0*

## Message Queuing

Although most of the applications in this book are implemented with COM, some tasks require an asynchronous message-based service. A message, in this context, is simply an arbitrary data structure that we wish to forward to a remote computer. Like an email message, we do not want to hold program execution while we wait for the remote machine to respond. Instead, a store and forward mechanism allows us to asynchronously pass messages. The sending program is able to continue once it is sure the message has been committed to a queue. This is useful in high volume situations such as e-commerce engines. Requests are sent as messages to the engine, and, once sent, the client is free to continue even when the server has a backlog. The backlog can then be cleared when demand drops.

The Microsoft Message Queue Server (MSMQ) provides for reliable communications through message passing. Copying the structure to a local queue sends a message. If the local machine is unable to connect with the desired recipient machine, the message remains in the queue until it can be sent. Once a message arrives on a remote machine, it is again placed in a queue, where it remains until the receiving application can consume the message. Providing a second form of queuing further enhances reliability. Messages that must survive a system shutdown or crash are automatically written to disk when placed in a queue and can consequently be recovered following a restart. In cases where the programmer wishes to trade reliability for throughput, however, MSMQ can be instructed to maintain the message in memory without writing it to disk. MSMQ even allows for the inclusion of messaging with the context of a transaction, extending the integrity of database transactions to include messaging.

*Reliable messaging and messaging transaction present difficult choices for system designers, particularly when used across a high latency network like the Internet. You must balance the need for integrity and reliability against the substantial performance penalties imposed by these features.*

MSMQ is hardly the first general-purpose messaging middleware package on the market. In fact, products like MQ Series from IBM and DEC MessageQueue are available for numerous operating systems. Because of the popularity of messaging middleware in the implementation of legacy mission-critical applications, there is a high degree of interest in integrating MSMQ with other messaging systems. Level 8 Systems offers products permitting MSMQ to be bridged with other messaging middleware products.

*For more information on interoperability, see the Level 8 Systems home page at*
`http://www.level8.com`

### Universal Data Access

Microsoft's goal of unifying access to disparate data stores has evolved through a number of technologies and names. Open Database Connectivity (ODBC), is a platform standard API for addressing relational databases (although ODBC drivers are also available for non-relational stores like text files and Excel spreadsheets). OLE DB, Microsoft's COM-based successor to ODBC, was a significant step forward. It offers a standard API for any data store capable of representing data in a rows-and-columns format, and the API was implemented as a COM object model. Subsequent to the initial introduction of OLE DB, efforts were made to provide efficient access to remote data sources. Many acronyms grew up around OLE DB. Eventually, these confusing terms were brought together under the name Universal Data Access (UDA) in Windows DNA. Clients use ActiveX Data Objects (ADO) as the client interface to Universal Data Access. Beneath ADO, UDA provides a number of abstract services. The simplest UDA components are data providers, representing a single physical store. Service provider components use one or more data providers to offer more complicated features such as cross-source joins. Command processors take some arbitrary command in a data retrieval command language, typically SQL, and use the service and data providers to satisfy the request encoded in the command.

Universal Data Access is of special interest to Web developers because of the way it offers efficient access to remote data through a connectionless protocol (HTTP). Data retrieved from the database server is packaged as a block of MIME-encoded binary data and passed back to a UDA component on the client. That component converts the MIME-encoded data to a local cache. This cache is a disconnected recordset that permits the client to work with the data without maintaining and using a persistant connection across a potentially low speed network link. So, subsequent requests (for example to scroll) from a client ADO component are satisfied through reference to the local cache. Only when the cache must be refreshed is another connection is made with the server.

## Windows DNA and Current Practice

What does this mean to us today? Windows DNA is the least futuristic of the three technologies we shall examine. Major pieces of the initiative are either available today or are evolutionary enhancements of currently available technologies. We can – and will – actually work with some of the technologies that fall under the Windows DNA umbrella.

Perhaps the most important lesson of Windows DNA is the importance of distributed programming to future systems. Although current practices like client-server computing and Distributed COM are properly considered forms of distributed computing, bringing the integrity and reliability achieved in monolithic applications currently requires substantial custom programming. Windows DNA not only delivers standard operating system services to address these concerns, but it makes them easily available to application programmers. This encourages system designers to build applications that fully utilize the distributed resources of a modern network. The control of the old centralized computing model is blended with the power and personalized access to resources in the PC model to achieve something more powerful than either model alone.

Windows DNA is component based at every level. Programmers who embrace the model of building software by coordinating discrete software components can easily gain the benefits of Windows DNA. The introduction of a directory service highlights the importance of a central store to which applications can go to discover and locate resources at runtime. It is not hard to see that if applications can dynamically discover resources and enlist them to accomplish their tasks, distributed applications will become more fluid. They will locate, access, and release the resources available to them on the network as and when needed.

# Millennium

Unlike Windows DNA, Millennium is a research project being conducted by Microsoft's research division. This project is an investigation into the issues surrounding an inherently distributed operating system. It assumes inherently distributed applications – the resources of the network not only enhance the performance of an application, they are *required* for its execution. Where Windows DNA is a vision of improving and extending existing, PC-centric networks, Millennium is a vision of a radically different computing environment. A system organized around Millennium's principles makes dynamic and transparent use of computing resources without prior configuration by the system designer. Windows DNA requires programmers and system administrators to manually partition systems for optimal performance. Such partitioning is explicit and obvious to those who use the system. In Millennium's vision, the ability to distribute computing tasks is implicit in the operating system. Individual computing resources are important mainly in the context of the network.

> *Like all long-term research projects, Millennium is subject to evolution and change. For the latest information on the project from Microsoft Research, see the Millennium Web site at* `http://www.research.microsoft.com/sn/Millennium.`

## Millennium's Goals

The nature of a distributed operating system in Microsoft's long-term vision can best be understood through the goals of the Millennium project:

- ❑ **Automatic distribution** – the operating system should determine how tasks in the application are distributed and make remote resources available as local resources
- ❑ **Scalability** – the operating system should consist of one logical system image, and any application should be able to scale as needed within the network
- ❑ **Fault tolerance** – the system and applications that run on it should adapt dynamically to failures and loss of connectivity without loss of data or functionality
- ❑ **Self-tuning** – the system should reallocate resources and redistribute application tasks based on observed application performance
- ❑ **Self-configuring** – the system should automatically incorporate new resources as they are connected to the network
- ❑ **Security** – despite a single system image, users and service providers can specify access control permissions for resources and users; the system should also allow non-hierarchical trust domains
- ❑ **Resource control** – users and service providers can place constraints on resources belonging to different trust domains for reasons of security

> *While some of these goals can be met with Windows DNA services and clustering, self-tuning and self-configuring reach their full potential under Millennium.*

These goals imply certain approaches. Four key principles may be derived from the Millennium project.

- ❑ **Abstract and automatic distribution of tasks** – the system performs distribution tasks, freeing programmers to focus on the problem at hand. Programmers and applications are unaware of the location of resources enlisted by the system on their behalf.
- ❑ **Dynamic enlistment of resources** – specific hardware resources and software services are bound to the application as needed at runtime.

❑ **Abstract locality** – neither applications running on nor programmers using the system know where computations and storage reside; the system acts as a middleman, locating required resources.

❑ **Automatic performance tuning** – the system must continually monitor the execution of applications and dynamically adjust the distribution of tasks in order to optimize system and application performance.

Web programmers may look on Millennium as an idealized version of the Internet. Presently, we manually search for servers and sites offering the data and services we require. The Domain Name System abstracts locality, converting a named resource into a physical location. Although the Internet does not self-tune its performance, the distributed nature of routing provides a crude sort of dynamic adaptation.

## Millennium Prototype Projects

Millennium is investigating the issues of distributed operating systems through three prototype projects using some current technologies. Each of the three prototypes uses a different technology for decomposing applications into tasks:

❑ **Coign** which uses COM components
❑ **Borg** which uses Java classes
❑ **Continuum** which uses COM+ components and is more dynamic than Coign in its approach to partitioning

> *As this book goes to press, Borg is no longer listed on the Millenium Web site. Whether this means Borg has been abandoned, subsumed into one of the other projects, or simply removed due to the on-going law suits between Sun and Microsoft is unknown. It is listed here because it reflects work previously done by Microsoft and illustrates some important points.*

Having seen the aims of Millennium, let's take a look at how each of these projects uses a different approach to meet the goals of the Millennium Project, and then see what we can learn from the ways in which these projects are trying to advance distributed networking.

### Coign

The Coign prototype implementation performs automatic distribution using COM components as the fundamental means of partitioning an application. Any application built from COM components, whether designed as a distributed application or not, can be partitioned by Coign. An important point to note is that the Coign system does not need access to the source code for the components, nor do the components have to be built with special libraries linked to them. Coign watches while the user works with the application, notes how often components are accessed and how they interrelate, then develops a scheme for distributing the components across available computers on a network.

A Coign developer runs a tool to insert run-time instrumentation into the binary code of the components. Next, he executes the application, presumably running through scenarios reflecting typical application use. Coign builds a model capturing inter-component dependencies. When deployed, a small, residual piece of the Coign runtime code embedded in the component binaries distributes the components in such a way as to minimize component communication costs. These costs reflect network latency and available bandwidth between partitioned components.

At the time of writing Coign did not adaptively self-tune, although users could alter the distribution of components by repeating the modeling process. Since the process does not require the source code for the component, the profiling process does not compromise the intellectual property of the application.

Coign runs on Windows NT and was tested with three applications, a commercially available photo editing application, a word processor, and a component-based intranet application intended as an instructional resource for developers. The developers of the last application manually partitioned the application. Re-partitioning using Coign reduced inter-component communication costs by 54%.

## Borg

This prototype aims to provide a single system image (SSI) of a distributed Java virtual machine (VM). Java classes are distributed beneath the SSI VM to enlist network resources in the execution of a single Java application. Programmers of a Java application running under Borg wouldn't derive their classes from any special base classes, make special distinctions regarding distribution, or otherwise know in any way that the classes their application would execute in a distributed environment. A single system image VM provides the benefits of distributed computing without explicit programming effort. A prototype of Borg has been successfully demonstrated.

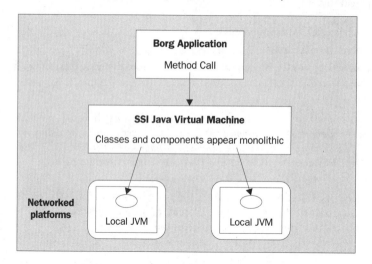

*One reason why Borg may no longer be a separate project is that the Microsoft JVM can expose Java classes as COM components. Once that is done, there is little difference between Coign and Borg.*

## Continuum

Like Borg, Continuum is a single system image prototype. Whereas Coign produces a static distribution of computing resources, Continuum uses the features of COM+ to allow it to dynamically migrate components from one computer to another while the application is running. Continuum would allow an application to be continually re-tuned in response to changes in the network environment.

## *Observations*

These three prototypes share three fundamental principles:

- ❑ **Automated partitioning** – Each prototype examines how an application uses components to accomplish its goals, then compares this to the computing resources available to it and partitions the application into groups of components. The groups are distributed to computers that can efficiently host them.
- ❑ **Self-tuning** – The prototypes decide the optimum allocation of available resources without operator intervention. Continuum goes a step further, performing this task while an application runs. If successful, Continuum would continually balance network resources as devices are added and removed, or if they are heavily loaded.
- ❑ **Abstract locality** – A user of these systems sees a single logical application and computer. Only the system knows where the resources that make up the application actually reside.

All three projects move application development to a higher level of abstraction, pushing physical network considerations into the runtime system. All are SSI implementations in that the user experiences a single, monolithic computing entity. Coign attempts aggressive optimization of commercially available applications by splitting up locally hosted COM components and efficiently distributing them. Continuum goes a step further, although it requires that the application be built from COM+ components and therefore cannot be used with today's commercial applications. Continuum performs the same task of automated partitioning as Coign, but where Coign does it once in a test setting, Continuum performs it dynamically in a production setting. As available resources change, Continuum moves components to balance the system.

## *Millennium and Current Practice*

Today, components and abstract locality are the most relevant features of the Millennium project. The partitioning and self-tuning features are exciting, but well beyond anything we will be able to do in current practice. Millennium, at its heart, relies on software built substantially from components. This is something we can do today, and which is becoming increasingly popular. In fact, Coign was tested in part on commercially shipping software. If Millennium's view of the future is correct, we can start down this road immediately.

Abstract locality is a bit more difficult to approach. Millennium carries this to an extreme; not only does the user not know where resources are located, he can only presume that the system is distributed, because Millennium presents a single system image, hiding the location of its resources. This is beyond current production practice. One lesson we can learn, however, is the value in delaying the firm commitment of resources until they are needed. Monolithic applications include resources within them, and client-server applications often explicitly specify the location of resources in their configuration, while Millennium hides the location of resources. Using directory services, you can specify the nature and location of resources in such a way that well-written applications can determine what they need and where it is located on a just-in-time basis.

# Jini

Jini is Sun Microsystems' experimental foray into providing highly dynamic network services to heterogeneous computing devices. Jini begins with the Java programming language but goes far beyond Web page applets. Jini is an architecture for distributed computing, influenced by the Linda system pioneered at Yale University
(http://www.cs.yale.edu/HTML/YALE/CS/Linda/linda.html).

Linda is a programming language with supporting tools that allow programmers of distributed applications to specify how to combine remote resources in such a way as to accomplish the goals of the program. Jini aims to provide a means for users – human and computational – to discover services provided by resources on a network. 'Resources' not only embraces PCs, but also standalone storage devices, printers, and other network-enabled appliances. Jini **federates** these groups of devices into systems that can be viewed, managed, and accessed as easily as the local resources of a PC. By this Jini means that combinations of resources are enlisted at runtime to accomplish specific tasks. The notion that they can only accomplish the task by combining resources is what federation means. The core resource element in a Jini system is a **service**. Do not confuse this with the definition of service provided in the introduction. Jini services are very specific, and largely pertain to narrowly defined network or operating system resources. Our meaning is closer to application modules. Clients – users and devices – search for Jini services by contacting a well-known lookup service, which in turn can reference other lookup services or indicate the source of the service desired by the client. Clients then **lease** a particular service for a specified duration. Clients accomplish tasks by leasing all the services required to accomplish some task.

Jini assumes that all devices support a Java Virtual Machine (VM) and that all services are provided by Java components. This enables Jini to build on the services being rolled out for Java, and allows components to travel between Java VMs. Unfortunately, this means that all prospective Jini systems must be built from programs written in Java, thereby eliminating direct use of legacy systems written in other languages.

## System Services

Like the designers of Windows DNA, Jini's architects recognize the need for system services that are more advanced than basic operating system services, like file and print services. Jini begins with the services offered by common Java technology:

- ❑ Java VM – execution and runtime services for downloaded byte codes
- ❑ Remote Method Invocation (RMI) – invoking the methods of Java classes on remote machines
- ❑ Security – control over what actions downloaded code can take
- ❑ JavaBeans – a component software technology
- ❑ Java Naming and Directory Interface (JNDI) – network directory services
- ❑ Java Transaction Service and API – specifications for building transactional services in Java

*I'm using a very broad definition of 'services' here. Sun sub-classifies these services into infrastructure, programming model, and services. The distinction is not important for our purposes. Suffice to say we are only concerned with the features offered by Jini/Java to the builders of applications and business systems.*

Jini adds enhancements to the Java platform as well as new services:

- ❑ Extended RMI – JDK 1.2 enhancements to RMI to fully support the Jini vision, distributed garbage collection for example
- ❑ Discovery – a protocol for advertising or finding the availability of a service on a Jini system
- ❑ Distributed Security – access control lists for users of a system and the rights granted to them
- ❑ Two Phase Commit – reliable database commits between distinct databases
- ❑ Events – a distributed mechanism for signaling events on remote objects
- ❑ JavaSpace – the server that enables clients to locate Jini system services and reserve access to them

As you can see, Jini is more than simply communicating between components on remote machines. It builds applications by forming federations of network services, enlisting them in the common cause of some application task. It provides a robust framework of platform capabilities that programmers can draw on in a just-in-time basis. The full system is extremely dynamic and capable of adjusting to fluctuating network configurations. Jini, therefore, marries the advantages of component software to the advantages of reliable access to network services to raise application programming to a higher level of productivity and performance.

## JavaSpaces

The provision of services in Jini is accomplished through the flow of objects between servers and clients. The entire Jini model relies on the location and negotiation of services on behalf of a client. A client application must find a service it requires, reserve that service, and use the service implementation provided by a server. JavaSpaces servers act as the broker matching clients with services. They are the middlemen between clients and service providers, providing a common clearing house for the entire network.

A JavaSpaces server contains **entries**, each of which is a Java object implementing a well-known interface. An entry contains **fields**, each of which is also a Java object. Servers offering a service in a Jini system write an entry to a JavaSpaces server, thereby copying the objects into the server. These objects are proxies for objects maintained by the service provider. Consider the following, highly simplified Jini system:

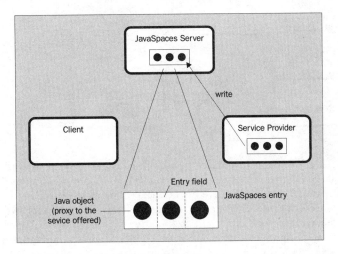

### Locating a Service

A client desiring service may locate a provider in one of two ways. Firstly, a client may request that a JavaSpaces server notify it when a particular service becomes available. This notification is accomplished using the distributed event service. Alternatively, a client may actively search for a service by presenting a template to a JavaSpaces server. A template contains entries and wildcards. If the entries in the template match entries residing in the JavaSpaces server, a match is found. An entry in the server and a template entry match if the two entries are of the same Java class and if the public fields of the entries contain the same values. Wildcards are strictly a 'don't care' entry placeholder.

Templates are presented using one of two operations: read and take. In a read operation, matching entries are copied to the invoking client without changing the entry on the server. In a take operation, the entry is removed from the JavaSpaces server after it has been copied to the client. Continuing with our simple system:

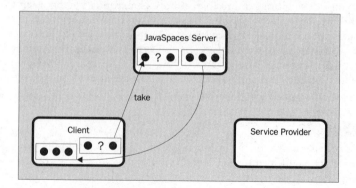

### Accessing a Service

Once the client has obtained an entry from the JavaSpaces server, it has access to the service it needs. The entry obtained may implement the service locally, or, more commonly, act as a proxy, communicating via RMI with the server that originally wrote the entry to the JavaSpaces server. Finally, our simple client obtains services:

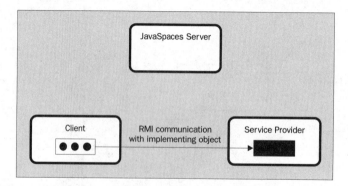

These are just the simplest elements of JavaSpaces. Large Jini systems require a number of features to support scaling to very large environments and provide for a robust, nonhierarchical system. Jini also provides a number of advanced features that are beyond the scope of our discussion. Two examples related to system scaling are JavaSpaces server replication and service lookup forwarding. JavaSpaces servers may replicate their entries to other servers in the interest of keeping lookups localized within network segments, which also improves performance and reliability when network segments fail. A JavaSpaces server may also forward a lookup request to another JavaSpaces server to facilitate location, while objects may break a problem down into smaller pieces and do lookups of their own using additional JavaSpaces servers. Overall the JavaSpaces specification provides for a powerful system based on the brokered flow of objects between hosts in a Jini system.

## Leases

A fundamental problem with distributed systems is that one party to a remote computation can fail, or the network connectivity between the two parties can be broken. When a client is lost, the server may maintain unused resources indefinitely. A lost server may cause the client to wait indefinitely for service. A mechanism must be added so that parties to a distributed computation can detect an unannounced loss of service. Some distributed systems use periodic polling to determine if the parties are still in communication. Others set a 'time to live' in the granted object. Jini uses the concept of **leases**.

A client guarantees access to a service by obtaining a lease. A lease is granted for a particular duration, typically negotiated between the client's desires and the server's willingness to maintain the resource. While the server will typically grant the lease for the term desired, a client may make an unreasonable request, or a server may be more constrained than expected, so negotiation allows servers the opportunity to downgrade the duration of what is asked. Negotiation is simpler than it sounds. A client asks for a particular lease, and the server agrees or offers something less. Using duration as the unit of measure for a lease rather than an absolute time avoids the need to globally synchronize clocks in a Jini system; indeed, it makes the federation of Jini systems possible. Consider a Jini system in which all clocks have been synchronized. Now, suppose a client wishes to have a service in another Jini system, if the two systems have differing clocks, who synchronizes with whom? Using duration eliminates the need to make sweeping synchronization changes. Once obtained, a client may renew a lease if the service is still needed. Leases may be exclusive or shared depending on the nature and implementation of the service. Clients may also cancel leases, permitting the early cleanup of resources.

An additional feature of leases is that they allow brokers like JavaSpaces, or application-specific entities, to negotiate leases on pools of resources in the interests of efficiency. A server can pre-allocate a pool of objects in order to respond faster to new service requests. When a third party claims a resource holding the lease, the lease simply travels with the resource, and the broker need not further concern itself with the resource's leasing arrangements.

## Jini and Current Practice

Jini seems to have struck a nerve in the networking community. In addition to the interest in all things Java, Jini has attracted particular interest in its ability to connect dissimilar devices on a common network. Even if the more advanced features of Jini – the ability to federate distributed resources for the purposes of an application – are never realized, this feature is likely to be pushed forward into the marketplace by Sun.

What we as application developers can take away from Jini's example is the idea of advertising services. You can see how this would complement the idea of finding the location of a resource as needed. If the provider of some sort of programmatic logic were to advertise it in a form that other applications could understand, applications could ask for the location not of a named program or device, but for the location of a program or device that accomplishes a particular logical task. Jini focuses on specific devices and fine-grained components. We can do something a bit easier by finding a way to classify our server-based programs according to the logic they carry out.

# Back to Reality

Hopefully, this brief excursion into the future was exciting. Unfortunately, upon returning to mundane reality, we still have to implement Web-based systems and we only have current technologies, languages, and networks.

Some of the technologies we've seen, such as component software, are currently available, so we will make extensive use of them. Others, like automatic component profiling and distribution, must wait for future operating systems and platforms. Somewhere in between lie functions we would like to have for developing Web based applications and which can be implemented using currently available programming techniques.

So that we can properly identify where we want to make improvements, we should take a quick look at some of the weaknesses in our available technologies.

# Where Are Our Present Weaknesses?

Before embarking on the task of identifying the functions of these future technologies that we can implement, we should ask why we need additional services at all. Many powerful Web and intranet sites exist using nothing more than the basic internetworking standards – HTTP, CGI, HTML, and so forth. So why do we need new techniques?

## Dealing With Increased Complexity

Powerful sites addressing serious problems are easily as complicated as a stand-alone application. Moreover, they have the added complexities inherent in distributed systems. Unmanaged complexity is a weakness of distributed systems. Resources become less and less useful as knowledge of their meaning and capabilities is lost to later-deployed clients.

Because Web-based applications are easily fielded and require no one's permission to add to the Internet (other than the obvious requirement of obtaining a domain name), servers and services quickly blossom and mutate. Presumably someone understands what they can do, but there are many more clients who could use them but who will never know these particular capabilities are available. Functions will be needlessly reimplemented again and again simply because no mechanism has been defined to advertise what is available. This is barely tolerable in the case of the public Internet; but it is a complete recipe for waste and disaster in a corporate intranet.

## Inflexible Applications

Applications are often written with a particular client in mind. Alter the needs of the client and you either have to re-write the server or create a new, highly similar service.

## Duplication of Data

New servers often duplicate large bodies of existing code because of minor changes in needs and specifications. This duplication of code can be seen as wasteful.

## Moves Towards Automated Web Tasks

If we wish to automate a previously manual Web-based application, we have a new problem. Our previous server generated HTML for human consumption, but when the consumer is an automated application, HTML is far harder to consume.

## Distributed Development and Implementation Teams

Disasters frequently occur when services are provided by some organization not under the control of the prospective client.

For example, you may be building an extranet supply chain application, in which case you must rely on an external partner for some of your application's services. When coordination is informal or nonexistent, services will move, change, and disappear. The administrative overhead of keeping pace with the changes rapidly snowballs. We need to add techniques and services that let us build flexible, robust, fault tolerant distributed systems that can change over time along with our needs. More importantly, we need to do this without requiring human coordination.

Hopefully, the future systems we have just examined will give us some ideas we can use to solve these problems.

# So, What Can We Learn From The Future?

It was all very interesting looking at the aims of these research projects, but we cannot wait for them to come to fruition, especially not when we live and work according to the accelerated rate of Internet time. You aren't likely to have bought this book for a prediction of the future technologies, so let's see what the common threads of these different efforts are so that we can crystallize our thoughts on how we are going to build *our* distributed cooperative applications *today*.

The three systems we have considered – and they are by no means the only visions growing in the field of computing – are highly dissimilar:

- ❑  The Microsoft systems use COM as their bedrock, while Jini is all about Java.
- ❑  Millennium is organized around single system images, while Jini looks for highly fluid systems of dissimilar resources.
- ❑  Windows DNA is in the process of fruition, using many tested technologies, while Millennium and Jini are clearly in the realm of blue-sky research.

# Common Threads

Having noted some differences, these systems face the problems common to all distributed systems and draw their solutions from the same existing research literature. Not surprisingly, then, some common threads are discernable. The main five are:

- ❑  Components as the building blocks of applications
- ❑  Abstraction of the location of services, and the dynamic discovery of location at runtime
- ❑  Dynamic use of resources for a task, and the ad hoc release of resources
- ❑  Formal description of desired resources at runtime
- ❑  Distribution of the programming task across multiple resources of the network

Let's take a closer look at each of these threads in turn, what they mean and how they affect us developing distributed cooperative applications. Unsurprisingly, these common threads address the weaknesses we have just outlined. So, let's look at the problems that each of these threads is trying to solve, and how they aim to do so using these common threads.

## Component Software

### Problem:

Object oriented computing swept over commercial practice in the 1980s with a mixed record of achieving its claimed objectives. Its model, however, proved useful and powerful. Data could now be packaged with the programming logic needed to properly handle it in a single, well-defined entity. Complicated programs could be built from the interaction of simpler packages operating black-box style through compiler-enforced interfaces. In practice, however, this was seldom realized. Access to source code tempted many programmers to modify code rather than use inheritance as rigorously as they might otherwise have done. Even when code was reused through its interfaces, language dependencies meant implementations in one language, e.g. C++, could not be used by applications written in another language, e.g. Visual Basic. Vendor specific dependencies further restricted the scope of reuse.

## Solution:

In the slightly mutated form of components, object orientation is proving to be a big boon to programmers. Language neutral component technologies such as COM permit the broadest possible reuse. A genuinely useful third-party component quickly finds use in a variety of applications. All the systems we have considered are built from components. Applications are built by assembling and coordinating the activities of components. These components are built, compiled, and tested separately from the using application, often by third parties. The result looks to the user like a single application, but is really the assembly and reuse of standard components. Complexity is managed by allowing the programmer to focus on the task at hand, relying on the components for large bodies of detailed code implementing lower-level operations. Clients and servers are coordinated through agreement on programmatic interfaces.

# Abstract Location

## Problem:

When you first learned to program a client–server application, you likely hard-coded the network location of the server into your code. The name of the server application and its specific network address was written into the client. It became apparent that this would not work in a real application, since servers can be renamed and addresses often change. In response, you might have adopted some sort of initialization scheme. You may have asked the client to read the name and address from a text file, or asked it to look up the same information from the Windows registry. Perhaps this information took the form of command line parameters needed to start the client executable. Clients and servers are less strongly coupled, but this will not suffice for the highly dynamic systems we envision. Using this approach, the information is provided in arbitrary ways. The client programmer must know where to look for the information. There is no standard place to look for the information or – in the case of the registry – standard way of naming these places within a well-known data store. Moreover, knowledge of what a particular server offers is assumed. Taking this approach, clients were therefore built largely in parallel with their servers, or, at the very least, built by a team with intimate knowledge of the server.

## Solution:

Microsoft wants us to use Windows DNA as the infrastructure for enterprise-scale, mission-critical systems. Consequently, we cannot count on initializing our knowledge of resource location by restarting our clients. The Active Directory in Windows 2000, or some other vendor's LDAP-capable directory service implementation, provides a persistent yet readily queried store for configuration information, including the location and parameters of our servers, which saves us from having to hard code our resources. Information entered by network administrators is copied at intervals to other directory servers, ensuring every client can get the information from a local source well-known to it. Clients can then turn to this source for information about the network and its resources.

Millennium takes this a step further. It doesn't just allow you to move services around the network and reference them from a directory service, rather it is built on the idea of hiding the location and nature of these services from you! It goes beyond the concept of directories, in that it does the querying and location for the using application. The result is a single system image rather than a map to distributed resources. Although at the time of writing it was not yet possible with current production technology, Coign may someday allow for the dynamic partitioning of resources, so the system demands the ability to locate services on an ad hoc basis.

Meanwhile, JavaSpaces is an indispensable piece of Jini, and its reason for existence is the dynamic discovery of and connection to services by clients at runtime.

# *Dynamic Resource Enlistment*

## *Problem:*

A fundamental assumption of all these systems is a reliable network that is always 'up' built from individual nodes that come and go with little or no coordination.

Stand-alone applications linked third party libraries of compiled code together in an iron-clad contract for life. The introduction of dynamically loaded libraries added some dynamic acquisition to the programmer's arsenal, but often applications were compiled with early-bound knowledge of services and loaded libraries when the application started. Going to a Web-based programming model forces us to be more fluid in our thinking, open to unsettled environments. When we request a service from an HTTP server it may not be available. Web servers that permit us to maintain a measure of state in an inherently stateless protocol require us to periodically renew our interest in the server. The contract between a client and a Web-based service is not so tight as in older models, and requires more flexibility on the part of all parties.

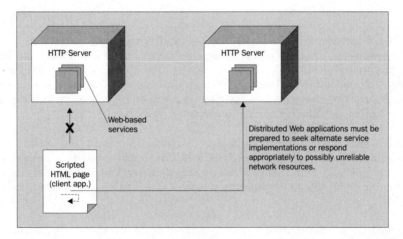

The HTTP protocol is stateless by design. A client cannot therefore count on a server-based resource being available at some time in the future simply because it was available for a prior request. Resource location, consequently, must be performed as close to the time of use as possible, and client-side code must be prepared to take appropriate action if a desired service is unavailable.

Web applications that span multiple server-side pages or scripts require that servers offer some kind of session state information for each client. In a small-scale ASP application, this is held in the `Session` object. The server, like the clients, cannot know whether the client is still interested in the session (clients leave abruptly and fail unexpectedly, after all), so all session state mechanisms are time dependent. If a client relies on server-side state, it must periodically renew contact with the server to ensure that session state information is not destroyed. These are factors you must consider when designing distributed applications using Web technology.

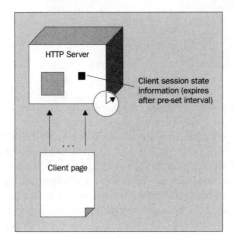

## Solution:

Component software and transaction services in Windows DNA provide for the difficulties of enlisting multiple resources. Should a particular service implementation be offline, a client application may try to find other implementations through the directory service. Should all implementations of a needed service be down, then an application can abort the operation (or rollback a transaction). The Web-based interface implies script-based clients, which call for services dynamically and employ late binding of component interfaces.

Millennium's single system image metaphor implies dynamically enlisted components, else it wouldn't be fault tolerant. After all, with SSI, the client is denied knowledge of network resources (as the Millennium runtime is solely responsible for coordinating distributed resources), so the Millennium system must be able to dynamically replace a lost resource with a newly created replacement.

Jini goes a step further. Its programming model, you'll recall, involves solving problems through the federation of services and the flow of objects from host to host. Efficient use of resources implies that clients acquire leases only as needed and for the minimum duration necessary. Applications on Jini systems must inherently be programmed to solve problems through the dynamic creation, flow, and destruction of resources.

## Description of Required Resources

### Problem:

Given the need to acquire services as we need them, how do we tell the server what it is that we need? In common Web-based applications, the service is implied by the URL requested. An ASP or CGI script is known to implement a particular service; by requesting the resource, you implicitly request the service. Nothing, however, prevents a new service from being created using the old URL, and the result is a broken application. URLs are intended to name a resource; any information regarding what is expected of the client and server – the contract between them for service – is strictly implied. A URL does not explicitly define an interface to a service. Something better, and more descriptive, is needed.

*Solution:*

Both Windows DNA and Millennium have COM at their hearts, so resource description is based on interface. When you want a particular set of functions, you ask for the interface that implements those features. If you have an interface pointer, you expect a particular set of features and behavior. This is the programming equivalent of a legal contract in the real world. Any server implementing the interface is bound to the documented semantics of the interface. If a designer wishes to modify the interface or its semantics, he is required by the rules of COM to offer a new interface. Millennium's Borg prototype and Jini use Java, which also works with interfaces that are implemented by Java classes.

## Task Distribution Across Networked Resources

*Problem:*

The whole point of distributed applications is to spread the programming load across the network, placing responsibility for accomplishing tasks with the host best able to serve the need.

*Solution:*

Windows DNA takes some steps in this direction, although most task distribution must be manual. MTS and clustering services in Windows DNA allow the creation of multiple tier applications, leaving system architects to make appropriate decisions regarding task allocation.

Millennium's Coign takes the opposite extreme – this prototype has task distribution at its core. Moreover, this partitioning is largely autonomous.

Jini falls somewhere in between. Like Windows DNA, task distribution is largely a matter of system architects making decisions at design time about the hosting of services. With the ability of Java objects to flow between machines through JavaSpaces, however, programmers are given better tools with which to alter partitioning. Services may be manually moved to another host, with the new host broadcasting its availability through the JavaSpaces in its Jini system.

So, we have seen these five common themes through the different systems we have studied. How can these ideals be seen in terms of what we can actually implement today?

# What is Practical Today

Clearly, the practicality of implementing these common threads with today's technology varies depending on what we are talking about. Some are proven capabilities, some are possible in rudimentary form using a combination of existing technology and programming conventions, and some things will simply have to remain in the realms of research experiments for some years to come. Let's consider each of these problems and solutions, which we have met in the form of the above common threads, and see what we can do today with today with commonly available operating systems and languages.

While we have been stressing the fact that these ideas are taken from research projects, you will no doubt have seen some parallels with technologies that are available today and techniques that we can use to achieve similar ends. This is where we actually get to see how these projects can influence our development directly today.

## *Where and How We Can Use Component Software*

The three future technologies we examined have components at their core for a reason: components offer many benefits. During the design phase of a project, we obtain the following benefits:

❏ **Abstraction** – high level goals are accomplished by coordinating the activities of a series of 'black box' components. The implementation is deferred for later, or even passed off to a third-party for development or purchase.

❏ **Delegation** – at the highest level, you can specify an interface in terms of preconditions, semantics, and results. The task of implementing the interface can be delayed until later.

During implementation, we see more benefits from components:

❏ **Cost** – encapsulation reduces the number of bugs due to closely coupled 'spaghetti' code. Errors in data integrity can be avoided because the data is accessed solely through code methods intended to enforce the business rules that define the nature and integrity of the data.

❏ **Availability** – A thriving market of third-party, general purpose components exists. We buy implementations of common tasks like charting and grid displays rather than build them.

❏ **Reuse** – once a component implementation of custom business logic is built and tested, other applications dealing with similar aspects of the business simply use that component. Not only do they avoid redoing work accomplished by others, but all users are assured of a consistent implementation of the rules of the business.

Component software is all around us. Microsoft Internet Explorer is an application built completely from software components and many Windows applications use components to some extent. In addition to COM, JavaBeans is another viable component software technology that is already used, and if we extend the definition to primarily distributed technologies, we can include CORBA in our list. There are also some other, lesser-used technologies such as IBM's SOM and the late, lamented OpenDoc technology stemming from the Macintosh world. Component software aids rapid application development though the ability to reuse proven implementations without resorting to the source code. So, the issue is not whether we can use component software in our designs, rather where and how.

Interoperability is a key issue. COM is primarily a Microsoft Windows-only technology, and despite the existence of a number of commercially available ports of COM to other operating system, the vast majority of COM-based projects are written for Windows. CORBA, meanwhile, suffers from slow growth, perhaps due to the fragmented implementations of the common CORBA standard. Finally, Java is just getting started, and cross-platform portability is a question best answered with a tentative "Yes, but..." reply.

The guideline for practicing Web developers, then, must be to restrict the use of components to a tier wholly under the control of the development team to remove problems of interoperability.

COM components can be a tremendously valuable asset to server-side development, or in cases where the client is known to run on a platform where COM is available. We will make extensive use of pre-built COM components in this book in just this way.

> Avoid using a given component technology across boundaries, and do not
> assume that clients and servers share a common component technology. Use
> components within the 'black boxes' of your networked system to speed
> development, and leave distributed component technology on public
> networks for the future.

Distributed component technologies like DCOM and CORBA are best used within a controlled
environment like a low latency LAN. In wide area networks, latency and heterogeneous technologies
rear their incompatible heads. In such cases, you need a more flexible, platform neutral mechanism
for allowing resources to interact.

## Isolating Applications from Configuration Issues

The future technologies we looked at allowed for the dynamic discovery of resource location through
reference to a single well-known point of reference. The Active Directory in Windows DNA, the SSI
in Millennium, and JavaSpaces in Jini implemented this task for us. They provided a flexible and
open ended repository for application-defined information. All clients on the respective systems have
access to the repository through a common API. In current practice, the best solution to this problem
is directory services as we saw in DNA.

Directory technology is just coming into common use. LDAP – Lightweight Directory Access
Protocol – is a valuable open standard for access to directories in a Web environment, but it is still
new. Directories, as we will see, are so much better than initialization files and other schemes in the
construction of large, robust production systems that we will use them in this book when we need to
find a given resource. Web programmers should become accustomed to writing applications so that
they are location-independent and rely on directory queries to find resources. If you do this, your
applications will automatically respond to changes in the network. The network administrator updates
an entry, and your application will respond by following the new information to the resource it
desires.

What can we put in our directories? Certainly we can discover the network location of services by
searching through well-known directories. By joining directories in a hierarchy, we can control the
scope of our search. Depending on the importance of a computation, we might want to limit our
search for resources to a local workgroup or expand it to encompass all directory servers in an
organization. As we expand the scope of our search, we implicitly expand the scope of the resources
we might consume. Alternatively, we might know that a service is hosted somewhere within a
particular organization foreign to us. In that case, we will wish to go directly to the directory server
for that organization with our query.

We not only want to know where something is located, but also just what service it provides for us.
The level of the directory hierarchy closest to the resource is best situated to know the current
location and condition of the resource. We can provide some limited information regarding the
capabilities of the implementing host for the service. There is no established scheme for doing this,
however, so we will have to establish some design principles of our own and rely on adopting them
throughout the network. Chapter 2 will show you a particular scheme that works with the other
techniques presented in this book. Hopefully, our tentative efforts will prove sufficiently useful that
standards will come in time.

## What Does Dynamic Resource Enlistment Mean Today?

Web developers utilize dynamic enlistment of resources every time they build a client that uses CGI scripts or Active Server Pages. The server has no prior knowledge that a client request is coming and typically does not maintain significant state for the client following the request. Think of a URL as naming a computing resource instead of simply a Web page. The client claims resources based on a name – the URL – then uses them, and loses the resource immediately. HTTP is an inherently stateless protocol, however, and what state is retained in applications depends on a variety of techniques.

Web servers that allow developers to maintain session state information typically do so through the use of client-side cookies and proprietary techniques on the server. But developers cannot assume that all users of their applications will have cookie support enabled in their browsers. Worse, these techniques fail utterly when we try to scale the application through the use of server farms (multiple HTTP servers to which requests are routed round-robin fashion, or according to some other algorithm). Commercial grade servers such as Microsoft Site Server or Netscape Enterprise Server use other techniques to provide a central repository that all the servers can access. Site Server uses a proprietary database with extensive in-memory caching, while Enterprise Server resorts to an LDAP directory server. You can see that we are once again headed in the direction of the futuristic technologies and there is a very good reason for this. Everyone is working from the same body of research literature, and talented programmers tend to converge on the same good answers, differing only in particular details or over differing requirements. So, where does this leave us?

Jini-style leases are plainly outside the scope of today's implementations. This limits the reliability of Web applications that share a significant amount of the computational burden between the client and server. Jini lets us lock in the availability of a resource for a specified period of time. Lacking that, we must employ measures that promise the same reliability.

We will restrict ourselves to conventional, stateless client-server interactions for the most part. Dynamic enlistment, in the sense of late binding of components in scripts implementing services, will also be used. Wherever possible, we would like to take advantage of abstract location in finding our components as well, but the current state of the art limits this. In our case, COM components, the Windows system registry lets us avoid hard-coding the specific location of a component or the name of its implementing DLL, but this is not nearly as good as a central directory service.

## How Can We Describe Required Resources?

Defining the specific features and data formats we require of an interface (resource description) is a particularly difficult problem. Component technology relies on the assumption that all parties understand an interface if they share an identifier for the interface. We've decided not to share components between partners on a distributed network so as to permit us to use dissimilar platforms without worrying about bridging component technologies. As a result, we need something better, some neutral means of describing what it is we require of a service. Ideally, we should be able to discover the nature of an interface – learning its contents and capabilities as we go. The artificial intelligence community has made some efforts along those lines, but they are far from standardized. The expert systems community, for example, is working on a knowledge description format (KDF), which will be a standard way to define facts and queries. Fortunately, we don't need real intelligence, just a convention for describing data and referring to data formats in terms of the syntax used to describe them. For example, we might wish to say, "Here is a person's name – last name, first name, middle initial – now look him up and give me his address and phone number. Be sure to tell me what strings make up the street, city, state, and so forth in the address".

In the coming chapters I will introduce you to the **Extensible Markup Language (XML)**, a tagged, text-based scheme for describing data. I will go into more detail in Chapter 3, but for now let's say that XML is entirely text based. It allows users to create new tags very much in the way HTML defines tags. It is a simple and flexible method of marking up proprietary information in a way that allows receiving applications to precisely locate the data they require. As a result, it is rapidly growing in popularity. I will also introduce you to a proposed draft standard for describing XML schemas. These are XML documents that define the permissible tags and sequences of tags in other XML documents that conform to the schema. More importantly, I will present some techniques and conventions proprietary to this book. These will deal with some commonly encountered problems and provide solutions intended to increase the fault tolerance of your Web-based systems. These techniques will be kept simple, as I believe that is the key to their adoption. Agreement on these basic principles by you and the developers of the services with which your applications interact will permit you to build robust applications that degrade gracefully.

## How Far Can We Go in Partitioning Systems?

Sadly, the answer here is simple – we are limited to manual partitioning using multiple tier architecture, segmented by the human designers of the systems. This is because the autonomous partitioning promised by Millennium is well outside the scope of current practice, while migrating components such as Jini's rely on a common component software technology. We will gain the benefits of partitioning mainly through the goal of making it easy for servers to cooperate. The techniques described in this book are intended to help you build servers that can be reused by other applications and development teams.

In the sense that you are more likely to partition a system if you can leverage the power of existing servers, we promote partitioning. Where we are able to describe the capabilities of the services hosted by a particular server, we increase the number of clients who can make use of the partitioning scheme. We are not restricted to a single client with implicit knowledge of the scheme; we can open the distributed resources to any client that can read our descriptions. How well these services utilize network resources, however, will depend on the skill and insight of their designers.

We have looked into the future at projects in development now. We have seen the principles that they want to employ in distributed applications. Finally, it is time to articulate a philosophy for building cooperative network applications. To do this we will introduce The 5 Principles for Building Cooperative Network Applications.

# The 5 Principles of Cooperative Network Application Development

Having looked at the ongoing projects for the future of distributed systems, (finding common threads between them and noting the problems they address) we can distill what we have learnt easily into 5 overall principles. The 5 Principles Of Cooperative Network Application Development will encompass the goals we need to achieve in developing applications that will promote the reuse of application code and the viability of applications in the face of change in needs and applications.

So, here they are, our 5 Principles of Cooperative Network Application Development:

1. **Applications Will Be Built From Coarse-Grained Services** – applications will be implemented by coordinating the discrete results obtained from server-based modules that are larger than individual components and which answer a specific question, problem, or task.

2. **Services Will Be Discovered By Querying Directories** – applications will find the location and name of the services they need at runtime by querying a directory. They will ask not for a specific implementation, but rather for any service implementation that addresses a particular question, problem, or task.

3. **Services Will Be Provided As Self-Describing Data** – applications will deal with services by exchanging structured data. The data will be written according to vocabularies defined for the problem or task that the service addresses.

4. **Services Will Be Enlisted On A Transient Basis** – applications will find and use services in a small number (preferably one) of round-trips and will not require state to be held between round-trips. Neither application nor service will assume any long-term availability of the other partner in the exchange.

5. **Services Must Support Extension And Degrade Gracefully** – services must take future enhancement into account, both on the part of their own logic and exchange formats and those of other applications and services. When encountering a new version of exchange data, it should make as much use as possible of the data. Applications and services must never break if they do not receive exactly the format they expect.

Of course, these principles must observe what is readily practical, both in terms of current technology and the likelihood of heterogeneous platforms in the network. So let's consider each of these in turn. We'll consider how to go about attaining these goals and how they relate to the common threads we observed in the technologies we looked at earlier.

# 1. Applications Will Be Built From Course-Grained Services

We've seen that software components, while useful tools, are reusable only in applications for platforms supporting the component technology in which they were built. There is no use in trying to use a COM component on a Unix platform. (Of course, some Unix platforms have COM ports built for them, but generally speaking COM is a Windows technology.) In our case, where a development team will create just one part of an application, or where new clients are created for existing servers, we cannot count on being able to use components in a way that spans the various tiers of our applications. Instead, we will turn to **services**. A service is an arbitrary collection of application code that is confined to one tier and accomplishes one well-defined task. It is bigger than a component; indeed, we will frequently use components to build services for the reasons we have enumerated elsewhere. Yet, it is smaller than an application. Services model one useful part of a problem domain. If they are too small, the overhead of translating data to and from a neutral data format will place a burden on performance. If they are too big, services risk the problems of monolithic applications.

*Compare our definition to that of services under Windows DNA or Windows NT. The services there are either applications that run with certain hooks into the operating system – a Windows 32 API service – or component frameworks like ActiveX Data Objects (ADO) for data retrieval. Both are bigger than a single component. ADO fails our definition only because it can rely on using a proprietary component technology across application boundaries. Apart from that, however, it would fit – it uses the interaction of several components to answer a specific problem: "Get me a result set based on a SQL query".*

Often our services will model some major object in the underlying business model – customers for a sales application, or a factory line for a manufacturing application for example.

Services are usually implemented as a server-side page or small group of cooperating pages. They are characterized by a well-known data format that represents the service's object. A collection of related objects might be offered to provide a wide range of functionality. For example, a service might offer HTML in addition to its data-only formats to permit its use by ultra-thin clients such as hand-held devices. The thin client would lose the benefit of being able to manipulate the data programmatically in exchange for not having to support the overhead of the data-only formats. While it could conceivably parse and manipulate HTML, that language is marked up for presentation, not semantic meaning. It would be easier to support a different exchange format than to try to use HTML as the basis of your data markup. In short, adding HTML support, a seemingly regressive move, allows simple platforms to participate in a limited fashion provided they support a standard Web browser. Access to our services, however, will always be via open protocols. By abstracting a major object this way, we retain some of the benefits of the object-oriented model while reducing our dependency on proprietary component technologies.

Since a service is developed and maintained by a single organization, and hosted on a site under their control, we can use more proprietary technologies within the service to maximize our productivity. We expect to use component software within our services. (Often, we will be providing a wrapper for some sort of legacy software or database to avoid major rewriting efforts.) We can also utilize the full range of features of the host operating system and Web server to obtain the most value from our site. When we cross the line to another service or to a client, however, we understand we may be crossing organizational boundaries and we retreat to open standards and formats.

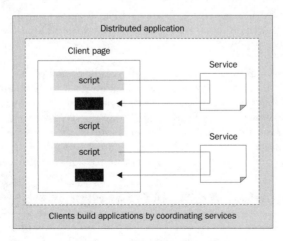

Note how this relates to the use of components in the future technologies we reviewed earlier. We cannot directly rely on components for the reasons we have seen, but we wish to use encapsulated bits of logic. Our applications will be built from reusable services. Within services, we rely on components. Applications use clean interfaces to reach services, and services use clean interfaces to reach the components within themselves. We are enjoying the benefits of encapsulation and delegation on both a large (service) and small (component) scale.

# 2. Services Will Be Discovered By Querying Directories

The network location of our services and the data formats they offer define access to our services. We must isolate these from any local conventions. While directories are still far from mature or widely deployed, we will make these the cornerstone of our service location strategy. They are pivotal to implementing location abstraction and dynamic discovery of resources. They are a resource that is useful only if it is visible to all users of the network. Consequently, we can safely assume this service will receive managerial attention at the highest levels of the information systems organization. Its structure, and the location of its servers, will be the subject of much discussion and consensus building within an organization, and it is the one area where we can safely assume global agreement and understanding within the organization.

The directory will store more than just the location of our services. It must define the capabilities of the services in terms of the business problem they address. As we shall see in later chapters, this will include a great deal of information regarding the formats in which data is offered.

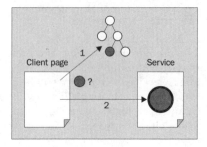

We will try to define useful directory structures and tools with which to peruse our directories. Every application must be written to browse our directories in search of information about desired services, so we shall try to standardize this task as much as possible.

Although not as aggressive as Millennium, this principle directly relates to one of the common threads we saw in the three future systems. That is the thread about abstract location and dynamic discovery of data. Provided you scrupulously adhere to this principle in your own distributed systems, you can gain some of the benefits we saw in Jini and Windows DNA. Your applications will be flexible, surviving changes in the location and availability of resources. In the next chapter, I will provide you with a scheme for using the Active Directory to implement this principle. After you have made use of it a few times, it will become second nature, an organic part of your programming style.

# 3. Services Will Be Provided As Self-Describing Data

Why do I make so much of data exchange formats? After all, I am an adherent of object-oriented methods as they are expressed in component software, and these methods try to shield the consumer of data from its format wherever possible. The exception is needed due to the fact that we are isolating components within a service as we have defined that term.

When we hop across the platform boundaries between service pages and their clients, we must represent the object our service implements in a form readily accessible to *all* clients. Despite the advances in distributed object-based computing in recent years, we are still left with static data structures.

We can define the characteristics of the object in terms of metadata, and each specific object instance will be represented by a data structure that conforms to that metadata definition. Since we want exceptional flexibility and robust response to errors (see principle 5, below), we shall use self-describing data. That means that each discrete element of data is marked (tagged) with some universally recognized means of labeling the data. A consumer of the data will always know what data element it is processing (regardless of its expectations) and where the element ends because the element is tagged, beginning and end, with labels denoting what element it is. Any consumer that understands the vocabulary of the service is thus able to understand what the provider of the data is trying to communicate.

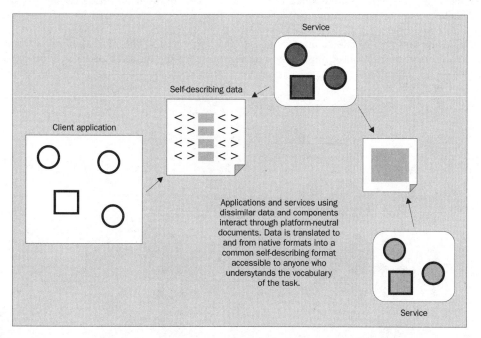

Applications and services using dissimilar data and components interact through platform-neutral documents. Data is translated to and from native formats into a common self-describing format accessible to anyone who undersytands the vocabulary of the task.

Traditionally, data is passed in a binary format where the structure of the data is shared by implication. That is, if two parties to a communication have the same message or operation in common, it is implied that they both understand the format of the data. The size, data type, and order of fields within a data structure are closely defined by design. Uncoordinated changes to data organization on the server break the client. You may have been part of a programming team working on a large client-server application in which parts of the application were assigned to different programmers. After writing the client to handle a particular data structure, you found your application broken one day. Upon investigation, you found that another programmer, responding to an enhancement request or bug report, had added a field or modified the length of an existing one without telling you. Your part of the program broke because of an arbitrary change in the data. Now, imagine the server and its structures are shared by many programming teams widely separated in geographic space and time and you can see the potential for trouble.

The use of tagged data minimizes this kind of trouble and maximizes the amount of useful sharing we can do. A consuming client or service can ignore changes it does not understand in a data structure. While we will have well-known formats, we will also tag each field within a structure. Each field is clearly delimited with the name of the field. Where fields are nested in a structure, this is made clear by the order of the delimiters. Thus, we will always be able to check for integrity on a field-by-field basis and ensure our code is responding to the data it is actually receiving, not responding to data it *assumes* it is receiving.

# 4. Services Will Be Enlisted On A Transient Basis

We must design our applications so that any persistent state is maintained solely on the tier that is interested in the computation. That is, a shopping agent is the party interested in the identity of the shopper and the shopping list, so the agent should maintain this information, not the vendor services it accesses. This works with the stateless nature of HTTP. It also allows us to minimize the dependencies between machines on our networks.

Services may come and go and clients may change their requirements. Therefore, wherever possible, a service should be written so that it need only maintain state for the duration of a single interaction with a client.

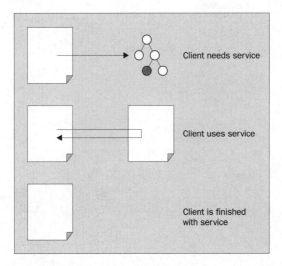

This will not always be possible, but it is the goal for which you must aim. Applications will be written as collections of clients that enlist services by making HTTP requests to obtain data. Once data is delivered, the association between the service and the client is assumed to be severed. Rather than put our efforts into ensuring state is properly maintained in a distributed system, we will devote ourselves to ensuring state need never be maintained. A client will obtain a cache of data sufficient for its needs.

From an organizational standpoint, this principle recognizes that differing development teams will change their priorities over time. An agreement reached today for maintaining state may not hold true tomorrow. This principle strives to eliminate the need for such agreements. This directly parallels the dynamic use and ad hoc release of resources we saw among the common threads of Windows DNA, Jini, and Millennium. Since we do not have the lease mechanism of Jini or the iron control of Millennium's single system image, we will limit the duration over which we must hold resources so as to minimize the chances of losing those resources while we need them.

# 5. Services Must Support Extension and Degrade Gracefully

Remember that one of our underlying problems is that independent development teams are at work. Time, distance, and organizational boundaries separate these teams. We have to expect some errors in the implementation of the data format. Even without errors, differing versions of the data will be common in wide area networks as new implementations are released. If each piece of data is tagged using some common convention, we can write code that checks to see what is coming next and respond appropriately.

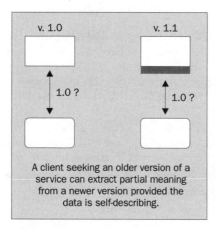

A client seeking an older version of a service can extract partial meaning from a newer version provided the data is self-describing.

Since different organizations have different views of common objects, we want to express our data in a way that will describe what pieces of data are held in common, and what pieces are specific to the offering organization. Similarly, data formats evolve over time, so we want to describe how the format has changed. That way, when a client accesses a service that offers data in a form slightly different from the form that the client would ideally like to see, it can still extract some information from the exchange. In later chapters, we will be introducing the Extensible Markup Language (XML), seeing how it is beneficial for our purposes, and presenting some principles for addressing the issues of format evolution and overlapping views of data. We will make use of its tagged, self-describing nature to express our problem vocabularies. Since it is written entirely in text, we can confidently assume that any computing platform we encounter will be able to read our data structures. In Chapter 4, I will introduce some conventions that allow you to express collections, version evolution, and specialization of a general format in terms of an XML document.

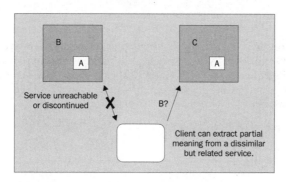

Service unreachable or discontinued

Client can extract partial meaning from a dissimilar but related service.

# Summary

Cooperative network applications make life easier for practicing intranet developers who work in real organizations with real issues of management and legacy code. I've set out five ambitious principles to follow in your practice of distributed computing with Web technologies. The chapters to come will present the tools and techniques you will need to follow these principles. We've defined cooperative network applications to be those that work in harmony with good network practices. They are built with a design philosophy that promotes the flexible sharing of data, ease of administration and maintenance, and reuse of deployed server-side applications.

We set out to develop some simple principles for building cooperative applications in a dynamic, even chaotic networking environment. We took our cues from three future network technologies: Microsoft Windows DNA, Microsoft Millennium, and Sun's Jini. We examined the goals of each and the highlights of their technology. Throughout, our objective was to identify common threads that might provide insight into our task. When we were finished, we found the following points common to these technologies:

- ❑ Component software
- ❑ Abstract service location and dynamic discovery of location at runtime
- ❑ Dynamic, ad hoc use of resources in the accomplishment of computing tasks
- ❑ Formal description of desired resources at runtime
- ❑ Distribution of the programming task across the network

Learning from these visions, we developed a philosophy for building cooperative applications. The limits on our philosophy are that it must work within currently available technologies and platforms, and must not require central control over development. We assume network applications are built by isolated development teams who cannot count on direct control over the code and interfaces to other applications and services. And we have defined The 5 Principles of Cooperative Network Application Development:

- ❑ Applications will be built from coarse-grained services that implement a unit of processing larger than components
- ❑ Services will be discovered by querying directories
- ❑ Services will be provided as self-describing data
- ❑ Services will be enlisted on a transient basis
- ❑ Services must support extension and degrade gracefully

The next six chapters build on these principles. Each chapter introduces a new technology or approach to implementing our philosophy. After that, we'll put these principles into practice as we build some applications in the course of three hypothetical case studies. Along the way we'll develop a few utilities you might find useful as the starting point for a personal tool set for developing cooperative network applications.

# 2

# Directories

In order for the loosely coupled network applications we have introduced to work as we envision, behaving cooperatively, we will need help finding the data and services. The old methods of pointing to a specific server or initializing an application from a file will not suffice in a network undergoing continuous change. Decentralized clients need to get a centralized view of the network from a globally accessible source. Fortunately, a technology which will be new to many PC programmers, and which has actually been some time in arriving, will help us. This technology is **directory services**.

In this chapter we will learn the basics of directories: what they are, how they function, and how we can reach them. In particular, we will learn a bit about the **Lightweight Directory Access Protocol** (**LDAP**) and how to locate a networked object's information in a directory. We will look at the particulars of the Active Directory, Microsoft's implementation of directory services for Windows 2000, as an example of how to use a directory service to locate services as part of our distributed application development strategy. We will give specific examples using a particular component library, the **Active Directory Service Interfaces** (**ADSI**) for accessing the Active Directory from script. Finally, we will see how an existing item in the Active Directory schema can be put to use helping our applications find the sources of data they will require.

Although we will gain a certain amount of background information regarding directories and LDAP in this chapter, our focus is entirely on locating one of our ASP-based services when we have only provided a specific class or data. Once found, we want to know how to connect to the service, what language it speaks, and how we pose queries to it.

> *Windows 2000 is in beta as we go to press. If you do not have access to this software, rest assured you can still make use of the scheme we present. This chapter will provide valuable background information on directories, as well as presenting the technique we shall use throughout this book. The software that accompanies this book, which may be downloaded from http://www.wrox.com and http://webdev.wrox.co.uk/books/2270, includes a stub version of our directory component. This stub can be used with the rest of the software in the book in the absence of Active Directory software. Even if you do not have Active Directory or some other LDAP-complaint directory service, it is important to plan for this and build applications that are directory ready. We will shortly see why this is so important and why it deserves to be one of the five principles.*

# Directory Basics

A directory service is much like a telephone directory. Finding a directory is easy; we usually have a copy at home and a copy at work to help us find local telephone numbers, and when we want a number that is outside our area we can call a service provided by the telephone company. We simply provide some information that helps us find the number we are looking for, and when we find the entry it gives us everything needed to reach the party represented by the entry.

Continuing the analogy, a telephone directory contains information about many types of objects. We think all the entries are alike, but we have entries for offices, stores, individual people, even other services that will yield still more information. In addition to telephone numbers, most printed directories provide addresses, maps, and some textual information. A telephone directory has a simple organizational scheme but is able to store information about many things and let us retrieve it.

In computing terms, a directory is a specialized repository of information that describes the nature and network location of devices, users, and services on the network and has some sort of programmatic interface to the repository. One of the key things that differentiate directory services from other types of data store is that they are highly optimized for frequent read access. Although there is obviously a mechanism for writing entries, the information is queried far more frequently than it changes. In addition, we typically do not make ad hoc queries of a directory. We tend to know what we are looking for and either navigate to it in a hierarchical fashion or perform a search on certain specific attributes. It is worth noting that Directories are not object brokers, such as are found in CORBA, although object brokers share some functions with directories. Finally, directories do not generally connect you to particular resources, but rather tell you where to find them and how you should connect.

It is fair to say that directories aren't restricted to a single structure. In practice, however, most directories do adopt a tree structure. This tree structure is very similar to how the file system on your computer is organized. For example, if you open Windows Explorer you see the various drives on your computer. In your hard drive you will find a list of folders, within which there may be other folders, and possibly some files. You can keep drilling down until you just get to a folder containing the files you are interested in.

The tree structure makes it very easy to name things and navigate to them. For example, I could have two files, both about this chapter, on my C drive called `Chapter2.doc`, but using their pathnames I can distinguish the document:

```
C:\My Documents\original\Chapter2.doc
```

where I made notes for what the chapter would contain, and the final version you are reading now:

```
C:\Books\DDA\Chapter2\Final\Chapter2.doc
```

These pathnames show the exact location of the file in the tree structure. We can break this pathname down, in this case it is broken up by backslashes, although other types of tree could use forward slashes, commas etc. The folders in the tree's structure can be considered as **container** objects, each one branches out taking you to a more specific part of the tree, while the files are the **leaves** on the tree. If the tree is well designed, the containers tell us something about the type of files they contain.

For us, both the leaves and branches on the tree are objects of interest in the network. Unlike a file system, both the leaves and containers of a directory can contain information. When we are talking about a network, instead of using the term folders we often use the term **nodes**, these nodes within the tree represent objects that contain other objects. Some of the containers are domains, while others are particular computers. For example, I could find my computer on a network using a path like this (which is rather similar to the way I could identify a file on my computer giving the pathname):

`WinNT://DOMAINNAME/COMPUTERNAME`

The IETF (Internet Engineering Task Force) added the idea of domain naming so those directories written to an early standard, X.500, could be rooted within the domain name system of the Internet. Thus, an object in a directory housed on the fictional `MegaWidgets.com` server is said to reside within the `MegaWidgets` domain, which is in itself a part of the `com` domain of the Internet. Within a domain, other containers may be used to compose a structure that is useful to the owning organization and descriptive of the network. Here is a conceptual view of a generic directory:

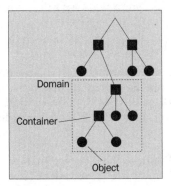

# Namespaces

The ability to offer a name and receive information about the named object is central to directory services. In fact, we say that a directory is a **namespace** – a bounded entity in which names are uniquely mapped to information. Since networks can be large and contain many items of interest, we need a formal method of naming the items in our directory. LDAP provides that through the idea of **distinguished names** (**DN**), which we meet shortly.

LDAP roots its namespace in the domain name system of the Internet. The top level containers are the top level domain names of the Internet. We can readily make our directory servers accessible to our external partners via the Internet using the proper distinguished name when our directory is so rooted.

We navigate through the namespace by specifying a path through the namespace. Consequently, any object can be identified by a combination of containers and a local name which, taken together, define the path through the directory needed to locate the object within the namespace. Some directories, notably Microsoft's Active Directory, also include the concept of **domains**. Each domain holds objects and containers for objects.

# Directory Servers

Information in a network ultimately comes from a server. A directory service consists of one or more servers providing directory look-ups. These servers must be accessible to all devices and users on the network to be useful. If we require all our clients to know the names of our directory servers, however, we will be repeating the mistake of hard-coding machine names. Everything can change in a network, even the number, nature, and location of directory servers. So, directory service APIs need a mechanism allowing clients to discover the directory servers available to them. For example, Active Directory provides a mechanism, as a part of the operating system, so that any machine can find the nearest directory server. Once found, we can use the directory schema to gain a sense of the network and expand our search to other servers. This is similar to how telephone directory assistance functions in the United States. You can call a single number from any telephone and reach the nearest directory. From there, you can obtain additional information – the area code – that allows you to compose the telephone number for the directory service of some remote area. You do not know where that service is located or how it is implemented, only how to find it, and from it, any other directory anywhere in the world. In this book we will be paying particular attention to Microsoft's Active Directory.

## Active Directory

Let's just clear up one frequent cause of confusion, Active Directory and ADSI might have very similar names but they are *not* the same thing. Active Directory is a directory store, and is just one of the things that you can access using ADSI. ADSI is out now, while Active Directory will be introduced with Windows 2000 Server (although it's actually already available with the Windows 2000 beta).

Active Directory forms part of the Windows 2000 Server operating system. It is intended to replace the NT domains of NT4 and is likely to be a very important directory on your network. Why? Because it's not just a directory, but it is *the* directory of network resources in a Windows network – which computers are in which domain, what printers, scanners etc. are located where, and who has security rights to do what. In other words, it's a central directory of everything you need to control your network. In fact (at least on the current beta version of NT5), if you decide to promote a server to be a domain controller you do so by installing Active Directory. So running Active Directory is synonymous with being a domain controller.

## Netscape Directory Server

We won't actually be using Netscape Directory Server in this book, but it deserves a mention because it is a widely regarded, scaleable, and general-purpose LDAP directory and was available at the time of writing. It traces its lineage to the original LDAP implementation at the University of Michigan. Netscape Directory Server can be used to store whatever you want. It is generally regarded as being highly scaleable and reliable, and conforms to LDAP version 3, an open standard that describes how the data in the server can be accessed. It's possible to access data stored in Netscape Directory Server using ADSI. We'll explain more about LDAP later in this chapter.

Having had an overview of Directory Services, let's take a look at how they are organized, using the concept of **Schemas**.

# Schemas

The schema defines the kind of information that can be stored in a particular directory. In an LDAP directory the schema defines this in terms of the object classes and attribute types that the directory can contain.

Each directory server in a particular network uses a common **schema**. The schema is made up of two types of rule, which define the schema, and help organize the information in the directory, these rules are:

❑ structure rules
❑ content rules

We've talked a bit about general structure of a directory service, now let's take a closer look at a schema using an example. Here we have a fictional directory for Wrox with details of Schema, Staff, and Books – everything. The diagram below shows a part of this tree:

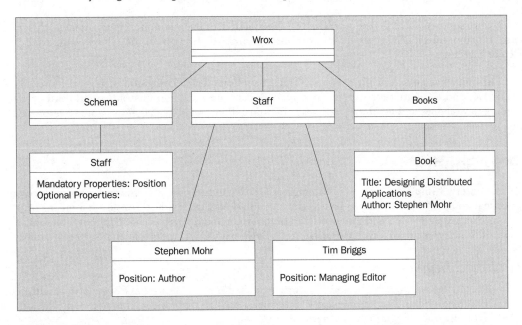

### Structure Rules

At the top level there's an object called `Wrox`, which is the company's domain. Below it in the tree structure is a container called `Staff`, which contains details of all the employees in the company. Obviously, we don't want to store information about our books in the same container as the staff, so we need some rules about what is allowed to go where. These rules will be implemented by the directory service, so that, if a client application tries to make a change to the directory that goes against these rules, the directory service will refuse to make the change. These types of rules are known as **structure rules**. Quite simply, they are the rules that define the structure of the directory.

### Content Rules

But we will also want to add detail to the objects. For example, we want to store each member of staff's position, e-mail address, department, etc. with the employee's record. These bits of information are known as **attributes** or **properties**. But, if someone new joins, who doesn't understand our system, he might accidentally try to add a release date or ISBN number to a member of staff. To prevent this happening (and any offence being taken due to such a mistake) we clearly need some rules that determine what information is allowed to be stored with each entry. Such rules are known as **content rules**.

Every entry in the tree is of some object class. It is the entry's object class that defines what attributes (the content rules) that the entry contains. Because the containers and leaves have attributes, information contained in the directory tree is not all held at one level; rather it is spread throughout the nodes in the tree.

So, it is these structure rules and content rules that are collectively known as the schema. In Active Directory each domain's schema is represented by entries stored in the directory itself.

The directory service uses the schema in satisfying namespace queries. Although most schemas will have common entries, such as those for users, computers, and protocols, there is no need for every directory that is connected to the Internet to share the same schema.

This is where we meet LDAP. The purpose of LDAP is to provide a common language, which servers can use to name things. Using LDAP, you can discover information about the schema supported by a particular directory.

Active Directory has an extensible schema. While it supports a rich collection of several hundreds of object classes and attribute types out of the box, with care, network administrators and third parties can define new classes and attributes. This is sometimes done to aid in managing unique resources or applications.

# LDAP in General

Given the different implementations of directories across the Internet, a common access protocol and programmatic interface is desirable. That is the role filled by LDAP. LDAP provides a means of talking to a directory service and attempting to obtain data about some object contained therein. Since most directories are hierarchical in nature, LDAP can use a standard format for path names.

## Distinguished Names

At the root of LDAP's syntax is the notion of distinguished names. As we have seen, a distinguished name (DN) uniquely identifies an object if it describes a path to that object from a known starting point. A DN is a series of comma delimited name-value pairs.

Domains are designated using the LDAP attribute for a Domain Controller, DC. The two kinds of high-level containers are Organization (O) and Organizational Unit (OU). Below this, all objects are named using a Common Name (CN). Thus, a server belonging to the Customer Service organizational unit of the fictional MegaWidgets company might have the distinguished name:

```
CN=PrintSrv, OU=Customer Service, DC=MegaWidgets, DC=COM
```

We can compose a DN for a container rather than an object if we wish to locate a container so as to enumerate all the objects contained within it. There is also the notion of a **relative distinguished name (RDN)**. The RDN for an object or container is that part of the DN which is specific to the item itself. The RDN for our server in the example above is CN=PrintSrv.

We will use DNs throughout this chapter. They are used as part of queries for objects and to bind to a specific object in order to obtain the attributes that describe it.

## Directory Access: The LDAP API and COM Components

The LDAP specification includes a C language API that all LDAP compliant directory services must support. We will not delve into this API in this chapter.

*If you are interested in LDAP pick up a copy of Implementing LDAP, ISBN 1-861002-211, from Wrox Press.*

Our development philosophy places strong emphasis on component software construction. Writing an entire component or plug-in to afford access to the Active Directory would undoubtedly be time consuming, and is not really necessary. Fortunately, Microsoft provides a library of components, the Active Directory Service Interfaces (ADSI), which performs this task for us. As we shall see, we will use ADSI for binding, although we will also need to use another component library, **ADO** (ActiveX Data Objects), for queries due to current limitations on the use of ADSI from Web scripts. We will retain the LDAP syntax, however, so that readers who wish to use the low-level LDAP API will have a point from which to start.

# Microsoft Active Directory

Microsoft Windows NT 5.0 – to be known as Windows 2000 Server when released – introduces an LDAP compliant directory service as part of the operating system, known as the Active Directory. Active Directory uses DNS or **Domain Name Service** as its naming and location service.

The Domain Name Service (DNS) is familiar to us all, and is defined in RFCs 1034 and 1035. It is designed to provide a human-friendly name for the location of computers on the Internet. DNS names are formed by names separated by dots, for example www.wrox.com. NT4 domains didn't necessarily have any connection with Internet domain names. This is important, because with Windows 2000 it will be possible to form domain trees and give the domains DNS type names, allowing it to integrate well with IP based inter- and intranets.

Active Directory supports the native LDAP API as well as ADSI and ADO queries. The Active Directory store may be replicated among a number of servers for fault tolerance or partitioned across multiple servers for scalability. It inherits the operating system's native security, which defaults to the Kerberos distributed security protocol in this version of Windows 2000. Other protocols, such as SSL and the native security system from earlier versions of Windows NT, can also be used, thereby affording maximum flexibility to system administrators.

# Structure

Active Directory scales by joining small-scale structures of computers into larger groupings. This mirrors the hierarchical nature of LDAP directories. This structure begins at the level of domains and continues through domain trees to forests.

## *Domain*

Windows NT security and administration has revolved around the notion of domains since the operating system was introduced. Although the default security model has changed, domains remain a building block for administering and securing Windows NT networks. A domain is simply a group of computers that share a common primary domain controller and use the same security schema.

Typically, domains reflect reliable, high-speed subnets. Domains may be configured to participate in trust relationships, so that a machine in one domain may access an object in another without having security credentials in the second domain. This becomes important as we join domains to create our organizational directory. The Active Directory Tree Manager automatically establishes the appropriate trust relationship when two domains are joined.

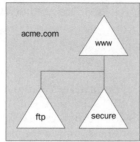

In Windows NT 3.x & Windows NT 4 one **Domain Controller** was set as primary (PDC) and Backup Domain Controllers (BDCs) were used to support the PDC. Active Directory has a multi-master model, in which the authoritative DCs accept change requests and then propagate them directly down the tree. This multi-master model combined with the transient trust relationship makes Active Directory a perfect platform for inter-site replication.

Domain controllers execute the Active Directory service. Depending on how we organize our directory, we may replicate the directory store between domain controllers for fault tolerance or partition the store so that the complete Active Directory contains many more objects than could be accommodated by a single domain controller. It is common for the domain structure of a network to reflect the organizational structure of the business operating the network.

Large domains may be divided into collections of organizational units (OU) to impose a more detailed structure on the directory. OUs may also be used to fine tune access and administration rights. OUs do not, however, affect the hosting of the Active Directory service.

Domains are important in another way. One of the advantages of having a directory is that it allows us to get away from having to remember machine names when we want to find something on the network. If we had to remember the names of our Active Directory servers, we would lose almost all of this advantage. We would be able to discover every machine *except* the directory servers. LDAP and the Active Directory address this through a technique known as **serverless binding**. From this starting point, we can walk up and down the directory to discover other domains and domain trees within the directory.

## Domain Trees

Just as a company joins groups into divisions, Active Directory allows us to join domains together to reflect a larger organizational entity. User and administrative rights may be granted for all domains or a select list of domains. Not only does this control access by users, it simplifies administration. Responsibility for administering the Active Directory can be delegated to individual domain administrators.

Domains are joined in a hierarchy to create a domain tree. Domains can contain other domains. For example, suppose Sales and Customer Service are domains that have been joined as children of the External Relations domain.

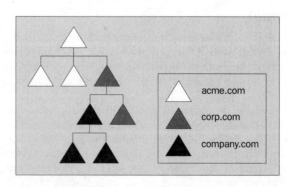

Now suppose an application in the Customer Service domain is searching for an object within its domain. The appropriate DN would include:

```
LDAP://DC=Customer Service
```

If it needs to search for an object in Sales, the DN would include:

```
LDAP://DC=Sales, DC=External Relations.
```

The application would either know the name of the domain it wishes to search, or would query the directory to obtain the names of all the domains.

So, when do we create a domain tree? All domains within a domain tree form a single DNS namespace. If we are joining networks that have separate DNS namespaces, two domain trees are called for. This has implications for directory searches, as well. A search using the **global catalog** (which is like an index for the directory) searches the entire directory. If we need to search based on an attribute that is not stored in the global catalog, however, we will only search objects in the current domain tree.

## Forest

Obviously, if we can have multiple domain trees in an organization's directory, there must be some overall grouping. This grouping is the forest. While two domain trees in the same forest do not share a DNS namespace, they must share the same schema and global catalog. When domain trees are joined, a trust relationship is established between the root domains of each tree in much the same way as occurred when we joined individual domains into domain trees.

## The Active Directory Schema

We have alluded to objects and their attributes. The collection of types of objects – classes – and their attributes is known as the schema for the directory. The schema applies to all levels of the directory. Active Directory contains a rich schema by default. An administrator may extend the schema by creating new classes of objects and new attributes for those classes, thereby extending his directory to become a general-purpose repository for information about networked resources. Classes in an LDAP-compliant schema may inherit from other classes. This allows us to progressively refine the information we publish in the directory by specifying only those attributes that are new to a newly created class. The new class possesses all the attributes of the class from which it was derived.

## Global Catalog

Occasionally, we will want to be able to find an object in the directory without knowing its DN. This might occur because we do not know what domain contains the object. Other times, we might wish to find all objects fitting a particular description. Provided we know the value of some key attributes, we can perform a search of the global catalog. The global catalog contains a partial copy of every object in the directory and as such acts like an index to the contents of the directory. For each class of objects, the Active Directory schema specifies a base set of attributes, which is stored in the global catalog. Administrators may add to these sets, and can specify which attributes are stored in the global catalog when creating a new class. While we can add attributes to the default list copied in the global catalog, adding attributes has an adverse effect on storage requirements and indexing time. At the extreme, if we stored all attributes we would have two copies of our directory! If we need to search outside the domain tree of the searching user, for an attribute not copied to the global catalog, we will need to repeat our search in each domain tree. The global catalog is maintained automatically by the directory replication system.

### Structure

Any particular object belongs to a single domain. An application executing on a particular machine traverses the directory structure through the use of distinguished names. If the desired object is in another domain, the application discovers the domain root and composes the appropriate DN from that root to the object. Subsets of the attributes of the objects in the directory are also stored in the global catalog. This permits rapid searching of the entire directory without walking the entire tree. Deciding what attributes to store in the global catalog is an important design issue if the catalog is to be kept to a manageable size.

Active Directory also has the concept of sites. These should not be confused with Web sites. Rather, they are subnets, usually for a local facility, like a LAN at a particular operating location. This is not, however, an LDAP structural element so we will not spend time on it here.

# Hosting and Replication

Large networks need multiple directory servers for several reasons:

❑ The loss of a single server should not result in the loss of the directory

❑ Loss of a portion of the network topology should not isolate a user from the directory simply because the directory server is no longer accessible from the isolated subnet

❑ Even under normal operation, it is simply not efficient to have all directory accesses traversing the entire network to reach a central directory server

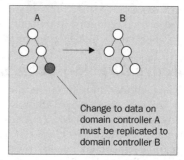

For these reasons, Active Directory allows multiple **domain controllers** to host the directory service. Keeping the information stored on multiple servers coherent is a task for the **replication** service. Permitting multiple directories to act as directory servers while resolving replication collisions from other servers is a concept know as **multi-master replication**.

Change to data on domain controller A must be replicated to domain controller B

## Domain Controllers

Each domain in Windows 2000 has a primary domain controller and zero or more back-up domain controllers. Each domain controller stores a copy of the domain's directory namespace. Since all computers must connect to the network at boot-up to obtain network resources they will connect with the domain controller, and subsequently will learn the location of all domain controllers in the domain. Therefore the directory is automatically visible to any computer entering the domain.

## Replication

Generally speaking, replication is automatic and should never explicitly concern the application programmer. It is the job of the network administrator to establish policies governing the frequency of replication. Changes made to the directory must, however, be reflected in the directory store at all other directory servers within the domain. If these changes affect the global catalog, they must be passed along to all domain controllers in the network.

To be realistic, it is not practical to replicate changes immediately to all servers in a large forest, particularly while clients are referencing the directory (although the changes must be replicated eventually). Moreover, as we shall see in a moment, any of the directory servers can make changes to their particular copy at any time. Thus, there is no guarantee of absolute consistency among replicas of the directory at any given instant. Over time, however, the replicas are reconciled and the directory becomes coherent. Active Directory uses sophisticated mechanisms to ensure replication updates between servers are dampened and do not propagate endlessly across loops in the directory topology. Similarly, great care is taken to resolve collisions – the situation that occurs when two replicas contain differing updates of the same object.

## Multi-master Replication

There is no single master domain controller in the Active Directory architecture. Nor is there a single server controlling the replication of changed directory objects between servers in the forest. Instead, all domain controllers hosting the directory service are seen as peers. We say that the Active Directory uses multi-master replication. This affords a high degree of availability as no single server failure results in loss of the directory service. Additionally, clients making changes to directory objects are using a server close to them in network terms. Because there is no need for all clients to use a single server to make changes, the processing load from directory changes becomes distributed across all the servers hosting the directory.

When a domain controller writes a change to a directory object, it also writes an Update Sequence Number as part of a single, atomic transaction. This is simply a sequential series of integers numbering changes to the directory. These sequence numbers are broadcast between servers periodically, allowing servers to request copies of updates they have not yet seen. The sequence numbers are the primary source for determining which version of an object is current. This eliminates the need to enforce time synchronization across a large, distributed network. Timestamps are used, however, as tiebreakers when the sequence numbers are not sufficient to resolve a collision.

Since replication isn't instantaneous, application programmers should respect the possibility of changes to data and obtain all related pieces of directory information at the same time, and directory information should never be cached in the application itself.

# Client Access

Hopefully, you are now excited about using directories for maintaining configuration information. Having a robust store managed by the network eliminates many concerns formerly borne by the application programmer. We don't have to worry about configuration files or coordinating registry entries. We also don't have to worry about getting configuration changes on a server application out to all possible clients. How, then, can we get information from the Active Directory?

As we have already seen, the Active Directory is LDAP-compliant. We could therefore use the LDAP API for our purposes. This is a low-level API intended for C programmers. Web development, however, is inherently a high-level programming environment, so there would be loud sighs of relief if we could avoid writing bits and pieces of C code just to access the directory. Fortunately, because Active Directory is LDAP compliant, and ADSI includes an LDAP provider, we can use the ADSI object model to access Active Directory from Web page scripts.

*Although we will be using ADSI with the Active Directory, you are not limited to this directory service. You can already use ADSI as your interface to any LDAP-compliant directory with NT4.*

## Active Directory Service Interfaces

ADSI can be seen essentially as a set of definitions intended to unify directory access, in other words, as a set of common function calls. We shall be using the ADSI LDAP provider, which can be used to access any LDAP compliant directory.

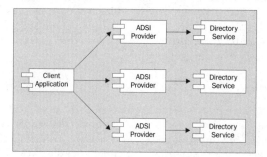

How this works in practice is shown in the diagram above. The client is the application that needs to make use of the data in the directory. The directory service is the directory, together (in some cases) with some software that makes that directory available to the outside world. In between is the ADSI provider. The ADSI provider is the component that is able both to communicate with a particular directory service, using that service's API, and to talk to clients using the standard ADSI methods. You can almost think of it as a language translator that allows clients that only understand ADSI to talk to directories.

The ADSI provider is actually a dynamic linked library (DLL), which means that communication between the client and the provider is extremely efficient. By contrast, the directory service will normally be in a different process, possibly even on a different machine, so talking to it is much slower. This means that it's useful to keep the number of calls to the directory service itself to a minimum. The ADSI methods handle this by caching a lot of information in the client's process, in something called a **property cache**.

By wrapping each directory object in a COM object, ADSI allows the client to appear as if it's talking to the object in the directory itself, even though it's actually talking to a COM object sitting in its own process space, created by the ADSI DLL. The COM object exposes the same properties as the directory object, and it also exposes methods to carry out useful operations, such as enumerating all its children if it's a container object.

We will be concerned with the LDAP provider here, although a WinNT provider is included with the basic ADSI distribution, which exposes a more limited set of objects from Windows NT 4.0 and Windows 2000 Server domain controllers. We **bind** to an object in the directory to access its attributes. Binding is the process of providing authentication to the directory in order to obtain access to the information contained within. When we do this via ADSI, the object in the directory is presented as an **automation object** (a COM object that exposes a dual interface and supports the late binding required by scripting languages). This makes it easy to manipulate directory objects from script in Web pages.

We can use one of two methods to bind to an object from script: the operating system's `GetObject()` method and the `OpenDSObject()` method of the `IADsOpenDSObject` interface. `GetObject()` uses the current user ID and security credentials when binding to an object. This is usually what we want to do, particularly if we are doing this from the client side of an intranet. When using `OpenDSObject()` we are required to provide a specific user ID, which we need for server-side access. `OpenDSObject()` also provides encryption to protect the data as it is transferred between the directory and the calling application.

Binding to directory objects from script is easy, but ad hoc directory searches are a problem for Web developers. ADSI provides the `IDirectorySearch` interface to help with this, but it is not accessible from script code because it is not a dual interface. Only early-binding languages like C++ can make use of this interface. Fortunately, a database provider component is available within the ActiveX Data Objects library that will let us search the directory using either LDAP or SQL queries from our Web pages.

### ActiveX Data Objects and LDAP

ActiveX Data Objects (ADO) are a collection of COM components for database access under Microsoft Windows. An interesting feature of ADO is that simply creating a COM component that exposes certain well-defined interfaces will provide us with access to non-relational sources. This enables us to query the directory as if it were a relational database simply by using the `ADsDSOObject` provider (DSO stands for Data Source Object). This provider (which comes with the ADSI 2.5 beta at the time of writing) is currently read-only, but that will be sufficient for our purposes. If you require write access, however, you can always use ADSI to bind to any object you find. Unfortunately the `ADsDSOObject` provider is only available with Windows 2000 beta 2 or later.

A thorough treatment of ADO can be found in *ADO 2.0 Programmer's Reference* from Wrox Press (ISBN 1-1861001-83-5), but the basic query access we require can be accomplished with a small subset of the ADO object model. As you might imagine in dealing with databases, we will need to create a **Connection** object specifying the source and user information. If you have dealt with SQL database programming, you will know that data is returned in a **Recordset**. We may also use an interface that might not be familiar to you, that of the **Command** object. This component interprets the command language we will be using. The `ADsDSOObject` provider is unusual in that it will accept either SQL or LDAP syntax. We'll use LDAP in the rest of this chapter to promote familiarity with that syntax, but we'll also give a SQL example in a little while for the benefit of those readers who may be well versed in SQL.

# ADSI Basics

Let's dive in and learn about ADSI programming. The basic tasks of ADSI access are:

- ❑ Locating a server
- ❑ Binding to a particular object
- ❑ Obtaining the values of that object's attributes

We also need to be able to enumerate all the objects in a particular container.

> *We'll work through enough ADSI to satisfy the requirements of our five principles. ADSI and the Active Directory are too rich and complex to fully explore in one chapter. A full examination of ADSI is found in* Professional ADSI CDO *(ISBN 1-861001-90-8) and* ADSI ASP Programmer's Reference *(ISBN 1-1861001-69-X) both from Wrox Press.*

# Serverless Binding

As we noted in our discussion of domains, Active Directory supports serverless binding, it uses the LDAP name `rootDSE` (which refers to the root of the directory tree on a particular directory server). So, an anonymous user can connect to the domain controller and retrieve attributes of the server with the following code in an ASP:

```
var rootDSE = GetObject("LDAP://rootDSE");
Response.Write("Domain: " + rootDSE.Get("defaultNamingContext"));
Response.Write("Current Server Time: " + rootDSE.Get("CurrentTime"));
Response.Write("DNS Host: " + rootDSE.Get("DnsHostName"));
Response.Write("Server Name: " + rootDSE.Get("ServerName"));
```

If the HTTP server is in a different domain from that in which the user logged-in, we could use the same approach on the client to retrieve the client's domain. Alternatively, if we want to explicitly connect to a known domain controller, the MegaWidgets domain for example, we should use:

```
var rootDSE = GetObject("LDAP:/MegaWidgets/rootDSE");
```

The first line of this ASP example is the most important, because this is the line which creates the object that implements the interface. We are telling the operating system to connect to a running directory object, creating a new COM object as a wrapper in response to the GetObject() call using our LDAP name as the name of the object. The domain controller presents the Active Directory service as such an object. Consequently, rootDSE is an object representing the domains' directory subtree.

> *Readers with some experience in COM programming may be interested to note that binding with all of the ADSI providers is implemented in the Active Directory using COM monikers.*

On my domain controller, named Vandenberg in the widgets domain, the result looks like this:

Domain: DC=widgets
Current Server Time: 19981106162743.0Z
DNS Host: VANDENBERG.widgets
Server Name: CN=VANDENBERG,CN=Servers,
  CN=Philadelphia,CN=Sites,CN=Configuration,DC=widgets

The rootDSE object supports a number of useful properties. The attribute defaultNamingContext is perhaps the most important as it allows us to find our domain; from there we can navigate through domain trees and even the entire directory forest. Note the ServerName attribute. My server, Vandenberg, belongs to the container Servers within the container Philadelphia, which is a site (hence is within the Sites container). A site is part of the network configuration, so Sites is contained in the Configuration container on the widgets domain. (Distinguished names can sometimes tell you more than you ever wanted to know.) One use for retrieving the time on the domain controller could be for reconciling times in specialized applications, or alternatively it could be to impress your friends. The rootDSE object supports the following attributes:

> *Note that some attributes can hold multiple values concurrently, which we term a **multi-valued** attribute*

| Attribute | Description |
|---|---|
| CurrentTime | Time set on the directory server. |
| SubschemaSubentry | DN for an object exposing the supported classes and attributes of the schema. |
| DsServiceName | DN for an object exposing the settings in the directory server. |
| NamingContexts | Multi-valued, DNs for all naming contexts in the server. Default values are Schema, Configuration, and the domain to which the server belongs. |
| DefaultNamingContext | DN for the domain to which the server belongs. |
| SchemaNamingContext | DN for the Schema container. |
| ConfigurationNamingContext | DN for the Configuration container. |
| RootDomainNamingContext | DN for the root domain of the tree containing this server. |
| SupportedControl | Unique Object IDs for extension controls supported by the server. |
| SupportedLDAPVersion | Multi-valued, major version numbers of the LDAP versions supported by this server. |
| HighestCommittedUSN | Serial number of the latest change notification to the directory. |
| SupportedSASLMechanisms | Security mechanisms supported for SASL negotiation. |
| DnsHostName | DNS address of the server. |
| LdapServiceName | Service Principal Name for the LDAP server. |
| ServerName | DN for the server object for this server in the Configuration container. |

In the table above, SASL refers to the Simple Authentication and Security Layer, a secure means of binding in which the client and the directory agree on an authentication protocol, like Kerberos, instead of passing cleartext passwords.

# Binding to a Directory Object

The technique we used to bind to the rootDSE object works for any object in the directory provided we know its distinguished name. Let's suppose I've forgotten my e-mail URL and wish to recover it the hard way. I can bind to my user object like so:

```
var rootDSE = GetObject("LDAP://rootDSE");
var me = GetObject("LDAP://CN=Stephen Mohr,CN=Users," +
    rootDSE.Get("defaultNamingContext"));
```

You'll quickly recognize the first line as we are recovering the domain name using serverless binding. In the next line, I bind to my user object. Starting at the lowest level, I know my common name (CN=Stephen Mohr), and I know all user objects are children of the Users container. The rootDSE object gives me the domain name to complete the distinguished name.

We can also bind to the global catalog at one of three levels: domain, domain tree, or forest. In each scope, the keyword for global catalog, GC, replaces LDAP. We simply need to get the right information to compose the distinguished name for each scope. For the domain we can use the following:

```
var root = GetObject("LDAP://RootDSE");
var domaincat = GetObject("GC://" + root.Get("defaultNamingContext"));
```

For the domain tree:

```
var root = GetObject("GC://RootDSE");
var treecat = GetObject("GC://" + root.Get("rootDomainNamingContext"));
```

The forest is slightly different. It is the root of the entire tree, so we don't have to specify what context to use. The GC container holds a single object to which we should bind. In VBScript we write:

```
Set root = GetObject("GC:")
For each child in root
   Set bindobj = child
Next
```

# Accessing Attributes

Now we know how to bind to any object at any level of the Active Directory we can turn to attributes. Returning to our email example, how do I get my URL once I've bound to my user object? The simplest means of querying for an attribute is one we've already seen. Once we have the object, we simply call the Get() method with the name of the desired attribute. Continuing with the code fragment we saw earlier:

```
var rootDSE = GetObject("LDAP://rootDSE");
var me = GetObject("LDAP://CN=Stephen Mohr,CN=Users," +
            rootDSE.Get("defaultNamingContext"));
if (me != null)
     alert(me.Get("mail"));
   else
     alert("Failed to find me in this domain.");
```

Once we have bound to my user object, we simply use that object's Get() method to obtain my mail attribute.

# Enumerating Objects

Sometimes, of course, we will need to enumerate a number of objects in a container. This will apply not only to containers, but also for multi-valued attributes such as lists. Here's some VBScript code to enumerate all the users in the Users container:

```
sub OnUsers()
    On Error Resume Next
    set ou = GetObject("LDAP://CN=Users,DC=widgets")
    ou.Filter = Array("user")
    for each aUsr in ou
        MsgBox(aUsr.Get("samAccountName"))
    next
end sub
```

Here, ou is a variable mapped to the Users container. We apply a filter so that we see only those objects in the container that belong to the user class. Objects of this class possess an attribute samAccountName that is the human-friendly name of the user. We use the enumeration feature of VBScript collections to define a variable, aUsr, which successively takes on the value of each user object in the collection.

> *As of beta 2 of Windows 2000 and the beta release of ADSI 2.5, there is some question of the ability of JavaScript to bind properly to collections. Consequently, much of our script in this chapter will be written in VBScript to work around this difficulty.*

Something similar is needed for multi-valued attributes. Since each multi-valued attribute returned is a collection, we have to enumerate each value of the attribute in turn. This subroutine in VBScript retrieves all the descriptions applied to my user account:

```
Sub OnGetEx()
    dim administrator
    dim descList

    Set administrator = GetObject("LDAP://vandenberg/CN=Stephen Mohr,+ _
        CN=Users,DC=widgets")

    descList = administrator.GetEx("description")

    For Each Desc in descList
        MsgBox(Desc)
    Next
End Sub
```

GetEx() always returns entries as a VBScript array, which is helpful when you do not know whether a value is multi-valued or not.

# Directory Queries

So far we've seen how to bind to servers and known objects. In the next few chapters we'll see that we won't generally know which specific server we want. Instead, we'd like to be able to search based on some particular attribute. For that, we need directory queries.

# LDAP Queries

We prefer to work with LDAP rather than the proprietary native APIs of different directory services because it is supported by many directory services. Consequently, readers who may not be using the Active Directory can take away some information they can use with their directory service. Moreover, this is an open networking protocol and we are building network applications. LDAP is therefore the 'natural' syntax to use with directory services.

## *Syntax*

The LDAP string for a directory query consists of the distinguished name for the root object of the search and several optional parameters:

```
<base DN>[;(filter)][;attributeList][;scope][;preferences]
```

### *Base Distinguished Name*

The distinguished name for the base of our search is what we've become accustomed to in terms of specifying some container or server. For example, if we wished to query the widgets domain on the server named vandenberg, the start of the LDAP string would be:

```
<LDAP://vandenberg/DC=widgets>;
```

### *Filters*

The filter allows us to set search criteria. We specify the name of an attribute (cn for the common name or objectClass for the schema of the object for example) along with an operator and a value, which may include literals and the wildcard character *. So, to restrict our search to user objects, we would use a filter of the form:

```
(objectClass=user)
```

We could use an asterisk in the place of user, as a wildcard for specifying any value, so long as a value exists. The operators supported are:

| Operator Meaning | Operator Symbol |
|---|---|
| and | & |
| or | \| |
| not | ! |
| equal | = |
| approximately | ~= |
| greater than or equal to | >= |
| less than or equal to | <= |

You can combine these to form complex criteria. Filters are built using a prefix notation in which the operator always precedes the arguments on which it operates. For example, if we wish to find all user objects with a surname of Smith, we would use:

```
(&(objectClass=user)(sn='Smith'))
```

### *Attribute List*

This is simply a comma-delimited list of the object attributes we wish to see in our search. If no attribute list is provided, all the attributes of the objects matching the search criteria will be retrieved. Specifying an explicit attribute list allows the Active Directory data provider to ignore other attributes. This improves performance and reduces the amount of data that is returned. For example, if I wanted to see the common name and Active Directory path for some object my attribute list would be:

```
cn, ADsPath;
```

## Scope

The portion of the directory we are searching could become quite large depending on the base distinguished name we've specified. As with all good search techniques, it is important to restrict the scope of our search in the Active Directory. Three levels of scope are defined. These are summarized below:

| Scope Identifier | Meaning |
|---|---|
| Base | Searches only the base DN provided; can return only zero or one object |
| OneLevel | Searches the immediate children of the base DN (excludes the object named by the base DN) |
| SubTree | Searches the entire subtree of the directory whose root is the object named by the base DN (includes the object named by the base DN) |

The SubTree scope is most useful if we are searching the home domain of the current user. The size of the subtree should be relatively small, and we can search without concerning ourselves about what organizational units or containers may have been created. This level of search is warranted because we expect the user to find resources closest to home. When he goes outside his domain in search of resources, we would expect him to be less likely to find services tucked away in odd corners. Instead, we would expect to search the immediate children of the domain. This presupposes that directory objects for services of use to a wide community are placed in the top level of a particular domain to make it easy for outsiders to find them (which is a good general rule to follow).

## Preferences

Preferences serve to configure the operation of the search. In most cases, the default values are fine. If, however, we are expecting a very large number of possible objects in response to a query, we may wish to set some limits. The ADSI documentation enumerates a number of possible preferences. Here are the preferences supported by the Active Directory:

| Preference Name | Data Type | Meaning | Default value |
|---|---|---|---|
| Asynchronous | true/false | true if searches should be asynchronous | false |
| Deref Aliases | true/false | Resolve object aliases when found | false |
| Size Limit | integer value | maximum number of returned objects | no limit (0) |
| Time Limit | integer value | maximum time in seconds to search before returning | no limit (0) |
| Column Names Only | true/false | return only the names of attributes | false |
| SearchScope | 0 (base), 1 (OneLevel), 2 (SubTree) | directory scope of the search | 2 |

*Table Continued on Following Page*

| Preference Name | Data Type | Meaning | Default value |
|---|---|---|---|
| Timeout | integer value | timeout period for the binding | none (0) |
| Page Size | integer value | size of ADO database pages for results | none (0) |
| Chase Referrals | true/false | send a referral message to the client when naming contexts are crossed, e.g., the search crosses a domain boundary | false |
| Cache Results | true/false | Retain search results in a client-side cache | true |

The information given for the Deref Aliases preference is for searches using ADO. ADSI searches use an enumerated value for this preference, which can be any of the following:

❑ never(0) – do not dereference when searching
❑ searching (1) – dereference aliases when searching subordinate entries of the specified base, but not when locating the base object
❑ finding (2) – dereference when locating the base object, but not when searching subordinates
❑ always (3) – dereference both when finding the base object and when searching subordinates.

## An Example in ADO

Let's pretend I'm still searching for my e-mail URL. We'll do an ADO search against the directory with the Active Directory provider. For clarity we'll go directly to my domain controller rather than finding it through a serverless binding. That way, we avoid having to make another search to locate the domain controller.

```
Sub OnQuery()
    dim dbConn, dbRecordSet

    Set dbConn = CreateObject("ADODB.Connection")
    dbConn.Provider = "ADsDSOObject"
    dbConn.Open "Active Directory Provider",
            "CN=SearchUser,CN=Users,DC=widgets", +
            "pwd"

    Set dbRecordSet = dbConn.Execute("<LDAP://vandenberg/DC=widgets>;
                            (&(objectClass=User)(mail=s*));cn,
                            mail;SubTree")

    While Not dbRecordSet.EOF
        MsgBox(dbRecordSet.Fields(0).Value + " " +
                dbRecordSet.Fields(1).Value)
        dbRecordSet.MoveNext
    Wend
End Sub
```

We use the standard `CreateObject()` call for creating an ADO Connection object. We have to tell the connection object which database provider to use, which is `ADsDSOObject` for the Active Directory provider. Next, we have to open a connection to this provider specifying user credentials. `Active Directory Provider` is the system name for the Active Directory provider. The next two parameters are the user credentials. This code assumes you have created a user named `SearchUser` with the password `pwd` who has access to the directory. Note that we name the user with an LDAP DN.

Once we have an open connection, we obtain a recordset object containing data by executing our LDAP syntax command. We specify a base DN of the `widgets` domain on the `vandenberg` domain controller. For a filter, we're looking for any object that is a `User` object and that has a `mail` attribute beginning with 's'. We tell the provider that we are interested in the `common name` and `mail` attributes so as to reduce the amount of data that is returned. Since I'm not sure where my `User` object is (remember, I'm having trouble remembering my e-mail URL), we'll search the entire subtree, which in this case will be the entire domain. All this is in the line:

```
Set dbRecordSet = dbConn.Execute("<LDAP://vandenberg/DC=widgets>;
                                  (&(objectClass=User)(mail=s*));
                                  cn, mail;SubTree")
```

Finally, we iterate through the recordset by seeing if the recordset has reached the end of file (`EOF`). If it hasn't, we display the attributes of one row and direct the recordset to move to the next row of data returned.

```
While Not dbRecordSet.EOF
    MsgBox(dbRecordSet.Fields(0).Value + " " + dbRecordSet.Fields(1).Value)
    dbRecordSet.MoveNext
Wend
```

# SQL Queries

We can also use SQL as our query language if that suits us. The syntax for a SELECT statement is:

```
SELECT [ALL] attributelist FROM base_DN WHERE criterialist
```

The criteria are written with normal SQL syntax, not LDAP filter syntax such as we used in our sample above. Everything in our LDAP example stays the same except the command line:

```
dbConn.Execute("SELECT cn, mail FROM 'LDAP://vandenberg/DC=widgets' WHERE
                objectClass='User' AND mail='s*'")
```

Note we are no longer using angle brackets around the base DN. Note also that the SQL string has no place for preferences. If we wish to alter the defaults, we need to explicitly create a command object. Since the default for SQL searches using the Active Directory provider is `SubTree`, let's rewrite our example to set the scope to `OneLevel`:

```
Sub OnQuery()
    dim dbConn, dbRecordSet, dbCommand

    Set dbConn = CreateObject("ADODB.Connection")
    dbConn.Provider = "ADsDSOObject"
    dbConn.Open "Active Directory Provider",
                "CN=SearchUser,CN=Users,DC=widgets", +
                "pwd"
```

```
      Set dbCommand = CreateObject("ADODB.Command")
      dbCommand.ActiveConnection = dbConn
      dbCommand.CommandText = "SELECT cn, mail FROM
                      'LDAP://vandenberg/CN=Users,DC=widgets' WHERE
                      objectClass='User' AND mail='s*'"
      dbCommand.Properties("SearchScope") = 1 rem 1 level - immediate children
      Set dbRecordSet = dbCommand.Execute
      dbRecordSet.MoveFirst

   While Not dbRecordSet.EOF
      MsgBox(dbRecordSet.Fields(0).Value + " " +
            dbRecordSet.Fields(1).Value)
      dbRecordSet.MoveNext
   Wend
End Sub
```

Of course, since we restricted the scope to the immediate children of the base DN object we had to be more particular in terms of our base DN. Fortunately, all this searching refreshed our memory.

# Network Applications and Directories

We now have a working knowledge of the Active Directory, LDAP, and how to manipulate and search the directory through script code. Remember from the last chapter that the second Principle of Cooperative Application Development is:

**Services will be discovered by querying directories.**

Remember, this principle is intended to protect our applications not only from changes to the location of resources such as services, but also to shield us from having to know what services deal with what kinds of business problems. You want to tell the directory what problem you want to solve and have it tell you what service will help you and where to find it.

*Here we are using our definition of a 'service' – a programming module bigger than a component, usually implemented as a server-side ASP or CGI script. You should not confuse this with the operating system concept of services.*

Generalizing, there are three points involved in making this principle work:

1. We can describe our services by using some class of objects in the directory

2. With an appropriate search, we can find objects representing the services that supply the data we need

3. Once we have these objects, we can look at their attributes and find out how to access them

To make this work in practice we will need to establish some simple conventions.

# Service Binding

We will frequently talk about binding to a service in the course of discussing networked applications. What does this mean? Generally speaking, this means that a client application locates the server hosting the service, establishes a connection, and provides some specific parameters to establish a conversation.

In our expansion upon The 5 Principles of Cooperative Network Application Development, we will particularly mean:

❑ Finding an HTTP server and some page on it
❑ Finding out enough information to send a query to that page

As you can see, these correspond to the second and third points we just raised as being important when discovering services by querying directories. The result of this is that some desired information is retrieved in a format we are prepared to accept.

# Discovering Services

Over the course of the next few chapters, we will develop a method of talking about objects through the use of the Extensible Markup Language (XML). But don't let that throw you, for now, it is enough to say that we want to offer services implemented as Web pages, usually Active Server Pages (ASP) generating the data we need. Our client-side pages will request the pages that provide a service through HTML forms or other mechanisms, and we will use XML to reconstitute the objects for which we asked.

Each such service page will be said to speak one or more 'vocabularies'. Our clients will query the Active Directory for the vocabulary they need. Sometimes, our clients will not be able to find an exact match, but our technique will permit it to use a vocabulary that overlaps with the one it wants. As you can imagine, this really strengthens the sense of cooperation and flexibility that we are aiming for. To achieve this, each service will list all the vocabularies it generates in the Active Directory. Clients will query first for the desired vocabulary, then, if that vocabulary is not found, go back to the directory and query it for a vocabulary that is good enough.

## Vocabularies

Each vocabulary has a name. XML, as we shall see, is a language for defining other languages. Each such language is called a vocabulary. Thus, our queries will look for the name of the vocabulary as an attribute of some class in the Active Directory.

## Existing Classes

The default Active Directory schema contains literally hundreds of object classes and attribute types, including a class called `Connection-Point`. This is the basis for all objects and classes to which some other object can connect. It is an abstract class, which means we cannot actually create any directory objects from it. There is also a derived class, `Service-Connection-Point`, which is described as holding binding information that allows one to connect to a service in order to make use of its services. `Service-Connection-Point` might seem to be ideal, however it is actually intended for use by for major services like LDAP itself. Also, servers hosting network services like HTTP and LDAP publish records to Domain Name Servers that help DNS map service names, like `www.somesite.com`, to an IP address. So, using this class properly would mean tinkering with th enterprise's DNS server. We'd like to avoid this. Should we, then, consider extending the default Active Directory schema?

The first thing you run into when extending the schema is the need for an object identifier (OID), which is a globally unique number that identifies the class to the directory. Using the OID properly requires applying to an international standards organization for a block of OIDs. This is not strictly necessary if we won't be exposing our directory service to outside clients, and our applications distinguish between internal and external searches. Providing that this is the case we can get away with using any OID not in use on the network. Such an approach, however, is definitely working around the rules. Clearly, extending the directory schema by the rules is a rare and difficult process. Extending the schema also means creating a class that will become a permanent part of your organization's directory. This may entail more authority than you can muster. It also has ramifications for storage space and search performance. For these reasons, schema extension is often discouraged. We need not give up hope, however.

## Our Usage of Service-Connection-Point

`Service-Connection-Point` has a most interesting attribute called `Service-Binding-Information`. This is implicitly defined information that describes how a client connects to the service. Since applications are assumed to have shared knowledge regarding the use of a service, it is not much of a stretch to assume our clients have knowledge that our services are not well-known services and, therefore, will not bother the DNS server for service records. We can thus get a free ride on `Service-Connection-Point` – it is always found in the Active Directory and is (in spirit at least) intended for the sort of thing we are doing. While purists may question our usage of this class, it is an effective ad hoc solution.

What are the things we need to know about our object servers? There are three things we definitely need:

- ❑ The URL of the page serving the information
- ❑ A page where users can get more information about the service, including how to query it
- ❑ A list of the vocabularies our service generates

The first two are accommodated by attributes of `Service-Connection-Point`. We shall use `WWW-Home-Page` for the URL of the page serving the information and `WWW-Page-Other` as the page where users can get more information about the service, including how to query it. For the last item we shall use `Service-Binding-Information`, a multi-valued attribute. We shall also use the `Service-Class-Name` attributes of the Active Directory schema to provide a single value we can use as a filter. All attributes are strings.

## Adding a new Service Object to the Directory

We can use a utility called the Active Directory Browser (`adsvw.exe`) to add new objects to the Active Directory. Upon starting this utility, you must specify in the first dialog box that you want a new object, not a search. Let's illustrate this process by adding a hypothetical service that generates documents representing customers maintained in a database by the Customer Service department of some hypothetical company. We simply navigate to the Customer Service OU in our directory and click on Add Item on the Edit menu. This gives us the following dialog box:

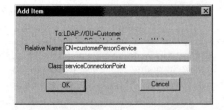

Note that we've given the service a CN and specified the class of our object. Also note that serviceConnectionPoint is the LDAP display name format of the class we know as Service-Connection-Point. Once we have clicked OK, Active Directory adds this object to the **Customer Service OU**. We can then modify the properties of the object to reflect where the services are found. Suppose we generate the customer documents with the page customers.asp in the custsrv site on our server called vandenberg. We explain the usage of this syntax to programmers on the page CustomerService.html. We select url (the LDAP display name for the WWW-Home-Page attribute), provide the URL for the customers.asp page, and click **Change**.

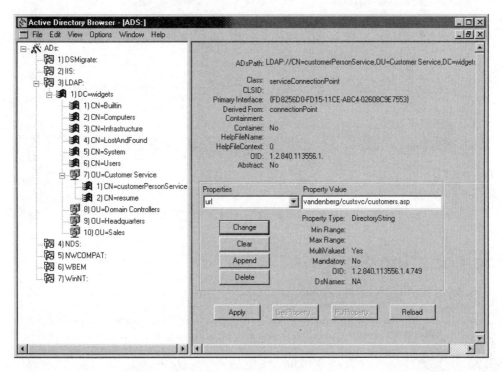

Note the **CN=customerPersonService** object in the tree structure in the left-hand pane of the figure above. We do the same to assign the value vandenberg/custsrv/CustomerService.html to the WWWHomePage (or WWW-Page-Other in the descriptive form) attribute. Now assume that customers.asp generates data in two syntaxes: a basic customer vocabulary and a more detailed custsrvcustomer vocabulary that is specialized from the basic vocabulary. The nature of these vocabularies is not important for the moment. Their meaning will become clear over the next two chapters, but assume for now that they are merely labels denoting a data format. If you select the serviceBindingInformation attribute, provide **customer**, but click **Append**. Now change the value to **custsrvcustomer** and click **Append** once more. The attribute serviceBindingInformation now contains a list of the two vocabularies. Finally, select serviceClassName and provide the name **xmlCustomerServicePerson**. We have completed specifying the minimal set of information for our new service.

> *We will be using the Extensible Markup Language (XML) as our data representation format.*
> *This will be described in the next chapter. For now, let us simply agree to begin all service class*
> *names with the prefix 'xml'. This will give us an easy filter criteria*
> *(serviceClassname=xml\* for example) to differentiate our services from any other service*
> *entries.*

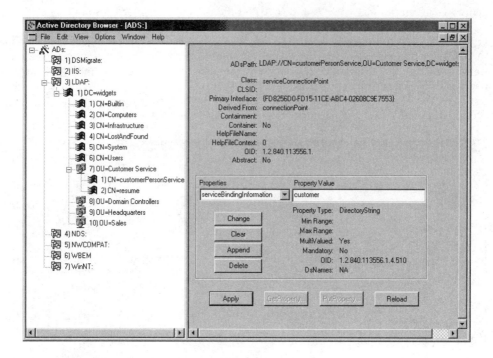

# Service Location Scriptlet

Now that we know how to locate information in the Active Directory, it is time to address the problem of locating servers that speak a vocabulary appropriate to a particular task. Ideally, we'd like to build a reusable component to do this for us. We could write a COM object in C++ or Java, but fortunately we won't need to resort to such extreme measures. Internet Explorer 4.0 and later supports a technique for exposing script as components. We will use this technique, which is called DHTML Scriptlets, throughout this book to build a toolkit of components that will help us implement our philosophy.

## What are DHTML Scriptlets?

Scriptlets are HTML pages containing DHTML script code. We can embed them in other pages much as we would a COM component. As a matter of fact, Internet Explorer will load a second instance of its browser COM component in order to load our scriptlet page. This host browser exposes the script functions as component methods. As a result, once we write some useful code, we can reuse it as a component simply by embedding it in a new page and scripting the embedded scriptlet page as if it were a COM component – which, from the containing browser's point of view, it is.

*The treatment of DHTML scriptlets presented here is sufficient for our purposes. A complete treatment of the subject may be found in* Instant DHTML Scriptlets *from Wrox Press (ISBN 1-861001-38-X).*

## Exposing an Interface

Suppose we have a page full of script functions that we wish to expose as a scriptlet object. Some of the functions and variables will be the methods and properties of the object we wish to offer to other scripts. Others will be private functions and variables necessary to the implementation of the public interface. Scriptlets use four simple rules for naming functions and variables in order to expose an interface:

- ❑ A variable with page scope (one that is declared outside any functions) and the prefix public_ is exposed as a read/write property
- ❑ A function with the prefix public_get_ is exposed as a read-access property
- ❑ A function with the prefix public_put_ is exposed as a write-access property
- ❑ A function with the prefix public_ is exposed as a method

Consequently, from VBScript, we might have the following examples:

```
Rem a read/write property
dim public_size = "large"

Rem private variable holding the value of the color property
dim privateColor

Rem read accessor function for color property
function public_get_color()
   get_color = privateColor
end function

Rem write accessor function for color property
function public_put_color(newValue)
   Rem insert range and validity checking here
   privateColor = newValue
end function

Rem ColorBook method
function public_ColorBook()
   Rem implementation code here
end function
```

## JavaScript Objects

JavaScript offers a simpler approach than VBScript. JavaScript actually embraces the notion of objects, although not as elegantly as Java or C++. We declare an object, then set its methods to some functions we've written. This sounds more confusing than it really is. Suppose we want to have a class named Monkey, with methods named Eat, Sleep, and Drink. First, we write functions implementing the behavior we want for each method. To keep things clear, we'll use the same names as the methods:

```
function Eat(food)
{
   // Some implementation code here
}

function Drink(beverage)
{
   ...
}
```

```
function Sleep()
{
    ...
}
```

Now we write a constructor function with the same name as the class, which in this case is `Monkey`. Within the constructor, we use the keyword `this` to refer to this object. JavaScript allows us to declare methods by using them in an assignment, but from where does the implementing code come? If we assign the functions we've written to the newly declared methods, the functions will be called whenever some user of a `Monkey` class instance calls the method, say, with the line `mySimian.Sleep()`.

```
function Monkey()
{
    this.Eat = Eat;
    this.Drink = Drink;
    this.Sleep = Sleep;
}
```

There's one more thing we need to do to make this class accessible as a scriptlet in JavaScript. We must declare a variable named `public_description` as an instance of our class. This must be a global variable, so be sure to declare it outside the scope of any function. This will limit us to one class per scriptlet page because `public_description` is a keyword variable:

```
public_description = new Monkey;
```

Properties can be exposed using either of two approaches. If you want to expose an internal variable directly, you can do so with the following line in the constructor function:

```
this.property = variable;
```

Alternatively, if you want to expose a variable with some validity checking, or if you wish to expose a calculated value as a property, you can supply accessor functions. These take the form of the public property name preceded by the word `get_` or `put_`. Thus:

```
this.get_propertyname = readfunctionname;     // read access
this.put_propertyname = writefunctionname;    // write access
```

Therefore, our `Monkey` could expose a preference for food with the following:

```
var myfood = "banana";

function Monkey()
{
    this.Eat = Eat;
    this.Drink = Drink;
    this.Sleep = Sleep;
    this.favoriteFood = myfood;
}
```

We could even have a very fickle `Monkey` that randomly states a preference:

```
function Monkey()
{
   this.Eat = Eat;
   this.Drink = Drink;
   this.Sleep = Sleep;
   this.get_favoriteFood = randomFoodSelection;
}
```

```
function randomFoodSelection()
{
   var fRandNum = Math.random();
   if (fRandNum >= 0.5)
     return "banana";
   else
     return "beluga caviar";
}
```

Note that our last example creates a read-only property because we have provided no `put_favoriteFood` function.

## Embedding a Scriptlet in a Web Page

Using a scriptlet in another page is very similar to embedding a typical COM component. Again we use an <OBJECT> tag, but there is a particular MIME type to specify, where we have `type=text/x-scriptlet`:

```
<OBJECT id=mySimian style="BORDER-LEFT: medium none;
   HEIGHT: 0px; LEFT: 0px; TOP: 0px; WIDTH: 0px"
   type=text/x-scriptlet VIEWASTEXT>
   <PARAM NAME="URL" VALUE="Monkey.html">
   <PARAM NAME="Scrollbar" VALUE="0">
</OBJECT>
```

We give it an ID so we can refer to it in script. Since this particular scriptlet has no visible interface, we give it dimensions of zero. Most importantly, we list the type attribute:

```
type=text/x-scriptlet
```

This attribute tells Internet Explorer that it is dealing with a scriptlet. Now it needs to know what HTML page to load to implement the scriptlet, so we add a <PARAM> tag:

```
<PARAM NAME="URL" VALUE="Monkey.html">
```

When we want to use the scriptlet in some script code, we refer to it by its `id` attribute:

```
function OnSomeButtonPress()
{
   ...
   mySimian.Eat();
}
```

# Directory Walker Example

Now we know how to manipulate the Active Directory, build DHTML scriptlets, and create objects in the Active Directory to represent the services in our development philosophy. If all our Web developers had to know this in order to gain the advantages of using the Active Directory, they'd be less likely to use it. To get around this we can build and test a DHTML scriptlet that hides most of this. So long as they are aware of the basic concepts of the Active Directory, our component will give other developers the ability to obtain a URL for a service providing the vocabulary they specify.

## The Interface

We want the user of our component to be able to search for a service given a vocabulary. The component should be able to look in the user's home domain as well as his domain tree. We could give him the ability to look at the entire forest, as well, but that seems dangerous. If everyone searched there first, the directory service might suffer an unacceptable performance burden. We'll provide the user with the ability to root his search in some arbitrary container, so a developer with better knowledge of ADSI and directory concepts would be able to search the forest.

We also need to provide some utility properties. Security is an issue, so we provide read-write access to a user DN and password. You can create a stock user with read-only access or allow the user to provide this. We also expose the DN for the user's home domain as well as the DN for the root of the user's domain tree. This is useful for troubleshooting, and it permits a programmer with knowledge of ADSI to navigate through the directory.

So let's take a closer look at the interface. First we will list the properties and methods, then look at how to implement them. Here are the properties of the Directory Walker:

| Property | Description |
| --- | --- |
| User | user distinguished name |
| Pwd | user password |
| HomeDomain | DN for the current user's home domain |
| TreeRootDomain | DN for the domain that roots the directory tree containing the current user's home domain |

And here are the public methods of our component:

### SearchHome()

Searches the current user's home domain for a service providing a named vocabulary.

| Parameters | Description | Returns |
| --- | --- | --- |
| sVocabulary | Case sensitive name of the vocabulary for which to search | URL for the service providing the vocabulary, or an empty string |

### SearchTree()

Searches the domain tree of the current user for a service providing a named vocabulary.

| Parameters | Description | Returns |
|---|---|---|
| sVocabulary | Case sensitive name of the vocabulary for which to search | URL for the service or an empty string |

### SearchDirectory()

Searches the container specified by the user for a service providing the specified vocabulary.

| Parameters | Description | Returns |
|---|---|---|
| Sbase | DN for the container rooting the search | URL for the service or an empty string |
| sVocabulary | Case sensitive name of the vocabulary for which to search | URL for the service or an empty string |

## Implementing the Properties

Having seen what functions and properties we make available, how do we actually implement the functions providing access to our properties?

### User and Pwd

Remember that `User` is the user's DN and that `Pwd` is the user's password:

```
dim sUser
sUser = "CN=Administrator,CN=Users,DC=widgets"
dim sPwd
sPwd = ""

function public_get_User()
    public_get_User = sUser
end Sub

function public_put_User(sNewValue)
    sUser = sNewValue
end Sub

function public_get_Pwd()
    public_get_Pwd = sPwd
end function

function public_put_Pwd(sNewValue)
    sPwd = sNewValue
end Sub
```

Note that we've declared some private variables and given them default values. The Administrator user is common to all Windows NT and Windows 2000 installations by default, although hopefully you've changed the default, empty password on yours. We wrap these with generic accessor functions; we might wish to do some specialized error checking or attempt to bind to a given user DN to ensure it exists. For clarity, though, we'll simply accept what the client gives us.

### HomeDomain

Now consider the property for the user's home domain. This is actually determined when a client of this scriptlet tries to read the property:

```
dim sHomeDomain
sHomeDomain = ""

function public_get_HomeDomain()
    dim rootDSE
    sHomeDomain = ""
    On Error Resume Next

    Set rootDSE=GetObject("LDAP://rootDSE")
    sHomeDomain = rootDSE.Get("defaultNamingContext")
    public_get_HomeDomain = sHomeDomain
end function
```

This should be familiar to you from the example of serverless binding, which we saw earlier. We bind to the user's domain controller using serverless binding and retrieve the `defaultNamingContext` property.

### TreeRootDomain

We do something similar for the root of the user's domain tree as we did for the `HomeDomain`:

```
dim sTreeRoot
sTreeRoot = ""

function public_get_TreeRootDomain()
    dim rootDSE
    sTreeRoot = ""
    On Error Resume Next

    Set rootDSE = GetObject("LDAP://rootDSE")
    sTreeRoot = rootDSE.Get("rootDomainNamingContext")
    public_get_TreeRootDomain = sTreeRoot
end function
```

Once again, we bind to the domain controller, but this time we ask for the `rootDomainNamingContext` property. We do not, however, provide `public_put_` functions; these are read-only properties.

## Implementing the Methods

Having seen how to implement the properties, let's go on to look at the methods.

### SearchHome()

Here's the code which implements the `SearchHome()` method:

```
function public_SearchHome(sVocabulary)
    dim sBase, sURL

    sBase = "LDAP://" & public_get_HomeDomain()
    public_SearchHome = DoQuery(sBase, "SubTree", sVocabulary)
end function
```

We compose the DN for our search by using our accessor function to retrieve the current user's domain. With that in hand, we call a utility function, not exposed through our interface, to do the actual search. We'll specify SubTree scope so the search will automatically recurse through all containers below the DN. This may or may not be an effective solution depending on the specific layout of your directory.

### SearchTree() and SearchDirectory()

We do something similar for the other two methods, SearchTree() and SearchDirectory():

```
function public_SearchTree(sVocabulary)
   dim sBase

   sBase = "LDAP://" & public_get_TreeRootDomain()
   public_SearchTree = DoQuery(sBase, "SubTree", sVocabulary)
end function

function public_SearchDirectory(sBase, sVocabulary)
   public_SearchDirectory = DoQuery("LDAP://" & sBase, "SubTree",
                                    sVocabulary)
end function
```

### DoQuery()

Finally let's see how DoQuery() works:

```
function DoQuery(sBaseDn, sScope, sVocab)
   dim dbConn, dbRecordSet,sCmd
   DoQuery = ""
   On Error Resume Next

   Rem Connect to the ADSI service provider for ADO
   Rem User specified must have appropriate access rights
   Set dbConn = CreateObject("ADODB.Connection")
   dbConn.Provider = "ADsDSOObject"
   dbConn.Open "ActiveDirectoryProvider", sUser, sPwd

   Rem Filter specifies a service under the convention set forth in the book
   Rem (Chap. 2)
   sCmd = "<" & sBaseDN &
          ">;(&(objectClass=serviceConnectionPoint)
          (serviceClassName=xml*));url,serviceBindingInformation;" & sScope
   Set dbRecordSet = dbConn.Execute(sCmd)

   Rem Iterate through the vocabularies of each service found
   Rem and see if it matches the vocabulary we are looking for
   While Not dbRecordSet.EOF
      For Each vocabulary In dbRecordSet.Fields(1).Value
         If sVocab = vocabulary Then
            Rem Value is always a collection, hence this hack
            For Each child In dbRecordSet.Fields(0).Value
               DoQuery = child
            Next
         End If
      Next
      dbRecordSet.MoveNext
   Wend
end function
```

The line On Error Resume Next allows us to continue processing if VBScript throws a runtime exception. Otherwise, processing would grind to a halt. We're familiar with the mechanics of opening an ADO database connection by now, but look at the composition of our command string:

```
sCmd = "<" & sBaseDN & ">;(&(objectClass=serviceConnectionPoint)
        (serviceClassName=xml*));url,serviceBindingInformation;" & sScope
```

We have to wrap the DN for the root container of our search in angle brackets. Next, we provide a filter based on our convention: `serviceConnectionPoint` is the object class and the `serviceClassName` must start with the `xml` prefix. We are interested in the `URL` and `serviceBindingInformation` attributes of any objects we find. Finally, we tack on the scope passed in from the public method.

Things become a bit more complicated once we have a record set. The basic iterative loop should be familiar:

```
While Not dbRecordSet.EOF
    For Each vocabulary In dbRecordSet.Fields(1).Value
        If sVocab = vocabulary Then
            ... Rem some action here
        End If
    Next
    dbRecordSet.MoveNext
Wend
```

Our fields are `URL` and `serviceBindingInformation` (zero and one, respectively, in the `Fields` collection). Since the `serviceBindingInformation` attribute is multi-valued, we need to iterate through each attribute value found and compare it to the vocabulary name for which we are searching. After evaluating a row in the record set, we move to the next one.

There is, however, a small wrinkle. Each `URL` attribute is returned as a collection, although this is a single-valued attribute in the schema. Consequently, we have to get at the child value and return it as the value of the function. If a match is not found for the vocabulary, the default value (an empty string which we set at the outset) is returned.

```
If sVocab = vocabulary Then
    For Each child In dbRecordSet.Fields(0).Value
        DoQuery = child
    Next
End If
```

Remember, the `DoQuery` assignment only works because we know there is only a single value for this attribute. That's it then, we have covered the entire implementation of our DHTML scriptlet.

## Using and Testing the Directory Walker

We create a test page using the Directory Walker DHTML scriptlet by making an HTML page with the following `<OBJECT>` tag:

```
<OBJECT id=walker style="HEIGHT: 0px; LEFT: 0px; TOP: 0px; WIDTH: 0px"
    type=text/x-scriptlet>
    <PARAM NAME="Scrollbar" VALUE="0">
    <PARAM NAME="URL" VALUE="DirectoryWalker.html">
</OBJECT>
```

The type attribute is the standard MIME type for DHTML scriptlets, `text/x-scriptlet`. It has no visible interface, so we give it zero dimensions all around. The `URL` attribute is set to `DirectoryWalker.html`, which is the name of the page containing our scriptlet code.

Here's some JavaScript code that searches for the `customer` vocabulary in the user's home domain:

```
function OnHome()
{
    walker.User = "CN=Administrator,CN=Users,DC=widgets";
    walker.Pwd = "";
    alert(walker.SearchHome("customer"));
}
```

We set the `User` and `Pwd` properties of the scriptlet, then call `SearchHome()` with the name of the vocabulary. Given the way we defined the service object (we used the `url` attribute to record a URL for our service, and the `serviceBindingInformation` attribute to record the XML vocabularies the service can generate) in the directory, we get a response of `vandenberg/custsvc/customers.asp`. That will allow a client page to retrieve some customer information by formatting a query using a known convention we will see in the next few chapters and sending it as part of a request for `customers.asp`.

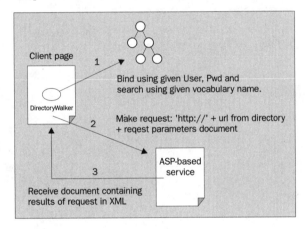

# Summary

Directory services are important to networked applications. Use of an LDAP compliant directory simplifies our programming task and helps us reuse existing services in our loosely structured network by giving us a mechanism for locating services and examining their capabilities. In particular, we learned the following:

- ❑ The nature and purpose of directory services
- ❑ The rudiments of LDAP
- ❑ Basic capabilities of the Active Directory in Windows 2000 and some of its schema
- ❑ Basic ADSI binding and directory searches using the Active Directory provider
- ❑ Conventions for representing our Web services in the Active Directory

We are demanding a commitment to directory usage from our organization as a part of our Web development philosophy. In return, we learned about DHTML scriptlets and built a utility component that hides much of the ADSI-related code and our conventions from other Web developers. Using this component, Web development teams should be able to insinuate their applications into the fabric of the organization's computing environment.

We've purposely skirted the topic of how our services will deliver data across the network. In passing, we said we would use XML. Now it is time to take up that topic and build more tools.

# 3

# Structured Data Exchange

Back in Chapter 1 we set forth the following principle:

### 3. Services will be provided as self-describing data

In the process of implementing our first principle, "1. Applications will be built from coarse-grained services" (that implement a unit of processing larger than components), we decided to isolate components at the service and client level. Methods on components will never be invoked across machine boundaries. They will only be invoked on the machine on which they reside – making them particular to a tier, thereby allowing us to keep our applications platform neutral. This means that some static representation for components will be required. This will take the form of structured data. According to our third principle, this data should be tagged and self-describing to promote the robust exchange of information. Since we want the widest possible acceptance of our formats, we should adopt an open standard as the mechanism for defining our exchange structures.

In this chapter we will be introduced to the Extensible Markup Language (XML), a recommended standard from the World Wide Web Consortium (W3C) for the markup of structured data. XML is text based and similar to HTML. Due to its elegant simplicity and the pressing need for structured data on the Web, XML is enjoying an explosion of popularity in the Web development community.

In the course of this chapter, you will learn:

- ❑ What problems XML is intended to address
- ❑ How XML came to be and who guides its development
- ❑ The rudiments of XML markup
- ❑ An object model for working with XML data
- ❑ How to move XML between services and clients

Since XML is an open standard, many talented people have dealt with the practical implementation of a parser for XML. Indeed, there are many parsers built for different programming needs. In line with our component software development philosophy, we'll get our practical experience in parsing XML by learning to use the Microsoft XML COM-based parser, MSXML.

There are, however, many other parsers that you could use instead of MSXML. For more information on other parsers check out `http://www.xmlsoftware.com/parsers/`

# The Extensible Markup Language

Web developers use a markup language every day – it's called HTML. Simply put, a markup language is a language in which the data you wish to represent is *marked up* with *tags* that not only delimit the data but also describe it. A fixed markup language, like HTML, breaks when a user wants to mark up some data that the language did not previously describe. There are times when we all wish to be able to create our own new tags for things that are not represented by HTML, and the arrival of XML makes our wish come true. It is a simple, relatively lightweight language (actually a meta-language) for creating new markup vocabularies. These vocabularies are the grammar and syntax of a markup language that allow us to express some information about an object in our particular business domain. This is essentially what we want to do in order to make our services self-describing – give each business object a vocabulary to describe what it contains. Since XML is text-based, it is easy to support on every platform. Since it is less complex and easier to implement than other markup languages, such as SGML, it is rapidly gaining widespread popularity. Let's start off with the basics, see what XML is, and see what it can describe.

## History

XML's predecessor was Standard Generalized Markup Language (SGML), a powerful language for describing the structure and content of electronic documents. First published in 1986, SGML is an international standard (ISO 8879). Fortunately for Web developers, some of the participants in the standards setting process recognized a problem with SGML. Some uncommon yet very powerful features of SGML were proving to be difficult to implement. They felt there was a need to implement a simpler version of SGML covering the most commonly used features of SGML. First proposed in 1996 by an SGML body within the W3C, XML proved to be the answer. XML became a recommended standard – the highest level of endorsement by the W3C – with version 1.0 of the XML specification, which was released in February 1998. The XML specification is maintained by the W3C XML Working Group, which continues to consider refinements and additions.

Web developers were quick to recognize the potential of XML. Both Netscape and Microsoft are offering support for XML in their browsers. Netscape's upcoming support (due to be released with their version 5 browser) is, at the time of writing, currently in the hands of the Mozilla open source effort. Meanwhile Microsoft made XML a strategic part of their development efforts when they made an XML vocabulary the basis for describing Web sites in their Channel Definition Format (CDF) push technology. XML vocabularies are rapidly proliferating. Microsoft promoted the Open Financial Exchange vocabulary for online banking, while the academic community has devised vocabularies for representing information in mathematics and chemistry. The uses for XML range from static document markup (e.g., MathML for marking up mathematical expressions) to dynamically created XML representations (e.g., the enterprise resource planning vocabulary from SAP, PeopleSoft, and Oracle).

## XML Overview

XML is, strictly speaking, a meta-language – a language for devising other languages. To avoid confusion, we will refer to a language developed using XML as a **vocabulary**. Vocabularies are a way of talking about some coherent body of data, such as a vertical market like manufacturing or finance.

The financial community, for example, needs to be able to mark up documents to describe things like transactions, transfer, payments, loans, and accounts. A financial vocabulary would let you transfer money between accounts by sending your bank a document marked with tags indicating what text specifies the account numbers and which provides the amount to transfer.

Vocabularies are formally defined as a set of production rules in a **schema**. The schema that is covered by the XML 1.0 specification is called a **Document Type Definition** (**DTD**), although there have been other developments in schemas that we will come back to later in the chapter. A schema defines the tags and attributes you may use in documents written to the schema's vocabulary and how you may combine tags.

An XML document that adheres to the rules in a DTD is said to be **valid**. In many data exchange applications, the vocabulary is informal and based on an implicit understanding between the communicating parties. When an XML document follows the basic rules of XML syntax but does not conform to a formal DTD, it is said to be **well-formed**.

XML will look very familiar to users of HTML. It describes the content and structure of the data much in the way HTML used to define the structure and content of Web pages before more descriptive tags like <FONT> and techniques like stylesheets became popular. Unlike HTML, however, XML is strictly about data. XML does not provide any information about how data might be presented to human users. Other standards, notably Cascading Style Sheets (CSS) and the Extensible Stylesheet Language (XSL), can be used for that. Since we want to isolate our services from changes in who uses them and how, this separation of data and presentation is ideal for our purposes.

XML was intended to be human-readable from the start. This has the happy consequence of making it easy for programmers to start encoding data using XML, as well as making it easy to debug XML-based applications. Like HTML, XML uses tags to delimit data. Tags are themselves delimited using angle brackets – for example, the following fragment is XML:

```
<POINT-VALUE>148.6</POINT-VALUE>
```

The data is the string 148.6, while <POINT-VALUE> and </POINT-VALUE> name and delimit the data. Tagged data may be nested, although they must not overlap. Like HTML, attributes may be added to tags:

> It is very important to remember that attributes *must* be enclosed in quotes. If you leave out the quotes, some XML parsers will not recognize the presence of the attribute.

So, continuing with our example, the following would be well-formed:

```
<TEST-RESULTS NUMBER="1">
    <TEMPARATURE>
        <POINT-VALUE EU="DEG F">148.6</POINT-VALUE>
    </TEMPARATURE>
</TEST-RESULTS>
```

While this would be incorrect because there are not quotes around the attributes and the tags overlap:

```
<TEST-RESULTS NUMBER=1>
   <TEMPARATURE>
      <POINT-VALUE EU=DEG F>148.6
   </TEMPARATURE></POINT-VALUE>
</TEST-RESULTS>
```

The attribute shows that our point value is unit of measure (engineering units in manufacturing terminology, hence EU) is degrees Fahrenheit. Without attributes, all we know is the value of some item of data and its name. Attributes permit us to provide additional descriptive information.

When we set out The 5 Principles of Cooperative Networked Application Development, we said that Services will be provided as self-describing data. XML is the mechanism by which we will create vocabularies that describe our services. The question arises as to what kind of agreement is needed for two parties to use XML? After all, minimizing the amount of coordination required between development teams is a key aim of our philosophy.

There are two issues here:

❑ The two parties must have a basic data type in common
❑ The two parties must have a vocabulary in common

XML uses text exclusively, which is probably the most widely supported data type in computing, so XML will be the basic data type that both parties use.

*Programmers who have developed applications for Asian-language users will note that text isn't quite as simple as I make it out to be. Textual characters sometimes need more than one byte to represent, or may be encoded in forms other than the one to which English language developers have become accustomed. Rest assured XML makes provisions for specifying the language encoding used. All parsers are required by the XML specification to handle UTF-8 and UTF-16 encoded characters. For simplicity, we'll stick with the default UTF-8 encoding.*

OK, so our parties must agree to use XML. XML is an open standard enjoying widespread acceptance, so this is not an unreasonable agreement. In fact, the enterprise as a whole should adopt the principle of using XML for structured data exchange. The choice of tools for working with XML, however, may be left to the individual organization or programming team.

The second point, that the two parties must have a vocabulary in common, is not so restrictive as it might seem. If the two parties are to communicate, they must share a common body of knowledge. A doctor will seldom wish to talk to an economist about the intricacies of international finance, but he can talk medicine to another doctor because they share knowledge of medicine. Parties interested in the same subject will tend to settle on common vocabularies.

*XML is working toward more formal methods of sharing vocabularies. We will come back to this topic and examine these methods in Chapter 5.*

That's it, what may have sounded like an ambitious principle can be achieved fairly simply. XML requires little sharing and coordination. The tools are simple and widely available. XML possesses the means to capture static data and its structure in a simple to use, widely accessible format.

*For a general treatment of XML, why not pick up a copy of XML Applications, by Wrox Press? (ISBN 1-861001-52-5)*

# Supporting Standards

Several complementary standards have grown up around XML to provide support for some of the key problems encountered in using XML and to solve other problems. Although not part of the core XML specification, these are important to XML users because they provide additional features and show where XML is heading. We will now look at a few of the supporting standards.

## XML Linking Language

Links between objects are a powerful part of HTML. It is this mechanism that lets a browser locate, obtain, and display a binary graphic file in the context of a text-based HTML file. The XML Linking Language, **XLink**, is intended to be an XML vocabulary for defining sophisticated links within XML documents. At the time of writing it was in working draft status with the W3C. XLink not only identifies a resource to link into the document, but also allows the semantics of the link and the role of the remote resource to be described. For example, we can use XLink to connect an XML document with a graphic image. The document might describe the image or provide notation to overlay on the image. A role can also be established for a linked resource, and this role is interpreted by the receiving application.

In the case of a graphic image depicting a medical X-ray, we might have a role `diagnostic` to denote that the X-ray is an actual patient diagnostic image, and a role `baseline` to denote an image of a normal, healthy individual for comparison.

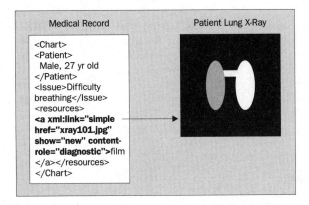

## XML Namespaces

Although markup items must have names that are unique within their DTD, there is no requirement for globally unique names. Obviously, such a requirement would be impossible to support. It is inevitable, then, that names will collide. As an example, it seems reasonable to suppose that `<NAME>` will be a fairly ubiquitous tag in XML documents. The meaning of the tag, however, will vary substantially. It is important to know whose definition the document author used. What is not so obvious, however, is that a document might be written using markup drawn from multiple DTDs. This comes about because document authors may wish to reuse particularly well-designed parts of DTDs or industry standard DTDs. In our own philosophy, we have indicated that there will be cases of overlapping, yet different, meanings. As we will see in the next chapter, such overlap is an important part of our strategy for reuse.

For whatever reason, it becomes necessary to qualify the **namespace** of the definition. A namespace in XML is a collection of names that may be used to identify elements (tags) and attributes. Indicating what namespace a particular tag comes from is what the XML Namespaces standard proposes to do. For example, we may use the <NAME> tag from a DTD for describing contacts and a <NAME> tag from a marketing DTD referring to branding of products, in the same document, both of which are intended for very different purposes.

XML namespaces became a W3C recommendation on January 14, 1999. A namespace associates a **namespace prefix** with a **local name** to develop a **qualified name**. The prefix is separated from the qualified name by a colon. The prefix identifies the entity providing the definition (such as the contacts DTD). This prefix is associated with a URI (URL link or other unique identifier) in a namespace declaration. A namespace declaration is given as an attribute of an element. A tag can contain multiple declarations, and the declarations apply to any nested tags. Let's qualify our hypothetical <NAME> element with a namespace:

```
<nm:NAME xmlns:nm="http://www.mysite.com/nameschema">
    <nm:FIRST>John</nm:FIRST><nm:LAST>Doe</nm:LAST>
</nm:NAME>
```

We've given the prefix nm to our namespace. It is associated with the URL http://www.mysite.com/nameschema in the attribute whose name is xmlns:nm. The prefix xmlns tells our XML parser that it is encountering a namespace declaration. The prefix we are going to use to identify the namespace follows the colon. Thereafter, wherever we use the prefix nm we know which namespace we are using. If our element included the attribute xmlns:gene="http://www.geneology.org/schema we could mix nm and gene to denote elements drawn from the two namespaces.

Since we use a URI to denote a namespace, we can use methods other than URLs to locate our resources. Sometimes it is sufficient to use an identifier for a well-known namespace without providing a URL. For example, Microsoft Internet Explorer 4.0 uses a universally unique identifier (uuid) to denote a namespace Microsoft developed to denote data types. Using this, it is possible to access typed values of attributes and elements in script code rather than the textual representation. In this case, Microsoft used a namespace to define strongly typed values for use in applications in Internet Explorer. For example:

```
<Product>. . .
<Weight>5.3</Weight><Price>3.99</Price>
. . .</Product>

<Product xmlns:dt="urn:schemas-microsoft-com:datatypes">. . .
<Weight dt:dt="fixed.14.4">5.3</Weight><Price dt:dt="fixed.14.4">3.99</Price>
. . .</Product>
```

Both fragments have the same text content regarding the price and weight of some product. The first assumes we know that price and weight are numbers and require us to perform the text to numeric conversion ourselves. The second, compatible with Internet Explorer 5.0, tells an XML parser that these are floating point numbers. We can write script that retrieves the numeric values from IE's parser and use them to calculate a unit price.

# XML Metadata

Any XML vocabulary is formed according to some rules whether they are explicitly defined in a schema or are simply understood implicitly. Because the schemas provide data about data marked up in a particular vocabulary they are known as **metadata**. Earlier in the chapter we briefly mentioned the type of schema that is covered in the XML 1.0 specification, Document Type Definitions. DTDs are written according to a modified form of EBNF (Extended Backus-Naur Form) notation, not according to XML syntax, thereby limiting their use by automated clients. If you wish to delve into a DTD, say to explore the structure of a new and unknown document, you must implement your own parser for DTD's. Since they are not written in XML syntax, you cannot simply use your XML parser.

Many XML users wish to discover vocabularies at runtime. This would be a powerful addition to the arsenal of XML tools. An automated producer of XML documents could ensure, at runtime, that it is generating XML according to the most recent version of the vocabulary. A consumer of an XML vocabulary previously unknown to the client could read the associated schema using an XML parser and glean some indication of the expected structure and content of documents written in that vocabulary.

Several submissions to and initiatives of the W3C attempt to address this issue by creating a schema language that employs XML syntax. We will be looking at three here:

- ❑ Resource Description Framework (RDF)
- ❑ XML-Data
- ❑ Document Content Description (DCD)

## Resource Description Framework

The most advanced of these three metadata efforts is the **Resource Description Framework** (RDF), a proposed recommendation of the W3C. More than just an XML syntax replacement for DTDs, RDF is an ambitious effort to define the nature, meaning, and origin of XML vocabularies. **XML-Data** is a less ambitious effort. It facilitates the description of schema, either syntactic, as in XML vocabularies, or conceptual, as with a database schema. XML-Data is a W3C note. Somewhere in between is the **Document Content Description** (DCD). DCD is an RDF vocabulary containing a subset of XML-Data. It is narrowly focused on the description of XML documents and is intended to be used as an alternative to DTDs. For example, it would enable you to define an XML vocabulary for financial transactions much as a DTD would. Unlike a DTD, however, a financial transactions DCD would let you specify richer information such as datatypes and the type of ordering of items in a list of transactions.

> *The W3C places a technical report in one of four categories. A Note is a dated, publicly available document of some idea. It does not represent any commitment on the part of the W3C. A Working Draft represents work in progress by the W3C. When a W3C group reaches consensus on an issue and proposes it for review as a potential recommendation, the draft becomes a Proposed Recommendation. When the review is complete and the result is approved by the W3C's director, the document attains the W3C's highest level of endorsement as a Recommendation.*

RDF is based on **resources**, each of which is identified by a URI, and their properties. A resource is some object or concept you wish to define and describe. These resources are the fundamental things you want to discuss in your XML document. Meanwhile property types identify the meaning, range of values, and list of objects to which a property can be applied. Properties as defined by RDF are much like properties in object-based langauges like C++. Associating a resource with a property and a specific value for the property makes a statement in RDF.

Here's a partial example of an RDF schema:

```
<rdf:Property ID="status">
   <rdfs:range rdf:resource="#proficiency"/>
   <rdfs:domain rdf:resource="#Programmer"/>
</rdf:Property>

<rdfs:Class rdf:ID="proficiency"/>

<proficiency rdf:ID="Beginner"/>
<proficiency rdf:ID="Intermediate"/>
<proficiency rdf:ID="Advanced"/>
```

We're saying that a property named status must belong to the class proficiency, and only applies to resources of the class Programmer. We go on to define the class proficiency and its allowable, enumerated values: Beginner, Intermediate, and Advanced. The definition of the Programmer class is omitted.

*If you feel that you've returned to the mathematics classroom as you read terms like "range" and "domain", you're not alone. RDF appears to be heavily influenced by mathematical set theory. The authors may be forgiven; after all, they are trying to create a format for creating rigorous definitions.*

Basic statements can be combined in RDF to build complex models of concepts. Because of its power, RDF is capable of performing many functions. Some envisioned in the working draft are enhancing Internet searches by providing RDF descriptions of sites for use by search agents, knowledge sharing, and content rating.

## XML-Data

XML-Data is organized around the idea of a schema. A schema contains tagged elements that may be grouped in some sequence or hierarchy. Such elements may be subtypes of other, less specialized elements, offering the notion of inheritance. Relations may be expressed by denoting some element as a key used by other elements. In addition to expressing document structure and relationships between elements, XML-Data allows elements to be more strongly typed, offering a capability similar to the Microsoft datatyping namespace we looked at in the last section. While XML-Data sheds much of the complexity and depth of RDF, it remains broadly useful for describing a wide range of schemas.

*Strong types in a programming language are those that refer to a specific data format, binary representation, and allowable range of values. Integers and floating point numbers are examples. Weakly typed variables are those for which a specific definition has not been given. A Dim statement in VBScript or a var statement in JavaScript declares a weakly typed variable. Weakly typed variables are flexible, allowing you to assign anything to the variable, but you must exercise care when performing an operation or submitting the variable as a parameter to a function.*

## Document Content Description

A more pressing need of XML users is to be able to express the DTD of an XML document in an XML vocabulary, thereby permitting the parsing of a document's structural definition using the same tools as those used to parse the document itself. DCD primarily focuses on this need. Where RDF and XML-Data let you address this need as part of a richer, more complex metadata scheme, DCD sticks to this task largely to the exclusion of the more complex areas. DCD uses a simplified version of the RDF model.

It uses XML elements to define the tags of an XML vocabulary and their attributes, as well as the order and cardinality of groups of elements. Like XML-Data, DCD permits strong typing of tagged elements.

| Effort | Purpose | W3C Status |
|---|---|---|
| Resource Description Framework (RDF) | Provide rich description of the properties, relationship, and meaning of Web resources | Recommendation (22 February 1999) |
| XML-Data | Define structure and contents of syntactic (e.g., XML) and conceptual (e.g., relational databases) schemae | Note (5 January 1998) |
| Document Content Description (DCD) | Specify the structure and content rules for XML documents | Note (10 August 1998) |

Any successful metadata initiative will provide the basis for powerful vocabulary discovery and reconciliation of overlapping data formats. Unfortunately, XML-Data and DCD are in the earliest stages of discussion. They will likely undergo a great deal of change and evolution before the W3C recommends a new approach to metadata in XML. All three also have a bigger drawback from the point of view of our five principles. Each provides a means of specifying metadata, but any use of these specifications will require serious programming effort. If you wish to do more than validate a document against the metadata rules provided for its vocabulary (e.g., explore the structure of an unknown vocabulary), you must write a lot of code that understands these proposals. In our view of pragmatic development in a loosely connected and coordinated network, it is unlikely that such an effort will be mounted until XML vocabularies are widely used. There is little incentive to develop a metadata capability until it can be applied to a syntax that forms the backbone of the environment. We will explore some simple, *ad hoc* techniques for addressing common metadata issues in the next chapter and these techniques will be informed by the standards we have discussed here, but will not require their formal use. In Chapter 5, we will revisit the issue of metadata using a partial implementation of DCD and XML-Data and see how it can improve our efforts to reconcile overlapping data vocabularies. We will see that being able to reconcile similar vocabularies gives us more flexibility in processing XML documents written in unfamiliar vocabularies. We can extract partial meaning if we have access to rich metadata about such documents.

# Basics of XML

The XML specification (version 1.0, dated 10 February 1998, may be found at `http://www.w3.org/TR/REC-xml`) contains many rich features. Entire books have been written regarding the composition and use of XML. An excellent source is *Professional XML Applications* from Wrox Press (ISBN 1-1861001-52-5). Nevertheless, XML is extremely accessible. Many of the more difficult features pertain rigorous use of XML DTDs and some of the more esoteric features of XML rather than application-to-application data exchange. The core of the syntax can be explained briefly and informally, which is precisely what I shall do here. This is all you will need to know to begin writing cooperative network applications.

# Documents

The top-level construct in XML is the **document**. Unlike our physical world notion of a document, an XML document is a very flexible thing. Some body of text is an XML document if it is well-formed according to the formal XML production rule for a document. This is more imposing than it seems. The production rule for an XML document essentially says that a document contains one or more elements. This is the heart of XML for our needs. To be rigorous, however, we must note that a document may also begin with a **prolog**.

The prolog consists of the XML declaration and an optional document type definition. The XML tells the application that this document is written in conformance with a particular version of the XML specification. At the time of writing the only correct format (because there was only one version of XML) for this was as follows:

```
<?xml version="1.0"?>
```

> It is very important to note that XML, unlike HTML, is case sensitive. While you can use a mix of case in the tags that you create, the Document Type Declaration requires the letters xml to be written in lower case.

You may also include information regarding the text encoding you are using. So for plain vanilla ASCII, the default, you would say:

```
<?xml version="1.0"? encoding="UTF-8">
```

Moving on, a document type declaration will refer to the formal definition of the structure of the XML vocabulary used to form the document, this can either reference an external Document Type Definition or include one in the form of markup declarations.

> It is very easy to get confused between a Document Type Definition and a Document Type Declaration. To clarify, just remember that a Document Type Declaration either refers to an external Document Type Definition or else contains one in the form of markup declarations.

The Document Type Definition (DTD) is written in a syntax other than XML and may appear within the document or in an external file. A document need not have a DTD to be well-formed, but it must have a DTD and strictly follow its rules to be **valid**. If the DTD is external to the document, which is most commonly the case, you would declare it thusly:

```
<!DOCTYPE name SYSTEM DTD_URL>
```

*Note the exclamation mark following the left angle bracket. The document type declaration is one of the few XML tags to use this notation.*

You replace name with the name of the root element and DTD_URL with a URL pointing to the external DTD. Therefore, if our document begins with an element called RECEIPT following rules in the file sales.dtd, our DTD within the document would be:

```
<!DOCTYPE RECEIPT SYSTEM "sales.dtd">
```

The keyword SYSTEM indicates that the following URL is a system resource – in our case, a local file. If the DTD is well known, e.g., an XML reworking of HTML, SYSTEM may be replaced with PUBLIC. This allows the parser to attempt to generate alternate URLs for the DTD.

# Elements

Elements are the workhorses of XML. They are delimited by start and end tags. A tag consists of an element name surrounded by angle brackets:

```
<RECEIPT>
```

An end tag has a forward slash immediately after the first angle bracket:

```
</RECEIPT>
```

One special exception is the empty element, an element defined to have no content. To save space, the start and end tags are replaced with a single tag consisting of an angle bracket followed by the name, a forward slash, and the final angle bracket. Thus:

```
<EMPTY_RECEIPT/>
```

An element may contain character data, other elements, or a mixture of the two (termed, not surprisingly, **mixed content**). This simple rule allows us to build everything from a simple nested tag to arbitrarily complex XML documents.

## Character Data

Character data is simply the content you wish to markup. In the following example, the character data is Thomas Atkins:

```
<PERSON>Thomas Atkins<PERSON>
```

## Element Content

This type of content consists of elements nested within the element. Elements so contained must begin and end entirely within the containing element in order to be well-formed. Here,

```
<EMPLOYEES><PERSON>Thomas Atkins</PERSON><PERSON>G. I. Joe</PERSON></EMPLOYEES>
```

is well-formed element content consisting of two <PERSON> elements contained within the <EMPLOYEES> element. As you can plainly see, overlapped elements are not well-formed, just gibberish:

```
<EMPLOYEES><PERSON>Thomas Atkins</EMPLOYEES></PERSON>
```

We can nest elements to any depth desired. Combining the inline and nested tags allows us to build complex structures. This ability will be quite important in Chapter 4 when we try to extend our data formats.

For now, consider the following XML describing a very small company:

```
<SMALL-COMPANY>
    <DEPARTMENT>
        <EMPLOYEES>
            <PERSON>John Doe</PERSON>
            <PERSON>J. D. G. Crater</PERSON>
        </EMPLOYEES>
    </DEPARTMENT>
    <DEPARTMENT>
        <EMPLOYEES>
            <PERSON>Amelia Erhart</PERSON>
        </EMPLOYEES>
    </DEPARTMENT>
</SMALL_COMPANY>
```

While we've arguably left out a lot of things we would need to describe this particular business object, we've also managed to include a great deal of structure. Our firm contains multiple departments, each of which contains employees. Employees are <PERSON> elements.

## Mixed Content

We can also mix data and elements for even greater complexity. This is akin to a structure in the C and C++ programming languages, or a record in Pascal. Simple items of information may be represented as data, while complex structures contained within our overall structure are marked up as elements. For example:

```
<PERSON>
    <NAME>
        <FIRST>Robert</FIRST>
        <LAST>Jones<LAST>
    </NAME>
    <AGE>30</AGE>
    He's a fine fellow
</PERSON>
```

Here we've mixed <NAME> and <AGE> elements with a comment on our person. The <NAME> element is itself a container of two other elements.

# Attributes

If you've written HTML, you're familiar with attributes. These are items descriptive of the element to which they are attached. When you define an HTML table, you might begin with the tag:

```
<TABLE WIDTH="100%" BORDER="1">
```

WIDTH and BORDER describe the table. Let's use attributes to redo our <PERSON> element from a few paragraphs ago, but remember these attributes *must* be kept in quotes:

```
<PERSON AGE="30">
    <NAME>
        <FIRST>Robert</FIRST>
        <LAST>Jones<LAST>
    </NAME>
    He's a fine fellow
</PERSON>
```

We've decided the person's age didn't need to be a separate element. There are no rules regarding when to use elements and when to use attributes, but you should remember that elements allow you to express structure, while attributes are structure-free adornments.

*Incidentally, if you need to use reserved characters like apostrophes or quotation marks within an attribute, you can make use of two of XML's predefined entities. An apostrophe may be referred to by the entity reference* &apos; *and a quotation mark by the entity reference* &quot; *we come back to entity reference in shortly. Angled brackets < > are denoted by the entities* &lt; *and* &gt;, *respectively.*

# Processing Instructions

A document can provide instructions to an application processing it through the use of **processing instructions**. A processing instruction is a single tag beginning and ending with an angle bracket and a question mark. At the beginning of the tag, after the question mark, the processing instruction has a name, followed by attributes. XML makes use of processing instructions. Here is a processing instruction for conveying what we think of a hypothetical document:

```
<?WhatToDo DoAction="justTrashIt" ?>
```

The name categorizes the instruction while the attribute conveys the information.

# Comments

Comments may be added just as in HTML:

```
<!-- This is a comment -->
```

Comments are intended to be source documentation, just as in a programming language. More importantly for our purposes, we are focusing on machine-to-machine communication. Comments won't be that useful to us.

# Entities

I mentioned the predefined entities &apos; and &quot; a short while ago. Entities are a useful way to define some body of XML once and refer to it later. Usually, you do this to avoid repeating lengthy sections of XML in a document. Every entity has to be declared before it can be used. You can do this in the document's prolog or in the DTD associated with the document. There are two kinds of entities: **internal entities** and **external entities**. An internal entity contains the content of the entity in the body of the declaration:

```
<!ENTITY age "Age of the person">
```

In this case, age is the name by which we will refer to the entity and "Age of the person" is the content. An external entity, by contrast, draws its content from some external resource. It works the same way as the DOCTYPE DTD declaration, being able to reference local (system) and disparate (public) external entities. For example:

```
<!ENTITY age SYSTEM "age.xml">
```

We use an entity by referring to it. An entity reference consists of the ampersand symbol followed by the entity name and a semicolon:

```
<AGE>
    <COMMENT>&age;</COMMENT>
</AGE>
```

Entity declarations may be added to the prolog of a document by including them inside square brackets within the DOCTYPE tag after the external DTD has been named. Here is an example of defining some entities in the prolog of an XML document:

```
<?xml version="1.0"?>
<!DOCTYPE SMALL_COMPANY SYSTEM "corporate.dtd"
    [<!ENTITY hq "Headquarters">
    <!ENTITY assembly "Assembly Line No.">
    <!ENTITY sales "Sales Office No.">]
>
```

*Entities are most useful when used within DTDs. Since we will be generating our XML programmatically, we won't find much use for entities in XML documents. Entities may be used in very flexible and creative ways within a DTD, and there are a number of options for use with entities that I have not covered here.*

# Document Type Definitions

A DTD is the formal specification of an XML vocabulary. A DTD consists of a series of production rules that describe how an XML document can be composed such that it is a valid document under that vocabulary. We will not be making much use of DTDs in the applications we develop in this book for several reasons. First, the syntax used in a DTD is not XML, so we would need to develop a parser distinct from the one we will be using to manipulate our documents. XML parsers have to understand DTDs, but they are not required to expose the information to outside users. More importantly, our XML will be generated by applications, not human authors.

There is also a subtler objection to the use of DTDs in our philosophy. There are some constructions of XML elements that make no difference to our applications, yet cannot be described in a DTD. For example, we might wish to say that each of several elements in a list must appear as children of another element. If we are initializing a local business object from an XML document, we don't care about the order in which the child elements appear. So this construction

```
<NAME>
    <FIRST>John</FIRST>
    <LAST>Doe</LAST>
</NAME>
```

is just as useful to us as this one:

```
<NAME>
    <LAST>Doe</LAST>
    <FIRST>John</FIRST>
</NAME>
```

We can initialize the properties of our name object in either order. Nevertheless, the DTD syntax gives us no way to express this. Consequently, the use of well-formed XML in preference to valid XML actually lets us write code that is more resistant to small errors, provided we don't abuse the privilege. If the programmers of the applications that will generate or consume a given vocabulary make a good faith effort to adhere to the rules of a vocabulary, we are better off with well-formed XML.

Nevertheless, a DTD gives us a way to express a vocabulary to other programmers. If your application is intended for a controlled setting and a DTD allows you to express all your rules, providing DTDs for document validation is a good way to stamp out errors. For these reasons, we should take a brief look at the syntax for writing DTDs. We will use DTDs throughout this book to express the vocabularies used in our sample code when those vocabularies are not trivial.

There are many tags and refinements that may be used in DTDs, but we will require only two: ELEMENT and ATTLIST. A lengthy discussion of DTD syntax and a thorough examination of this topic may be found in *Professional XML Applications* (ISBN 1-1861001-52-5).

### Declaring Elements

XML elements are defined using the ELEMENT tag. This tag takes the following form:

```
<!ELEMENT element_name rule>
```

The rule specifies the content of the element. It can be PCDATA (denoted by #PCDATA), a list of child elements, or some combination of the two. PCDATA, or Parsed Character Data, is text which contains no further tags and which the parser is expected to process[1]. There are also the explicit content identifiers EMPTY and ANY. Element lists and mixed content are more interesting. Lists are enclosed in parentheses, and you can even have lists nested within lists. If a strict sequence of child content is needed, the child elements and PCDATA will be listed in a comma delimited sequence. If they are alternatives to one another, they will appear separated by the pipe symbol, |. Here are some simple examples:

```
<!ELEMENT PERSON (NAME, ADDRESS, DESCRIPTION)>
<!ELEMENT DESCRIPTION #PCDATA>
<!ELEMENT NAME (#PCDATA | (FIRST, MI, LAST))>
```

Elements may be optional. We also need some way of specifying how many occurrences of a particular element may appear. This is handled by following the child item – an element or list – by a symbol according to the following table:

| Symbol | Cardinality |
| --- | --- |
| ? | optional, i.e., zero or one occurrence |
| * | zero or more (i.e., zero or *n*) occurrences |
| + | one or more occurrences |

---

[1] There is also CDATA, or character data, which the parser will ignore and which can contain any text, even tags – such as embedded HTML – that you wish to pass on to some application.

If the child item is not qualified by one of these symbols, it appears exactly once. Here are some more complicated element declarations:

```
<!ELEMENT NAME (FIRST, MI?, LAST)>
<!ELEMENT FAMILY (MOTHER, FATHER, CHILD*)>
<!ELEMENT PLACE_SETTING (SPOON+, FORK+, KNIFE, BUTTER_KNIFE?)>
<!ELEMENT CHAPTER (PARAGRAPH | ILLUSTRATION | BULLET_LIST)*>
```

The element PLACE_SETTING thus consists of one or more spoons, followed by one or more forks, exactly one knife, and perhaps a butter knife. CHAPTER consists of zero or more occurrences of paragraphs, illustrations, or bullet lists, in any order. We do not specify the order because we are using the OR operator and we can have multiple occurrences. Even the trivial case of a chapter with no content is also permitted because the * qualifier allows zero or more occurrences of the child list.

### Declaring Attributes

We specify the attributes that apply to a given element with an ATTLIST. This has the form:

```
<!ATTLIST element_name attribute_list>
```

The attribute list, in turn, takes the form of a sequence of triplets separated by whitespace. Each triplet is composed of the attribute name, the attribute type, and a default declaration. Attribute types may be one of the following: a literal string (denoted by CDATA), a tokenized primitive type, or an enumerated type. There are a number of tokenized types, but we will focus on NMTOKEN and NMTOKENS. An NMTOKEN type consists of one or more occurrences of characters drawn from this list: letters, digits, '.', '-', '_', and ':'. NMTOKENS simply refers to a series of NMTOKEN types separated by whitespace.

Default declarations tell us whether an attribute must appear in an element, and whether it has a default value if it is not specified. If the default declaration consists of #REQUIRED, then the attribute must always appear within the element. If it is #IMPLIED, no default value is provided. If the default declaration has the literal #FIXED followed by a value, the attribute must always have that value. If a value appears that is not qualified by any of the three literals, and the attribute is omitted in an element, the parser will act as though it is present with the default value.

Here is an example of an element declaration describing a person followed by the attribute list for that person:

```
<!ELEMENT PERSON (NAME, ADDRESS, JOB_TITLE)>
<!ATTLIST PERSON
      AGE       CDATA            #IMPLIED
      GENDER    (male | female)  #REQUIRED
      LOCALE    "our_town"       #FIXED>
```

Each person element can have an age attribute, must have a gender attribute taking either the value male or female, and must have the fixed locale attribute our_town. The following XML elements conform to this declaration:

```
<PERSON GENDER="male" LOCALE="our_town">...</PERSON>
<PERSON AGE="29" GENDER="female">... </PERSON>
```

In the second case, since the LOCALE attribute does not appear, the application must assume it has the value our_town.

So, here's a sample DTD for a person:

```
<!ELEMENT PERSON (NAME, ADDRESS, JOB_TITLE)>
<!ATTLIST PERSON
      AGE            CDATA                  #REQUIRED
      GENDER         (male | female)        #REQUIRED
      HAIR_COLOR     CDATA                  #IMPLIED>

<!ELEMENT NAME (FIRST?, MIDDLE?, LAST)>
<!ELEMENT FIRST (#PCDATA) >
<!ELEMENT MIDDLE (#PCDATA)>
<!ELEMENT LAST (#PCDATA)>

<!ELEMENT ADDRESS (STREET1, STREET2?, TOWN, STATE)>
<!ELEMENT STREET1 #PCDATA>
<!ELEMENT STREET2 #PCDATA>
<!ELEMENT TOWN #PCDATA>
<!ELEMENT STATE #PCDATA>
```

Here are two XML documents that conform to this DTD. The example assumes the DTD given in the text is saved as a separate file named `person.dtd` somewhere on the user's system.

```
<?xml version="1.0" ?>
<!DOCTYPE PERSON SYSTEM "person.dtd">
<PERSON AGE="19" GENDER="male" HAIR_COLOR="brown">
    <NAME>
        <FIRST>John</FIRST>
        <LAST>Doe</LAST>
    </NAME>
    <ADDRESS>   '
        <STREET1>1120 Mortified Road</STREET1>
        <STREET2>Apartment 66</STREET2>
        <TOWN>Boxwood</TOWN>
        <STATE>New York</STATE>
    </ADDRESS>
    <JOB_TITLE>Chief Slacker Inspector</JOB_TITLE>
</PERSON>
```

```
<?xml version="1.0" ?>
<!DOCTYPE PERSON SYSTEM "person.dtd">
<PERSON AGE="34" GENDER="female" >
    <NAME>
        <FIRST>Rebecca</FIRST>
        <MIDDLE>Ann</MIDDLE>
        <LAST>Morris</LAST>
    </NAME>
    <ADDRESS>
        <STREET1>123 Sand Street</STREET1>
        <TOWN>Hereford</TOWN>
        <STATE>New York</STATE>
    </ADDRESS>
    <JOB_TITLE>Production Manager</JOB_TITLE>
</PERSON>
```

Devising a DTD is a matter of analyzing the object in question and anticipating what properties of that object will need to be manipulated. It is rather like developing a database or directory schema. The question of whether some property of the object should be an attribute or element is one which cannot be resolved definitively. It is also a matter of analysis. Skill in composing useful DTDs comes only with practice.

# Working with XML

We need a way to manipulate XML documents programmatically. We'd like to avoid writing our own parser, and we'd like to be able to use an existing parser from script. Fortunately, the W3C has been at work formulating a generalized model for dealing with structured documents like HTML pages and XML documents. With the model in hand, we turn to an ActiveX component from Microsoft that implements a parser and exposes an object model that implements and extends the W3C model. This will allow us to focus on using XML rather than building the tools to manipulate XML. This is exactly in line with the common thread of component software we noted in Chapter 1.

# Document Object Model

The W3C is working on a series of object-oriented interfaces for manipulating structured documents such as XML. These interfaces are collectively known as the Document Object Model (DOM). The XML parser we will be working with in this book follows the DOM, providing Web page script writers with a simple means of manipulating XML content once it has been parsed.

*Version 1.0 of the DOM, Level 1, became a recommendation of the W3C on 1 October 1998. The specification may be found at http://www.w3.org/TR/REC-DOM-Level-1.*

## DOM Interfaces

The DOM represents documents as a hierarchy of nodes. Nodes may offer specialized interfaces depending on their type. Interfaces in this context is in the general sense of an API, not COM component interfaces. The DOM takes no position on specific technologies. Since nodes are central to the DOM, all interfaces stem from and extend the basic Node interface. This allows for a simple, flat view of the DOM interface hierarchy for use when performance may be an issue and you want to minimize the number of interfaces you must obtain and use. The following interfaces must be supported by all implementations of the DOM. They are required for manipulating documents written in HTML.

| Interface | Purpose |
| --- | --- |
| DOMImplementation | Permits an implementation to be queried regarding feature support |
| DocumentFragment | Lightweight object intended to hold some subset of a document |
| Document | Represents a complete structured document |
| Node | Primary datatype of the DOM, it represents a single node in the document tree |

| Interface | Purpose |
| --- | --- |
| NodeList | Ordered collection of nodes accessed by an ordinal index |
| NamedNodeMap | Unordered collection of nodes accessed by node name |
| CharacterData | Extends Node by adding methods specific to processing character data |
| Attribute | Extends Node with attributes peculiar to element attributes |
| Element | Extends Node with methods and attributes peculiar to elements |
| Text | Extends Node with a method for splitting character data |
| Comment | Extends CharacterData; does not presently offer additional features |
| ProcessingInstruction | Extends Node with attributes peculiar to processing instructions |

The DOM also provides for throwing exceptions in languages that support them.

## Extended Interfaces

The basic set of interfaces we listed in the preceding section is adequate for HTML. We, however, are interested in XML. The DOM provides an extended set of interfaces to manipulate features found in XML.

| Interface | Purpose |
| --- | --- |
| CDATASection | Extends Text and represents character data which would be interpreted as markup but which should be passed on unparsed; presently offers no additional features |
| DocumentType | Extends Node with attributes for the prolog information |
| Notation | Extends Node with attributes for the target (e.g., "xml") of processing instructions and binary resource types |
| Entity | Extends Node with attributes peculiar to entities |
| EntityReference | Extends Node to represent a reference to an entity; does not presently add features |

## The JavaScript Binding

The DOM specification provides for an implementation of the preceding interfaces in JavaScript. This binding provides objects for each of the interfaces presented in the preceding sections, as well as the exception mechanism and the exception code enumeration. We're going to be manipulating the DOM from JavaScript, but we will be making use of a specific implementation offered by Microsoft. I will therefore discuss the JavaScript approach in terms of this specific implementation, noting where the two differ.

# Microsoft XML Component

Microsoft used XML as the basis for representing the structure of Web sites in their version of push technology. The Microsoft XML component technology was first offered with Internet Explorer 4.0. In the absence of a recognized standard, Microsoft designed their own interfaces for the first version of MSXML, which shipped with IE4. A subsequent version of the component, which follows the DOM, is now available. This DOM-compliant component is installed with Microsoft Internet Explorer 5.0.

This component, often only referred to as MSXML, offers a variety of COM interfaces. (Some of these are for backward compatibility with the previous version of the component.) All the DOM interfaces are provided, but the most commonly used set of interfaces is a flattened version that works with all the specialized nodes as implementation instances of the core Node.

## MSXML Scripting Object Model

In the MSXML scripting object model, an XML document contains nodes. For navigation throughout the hierarchy, the document object points to a root node. The root node, and every node under it, points to a node list object, which is simply a collection of nodes. This list can be reached through either of two interfaces. One is designed to deal with the nodes in sequential order, while another accesses nodes based on their names. The Document also has an error object for reporting faults in parsing. This is shown in the following diagram, with one node expanded to show the node to node list relationship.

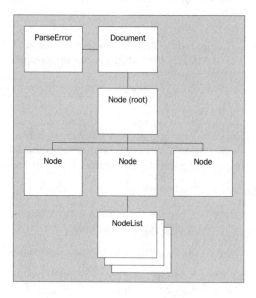

### Document Object

This object represents an XML document and provides control over the operation of the component itself. The document is the XML document and MSXML is a component implementing this object. As an implementation, it needs to let users control such things as how it loads lengthy documents. Where the DOM refers to variables within interfaces as attributes, MSXML refers to properties. We'll use that term in the reference tables that follow.

| Properties | Meaning |
|---|---|
| text | The text content of the entire document; read-write |
| xml | The xml source of the entire document; read-only |
| docType | A node representing the < ! DOCTYPE> tag, if any; read-only |
| implementation | A reference to the DOM implementation interface; read-only |
| documentElement | The root node of the document; read-write |
| readyState | A value denoting one of five possible states of the object; read-only (see the following table for the five possible states) |
| parseError | An error object containing the state of the last error generated by the parser; read-only |
| url | The url of the loaded document; read-only |
| async | TRUE for asynchronous download of the document (default), FALSE for synchronous download; read-write |
| validateOnParse | TRUE if the parser should validate loaded documents; read-write |
| resolveExternals | TRUE if the parser should resolve XML references to external entities, DTDs, and schemae; read-write |
| preserveWhiteSpace | TRUE if the parser should retain whitespace exactly as it appears in the document, FALSE if it should collapse multiple spaces into one and remove line breaks; read-write |
| onreadystatechange | Allows the script to register an event handler for the readystatechange event; write-only |
| ondataavailable | Allows the script to register event handlers for the dataavailable event (used in conjunction with asynchronous downloads); write-only |
| ontransformnode | Allows the script to register event handlers for the ontransformnode event (used with styled formatting); write-only |
| documentNode | The root node of the document; read-only |
| readyState | A value denoting one of five possible states of the object; read-only |

The values taken on by the `readyState` property are as follows:

| State | Code | Meaning |
|---|---|---|
| UNINITIALIZED | 0 | No document has been loaded by the parser |
| LOADING | 1 | The document has been read but not parser |
| LOADED | 2 | The document has been loaded and is now being parsed |
| INTERACTIVE | 3 | The document is partially parsed and the object model is available |
| COMPLETED | 4 | The document has been loaded and parsed |

The document object will have a `readyState` of COMPLETED whether the document was parsed successfully or not. You should check for this state only to see if a complete object model is available for scripting.

Next, here are the Document Object's methods:

| Methods | Use |
|---|---|
| createElement(tagName) | Creates an Element node with the given name |
| createDocumentFragment() | Creates a DOM DocumentFragment node (used to exchange DOM subtrees between documents) |
| createTextNode(data) | Creates a text node with the given content |
| createComment(data) | Creates a comment node with the given comment |
| createCDATASection(data) | Creates a CDATA node with the given content |
| createProcessing Instruction(target, data) | Creates a PI node whose target (portion immediately following the ?) and data content is given |
| createAttribute(name) | Creates an attribute with the name supplied |
| createEntity Reference(name) | Creates an entity reference node with the given name |
| getElementsByTagName (tagName) | Returns a node list containing all elements whose name matches tagName |
| createNode(type, name, namespaceURI) | Creates a new node object with the given type (integer enumeration or string name, e.g., "ELEMENT"), name, and namespace URI |
| nodeFromID(idString) | Returns the node whose ID attribute matches the parameter |
| load(xmlSource) | Loads an XML document from a URL |
| abort() | Cancels an asynchronous download in progress |

| Methods | Use |
|---|---|
| `loadXML(strXML)` | Loads a document from a string representation |
| `Save(destination)` | Saves the document to destination, which may be a file name, ASP Response object, XML document object, or a custom COM object supporting persistence. |

### Node Object

This is the workhorse of the MSXML object model. It represents elements and attributes in the document. It captures the features of the specialized interfaces of the DOM such as `Element` and `CharacterData`. It also allows us to implement the same functionality offered by the DOM's `DocumentFragment` interface. When you move a Node within a document, the entire subtree anchored by the Node moves with it.

| Properties | Meaning |
|---|---|
| `nodeName` | Name of the node; read-only |
| `nodeValue` | Value stored in the node; read-write |
| `nodeType` | An enumeration denoting the type of he node, e.g., `ELEMENT`, `ATTRIBUTE`; read-only |
| `parentNode` | The node whose child this node is; read-only |
| `childNodes` | A node list of all children of this node; read-only |
| `firstChild` | First child of this node; read-only |
| `lastChild` | Last child of this node; read-only |
| `previousSibling` | Preceding node at the same level of the tree; read-only |
| `nextSibling` | Following node at the same level of the tree; read-only |
| `attributes` | Named node map of all attributes of an element node; read-only |
| `ownerDocument` | Document that contains this node; read-only |
| `nodeTypeString` | The type of the node as a string, e.g., Element; read-only |
| `text` | Text content of the node and its child subtree; read-write |
| `specified` | `TRUE` if the attribute node was explicitly provided; `FALSE` if a default was provided; read-only |
| `definition` | A node in the DTD or schema that defines this node; read-only |
| `nodeTypedValue` | Returns the native datatype value of the node, e.g., a numeric value if the `dt:dt` attribute is a numeric type; read-write |
| `dataType` | The enumerated type of the node; read-write |
| `xml` | The XML source for the document as a string; read-only |

| Properties | Meaning |
|---|---|
| parsed | TRUE if the node's subtree has been parsed; read-only |
| namespaceURI | The value of URI in the namespace declaration attribute |
| prefix | Namespace prefix of the node |
| baseName | Node name with the namespace prefix stripped off; read-only |
| childNodes | Collection of nodes consisting of the child elements of an element; read-only |
| nodeName | Name of the node; read-only for elements, read-write for all others |
| nodeType | Enumeration for the type of node represented, e.g., element, attribute, PCDATA, etc; read-only |
| nodeValue | Value of a node; read-write |
| parentNode | The immediate ancestor of the current node; read-only |
| specified | TRUE if a node's value is specified, FALSE if it is implied; read-only |

Information from a DTD is only available for entities and entity references. Element and attribute definitions are available when using the XML schema preview.

Since nodes represent many different types of constructs in XML, the nodeType property takes on a variety of values to denote the kind of construct the node is representing:

| Value | XML Type |
|---|---|
| 1 | Element |
| 2 | Attribute |
| 3 | PCDATA |
| 4 | CDATA section |
| 5 | Entity reference |
| 6 | Entity |
| 7 | Processing instruction |
| 8 | Comment |
| 9 | Document |
| 10 | Document type |
| 11 | Document fragment |
| 12 | Notation |

| Methods | Use |
| --- | --- |
| `insertBefore(`<br>`  newChild, refChild)` | Inserts `newChild` into `childNodes` immediately before `refChild` |
| `replaceChild(`<br>`  newChild, oldChild)` | Replaces `oldChild` with `newChild` in the `childNodes` list |
| `removeChild(childNode)` | Removes `childNode` from the `childNodes` list |
| `appendChild(newChild)` | Adds `newChild` to the end of the `childNodes` list |
| `hasChildNodes()` | Returns true if the node has children |
| `cloneNode(deep)` | Creates a copy of the node; if deep is TRUE, the node's subtree is copied as well; if deep is FALSE, only the node and its attributes are copied |
| `transformNode(stylesheet)` | Returns a string representing the transformation of the node and its subtree according to the XSL rules in stylesheet |
| `selectNodes(queryString)` | Returns a node list of nodes matching the XSL query `queryString` |
| `selectSingleNode(queryString)` | Returns the first node matching the `queryString` XSL query |
| `transformNodeToObject(`<br>`  stylesheet, outputObject)` | Returns the result of applying the rules in stylesheet to the node as either a Document object or a stream |

### Node List Object

This is a collection object representing the children of a particular node. It is fundamental to traversing the document's hierarchy.

| Property | Meaning |
| --- | --- |
| `index(index)` | The node at position index within the list; default attribute |
| `length` | Number of nodes in the node list |

| Method | Use |
| --- | --- |
| `nextNode()` | Gets the next node in the list |
| `reset()` | Resets the position of the list iterator |
| `Item` | Returns a node given an ordinal index. |

### Name Node Map Object

This is a collection object that allows you to access member nodes by name. It is especially useful when dealing with attributes, because we will typically be searching for a particular attribute.

| Property | Meaning |
| --- | --- |
| index(index) | The node at position index within the list; default attribute |
| length | Number of nodes in the node list |

| Method | Use |
| --- | --- |
| getNamedItem(name) | Gets the node whose name is supplied |
| setNamedItem(newItem) | Adds newItem to the list |
| removeNamedItem(name) | Removes the named node from the list |
| getQualifiedItem (baseName, namespaceURI) | Gets the node named by the namespace qualified name (i.e., namespaceURI:baseName) |
| removeQualifiedItem (baseName, namespaceURI) | Removes the node named by the namespace qualified name |
| nextNode() | Gets the next node in the list |
| reset() | Resets the list iterator |

### Error Object

The Error object contains properties regarding the last error, if any were detected during parsing. It is accessed through the parseError property of the Document object.

| Properties | Meaning |
| --- | --- |
| errorCode | Code for the last error detected by the parser (default property); read-only |
| url | URL for the XML document parsed; read-only |
| reason | Text describing the last error detected; read-only |
| srcText | The XML surrounding the error; read-only |
| line | Line number in the XML where the error occurred; read-only |
| linepos | Character position within the line where the error occurred; read-only |
| filepos | Absolute file position in the XML document where the error occurred; read-only |

Note carefully the `errorCode` property. The `readyState` property of a document has the value `COMPLETED` (4) when parsing terminates regardless of whether an error occurred. Therefore, after loading a document we must check that `errorCode` has the value `zero`. Since `errorCode` is the default property, the following lines are equivalent:

```
if (myparser.parseError.errorCode == 0)
```

```
if (myparser.parseError == 0)
```

# Navigating XML

In order to navigate data in an XML document we must first create an instance of the MSXML parser and load the XML into it, before we can traverse through the tree that it creates from document.

### Creating an Instance of MSXML

No matter what we want to do, we will need an instance of the MSXML parser component. There are two ways to do this. We can create it in JavaScript with the following line:

```
var parser = new ActiveXObject("microsoft.xmldom");
```

This is very common way to create and instance of MSXML, however, we will be using another technique. This is because we are going to be using a single instance of the parser throughout the page, so we'll simply embed an instance of the component in the page and retrieve it when we need it. The HTML to embed it is:

```
<OBJECT classid="clsid:E54941B2-7756-11D1-BC2A-00C04FB925F3" name="xmlDOM">
</OBJECT>
```

This is the standard syntax for embedding an ActiveX component in Microsoft Internet Explorer. The attribute `classid` specifies the unique identifier of the control. Netscape handles things a bit differently. First, there is no native support for ActiveX controls, so you will need the ScriptActive plug-in from NCompass Labs (`http://www.ncompasslabs.com`). Netscape also uses the `<EMBED>` tag in preference to `<OBJECT>`. You could then write a version that will work in either browser:

```
<OBJECT classid="clsid:E54941B2-7756-11D1-BC2A-00C04FB925F3" name="xmlDOM" >
<EMBED name="xmlDOM" classid="clsid:E54941B2-7756-11D1-BC2A-00C04FB925F3"
name="xmlDOM">
</OBJECT>
```

Netscape will ignore the `<OBJECT>` tag and read the `<EMBED>` tag, while Internet Explorer will ignore the `<EMBED>` so long as it is nested inside the `<OBJECT>` tag. Once we have an instance of the component in the page, we retrieve it in a function with the line:

```
var parser = document.all("xmlDOM");
```

The variable `document` in this case is part of Internet Explorer's object model and it refers to the HTML page, while the `all` property is the collection of all HTML elements on the page. We then retrieve the named element `xmldom` – our `OBJECT` – from this collection for use.

## Loading XML into MSXML

Having created an instance of the parser, we can load a document in one of two ways. Using either the load() or loadXML() methods of the Document object. The load() method takes a URL to the XML document that we want to load, while the method loadXML() takes a string representation of the source XML and loads that.

## Navigating the Parse Tree

Once a document is loaded and parsed, MSXML has a parse tree ready for our examination. Each node of the tree represents an element or attribute of the XML document. We must walk this tree if we want to extract the information encoded in the document. This is simple. The parser is the top level Document object. Its root is the outer-most element. Each node, from the root on down, has a nodeList in its childNodes property. We simple walk this list and expand each node in turn. The following code for the TraverseTree() JavaScript function in the page BasicXML.htm starts us on our way:

```
function TraverseTree(document)
{
    var root = document.documentElement;
    ProcessNodeSimple(root);
}
```

Given a document, we obtain the root node and pass it on to ProcessNodeSimple(), a function designed to expand nodes:

```
function ProcessNodeSimple(node)
{
    for (var i = 0; i < node.childNodes.length; i++)
      ProcessNodeSimple(node.childNodes(i));
}
```

ProcessNodeSimple() uses recursion to perform a depth-first traversal of the tree. Simply put, we expand each node all the way down through its immediate children until we reach the bottom, then we pop back up and expand the next child node all the way down to the bottom of its subtree. When control returns to TraverseTree(), we have expanded every child node of the root and we are finished.

> *You may be wondering what the effect of* node.nextNode() *and* node.previousNode() *on the* nodeList *position would be. Calling either method has no effect on the position of* node.currentNode(); node.currentNode() *returns the same* Node *object before and after the call. So, these methods provide us with a way of looking ahead or behind without disturbing our processing.*

This code is simple, but somewhat less than exciting. Unless you step through it in a debugger, you won't see anything. Clearly, we are going to have to do a little more work to be able to use XML for something useful. So, how about we write some code that displays an HTML representation of the nodes we find in our traversal? Before we move on to that task, however, let's observe two things about structure that this little exercise exposes. Consider the sample XML below:

```
<TEAM>
    <PERSON AGE="38">
        <NAME>John Connor</NAME>
    </PERSON>
```

```
<PERSON AGE="18">
    <NAME>Thomas Atkins</NAME>
    <FAVORITE_COLOR>green</FAVORITE_COLOR>
</PERSON>
</TEAM>
```

We have two PERSON elements contained within the TEAM root element. First, note that calling node.nodeValue for some variable node will return a string concatenating all the values for contained elements. If you invoke this method on the second person's NAME element, you'd get "Thomas Atkins". If you invoke it on the second PERSON element, however, you would get "Thomas Atkinsgreen". Both NAME and FAVORITE_COLOR are contained elements of that PERSON instance, so their combined values are considered the value of the PERSON element's node.

Secondly, if you do step through this in a debugger, you will see processNode go one level deeper than you may be expecting. Expanding the first PERSON element, you get down to the NAME element. nodeName is "NAME", and nodeValue is "John Connor". childNodes.length, however, is 1, so we process this node. This time, nodeName is "" and nodeValue is still "John Connor". The key is that the element's character data is a node type, PCDATA. If you checked the value of nodeType, you would see a value of PCDATA (3). The nodeType property, then, is the key to telling when we have reached a leaf node of the parse tree.

## Working with Nodes

Let's modify our tree traversal code so that we output formatted HTML to a <DIV> in a Web page. The HTML will identify each node by type and supply indenting to indicate the nesting structure of the XML document. For our sample XML from the navigation section, the results in our Basicxml.htm page will look like this:

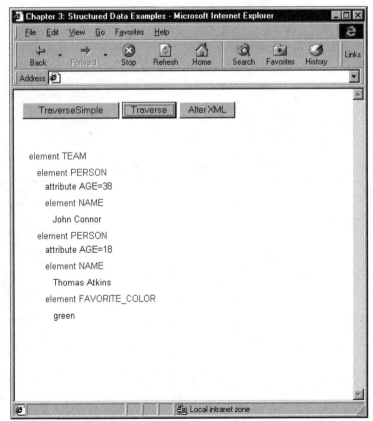

*Remember that the code for this section can be downloaded from the Wrox Web site, along with all the other code for this book, at* http://www.wrox.com. *You can also try out this example at* http://webdev.wrox.co.uk/books/2270/

As you can see, we have three buttons on BasicXML.html TraverseSimple, Traverse, and AlterXML, we come to each in turn.

The instance of MSXML in the BasicXML.html page loads the sample XML and provides a parse tree for us to work with. We walk this tree if we want to extract the information encoded in the document. The parser is the top-level Document object, and its root is the outer-most element. Each node, from the root on down, has a NodeList in its childNodes property. We simple walk this list and expand each node in turn. If you click on the Traverse button in BasicXML.htm, you will be taken to the OnTraverseSimple() function. It loads a simple document into the parser and calls the function TraverseTree() to walk the entire tree, although this will not actually display anything in the browser window:

```
function OnTraverseSimple()
{
   parser.async = "false";

   parser.loadXML('<TEAM><PERSON AGE="38"><NAME>John
          Connor</NAME></PERSON><PERSON AGE="18"><NAME>Thomas
          Atkins</NAME><FAVORITE_COLOR>green</FAVORITE_COLOR></PERSON></TEAM>');
   if (parser.readyState == COMPLETED && parser.parseError == 0)
      TraverseTreeSimple(parser);
   else
          alert("Parser detects error: " + parser.parseError.reason);
}

function TraverseTree(document)
{
   var root = document.documentElementNode;
   ProcessNodeSimple(root);
}
```

The major change between TraverseSimple and Traverse is shown when we come to ProcessNode(), having parsed the tree, we will now display something – as shown in the screen shot above.

```
function ProcessNode(node)
{
   tabsize += 12;
   linesize += 4;
   switch (node.nodeType)
   {
      case ELEMENT:
         . . .
         break;

      case PCDATA:
         . . .
         break;

      default:
         HandleOther(node);
```

```
            break;
        }
    tabsize -= 12;
}
```

First, we use the `nodeType` property to determine what sort of node is at hand. We are primarily interested in ELEMENTs, ATTRIBUTEs, and TEXT nodes (for the character data value of elements). Everything else will receive default treatment. You can easily see where we address ELEMENTs and PCDATA, but where are attributes handled? You may recall that `Node` has an `attributes` property. All attributes of an ELEMENT are found there as nodes. They will not appear in the `childNodes` collection, so we must handle them during the course of processing ELEMENTs. The code looks like this:

```
    . . .
    switch (node.nodeType)
    {
        case ELEMENT:

            // List the name of the element
            ListLine("element " + node.nodeName, "red");
            linesize += 4;

            // Handle attributes for the element
            tabsize += 12;
            for (var j = 0; j < node.attributes.length; j++)
            {
                var attribute = node.attributes.item(j);
                ListLine("attribute " + attribute.nodeName
                    + "=" + attribute.nodeValue, "blue");
                linesize += 4;
            }
            tabsize -= 12;

            // Expand child nodes
            for (var i = 0; i < node.childNodes.length; i++)
                ProcessNode(node.childNodes(i));

            break;

        . . .
    }
    tabsize -= 12;
}
```

We have developed a simple `ListLine()` function for writing the findings to the page. The variables `linesize` and `tabsize` are global variables controlling placement on the page.

The important thing to note here is that we:

❑ Write the name of the element
❑ Write out any attributes
❑ Then expand the child nodes

Note that if there are no attributes, `node.attributes.length` will be zero and nothing will be listed.

Here is the `ListLine()` function we devised to make use of inline style sheets to supply a particular font and position on the page.

```
function ListLine(text, color)
{
    var str = '<DIV style="font-family:arial,sans-serif; font-size:10pt; color:'
        + color
        + '; position:relative; left:' + tabsize
        + '; top:' + linesize + ';">'
        + text + '</DIV>';
    oDisplayArea.insertAdjacentHTML("beforeEnd", str);

}
```

PCDATA handling is simple:

```
case PCDATA:
        // List the value
        ListLine(node.nodeValue, "black");
        linesize += 4;
        break;
```

In the case of the rest of the node types, we simply want to display the element name and the value:

```
function HandleOther(node)
{
    ListLine(node.nodeName + " " + node.nodeValue, "black");
}
```

## Creating XML

So far we've read a previously created XML document and parsed it. Now we'll use the MSXML object model to create new XML fragments and manipulate documents. Recall the simple XML document we used for our traversal examples:

```
<TEAM>
    <PERSON AGE="38">
        <NAME>John Connor</NAME>
    </PERSON>
    <PERSON AGE="18">
        <NAME>Thomas Atkins</NAME>
        <FAVORITE_COLOR>green</FAVORITE_COLOR>
    </PERSON>
</TEAM>
```

We've taken a dislike to John Connor and want to replace him. So, we'll add a function to `BasicXML.htm` called `OnAlterXML()` that gets called when the user clicks on the Alter XML button; getting rid of John Conner and replacing him with Jack Benny. To achieve this, we need to create a new PERSON node. Notice however, that also means we'll need a child NAME node. While we're at it, let's create a FAVORITE_COLOR element for our new person. We also need to set the AGE attribute on our person. The most important method we need is part of the Document object:

```
createElement(nodeName);
```

In our case, we create a new PERSON element. To create a new PERSON element we need an instance of MSXML, then we create a PERSON node. This is done with the following line of code:

```
var person = parser.createElement("PERSON");
```

The variable parser contains our document object. Now let's set the AGE attribute. We need to create an attribute node, add it to the attributes collection of the node we just created, and set its value. We do this in three steps:

```
ageAttr = parser.createAttribute("AGE");
person.setAttributeNode(ageAttr);
person.setAttribute("AGE", "39");
```

We once again need the instance of MSXML to create a new node, this time of type ATTRIBUTE. We use setAttributeNode to add it to the attributes collection, then call setAttribute to give the attribute a value. That method takes the name of the attribute and a value. If it finds the named attribute, it sets the value.

Now that the person element is created, we want to create its child elements. The pattern we will follow is this: create a node, create the TEXT node for that node's value, and associate the two. For NAME and FAVORITE_COLOR, that looks like this:

```
var name = parser.createElement("NAME");
var nameVal = parser.createTextNode("Jack Benny");
name.appendChild(nameVal);

var favoriteColor = parser.createElement("FAVORITE_COLOR");
var colorVal = parser.createTextNode("green");
favoriteColor.appendChild(colorVal);

person.appendChild(name);
person.appendChild(favoriteColor);
```

Note that PCDATA (pure text) elements do not have names. The method appendChild permits us to establish the parent-child relationship by adding the NAME element as a child of the PERSON element.

We have now created our new PERSON element, with its attributes. However, we originally decided to *replace* the PERSON element possessing the PCDATA value "John Connor". We know this is the first child element of the root TEAM element, so we finish by getting the root node, replacing its first child with the new node (thereby replacing John Connor with Jack Benny), and sending the document off to our TraverseTree() function for display in the document:

```
var root = parser.documentNode;
root.replaceNode(root.childNodes.item(0), person);

// Send results to the Web page
TraverseTree(parser);
```

Here is a complete listing of the function we have analyzed so you can study the code in context:

```
function PersonReplacement(parser)
{
    var ageAttr;
    var person = parser.createElement("PERSON");
```

```
    ageAttr = parser.createAttribute("AGE");
    person.setAttributeNode(ageAttr);
    person.setAttribute("AGE", "39");

    var name = parser.createElement("NAME");
    var nameVal = parser.createTextNode("Jack Benny");
    name.appendChild(nameVal);

    var favoriteColor = parser.createElement("FAVORITE_COLOR");
    var colorVal = parser.createTextNode("green");
    favoriteColor.appendChild(colorVal);

    person.appendChild(name);
    person.appendChild(favoriteColor);

    var root = parser.documentElement;
    root.replaceChild(person, root.childNodes(0));

    TraverseTree(parser);
}
```

The XML document now looks like this:

```
<TEAM>
    <PERSON AGE="39">
        <NAME>Jack Benny</NAME>
        <FAVORITE_COLOR>green</FAVORITE_COLOR>
    </PERSON>
    <PERSON AGE="18">
        <NAME>Thomas Atkins</NAME>
        <FAVORITE_COLOR>green</FAVORITE_COLOR>
    </PERSON>
</TEAM>
```

This is shown when we click
the **AlterXML** button of
`BasicXML.html`:

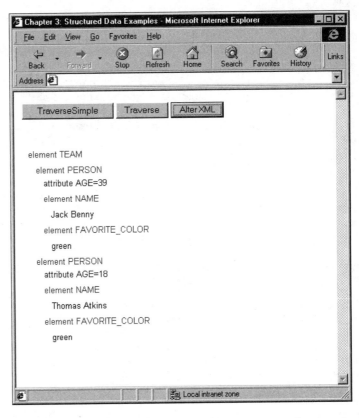

We started out with an existing XML document. We could just as easily create a new document using the MSXML object model. This relies on the fact that the Document object is a Node itself. We simply create a new element node and set the parser's `documentElement` property to the new node. Since the list is empty, the new element becomes the root of the document:

```
function CreateXMLDoc()
{
    parser.async = "false";

    var newroot=parser.createElement("TEAM");
    if (newroot != null)
        parser.documentElement = newroot;

    // Add child nodes here
}
```

# Exchanging XML over Networks

Now it is time to consider how we will move XML documents between clients and servers. Our focus is on network applications built as Web applications. The use of HTTP is most convenient but imposes some limitations. We will see that there are several alternatives. Different techniques will be required depending on the nature of the client and the size of the document. Since we will be using XML as a mechanism for exchanging structured data, the size of our documents will vary widely.

# HTTP

Many of our applications will use HTML documents in Web browsers for the client. Even when we construct an entirely automated client, such as an agent, HTTP is so readily accessible that it is the easiest solution. Indeed, MSXML's Document object provides the `load()` method for obtaining XML via HTTP. We must look at this more closely, however. While this method will bring XML down from the server, how do we get XML generated on the client to the server?

HTTP provides two means of getting client data to the server. These are the GET and POST operations.

## GET

In this case, named parameters are sent to the server as a series of name and value pairs appended to the document name in the URL. The URL takes the form:

```
http://doc_name?parm_name1=parm_value1&parm_name2=parm_value2...
```

Since ASP allows us to retrieve the entire string of parameter pairs, we can even dispense with naming the parameters. Thus, we might send:

```
http://MyServer/XMLConsumer.asp?<PERSON><NAME>John</NAME></PERSON>
```

Our ASP would retrieve the XML in the request – `<PERSON><NAME>John</NAME></PERSON>` – with the line:

```
var sXML = Request("QUERY_STRING");
```

After processing the XML and generating a reply of its own in XML, it would answer with a pure XML document. We might then use the client-side code:

```
parser.load("http://MyServer/XMLConsumer.asp?<PERSON><NAME>John</NAME></PERSON>");
```

This is a powerful line of code. MSXML performs a GET, transmitting the XML string. The receiving ASP performs some processing and returns an XML document that the parser loads. After this line completes, we have our reply in a parse tree, ready to navigate. This is simple and effective.

Unfortunately, there are some significant drawbacks. First, URLs cannot contain non-alphanumeric characters. Such characters must be converted to the form %xx, where xx is the hexadecimal code for the character. Thus, if our PERSON in the example above had a last name, we would need to convert the URL as follows:

```
http://MyServer/XMLConsumer.asp?<PERSON><NAME>John%20Doe</NAME></PERSON>
```

This requires us to remember to preprocess our XML-based requests before transmission. There is another limitation on the use of the GET operation. Servers have an upper limit on the length of URLs that varies from server to server. For IIS, we can transmit approximately 2K worth of character data in a URL before encountering difficulty. For small amounts of XML, GET is a simple and effective solution.

## POST

This operation alleviates most of the two limitations inherent in a GET. POST is used with HTML forms. When the form is transmitted to the server, the URL is sent in one HTTP message, followed by another message with the form element values. There is no length limit and non-alphanumeric characters may appear. The exception is the use of some characters that HTML reserves for itself, like angle brackets and quotation marks. Unfortunately for us, MSXML does not provide a POST version of the load method. So, we will discuss an approach that avoids this in a moment. For the time being, let's look at how we get our XML to the server via a POST.

Assume we want to use a form that existed prior to our commitment to XML for a data exchange format. We wish to use it with a new, XML-enabled service. The following form might have been used to add people to a corporate database. It is the page PersonFormA.htm and it can be downloaded from our site at http://www.wrox.com and run from http://webdev.wrox.co.uk/books/2270:

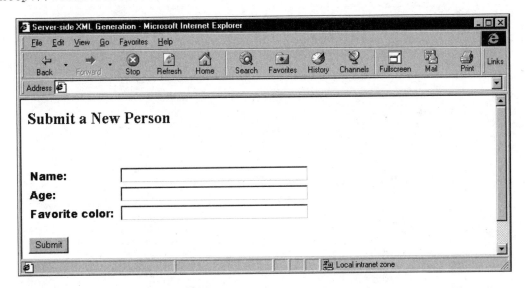

Its purpose is to use a POST operation to send the values of the form fields to the ASP PersonHandler1.asp. The relevant section of HTML looks like this:

```
<form method="POST" action="PersonHandler1.asp">
  <table border="0" width="70%">
    <tr>
      <td width="28%"><font face="Arial Black">Name:</font></td>
      <td width="72%">
        <input type="text" name="NameText" size="39">
      </td>
    </tr>
    <tr>
      <td width="28%"><font face="Arial Black">Age:</font></td>
      <td width="72%">
        <input type="text" name="AgeText" size="39">
      </td>
    </tr>
    <tr>
      <td width="28%"><font face="Arial Black">Favorite color:</font></td>
      <td width="72%">
```

```
            <input type="text" name="ColorText" size="39">
      </td>
    </tr>
  </table>
  <div align="left"><p><input type="submit" value="Submit" name="B1"></p>
  </div>
</form>
```

The POST operation is specified in the method attribute of the <FORM> tag, while the target URL is the action attribute. Of course, the ASP does not receive XML. It receives a collection of field names and values. In ASP, this is represented by the Form collection of the Request object. Assuming it understands the XML vocabulary for people, we can generate the XML on the server as follows:

```
var sXML = new String("<PERSON");

// Collect the pieces of data
if (Request.Form("AgeText") != "")
   sXML += ' AGE="' + Request.Form("AgeText") + '"><NAME>';
else
   sXML += "><NAME>";
sXML += Request.Form("NameText") + "</NAME>";

if (Request.Form("ColorText") != "")
   sXML += "<FAVORITE_COLOR>" + Request.Form("ColorText") + "</FAVORITE_COLOR>";

sXML += "</PERSON>";
```

If we added some values to the form, the resulting XML would look like this:

```
<PERSON AGE=26>
<NAME>Chris Hindley</NAME>
<FAVORITE_COLOR>Red</FAVORITE_COLOR>
</PERSON>
```

The Request object is offered by ASP to represent the information sent from the client. Its Form collection permits us named access to the values of our form elements. We retrieve these values and wrap them in our tags. This approach permits us to use pre-existing Web forms and keep all XML-aware pages on the server.

This is not entirely satisfying, however. In Chapter 1 we envisioned a network of loosely coupled clients and servers. The job of generating XML for requests truly belongs on the client. After all, if we force the server to do the work, we've saddled the server with knowledge of the client, precisely what we want to avoid by using XML. If the client sends over XML, the server doesn't need to know anything about the client. Let's revise the page containing the form so that it contains the following HTML (this source is found in PersonFormB.html):

```
<table border="0" width="70%">
  <tr>
    <td width="28%"><font face="Arial Black">Name:</font></td>
    <td width="72%">
        <input type="text" name="NameText" size="39">
    </td>
  </tr>
  <tr>
```

```
            <td width="28%"><font face="Arial Black">Age:</font></td>
            <td width="72%">
                <input type="text" name="AgeText" size="39">
            </td>
        </tr>
        <tr>
            <td width="28%"><font face="Arial Black">Favorite color:</font></td>
            <td width="72%">
                <input type="text" name="ColorText" size="39">
            </td>
        </tr>
    </table>

    <form method="POST" action="PersonHandler2.asp" name="PersonForm">
        <input type="text"
            name="XMLValue" style="display:none" size="20">
    </form>

    <div align="left">

    <p><input type="button" Value="Submit" name="B1" OnClick="OnClick()"></p>
```

Our intent is to pass an XML document rather than a collection of HTML form values. We've made a number of significant changes here. First, we moved the HTML form elements outside the form itself. The values of all elements within the form are transmitted with the POST operation. Since we're generating the XML on the client, we don't want to consume network resources sending the raw data in addition to the XML. Our form now consists of one text box with the display:none style. This means it is not visible in the browser. We are using it simply as a place to store the XML we will generate. We also have a button outside the form. We associate it with the following a script through the OnClick attribute:

```
function OnClick()
{
    var sName, sAge, sColor, sXML;
    var oForm = document.PersonForm;

    // Obtain form element text
    sName = document.all("NameText").value;
    sAge = document.all("AgeText").value;
    sColor = document.all("ColorText").value;

    // Build an XML fragment
    sXML = "<PERSON AGE=&quot;" + sAge + "&quot;><NAME>" + sName + "</NAME>";
    sXML += '<FAVORITE_COLOR>' + sColor + '</FAVORITE_COLOR></PERSON>';

    // Set the hidden form element and force a submit
    oForm.elements("XMLValue").value = sXML;
    oForm.submit();

}
```

Note that we need to use the &quot; HTML entity to ensure the quotation marks around attribute values survive passage through HTTP as form element parameters. Named forms enjoy an unusual relationship with the containing document in Microsoft DHTML. The form may be referenced by name just as if it were a property of the document. Thus, the line

```
    var oForm = document.PersonForm;
```

is equivalent to

```
var oForm = document.all("PersonForm");
```

Since our form elements are outside the form they must be retrieved from the `document.all` collection. Once we have their values, we build an XML string and copy it to the hidden element in our form:

```
oForm.elements("XMLValue").value = sXML;
```

We then call the submit method of the form, causing our XML to be sent to the server (`PersonHandler2.asp`). The server retrieves the XML with the line:

```
sXML = Request.Form("XMLValue").item(1);
```

Now we must turn our attention to the problem of returning XML to the client. With the GET operation, we could simply stream XML back to the client and rely on MSXML catching it in its load method. (In Chapter 6 we will look at some components that will allow us to retain that approach.) For now, however, let's solve the problem of getting the XML back without using anything more complicated than ASP and JavaScript.

Our technique involves writing the result XML into a hidden `<DIV>` on the returned page. We hard code the `<DIV>`, then insert ASP script code to write the XML we that appears when the page generated by the ASP arrives on the client. That page can then have a script that extracts the HTML in the `<DIV>` and passes it to MSXML. Here's the code to do this in an ASP:

```
<DIV STYLE="display:none" ID="XMLBuffer">
  <% //Rem Echo the XML POSTed from the client
    var sXML;
    sXML = Request.Form("XMLValue").item(1);

    //Rem Echo the XML to the client
    Response.Write(sXML)
  %>
</DIV>
```

Let's verify that we can retrieve this and parse it by returning to the XML expansion functions we used earlier:

```
function OnClick()
{
    var sXML = document.all("XMLBuffer").innerHTML;

    var parser = new ActiveXObject("microsoft.xmldom");

    parser.loadXML(sXML);

    //Preparatory stuff
    oDisplayArea = document.all("results");
    oDisplayArea.innerHTML = "";
    tabsize = 0;
    linesize = -15;

    if (parser.readyState == COMPLETED && parser.parseError == 0)
```

```
{
    var root = parser.documentElement;
    ProcessNode(root);
}
else
    oDisplayArea.innerText = "Error reading XML returned from server";

tabsize = 0;
linesize = -15;
}
```

Here is the result, when we click on the ViewXML button of the PersonHandler2.asp page, we can see that our XML has been returned to the client:

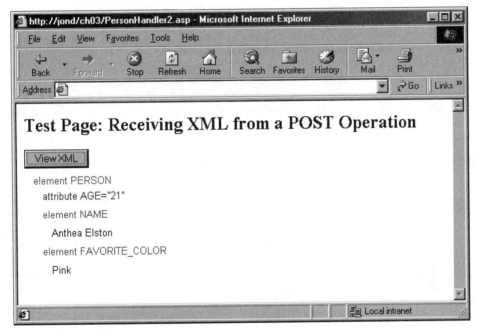

Internet Explorer believes the XML we created is HTML. We retrieve the XML as a string by obtaining the HTML from our hidden <DIV>. This string is then loaded into MSXML for parsing. This approach to passing XML to the server via a POST and receiving an XML reply is obviously a bit tricky. Admittedly, passing XML around this way appears to violate our desire to restrict the interface between producer and consumer to XML. We could, however, conceive of some module that generates pure XML as the general purpose case, with this ASP simply wrapping it in a convenient form. If requirements permit, you should devise short requests so that you can use a GET and receive XML directly into MSXML. That way, your service can work for all sorts of clients. If, however, you must have long requests and you do not want to resort to specialized components, a POST will work provided you observe the difficulties involved in passing XML in the guise of HTML.

# File Transfer

An approach sometimes used in document-centric applications is to use FTP as the means of moving XML between machines. This is well suited to bulk data transfer, but presents several problems. First, this is an inherently asynchronous, background transfer. Either the server runs a background process scanning some target directory for the arrival of files, or the client must send the server a message after the file has been transferred. Having done so, the client has no control over when the server actually looks at the XML. The same problem holds for the return path, only we are dealing with clients who may well be transient: browser sessions and software agents. Either technique involves real complexity when dealing with production systems. Either approach is a distributed protocol with all the attendant complexities. Robust protocols like FTP and HTTP require a good deal of effort to design, implement, and test. FTP is a well-known protocol, however, and off-the-shelf implementations are widely available. For some specialized applications the use of FTP may make good sense.

Much of the simplicity we hope to gain through our five principles will be given back if we have to develop a custom protocol that must be observed by all using parties. We fully expect clients and servers to be developed by different teams at different times. Developing a new protocol that addresses the issues we just raised flies in the face of this situation. Rather than do this in order to use FTP, we are better off designing our clients to use small, frequent requests, and our servers to deliver concise, narrowly targeted answers. This will permit us to do the bulk of our data exchange using simple HTTP operations.

## Component and Applet-Based Solutions

There will be occasions when basic, script driven HTTP exchanges will not suffice. Those cases must be handled through custom components. The idea is to encapsulate a customized communications method inside a component that can be scripted. For example, we might want to use a POST but receive the XML directly from the server. In that case, a commercially available HTTP component could be wrapped inside a scriptlet or COM component that exposes the returned XML string to MSXML. Alternately, we might wish to move MSXML inside the custom component and expose the parsed XML as a service to the scripts on the page. We will visit this particular scenario in Chapter 6. Finally, of course, there is the case of a completely custom client such as a software agent. In that case, it can implement any protocol it wishes and consume the returned data directly.

# Summary

We've explored XML as the mechanism for transferring the properties of our business objects between our services and clients. We looked at the general purpose of XML, proposed standards that will enhance it, and the basic syntax of XML and XML DTDs. These basics are only an introduction sufficient for our limited purposes. We should, however, remember that XML, as a whole, is much richer than what is presented in this chapter.

Since we want to handle XML data from application code, we looked first at the W3C Document Object Model, then at a specific implementation that loosely follows that model. The implementation, MSXML, is a COM component included with Microsoft Internet Explorer that can be used from JavaScript. We covered the following areas pertaining to MSXML:

- ❑ The object model overview
- ❑ Parser states and error handling

- ❑ Traversing the XML parse tree
- ❑ Editing XML documents
- ❑ Creating XML documents

Finally, we looked at several simple approaches to moving XML between networked platforms. Two HTTP-based techniques were examined in detail. We also considered the use of FTP and custom components.

At this point, we have a real start on implementing the five principles. We started by decreeing that applications will be built from services. The last chapter gave us the second principle, that of querying directories to discover services. This chapter showed us a self-describing data format, XML, which we can use to pass data between services and clients, and helps us with our third principle that services will be provided as self-describing data. We also worried about maintaining state between calls to services and worked hard to use GET and POST so that we could get our data without a complicated stateful protocol. This is important to principle four that Services will be enlisted on a transient basis.

Now that we can exchange data, we'll take on the fifth principle regarding extension and service degradation.

# 4

# Reconciling Data

The principle problem we will encounter when writing effective XML vocabularies is that data and meaning change depending on where – and when – you stand. Different user groups have different yet similar views of the same object. These views will evolve over time, necessitating changes to the vocabulary. We will also want to be able to offer collections of objects in an obvious way. Data reconciliation is the task of meeting these needs while maintaining the flexibility we expect from our five principles.

Remember we said that our applications must support extension and degrade gracefully – this was our fifth principle. As representation of data changes, either over time or due to different implementations used by varying development teams, we need to be able to perform some kind of reconciliation in order for our applications to be truly flexible and cooperative.

To deal with reconciling data, this chapter will be split into two sections:

- ❑ **Development guidelines**: We will develop simple guidelines for handling object specialization, collections, and vocabulary evolution in XML.
- ❑ **Creating a Data Splicer service**: In order to make life simpler for our prospective programmers, we will construct a utility scriptlet for manipulating XML documents written according to our guidelines.

Using the methods developed in this chapter, an intranet application requiring a particular vocabulary will be able to receive service from a more specialized server, pass the result to the utility scriptlet, and receive a parse tree consisting of the portion of the document written in the desired vocabulary.

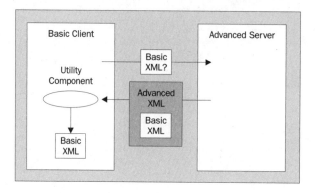

# How Data Changes

Our task in the last chapter was basic: given a document written by a server in a known format, the client manipulated the tree provided by MSXML to extract known items. The task we will encounter in the real world, however, is harder. What the client wants and what the server offers may overlap, but will seldom be the same.

Different users and programmers have different views of the world. Data describing an object, then, changes depending on who is doing the describing and when they wrote their server application. For example, a client might be written for a prototype application. Later, after the prototype proves successful, more advanced versions of the service may be written. In fact, some groups may specialize their implementations so that they provide additional information to feed clients of their own. The original client should still work, provided we are able to **reconcile** the data. In this book, the term will mean finding the common ground between two XML vocabularies. In our example, the more advanced vocabulary is reconciled by extracting the data pertaining to the original vocabulary. In cases where two vocabularies differ in some other way, reconciling such data will mean finding the common elements and providing a document in the client's vocabulary that is built from the extracted data.

On many occasions, we want to describe a **collection** of related objects. A collection exists solely to contain other elements. The contained elements are the items of interest. It is important to be able to distinguish between a tag denoting a collection and an element composed of other elements.

Data about an object commonly becomes more detailed or develops its interpretation as we travel deeper into an organization. It not only inherits the more basic features from the base description, but also adds or modifies features. This is termed **specialization**. We might define a generalized Automobile vocabulary for a car manufacturer, then specialize it by adding elements to create a Luxury Automobile to meet the needs of a particular product division.

Finally, document type definitions change over time. In the network environment we assumed at the outset of this book, we cannot guarantee that the client applications using a service will always be programmed employing the same version of the DTD that was used to program the server. The most common situation is when a server is updated with knowledge of a new DTD before all users receive updated clients. Nevertheless, we cannot rule out the possibility that we might encounter a server written to an out-of-date DTD tucked away in a backwater of the network. It is desirable, therefore, to agree on a common method for DTD **version evolution** so clients can stick to those elements they understand.

Let's take a closer look at each of these problems and develop some guidelines for handling the challenges they present.

# Development Guidelines

Having just seen some of the ways in which data changes, we must address each of these situations individually. In short then, we need to have data reconciliation techniques for handling the following three problems:

- ❑ Indicating a **collection** of data objects
- ❑ Reaching the generalized data object within a **specialized** data object
- ❑ Denoting snapshots of data relevant to different **versions** of the vocabulary

# Collections

We often need to consider groups of objects. A query against a database, for example, retrieves zero or more rows of information. A mailing list contains some number of addressees. A team is composed of multiple employees, and so forth. Programming is full of techniques for managing collections depending on the nature of the task. To achieve maximum flexibility and cooperation we should have a simple scheme for dealing with a number of possibly heterogeneous objects in some sort of collection.

What distinguishes a collection? Primarily, they have two notable features:

- ❑ There are multiple items
- ❑ Each item is a peer of the others

Thus, for example, we might talk about the collection of automobiles on a parking lot. The cars are dissimilar, but we are interested in them as cars. In this situation we are not interested in their engine and tires; the generalized `car` object is the element of interest. Anything we do to the collection – sort order, filter, enumerate – we do to the peer `car` object. So, our technique for dealing with collections in XML should make it easy to distinguish the peer objects in the collection. This is made a little more difficult in that an element in XML can contain other elements. Indeed, a great source of power in XML elements is their ability to nest elements to produce arbitrarily complicated structures. Our technique, therefore, must make clear the difference between a child element and the starting element of a generalized object within a more specialized one.

Collections are useful because they give us a way to manage a group of objects as a single object. Once we group the objects together, we can simply pass around the collection. Anything we do in XML to handle collections, therefore, should support this useful trait. So far then, we have the following requirements for handling collections in XML:

- ❑ multiple objects
- ❑ easily distinguished peers
- ❑ handling groups as a single logical entity

Consider the following conceptual diagram:

We have a single collection object and three peer objects as members of the collection. Objects A, B, and C are clearly the items of interest. The three objects in the collection are dissimilar in structure, as we will see B and C nest other elements within themselves, but not in the same way. So how do we translate this into XML?

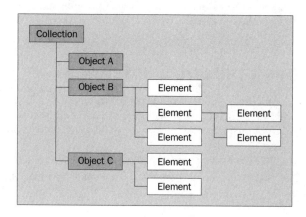

## Translating the Collection into XML

We can follow some simple steps to take our collection and make it well-formed XML.

- ❑ Establish a `<Collection>` element. This will be a reserved word in our technique. Note that any information about the collection will be recorded as attributes of this element. We'll return to this in a moment.
- ❑ Each peer object must have its root tag as an immediate child of the collection.
- ❑ Any element below this level is assumed to be part of the peer object's internal structure.

Note this does not preclude a collection of collections; in this case, each peer is a collection whose subordinate elements are in themselves peer objects. To handle a collection of collections, we must handle the outer collection and submit each peer object to our utility for handling collections.

Note how nicely this will work with MSXML. Each peer object is a node in the `childNodes` collection of the `Collection` node. We can return a peer object as a node, confident that the contained elements come with it. Similarly, we can return the `collection` node as a node and know that all the peer objects come along as well.

A collection of dissimilar purchase orders might look like this in XML using our scheme (omitting PCDATA for clarity of structure):

```
<Collection>
   <Purchase_order>
      <Product_code></Product_code>
      <Quantity_ordered></Quantity_ordered>
      <Unit_price></Unit_price>
   </Purchase_order>
   <Purchase_order>
      <Product_code>
         <Vendor_code></Vendor_code>
         <Vendor_ProdID></Vendor_ProdID>
         <Internal_ProdID></Internal_ProdID>
      </Product_code>
      <Quantity_ordered></Quantity_ordered>
      <Unit_price></Unit_price>
   </Purchase_order>
```

```
    <Purchase_order>
        <Product_code></Product_code>
        <Order_status></Order_status>
        <Quantity_ordered></Quantity_ordered>
        <Unit_price></Unit_price>
    </Purchase_order>
</Collection>
```

Once we detect the `<Collection>` tag, we have one of two options: iterate through `childNodes` returning peer elements, or, if we wish to handle the collection as a whole, return the node corresponding to the collection. In the first case, returning peer elements, the recipient of the node has to dive into the element's children to determine the object's structure.

At the beginning of this section, we indicated a desire to capture some information about the collection as attributes of the `<Collection>` element. Our five principles were designed to keep development simple, so we'll keep the list of global attributes to a minimum. These attributes are optional, but intended to facilitate processing when found.

The list of attributes for our `<Collection>` element are shown in this table:

| Attribute | Description |
| --- | --- |
| ObjectType | A string of the names of the root elements within the collected peer object; if more than one, the list is comma delimited; e.g., `automobile` for a collection of `<automobile>` vocabulary documents |
| Order | The basis for ordering the elements; allowable values are `sequential` (objects appear in the desired order) or the `name`(s) of the elements within the peer objects used to sort the peer objects. If other than sequential, the sort element list is followed by a semicolon and one of the following values: `ascending` or `descending`. e.g., `Order="color; ascending"` if the objects are sorted according to some `color` element in ascending order |
| Name | A name for the collection |

So, permissible examples illustrating some variations of the `<Collection>` element's attributes are:

```
<Collection ObjectType="PERSON" Order="LNAME" Name="Employees">

<Collection ObjectType="PERSON, RESOURCE">

<Collection ObjectType="Vendor" Order="STATE, CITY, STREET1, STREET2; ascending
    Name="Suppliers">
```

Although it will not be enforced in code, I would recommend using a value for the `Name` attribute that is plural and descriptive of the contents. Particular XML vocabularies may add their own attributes, but our utility for handling data changes will only understand the three attributes we have presented.

# Specialization

This is the most important and most common way in which data changes within an organization. It arises because different organizations and departments view the same object in different ways. An organization or department is interested in the attributes of an object that most closely pertain to their primary area of work. There is commonality, of course, when the same object is of interest to two or more groups.

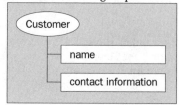

Consider the notion of a customer. Most businesses are interested in customers. A fast attempt at defining a customer object might look like this:

Of course, the DTD for the customer vocabulary would break contact information up into elements for street address, city, postal code, telephone number, and so forth. Nevertheless, it is hard to see how anyone in an organization could disagree with this formulation. On the other hand, it is hard to see how anyone could get any work done with something as simple as this. Here's what someone in customer service might do with our customer:

Note that while the purchase list is a collection of purchases, we're only showing one purchase in this diagram. The customer service department is still interested in the customer's name and contact information, but they must also deal with the type of service plan the customer purchased and what products he owns. This is clearly derived from the basic customer object, but we have *specialized* it for use by the customer service department. In the language of object oriented programming, Customer is the **generalized vocabulary** for Svc_Customer. While we were busy developing this, however, the manufacturing department came up with a different view of a customer:

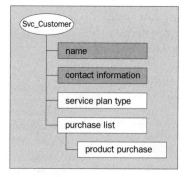

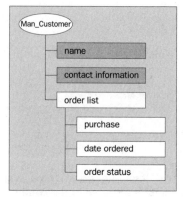

Manufacturing is interested in tracking the status of open orders. They have a collection of orders, each of which contains the product ordered, the date of the order, and the status. They have also *specialized* the basic customer object, but they added different attributes.

If every department worked in isolation, the specific XML vocabulary each devises wouldn't matter. However, in a fluid situation, we might want to visit each department's server. For example, suppose manufacturing was asked by customer service to look into a report of a defective product. Since the product was shipped, manufacturing no longer has the customer in their database. So, their application should be able to get the customer's name and contact information, since both objects overlap to this extent.

Assuming they didn't share their DTDs ahead of time, we'll have to locate the `Customer` hiding within a `Svc_Customer`. We can't expect the programmers in customer service to have programmed `Customer` or `Man_Customer` vocabularies into their server. Similarly, manufacturing might want to alert customer service to a new customer, in which case a customer service client application would have to do a similar extraction.

In all cases, the customer database at corporate headquarters should be able to add new customers as they originate in the sales department and update customer information regardless of which department takes the change. If a customer talking to the service department corrects a misspelling in his name, the customer shouldn't receive a letter from sales with the misspelling. In effect, all the departments should be sharing what they know about this customer.

To see how one of these teams might encode their customer details in XML here is an example for the customer service department. Their `Svc_Customer` object might look like this:

```
<Svc_Customer>
   <Customer>
      <Name>Horace Greeley</Name>
      <Contact_Information>
         <Address>123 Home Lane Greeley, CO</Address>
         <Phone>123-555-5555</Phone>
      </Contact_Information>
   </Customer>
   <Svc_Plan>Gold-Plated</Svc_Plan>
   <Purchase_List>
      <Product>Master Widget</Product>
   </Purchase_List>
</Svc_Customer>
```

# Version Evolution

Despite our best efforts at defining DTDs, we will discover a need for change at some later date. New features become of interest, mistakes are discovered, a more elegant encoding of the vocabulary is found. We need a way to indicate change to a recipient for different reasons:

- ❑ The receiving code may not understand the latest DTD. In that case, it must skip any information later than the version of the DTD it understands.
- ❑ The application needs to know that potentially different elements of an object pertain to the same object. For example, if the structure of an element changes between versions, we should ignore the earlier version's contents in favor of the newer.

We will represent version-controlled elements by adding an attribute, `Version`, whose value is the version number of the latest DTD in use. You can use a date string – vYYYYMMDD – or major/minor string, e.g., v1.02, as you wish, so long as your organization is consistent. One version is then clearly later than another, if its `Version` value string is greater than the other.

We also use an attribute, `EarliestVersion`, denoting the earliest version explicitly supported in the document.

The version attribute alone, however, is insufficient to indicate that groups of elements are from different versions. For that we shall have to resort to structure. Each set of sub-elements of a version-controlled object is pushed into a containing element whose name is the version number of the DTD used to encode it. Each such group contains the minimum amount of information needed to convey the changes from the prior version. Deleted elements are implicit, i.e., the receiving code must understand that the DTD dropped the element. This will work because the programmers worked from the new version of the DTD when they implemented the code, so the application reflects the fact that the element was dropped. Added or changed elements, then, are all that appear in a version container. Version groups must appear in ascending order of version. This permits a receiver to skip the remaining version groups once it finds one it does not understand. For example:

```
<Person Version="v19981019" EarliestVersion="v19980418">
    <v19980418>
        <Name>John Doe</Name>
        <Address>1234 Nowhere Lane, Philadelphia, PA 19102</Address>
    </v19980418>
    <v19980521>
        <Name>
            <First>John</First><Last>Doe</Last>
        </Name>
    </v19980521>
    <v19981019>
        <EmployeeType>Full-time</EmployeeType>
    </v19981019>
</Person>
```

In this example, the latest version is dated October 19th, 1998. The earliest version dates from April 4th of that year, when a person consisted simply of a name string and an address string. In May (v19980521), someone decided to break the name into its first and last components. In October (v19981019), this person was defined as an employee with a work classification. Presumably there will be a later version when someone discovers the value of breaking up the address.

How the receiving code handles the changes depends on the nature of the change. An up-to-date version for our example would skip the name until it found a version record dated v19980521. It would grab the first address string it found, since it knows that the address element hasn't changed since the first version. An alternative approach could be to use brute force. In which case, if a later version contains an element with the same name as an element in an earlier version, it replaces the earlier version.

In general, we want to read the latest version of an element without reading a version later than the one we are seeking. A programmatic approach with no special knowledge, however, will also work. Each version section adds or changes elements. If the program finds an addition, it adds it. If it finds a change, it replaces the older version of the element with the newer version. While this leaves us with "extra" elements when an element is dropped, it is permissible. The receiving application software will just ignore the outdated information. If an application proceeds in this way, it will end up with a current version of all the elements it cares about. Let's look at this in detail.

### Rules for Handling Versions

We can define a set of rules for how an application should handle the versioning which we have implemented:

- ❑ An element with a version attribute contains, as its immediate children, only version elements
- ❑ The immediate children of a version element represent the version-controlled properties of some object
- ❑ Version elements are written in ascending order
- ❑ If a later version contains an element with the same name as an earlier version, replace that element and all its children with the newer element and its children
- ❑ Add any element (and its children) not found in previous version elements
- ❑ Process only those versions that are less than or equal to the desired version

Applying these rules in code to a document with version information encoded according to our technique, results in an XML fragment for the object that contains the latest version of all properties passed. It will also, unfortunately, contain any properties that have been dropped by later versions. Luckily, this is not as great a problem as might appear at first glance. Any program receiving this reconciled XML document will traverse the parse tree assigning the values found to the properties of some internal object. If it finds an element name it does not recognize (because the element was dropped in later versions), it does nothing. Note we are talking about application code running on top of the reconciliation software. The latter adds new elements in the process of reconciliation, while the application software receives a reconciled version in which the version sections have been collapsed to provide a snapshot of the object that is current as of the specified version. The application is not doing reconciliation, so it ignores anything it doesn't recognize.

A greater risk is that later versions of services that are generating XML documents may omit elements that were supported by earlier versions. The reconciliation utility will be unable to provide the data conveyed by the omitted element. In that case, some properties expected by out-of-date application software receiving the reconciled document may be missed. This is where the `EarliestVersion` attribute comes into play. If the difference in versions between the generating and receiving software is so great that they cannot reliably communicate, the `EarliestVersion` attribute will have a value later than the version the receiving software is able to process reliably. If, on the other hand, the receiving software recognizes the value of the `EarliestVersion` attribute, it can expect to find all the properties it needs represented as elements in the XML fragment. To be as effective as possible, generating software *must* write all required elements for the versions it supports, including deleted elements.

> **Software should support a large range of versions – three or four – as a matter of course to ensure most clients will be able to find the data they need.**

To illustrate why this is important, consider the following example. A client was built to version 2 of some service. The client is still in use in some isolated pockets of the company, while the services that implement the vocabulary have moved on to version 4. The client might receive the following:

```
<Person Version="v4" EarliestVersion="v3">
   . . .
</Person>
```

The client, however, can't process anything later than version 2. It might recognize some elements from the later versions, but we cannot guarantee this. So, we are unable to reliably reconcile the offered data with the version understood by the client. If the service maintained compatibility with another generation, e.g., version 2, we would be able to reconcile the data for the client as we could take the data from the earliest version and ignore the succeeding versions:

```
<Person Version="v3" EarliestVersion="v2">
   . . .
</Person>
```

Having completed our look at how to deal with collections, specialization and version control, it is now time to move on to the second section of this chapter and build a service, that will become part of our toolkit; the Data Splicer.

# Building a Data Splicer

The general rules we set forth in the preceding sections would be too burdensome to support without some reusable utility software to support them. Writing the XML according to the rules isn't as difficult as reading it. The hardest authoring task is version control, and even this task is straightforward provided we segment our authoring code according to version. That is to say, the programmers developing and maintaining server software must take care that any changes they make are laid out to explicitly show the versions. Say we change the structure of the <Person> element with version 2 of some service. You'd want your programmers to be careful and write something like the following pseudocode:

```
// Original code
WriteOldProperties(myObject, sPersonText);

// Don't change the existing code, extend it
ModifyPropertiesForV2(myObject, sPersonText);
```

The usual temptation of maintenance programmers is to directly modify the property writing code so that it reflects the desired changes. Instead, you must get in the habit of leaving older supported versions alone and add the new information after them in order for your data to remain flexible, cooperative and re-useable.

Reading the XML is slightly more complicated. In all three cases we are presented with more structure than we want. Collections offend the least. Specialization and version control present the worst problems. In the case of specialization, we only want the structure we recognize; after all, our ideal case is a server that speaks exactly the format we need. More specialized XML is wasteful, because our application wouldn't use the more specialized data. Regarding version control, we really want a parse tree that contains an XML fragment shorn of all version elements and reconciling elements that have changed.

The solution, as we saw in Chapter 2, is a DHTML scriptlet. If you are working in a non-Windows environment, feel free to substitute the component technology of your choice. If you are a Java programmer, JavaBeans will work nicely. Since we are modifying our data, cutting it apart and reconstituting it, we shall call our utility scriptlet the Data Splicer. It will meet the following requirements:

- ❑ Given a node containing a specialized object encoded in XML and a less specialized version as well, extract all instances of the less specialized object – this will leave the most specialized object that can be handled by the application
- ❑ Given an XML document and the name of a collection, return the collection
- ❑ Create a collection node
- ❑ Accept a version-controlled element (and its contents) and return a node containing a reconciled version of the element

Before we go on, let's have an illustration of the last requirement. Recall our earlier Person document:

```
<Person Version="v19981019" EarliestVersion="v19980418">
   <v19980418>
      <Name>John Doe</Name>
      <Address>1234 Nowhere Lane, Philadelphia, PA 19102</Address>
   </v19980418>
   <v19980521>
      <Name>
         <First>John</First><Last>Doe</Last>
      </Name>
   </v19980521>
   <v19981019>
      <EmployeeType>Full-time</EmployeeType>
   </v19981019>
</Person>
```

We should be able to call some utility component method telling it we want a document reconciled to `v19980521` and receive the following:

```
<Person>
   <Name>
      <First>John</First><Last>Doe</Last>
   </Name>
   <Address>1234 Nowhere Lane, Philadelphia, PA 19102</Address>
</Person>
```

Now the Person object, that is current as of the requested version, can read the reconciled document without trouble. The Name element is broken into First and Last child elements, as expected.

Starting our implementation, we begin with the usual preliminaries for creating a scriptlet in JavaScript. We have a globally defined variable, ELEMENT, which contains MSXML's identifier for a node of type ELEMENT.

```
public_description = new DataSplicer;
var ELEMENT = 0;

function DataSplicer()
{
   code for the functions goes here
}
```

We define the scriptlet to be an instance of the class DataSplicer. Now it's time to add the functionality. So let's look at dealing with collections, specialization and version control while we are reading XML using our Data Splicer. Here's the interface we shall implement:

| Method Name | Meaning and Usage |
| --- | --- |
| MakeCollection() | Creates a Collection node and sets the attributes specified by our technique |
| FindNamedCollection() | Searches recursively through a subtree for a Collection element whose Name attribute is given |
| FindTypedCollection() | Searches recursively through a subtree for a Collection element whose ObjectType attribute bears the value specified |
| CollectionOrder() | This method returns the value of a Collection element's Order attribute |
| CollectionName() | Returns the string value of a collection's Name attribute |
| TypesInCollection() | Returns the string value of a collection's ObjectType attribute |
| Extract() | Finds a given node representing a generalized object within a given subtree and returns a reference to it |
| ExtractAll() | Finds all occurrences of a particular generalized element within a subtree. This method is useful for finding all the generalized types within a collection of specialized elements. Returns a collection of all instances of the generalized type that are found within the document. |
| CollapseVersion() | Performs version reconciliation on a versioned XML document, returning a collapsed version of the versioned document |

*A comprehensive reference to the interface, complete with parameters and return types is given in Appendix A. The usage will become more apparent as we proceed through the implementation. For the moment, you should focus on the tasks the interface performs for you.*

# Collections

We can assist our programmers in using collections by adding some simple methods to the Data Splicer. We need a method that will create a new collection element according to the rules we have just seen so programmers won't have to remember and apply all the rules consistently. You may remember that these rules were:

❑ Establish a <Collection> element. This will be a reserved word in our technique. Note that any information about the collection will be recorded as attributes of this element. We'll return to this in a moment.

❑ Each peer object must have its root tag as an immediate child of the collection.

❑ Any element below this level is assumed to be part of the peer object's internal structure.

As long as we're hiding the rules from our application programmers, we should also add a method to extract the attributes of a collection.

Since collections will typically be contained within a complex document, we might offer the ability to find a particular collection within a document and extract it. The rules we have devised are simple, but implementing them consistently is an error prone process when done repeatedly. Our convention relies on programmers applying the rules properly every time they use a collection. Some simple utility support will go a long way toward making our networked applications more reliable.

## Create a Collection

To start giving our scriptlet functionality we add a method, `MakeCollection()`, to create collections. This will be useful for clients who take some information and create a new XML document to pass on to another client.

```
public_description = new DataSplicer;
var ELEMENT = 0;

function DataSplicer()
{
    this.MakeCollection = MakeCollection;
}
```

We define the scriptlet to be an instance of the class `DataSplicer`, and we have a constructor function that assigns the method name `MakeCollection` to the JavaScript function `MakeCollection()`.

Our method will take a reference to the MSXML parser and parameters denoting:

- ❑ The class of object contained in the collection; it's `ObjectType`
- ❑ The `orderType`, `sequential`, or `field,names`
- ❑ The `Name` of the collection

```
function MakeCollection(parser, objectType, orderType, colName)
{
    var rCollectionNode = null;
    var regexpAsc = /\; *ascending/i;
    var regexpDesc = /\; *descending/i;

    rCollectionNode = parser.createElement("Collection");
    if (rCollectionNode != null)
    {
        rCollectionNode.setAttribute("ObjectType", objectType);
        if (orderType == "sequential")
            rCollectionNode.setAttribute("Order", orderType);
        else
            if (orderType.search(regexpAsc) == -1 &&
                    orderType.search(regexpDesc) == -1)
            rCollectionNode.setAttribute("Order", orderType + "\;ascending");
        if (colName != null && colName != "")
            rCollectionNode.setAttribute("Name", colName);
        else
            rCollectionNode.setAttribute("Name", objectType + "s");
    }
    return rCollectionNode;
}
```

We use MSXML to create a new node to hold our collection.

```
rCollectionNode = parser.createElement("Collection");
```

Next, we set up the three attributes. The `Order` attribute can be tricky. Recall that it either has to be the literal `sequential` or some tag name followed by a semicolon and either of the keywords `ascending` or `descending`.

```
rCollectionNode.setAttribute("ObjectType", objectType);
if (orderType == "sequential")
    rCollectionNode.setAttribute("Order", orderType);
```

If our `orderType` parameter isn't `sequential`, we need to search using the regular expressions we declared at the beginning.

```
var regexpAsc = /\; *ascending/i;
var regexpDesc = /\; *descending/i;
```

Basically, we're looking for the semicolon followed by zero or more spaces and either of the literals. The first slash in the declaration marks this as a regular expression. The second slash followed by the semicolon denotes the semicolon literal. Without the slash, the interpreter would read an end of statement condition and begin a new, and erroneous line. Next, we have a space followed by an asterisk to denote zero or more occurrences of the space character. The keywords ascending and descending must appear next. The final slash followed by the letter i is a switch telling the search method we want to ignore the case of the text we are searching.

```
else
    if (orderType.search(regexpAsc) == -1 &&
            orderType.search(regexpDesc) == -1)
        rCollectionNode.setAttribute("Order", orderType + "\;ascending");
```

If none of the keywords `sequential`, `ascending`, or `descending` appear, we provide `ascending` as the default, assuming that whatever was provided is the tag name on whose value the order is based.

```
if (colName != null && colName != "")
    rCollectionNode.setAttribute("Name", colName);
```

If no collection name is provided, we use the `objectType` with the letter `s` appended to denote a collection of these objects.

```
else
    rCollectionNode.setAttribute("Name", objectType + "s");
```

Finally, we return the node to the caller ready to accept new members for the collection.

## Locate and Extract a Collection

Given our approach to collections, there are two ways to search for a specific collection in an XML document: by the `Name` attribute and by the `ObjectType` attribute. While the former will be most common, the latter search is useful when examining the structure of some poorly understood XML document – you simply look for collections of objects you know about.

### Searching by Name

Searching by Name involves traversing the tree until a collection is found and then seeing if it has an attribute Name with the value for which you are searching. By now we are well versed in traversing an XML DOM tree with MSXML, but there is a small wrinkle here. We've allowed collections to contain collections, so we can't skip the children of a Collection element while searching.

Only an element can contain other elements, so we check the nodeType right away. If it is not an element, we can discontinue the search.

```
if (Node.nodeTpe == ELEMNT
   {
   ...
   }
else
   return null:
```

If it is an element, we see if it has the nodeName Collection, which you will recall is our convention.

```
if (Node.nodeName == "Collection")
{
   // Check the Name attribute
   . . .
}
else
   // Go through all the children until we find the target
   . . .
```

If we have a Collection element, we see if it has an attribute named Name. It need not have one, so we check to see if it is null:

```
if (attrVal != null && attrVal == name)
   return Node;
else
   . . .
```

If those conditions are met, we have our match and we return the node. If we do not, we must continue. We submit each child node in turn to our FindNamedCollection() function:

```
for (var i = 0; i < Node.childNodes.length; i++)
{
   tgtNode = FindNamedCollection(name, Node.childNodes.item(i))
   if (tgtNode != null)
      return tgtNode;
}
```

We do the very same thing if we have an element that is not named Collection. Here's the complete code for the Data Splicer's FindNamedCollection() method:

```
function FindNamedCollection(name, Node)
{
   var tgtNode;
   // Only elements can contain other elements
   if (Node.nodeType == ELEMENT)
```

```
    {
       if (Node.nodeName == "Collection")
       {
          var attrVal = Node.getAttribute("Name");
          if (attrVal != null && attrVal == name)
             return Node;
          else
          for (var i = 0; i < Node.childNodes.length; i++)
          {
             tgtNode = FindNamedCollection(name, Node.childNodes.item(i))
             if (tgtNode != null)
                return tgtNode;
          }
       }
       else
          for (var j = 0; j < Node.childNodes.length; j++)
          {
             tgtNode = FindNamedCollection(name, Node.childNodes.item(j))
             if (tgtNode != null)
                return tgtNode;
          }
    }
    else
       return null;
}
```

## Searching by Object Type

We do something very similar when we search by the ObjectType attribute as we did when searching for the name. Here's our FindTypedCollection() function:

```
function FindTypedCollection(objectType, Node)
{
   var tgtNode;
   // Only elements can contain other elements
   if (Node.nodeType == ELEMENT)
   {
      if (Node.nodeName == "Collection")
      {
         var attrVal = Node.getAttribute("ObjectType");
         if (attrVal != null && attrVal == objectType)
            return Node;
         else
         for (var i = 0; i < Node.childNodes.length; i++)
         {
            tgtNode = FindTypedCollection(objectType, Node.childNodes.item(i))
            if (tgtNode != null)
               return tgtNode;
         }
      }
      else
         for (var j = 0; j < Node.childNodes.length; j++)
         {
            tgtNode = FindTypedCollection(objectType, Node.childNodes.item(j))
            if (tgtNode != null)
               return tgtNode;
         }
   }
   else
      return null;
}
```

The only difference is which attribute we examine:

```
var attrVal = Node.getAttribute("ObjectType");
if (attrVal != null && attrVal == objectType)
   return Node;
```

Let's test our implementation so far with a test page intended to host the Data Splicer, `DataSplicerCont.html`. Remember, you can download the code from the Wrox Web site at `http://www.wrox.com`, or run the examples on our Web Developer site `http://webdev.wrox.co.uk/book/2270/`. You'll need a sample XML document, so create a variable, `colDoc`, and assign it the following value:

```
<SomeRoot>
   <SomeHeader>Filler</SomeHeader>
   <Collection Name="Persons" ObjectType="Person" Order="sequential">
      <Person><Name>John Doe</Name></Person>
      <Person><Name>Jane Smith</Name></Person>
      <Person><Name>Thomas Atkins</Name></Person>
   </Collection>
   <Collection ObjectType="Animal" Order="sequential">
      <Animal>Cat</Animal><Animal>Dog</Animal><Animal>Lemur</Animal>
      <Animal>Wombat</Animal><Animal>Koala</Animal>
   </Collection>
</SomeRoot>
```

You'll also need an instance of MSXML for a variety of functions in the page, so you should create a globally-scoped variable like this:

```
var parser = new ActiveXObject("microsoft.xmlDOM");
```

Then we load the XML and parse the document like this:

```
parser.loadXML(colDoc);
```

Submit the results of this call:

```
var rChildren = splicer.FindNamedCollection("Persons", parser.documentNode);
```

to the `TraverseTree()` utility function from the last chapter and you will find that you have indeed found John Doe, Jane Smith, and Thomas Atkins.

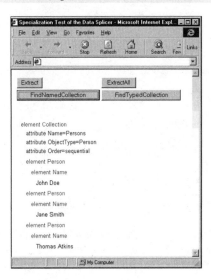

The call:

```
var rChildren = splicer.FindTypedCollection("Animal", parser.documentNode);
```

similarly, finds our cat, dog, lemur, wombat, and koala.

## *Determine Miscellaneous Collection Attributes*

Although any programmer with knowledge of both our collection conventions and the MSXML object model could readily retrieve the attributes of a collection, it is convenient to provide some utility methods to do this. These methods will serve to enforce the rules of our convention as well as making life a little easier for our application programmers.

We will provide methods for reporting the Name, Order, and peer ObjectTypes of a collection. Each method will check the passed node to ensure it is a collection. In addition, each method will provide any validation specific to the underlying attribute according to our convention.

Retrieving the Name of a collection is simple:

```
function CollectionName(node)
{
   if (IsCollection(node))
   {
      var attrVal = node.getAttribute("Name");
      if (attrVal != null)
         return attrVal;
      else
         return "";
   }
   return "Error: Node is not a collection";
}
```

If the node passed to our method is, in fact, a collection element, we check for a Name attribute. If found; we return it. If not, we want to indicate that it is unnamed, so we return an empty string. If the node is not a collection according to our rules, we return an error message.

How do we ensure, first, that a given node is a collection? We use a helper function, IsCollection(), to check this:

```
function IsCollection(node)
{
   if (node != null)
   {
      if (node.nodeType == ELEMENT && node.nodeName == "Collection")
         return true;
      else
         return false;
   }
   else
      return false;
}
```

This function returns true if the node checks out properly and false otherwise. We first screen to ensure the caller has not passed us a null parameter. Otherwise, we simply ensure that the node is an XML element and that it is named Collection.

Returning the `ObjectTypes` in a collection is similar. We could have gotten fancy and returned some sort of COM collection enumerating the individual types, but most collections will have only a single type. In that case, a COM collection would only make the programmer's task more difficult. If an application programmer is interested, he will likely be aware of our conventions and be able to parse out the types.

```
function TypesInCollection(node)
{
    if (IsCollection(node))
    {
        var attrVal = node.getAttribute("ObjectType");
        if (attrVal != null)
            return attrVal;
        else
            return "";
    }
    return "Error: Node is not a collection";
}
```

Retrieving the `Order` is harder. Getting the actual attribute is simple, as we have seen in the preceding two methods. The trick in retrieving the order lies in validating the `Order` attribute. Recall our rules for this attribute:

❑ If the order is `sequential`, the attribute must have the value `sequential`.
❑ If any other order is specified, the attribute has a value composed of the element used for sorting, a semicolon, and the word `ascending` or the word `descending`.

Here is the basic code for getting the `Order` attribute:

```
function CollectionOrder(node)
{
    if (IsCollection(node))
    {
        var attrVal = node.getAttribute("Order");
        if (attrVal != null)
        {
            if (attrVal == "sequential" || ValidateOrder(attrVal))
                return attrVal;
            else
                return "Error: Invalid order attribute";
        }
        else
            return "";
    }
    return "Error: Node is not a collection";
}
```

This is very similar to the other two methods. Note, however, this line:

```
if (attrVal == "sequential" || ValidateOrder(attrVal)) . . .
```

Testing for `sequential` is easy. Validating a more complicated sort scheme requires a helper function called `ValidateOrder()`:

```
function ValidateOrder(OrderAttr)
{
   var semiColonPos, orderDirPos;

   semiColonPos = OrderAttr.indexOf(";");
   if (semiColonPos > -1)
   {
      orderDirPos = OrderAttr.indexOf("ascending", semiColonPos);
      if (orderDirPos == -1)
         orderDirPos = OrderAttr.indexOf("descending", semiColonPos);

      if (orderDirPos > -1)
         return true;
      else
         return false;
   }
   else
      return false;
}
```

This is where our second rule is implemented. Note that the JavaScript method *String*.indexOf returns a value of -1 if the search string is not a substring of the string being tested. When we search for the order keywords ascending and descending, we only check the string following the semicolon to eliminate the possibility that the sort element name string contains semicolon. If either keyword appears, the attribute value is deemed valid. If no semicolon appears (the outer if statement), the attribute value cannot possibly be correct, so the function returns false.

# Specialization

Our discussion of specialization, earlier in this chapter, focused on representing a specialized object as an XML element that embeds the generalized object's XML representation within it. We'll spend most of our time implementing the ability to extract some generalized object element given some element containing it. Sometimes, though, it is also useful to extract all contained generalized representations within a document. After we develop the basic task – extracting a single instance – we'll apply it to the task of building a collection of contained base class XML representations. These two tasks allow us to reconcile a specialized document for an older version client application, disregarding the specialized information the client is not prepared to handle.

## Single Instance

Let's start simply and assume the XML document we are given contains zero or one instance of the requested object. All we have to do is traverse the tree until we find the named node and return it. We'll call our public method for handling specialization Extract().

Let's see what we have to do to locate and extract a base class. As we did in the traversal examples of the last chapter, we set up our recursive traversal. Extract will take the name of the element to find, termed toExtract, and the Node from which to start the search, startNode:

```
function Extract(toExtract, startNode)
{
   // startNode is either the root of the specialized object
   // or the root of a subtree containing the toExtract
   // node somewhere within it

   return FindNode(toExtract, startNode);
}
```

The tree traversal is a slightly modified version of our recursive traversal from Chapter 3:

```
function FindNode(targetName, Node)
{
    // Only elements can contain other elements
    if (Node.nodeType == ELEMENT)
    {
        if (Node.nodeName == targetName)
            return Node;
        else
            // Go through all the children until we find the target
            for (var i = 0; i < Node.childNodes.length; i++)
            {
                var tgtNode = FindNode(targetName, Node.childNodes.item(i));
                if (tgtNode != null)
                    return tgtNode;
            }
    }
    else
        return null;
}
```

We first check to see if the passed node is an element. In the initial call, Node will be the startNode from the Extract function. In subsequent calls, it will be some child node to examine. In the latter case, we can skip it if it is not an element, e.g., PCDATA. When we have an element, we recursively send each child off to FindNode. When the target node is located, we abort the process and return the node.

We can test this with our test page, DataSplicerCont.html. We will hand Data Splicer the sample Svc_Customer object we saw earlier and ask it to extract the base class Customer hidden within it. Here is the Svc_Customer object, just to remind you:

```
<Svc_Customer>
    <Customer>
        <Name>Horace Greeley</Name>
        <Contact_Information>
            <Address>123 Home Lane Greeley, CO</Address>
            <Phone>123-555-5555</Phone>
        </Contact_Information>
    </Customer>
    <Svc_Plan>Gold-Plated</Svc_Plan>
    <Purchase_List>
        <Product>Master Widget</Product>
    </Purchase_List>
</Svc_Customer>
```

Now, here is our onExtract() function for the Data Splicer:

```
function OnExtract()
{
    //Preparatory stuff
    oDisplayArea = document.all("results");
    oDisplayArea.innerHTML = "";
    tabsize = 0;
    linesize = 0;
    parser.async = "false";
```

```
parser.loadXML("<Svc_Customer>
    <Svc_Plan>Gold-Plated</Svc_Plan><Customer>
    <Name>Horace Greeley</Name><Contact_Information>
    <Address>123 Home Lane Greeley, CO</Address>
    <Phone>123-555-5555</Phone>
    </Contact_Information></Customer><Purchase_List>
    <Product>Master Widget</Product></Purchase_List></Svc_Customer>");

if (parser.readyState == COMPLETED && parser.parseError == 0)
{

    var target = splicer.Extract("Customer", parser.documentElement);

    if (target != null)
        TraverseTree(target);
    else
        alert("Customer not found in" + parser.documentElement.nodeName);
}
}
```

We'll use the same DHTML code as in Chapter 3 to output a formatted version of the XML to the page. Note that we've hard-coded the sample `Svc_Customer` XML document in our call to MSXML's `loadXML()` method. When the parser has completed its task, we hand the root `Svc_Customer` node off to the Data Splicer and ask it for `Customer`:

```
var target = splicer.Extract("Customer", parser.documentNode);
```

If `target` is not null, we know the splicer found `Customer`, so we submit that to our old DHTML output functions, starting with `TraverseTree()` from Chapter 3 to verify the result. This is what we see in the browser:

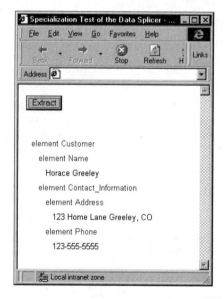

## Extracting All Instances

Now that we know how to extract one generalized object from a specialized object, let's take things a step further and build the ability to extract all such objects contained in a document. We might have a document that we know contains a collection of specialized objects. Having the ability to extract all instances of a generalized object representation allows us to send the collection to this function and receive a collection of the generalized representations.

*We have become used to talking about specialized objects and generalized objects. Note, however, that this is just our convention. The Data Splicer's* Extract() *method and the method we are about to develop give you the ability to locate and return any sub-tree of the parsed XML provided you know the name of the element anchoring it.*

Let's take a look at the conveniently named ExtractAll() method:

```
function ExtractAll(parser, toExtract, startNode)
{
   var rPeers;

   // Create a collection object
   rPeers = MakeCollection(parser, toExtract, "sequential");

   // Populate it with all instances of toExtract found in startNode
   FindAll(toExtract, startNode, rPeers);

   return rPeers;
}
```

We've had to add a reference to MSXML as the first parameter of the method. This is because we are going to create a new node for our collection. MSXML's document object is needed to do this. Proceeding into the body of the function, we make a call to MakeCollection() which was the first function we added to the Data Splicer. The collection that results will be named for the base class for which we are searching and will be ordered sequentially:

```
   rPeers = MakeCollection(parser, toExtract, "sequential");
```

The real work is in FindAll(). We might imagine that it is a slight rework of Find(), and we'd be correct:

```
function FindAll(targetName, Node, rCollection)
{
   if (Node.nodeType == ELEMENT)
   {
      if (Node.nodeName == targetName)
         rCollection.appendChild(Node);
      else
         for (var i = 0; i < Node.childNodes.length; i++)
            FindAll(targetName, Node.childNodes.item(i), rCollection);
   }
}
```

The novelty of this implementation over Find() is that we don't return when we find the first instance of the base class representation. We have to add it to the collection in sequential order and continue.

As with Find(), we call FindAll() recursively when we encounter an element that is not the target of our search. This takes us through the parse tree by going all the way down each branch, then returning to the top and repeating the process for the next branch.

```
   if (Node.nodeName == targetName)
         rCollection.appendChild(Node);
      else
         for (var i = 0; i < Node.childNodes.length; i++)
            FindAll(targetName, Node.childNodes.item(i), rCollection);
```

### Using Overlap in Related Formats

It may not be immediately obvious how this helps us as we build Web applications. After all, specialization in a language that does not support inheritance, e.g., JavaScript, is nothing more than cutting and pasting source code. We've made the assumption that we won't have access to the source, so why go to the trouble of working with specialization?

A general version of a class of objects provides some benefit to a client looking for the specialized version. For example, a client looking for the specifics of a customer in the context of a customer service setting can get basic contact information from a general customer service. Similarly, if all it can find is a highly specialized class for some other setting, e.g., manufacturing, it can extract the basic customer information it recognizes while ignoring the specialized information. So, a server can build on a pre-existing service by wrapping generalized information in its own specialized class. The ability to add and remove layers of specialization is how we will turn data format overlap to our advantage. If we find a service that is good enough, we can continue processing. If we find a service that is a good starting point, we can build on it. To do this we would simply call upon a pre-existing service to generate the generalized object's XML. Then we would embed this into the XML generated by our specialized application.

# Version Evolution

It is in the nature of software that no design is ever finished. No sooner is some body of software released than we identify a valid need to modify our data formats. Traditionally, we require our clients and servers to be synchronized by the version of the data formatted. If any effort is made to handle out-of-synchronization formats, it is limited to allowing a client to read a limited number of older versions. In the type of network environment we've assumed, we are likely to run into unsynchronized formats with great regularity.

We therefore need to be able to mark-up version-related information in the body of our XML. If we do this, a client can reconcile the data in a body of XML to the level it understands. It will extract what it understands and ignore anything from a later version. If our clients provide default information for each property, they will then be able to accept information from servers that offer an earlier version of the data format. Either way, our clients will be robust, and capable of handling data that is less than perfect from their point of view.

Data formats evolve through versions by adding new properties, dropping old properties, and changing the content and structure of old properties. We will develop a simple technique to handle each of these behaviors.

### Handling Versions

Recall our approach to version control for the XML representation of an object. Each object consists of a root element, e.g., <PERSON>, whose immediate children are the properties of the object. Children of the root may contain elements of their own, but these represent the internal structure of the properties – they are not properties themselves. For version control, we add a layer in between the root and the properties. This layer consists of elements whose names are the version identifiers. Their children are the elements representing the properties that were added or changed with that version. Deleted elements are not directly handled. It is assumed that an application receiving a version-controlled object understands the properties that are current as of some version it understands. Our version control scheme then serves to allow the application to initialize an object at any of the communicated versions. The following illustration is a conceptual diagram of this scheme Version 2 expanded Property A and added Property B. Version 3 added Property C. Assume, for the sake of argument, that version 3 drops Property B.

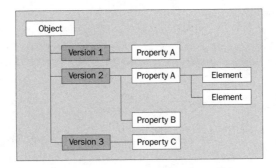

An application written to version 1 standards wants to be able to extract Property A. Another application written to version 2 standards needs the updated version of Property A as well as Property B. An up-to-date application needs the expanded Property A and Property C. Thus, a fully up-to-date application wants to see:

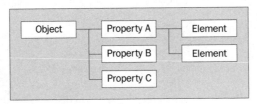

However, we said the third version dropped Property B. This is not a problem so long as our code initializes a local object in a manner similar to this:

```
. . .
switch  (node.nodeName)
{
   case "PropertyA":
      // Initialize structure from child elements of this node
      ...
      break;
   case "PropertyC":
      this.PropertyC = node.text;
      break;
}
. . .
```

That is, if we have some sort of object local to a particular tier that has to be initialized from an XML document, we should load the properties from a switch statement driven by the node names in the XML document. If a particular element appears, we set the corresponding object property. In our example, the code to initialize the object won't contain a case for Property B since the expected version no longer includes that property. The XML document will contain that element, but the receiving code will ignore it.

Let's look at some XML for a hypothetical, simple `Person` object. In version 1.0, the object contains only a `<NAME>` element. Version 2.0 comes about when we break the name into `<FIRSTNAME>` and `<LASTNAME>` and add `<SSN>`. We are asked to drop `<SSN>` on privacy grounds and add `<AGE>`, so we release version 3.0 of our `Person` DTD. A sample person object marked up for all three versions, assuming we use the major/minor version naming convention, would look like this:

```
<PERSON Version="v3.0" EarliestVersion="v1.0">
   <v1.0>
      <NAME>John Standish</NAME>
   </v1.0>
   <v2.0>
      <NAME>
         <FIRSTNAME>John</FIRSTNAME><LASTNAME>Standish</LASTNAME>
      </NAME>
      <SSN>111-22-1234</SSN>
   </v2.0>
   <v3.0>
      <AGE>102</AGE>
   </v3.0>
</PERSON>
```

After we get done reducing the version information, it would be presented to the third generation client application in this form:

```
<PERSON>
   <NAME>
      <FIRSTNAME>John</FIRSTNAME><LASTNAME>Standish</LASTNAME>
   </NAME>
   <SSN>111-22-1234</SSN>
   <AGE>102</AGE>
</PERSON>
```

The client receives the correct form of <NAME>, skips over <SSN> since it is not equipped to process that, and gets <AGE>. Let's write the code to implement this.

## Adding Version Support to the Splicer

Here's the CollapseVersion() function that takes a version-controlled object represented in XML and reconciles it to a given version:

```
function CollapseVersion(parser, objectNode, sVersion)
{
   var workingSetNode;

   if (objectNode.nodeType == ELEMENT)
   {
      // Create a new node to hold the working set

      workingSetNode = parser.createElement(objectNode.nodeName);

      for (var ni = 0; ni < objectNode.childNodes.length; ni++)
      {
         // If <= the version, reconcile it.  If > version, remove it
         if (objectNode.childNodes.item(ni).nodeName <= sVersion)
            ProcessVersionSet(workingSetNode,
               objectNode.childNodes.item(ni));
      }
      // Replace the given node with the working set in the document
      parser.replaceChild(workingSetNode, objectNode);
   }
}
```

First, we do some limited error checking to make sure the node we've been passed is, in fact, an element. If it isn't, the fragment of XML can't possibly be an object representation in our scheme. Next, we create a new element. This might seem unnecessary at first glance. After all, couldn't we do our reconciliation in the passed node by simply moving elements up from the version-controlled elements into the main object? Unfortunately, that would continually change the number of children in the element we were passed. Instead of having blocks of version-controlled properties, we'd have a mix of version-controlled properties and reconciled properties. It's a lot cleaner to build a working copy of the element we were passed, do our reconciliation into that element, then replace the given element with the working copy. This also has the happy side effect of removing the version-related attributes from the element in the document. The `createElement()` method of the parser makes the working node for us.

Having built the working copy, we look at the passed element. Each immediate child is a block of version-controlled properties. If the version is less than or equal to the version we were given, we send it off to be reconciled using the `ProcessVersionSet()` function, which we come to next. Otherwise, we ignore it as it contains changes from a later version the caller does not understand.

```
if (objectNode.childNodes.item(ni).nodeName <= sVersion)
        ProcessVersionSet(workingSetNode,
                objectNode.childNodes.item(ni));
```

Finally, having reconciled all the children, we replace the original node with the newly reconciled node.

```
parser.replaceChild(workingSetNode, objectNode);
```

The document that contained a version-controlled representation of the object now has an object current with all changes up to and including the specified version. The document can now operate on the object without concerning itself with version information.

Now we'll expand `ProcessVersionSet()` and see how it works.

```
function ProcessVersionSet(rootNode, versionSetNode)
{
    var foundNode;

    if (versionSetNode.nodeType == ELEMENT)
    {
        for (var ni = 0; ni < versionSetNode.childNodes.length; ni++)
        {
            foundNode = FindNode(versionSetNode.childNodes.item(ni).nodeName,
                    rootNode);
            if (foundNode != null)
                rootNode.replaceChild(
                        versionSetNode.childNodes.item(ni).cloneNode(true),
                        foundNode);
            else
                rootNode.appendChild(
                        versionSetNode.childNodes.item(ni).cloneNode(true));
        }
    }
}
```

Again, we do an error check to ensure we are dealing with an element. The heart of the function operates on each child element. These children represent the properties of the object we are representing in XML. Each child may have children of its own, in which case they are not properties of the object, but rather part of the complex structure of the property. Consequently, we can ignore everything but the immediate children. Recall that if we move a node, all its children go with it. Each property may or may not have depth, but we can think of them as atomic properties.

We can't simply move properties into the working set, denoted here by the `rootNode` parameter. That would work for the first block of version-controlled properties, but fail with later blocks, since new versions of properties already placed in the working set would conflict. Instead, we make use of the `FindNode()` function we developed earlier. We pass it the name of the current element, i.e., a property, and the working set. If it finds a match, it returns the node representing a property we previously placed in the working set. In that case, we replace it with a copy of the current property. If `FindNode()` doesn't find a match, it returns `null` and we know to simply append a copy.

```
foundNode = FindNode(versionSetNode.childNodes.item(ni).nodeName, rootNode);
if (foundNode != null)
    rootNode.replaceChild(versionSetNode.childNodes.item(ni).cloneNode(true),
        foundNode);
else
    rootNode.appendChild(versionSetNode.childNodes.item(ni).cloneNode(true));
```

We need to make a copy of the current property for the same reason we made a working copy of the overall object. `replaceChild()` and `appendChild()` move the nodes themselves and this would continually alter the `childNodes` property of the property block element. We make our copy using the `cloneNode()` method of the Node object.

If we create a test driver using our sample XML as the document –

```
<PERSON Version="v3.0" EarliestVersion="v1.0">
    <v1.0>
        <NAME>John Standish</NAME>
    </v1.0>
    <v2.0>
        <NAME>
            <FIRSTNAME>John</FIRSTNAME><LASTNAME>Standish</LASTNAME>
        </NAME>
        <SSN>111-22-1234</SSN>
    </v2.0>
    <v3.0>
        <AGE>102</AGE>
    </v3.0>
</PERSON>
```

– and ask the Data Splicer to collapse it to version 3.0 –

```
splicer.CollapseVersion(parser, parser.documentElement, "v3.0");
```

we end up with the desired result.

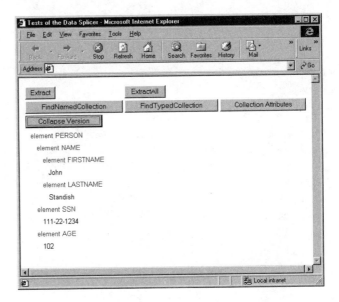

# Summary

Building on our use of XML to represent the objects offered by services in our system, we developed simple guidelines for handling common tasks related to such objects. These tasks are:

- ❑  Collections, a way of signaling to our clients that an element is a container for objects
- ❑  Specialization, a way of modifying a general class for use in a specialized area without losing the reuse potential of the general class
- ❑  Vocabulary evolution, a means of passing version information to reconcile version conflicts between clients and servers

Specialization will be a workhorse in our system. It is the technique by which we will promote reuse. More importantly, it helps us implement our fifth principle:

- ❑  **5. Services must support extension and degrade gracefully**

We can represent the data offered by an extended service through specialization. This works in reverse, as well. A service can degrade gracefully when approached by a simpler client by offering the generalized version of its data. Vocabulary evolution also allows services to degrade gracefully when we encounter a version conflict. This is a common occurrence in loosely organized networks. Whenever there is conflict between the producer of some data and the consumer of that data, you can use specialization and versioning to reconcile exchange data and find common ground between the two parties.

Collections are a convenient way to provide a software client with some information. Having a simple technique for representing collections of objects, a technique shared throughout our networked applications, allows programs to easily recognize what is being communicated and how it is ordered.

Since these techniques address common tasks in our development philosophy, we constructed another DHTML scriptlet for our toolset. The Data Splicer provides the basic methods for using the techniques we developed in this chapter.

# 5

# Metadata

We've taken an informal approach to structure in our XML so far. We've assumed an implicit DTD and enforced it through carefully written code. In fact, we allowed a violation of an implicit DTD when the error didn't change the meaning of the document. You may be wondering by now if this is such a good idea. After all, haven't we said that the teams working on our applications are only loosely connected? Shouldn't there be some way for them to learn how a specific vocabulary is put together?

In fact, we're going to see that validation is but one use for "data about data". We'll introduce metadata, see how we use it in XML today, and look ahead to its future. We'll see that these future uses of metadata can be more important to networked applications than validation. Indeed, these uses will enable us to build applications with fewer assumptions than we can today. In this chapter, you will learn the following:

- ❑ What is metadata?
- ❑ How is metadata used today?
- ❑ A brief overview of W3C metadata proposals, including RDF, MCF, XML Data and DCD
- ❑ How one metadata implementation can be used to dynamically generate HTML input forms

The W3C has a number of proposals before it dealing with metadata in one form or another. All are on or beyond the cutting edge in terms of use in production applications. For that reason alone, we must approach this chapter as an experiment. The support for metadata in parsers is also spotty. Nevertheless, we need to see how far we can take metadata in order to see why we should care about it. Once we've seen what we can do with metadata, we can begin to organize our applications so they may readily support whatever metadata proposals are ultimately adopted.

# What is Metadata?

We obey some structural rules whenever we write an XML document. The XML specification itself provides a syntax, which must be followed in order for the result to be considered well-formed XML. In addition, the vocabulary in which the document is written imposes more rules. It tells us the names of allowed tags and the attributes of those tags. It tells us the structure of our documents by telling us what elements may contain. Metadata's role is in telling us the rules of a vocabulary. A well-written vocabulary mirrors the application domain. A vocabulary about banking will inherently teach a layman something about the nature of banking. The syntactic rules of XML and the rules of any particular vocabulary are thus data *about* data. Philosophers long ago coined the term **metadata** to describe this. Our rules convey no information in the vocabulary, but they tell us what *may* be written under the vocabulary.

Obviously, metadata is important if we want to validate an XML document. We took an introductory look at DTDs in Chapter 3. Our chosen parser, MSXML, became a validating parser with version 5.0 of Internet Explorer, and we can use this feature to avoid syntactic errors in the data we exchange. Simply adopt a resolution in your organization that all documents must be valid, provide DTDs, and turn on the validation feature of MSXML. Apart from a small performance penalty, however, we won't see much change in our applications merely by enforcing the validity of our documents.

Metadata tells us about our vocabularies, so we should be able to use it to discover how new vocabularies work. While that is a utopian ideal, we'll see that we can make shrewd use of metadata in the service of our third principle: services will be provided as self-describing data. XML documents become truly self-describing when vocabulary metadata is available.

# How Metadata is Used Today

The only use of metadata in the XML 1.0 recommendation is in the use of Document Type Definitions (DTD). DTDs give us much of what we would like to know regarding a document. They completely specify the structure of XML documents. Elements and their attributes are discussed, optional items are noted, and so forth. DTDs are the only formally approved mechanism for validating XML documents. They suffer from one great flaw, however. DTDs are written using a syntax other than XML. You can't use the XML DOM to parse and traverse a DTD. Obviously, it isn't impossible to write a parser for handling DTDs as every validating XML parser must include a DTD parser. It is simply annoying and inconvenient. As a result, there is great interest in replacing today's DTDs with an XML vocabulary for describing metadata.

# W3C Proposals

Metadata is a broad topic within the W3C and is managed by the W3C Metadata Activity. The W3C's interest in metadata extends to more than just XML. One of the earliest efforts was PICS, the Platform for Internet Content Selection, an initiative to build a mechanism for applying rating labels to Web sites. Obviously, a rating scheme must be able to describe content to some degree, so PICS came to be a way to create general rating systems. Yet PICS was modest in scope; it only attempted to describe what could be encoded in HTML pages. This certainly simplifies the task, but it makes it unsuitable for use as a general purpose metadata language.

PICS also inspired other efforts. The broadest is the W3C's Resource Description Format (RDF). More recently, the XML community has advanced more specialized proposals such as XML Data and the Document Content Description (DCD) for XML. Another activity, XML Namespaces, is not precisely a metadata activity, but as we shall see it can provide us with interesting information. Since the XML namespaces activity is a W3C recommendation and is simpler than the proper metadata activities, let's begin there.

> *W3C documents are prone to frequent changes in status. You can find a summary of current status at* `http://www.w3.org/TR/`.

# Namespaces

We encountered XML namespaces briefly in Chapter 3. If you recall, we established that namespaces are a means of naming some vocabulary for the purpose of reusing elements it contains in another vocabulary. If someone has published an excellent vocabulary for describing demographic information and we are working on a vocabulary for an advertising application, we might wish to reuse the demographics tags within our own vocabulary. We should have a means of pointing back to some description of the vocabulary, both for the purposes of attribution and for maintaining a link to the authoritative source for the vocabulary. At a minimum, we want a way to identify a particular tag name usage as being defined in the demographics vocabulary. This prevents confusion when the same tag name is used by multiple vocabularies. If an element is marked as belonging to a particular vocabulary, the meaning should be unambiguous.

## *Declarations*

Let's review the syntax for XML namespaces. We declare a namespace as follows:

```
<tagname xmlns[:name]=URI>
```

The namespace applies to the named tag and its contents. If we are going to deal with a number of tags from the same namespace, it is convenient to declare the namespace at the highest possible level. Tags that are not qualified are assumed to belong to the containing namespace. Note that the URI need not refer to a DTD or other online definition. While that is useful, it is not a requirement. The URI must simply provide a unique designator for the namespace.

With that in mind, here are some valid namespace declarations:

```
<People xmlns:mynames="http://www.myserver.com/mynames/schema.html">
<Things xmlns:stuff="urn:someschema-things.com-things">
<Concepts xmlns:pr="urn:astronomical-schema:pulsars">
```

You may not be familiar with the prefix `urn`. It stands for **universal resource name** and is a specific kind of **universal resource indicator** (URI). Unlike a URL, which is another specific type of URI, a URN just provides a name. Presumably, the name is widely understood. In the examples above, the `stuff` and `pr` prefixes will be used to denote namespaces, but we have not provided any way for the curious reader to find out more about what they mean. Hopefully, they are as familiar to the recipient of the declarations as HTML and other universally recognized namespaces. If we want to use a number of namespaces liberally throughout a document, we should declare them early and provide a namespace prefix with which to qualify individual element and attribute names. If we want to have an XML document whose root element is `<TRANSACTION>` and which borrows names from the `BANKING` and `FINANCE` namespaces, we should declare both namespaces in the root element:

```
<TRANSACTION xmlns:bank="urn:financial-schema-BANK"
    xmlns:fin="urn:financial-schema-FINANCE">
  ... some usage of the namespaces here ...
</TRANSACTION>
```

## Using Namespaces to Qualify Names

Tags use namespace declarations in one of two ways. They explicitly use the namespace if the tag name is qualified by the prefix specified in the declaration. Our `<TRANSACTION>` example declared two namespace prefixes, `bank` and `fin`. Extending our `<TRANSACTION>` example:

```
<TRANSACTION xmlns:bank="urn:financial-schema-BANK"
    xmlns:fin="urn:financial-schema-FINANCE">
  <bank:institution>Shaky Finance Corp.</bank:institution>
  <fin:instrument>certificate of deposit</fin:instrument>
</TRANSACTION>
```

The `institution` element comes from the `BANK` namespace, while the `instrument` element comes from the `FINANCE` namespace.

Alternately, an element or attribute name is implicitly qualified by the namespace declaration in whose scope it appears. If we declare a namespace in some element, any element that is not otherwise qualified is assumed to belong to the declared namespace. Suppose we changed our `<TRANSACTION>` example just a bit:

```
<TRANSACTION xmlns="urn:financial-schema-BANK"
    xmlns:fin="urn:financial-schema-FINANCE">
  <institution>Shaky Finance Corp.</bank:institution>
  <fin:instrument>certificate of deposit</fin:instrument>
</TRANSACTION>
```

Note we've omitted a namespace prefix for the `BANK` namespace. The `institution` element has no prefix, but it is implicitly assumed to come from the `BANK` namespace because it is contained within the scope of that declaration.

## Searching for Namespace Declarations

Namespaces are only intended to uniquely name elements and attributes. Enumerating the namespaces used within a document can tell us something about the meaning of the document, however. The fact that a namespace is used within a document indicates that some meaningful term has been borrowed from another vocabulary. If we can identify the namespaces referenced in a document, we will see what domains contributed to its meaning.

The first task is to enumerate all the namespace declarations within a given XML document. We could certainly traverse the entire DOM parse tree and examine each attribute found for the substring `xmlns`. Fortunately, we don't have to go to that much trouble. MSXML supports the Extensible Style Language (XSL) draft, and XSL includes a powerful pattern matching language. We can use this to enumerate all the elements matching a particular pattern – in our case, every attribute that declares a namespace.

> *This topic is well over the cutting edge. Not only is XSL a work in progress, but the XSL pattern matching support in MSXML includes some extensions that have been submitted to the W3C as a note regarding a query language for XML. The syntax that follows will certainly change and is meant to indicate one way a query language can be used to help us in our search for metadata.*

Consider the following fragment of an XML document. We have included two namespace declarations within the root element.

```
<?xml version="1.0"?>
<TOP xmlns:i="urn:myschema-first" xmlns:ii="urn:myschema-second">
   ...
</TOP>
```

We can use the `selectNodes` method of the node object to apply an XSL pattern string to the document and receive an enumeration of all attributes matching the pattern. Assuming we've created an instance of MSXML in the variable parser and loaded the document above successfully, we can make the following call:

```
rNSDeclarations = parser.documentElement.selectNodes("//@*[nodeName() >=
                                                      'xmlns']");
```

The `selectNodes` method takes a string conforming to the rules of the XSL pattern matching syntax. Generally speaking, the string above breaks down into a search scope, an indication of what we are searching for, and a filter.

The scope is denoted by `//`, meaning the entire document starting from the root. A single slash `/` would denote the root itself, while `./` would indicate the current context. The context is the point from which we start the search. We are searching from the root element, but we want to look at the entire document.

The symbols `@*` mean any attribute. It will be our filter that is going to have to limit the search because we don't know exactly what attribute names we are searching for. This is because we can declare a namespace prefix, but there is no way we can know in advance what that will be.

Everything within the square brackets is the filter. `nodeName()` is a built-in function of MSXML that can be evaluated at runtime. It will give us the name of the attribute. The constraint `>= 'xmlns'` gives us any attribute that begins with the substring `xmlns`. This will match declarations that have prefixes defined, as well as those that do not define a prefix.

If we apply the selection call to the sample XML document, we find we have an enumeration of two items. These will be node objects, so we can get their `text` property (this is equivalent to `childNodes.item(0).nodeValue`). Calling it on each of our two namespace declarations yields:

```
urn:myschema-first
urn:myschema-second
```

If we called for the `xml` property of the node object instead of the `text` property, we would get the entire attribute declaration, e.g., `xmlns:ii="urn:myschema-second"`.

## Other Namespace Support in MSXML

The DOM support in MSXML allows us to look at the parts of an element or attribute name. The `nodeName` property gives us the entire qualified name. `prefix` gives us the namespace prefix, if any. `basename` yields the unqualified name. For the element `<ii:More>`, the results are:

| Property | Result |
|----------|--------|
| nodeName | ii:More |
| prefix | ii |
| Basename | More |

## *Enumerating Namespace Usage*

Now we'll put this all together to analyze an XML document for foreign namespace usage. We want to list all the namespace declarations in a document, together with the qualified elements and attributes taken from them and used in the document.

> *The following code comes from the sample file* `NSTest.html`. *All code samples are available for download from our Web site at* `http://www.wrox.com` *and this example can be run from our site at* `http://webdev.wrox.co.uk/books/2270/`.

The `selectNodes` call we saw before gives us a list of declarations:

```
rNSDeclarations = parser.documentElement.selectNodes("//@*[nodeName() >=
'xmlns']");
```

Now we have a collection of namespace declarations. We want to iterate through the collection and perform searches for qualified elements and attributes. We'll continue to use the `selectNodes` call and search the entire document. We obtain a collection of qualified elements with this call:

```
rQualElements = parser.documentElement.selectNodes("//*[nodeName() >= '"
                + declaration.basename + "':']");
```

Note we've dropped the @ character from the search pattern. The unqualified * character indicates that we are looking for elements. We use the basename of the declaration together with a colon to give us the qualifying prefix. Recall that the declaration has the prefix `xmlns`, and a basename consisting of the prefix to use to qualify names from this namespace. There's a problem, however. Since the XSL pattern matching syntax doesn't allow us to use wildcards in our `nodeName` selection, we may get some element names that aren't from this namespace. For example, if our prefix is `aa`, then a qualified node `zz:XYZ` will match the search. The collection we obtain from the search is guaranteed to include all the names for which we are searching, but may include other names as well. Consequently, before we list any element names, we have to test the element's prefix against the declaration's basename.

```
for (nj = 0; nj < rQualElements.length; nj++)
{
   element = rQualElements(nj);
   if (element.prefix == declaration.basename)
   {
      ListLine(results, element.basename, "blue", tabsize, linesize);
      linesize += 4;
   }
}
```

We use a similar approach to obtain the qualified attribute names:

```
rQualAttributes =
   parser.documentElement.selectNodes("//@*[nodeName() >= '"
      + declaration.basename + "':']");

   // some formatting code here

   for (nk = 0; nk < rQualAttributes.length; nk++)
```

```
    {
        attribute = rQualAttributes(nk);
        if (attribute.prefix == declaration.basename)
        {
            ListLine(results, attribute.basename, "red", tabsize, linesize);
            linesize += 4;
        }
    }
```

We'll use the following XML for our test document:

```
<?xml version="1.0"?>
<OUTER xmlns:pe="urn:schema-process-engineering" xmlns:xmit="urn:myschema-
transmission">
    <xmit:INSIDE xmit:more="extra">Filler</xmit:INSIDE>
    <pe:OPERATINGPOINT>
        128.4
        <pe:UNITS>deg F</pe:UNITS>
        <xmit:PADDING>xxxyyy</xmit:PADDING>
    </pe:OPERATINGPOINT>
<MIDDLE>
    <xmit:STUFFING>zzz</xmit:STUFFING>
    <pe:SETPOINT>
        129
        <pe:UNITS>deg F</pe:UNITS>
    </pe:SETPOINT>
    <pe:LIMIT>
        250
        <pe:UNITS>deg F</pe:UNITS>
    </pe:LIMIT>
</MIDDLE>
</OUTER>
```

Here's the result when we run NSTest.html:

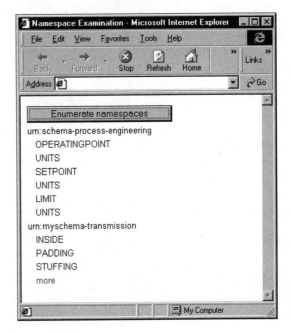

We can clearly see the **schema-process-engineering** namespace is used heavily. A human reader might be able to make something of the names, particularly if the namespace creator used names descriptive of a particular problem domain.

An automated agent might be given a list of namespace URIs in which a user is interested. Given that and a usage listing such as we produced above, the agent could assign a relevance priority to each document it encounters. Namespaces alone don't give much metadata, but they do give us a clue to what a document might be talking about. Here's the complete listing for our enumeration function:

```
function OnEnumNS()
{
    var parser = new ActiveXObject("microsoft.XMLDOM");
    var results = document.all("concordance");
    var rNSDeclarations, rQualElements, rQualAttributes;
    var declaration, element, attribute, ni, nj, nk;

    linesize = 4;
    tabsize = 0;

    results.innerHTML = "";

    if (parser != null)
    {
        parser.async = false;
        parser.load("namespace.xml");
        if (parser.readyState == COMPLETED && parser.parseError == "")
        {
            // namespace declarations
            rNSDeclarations =
                parser.documentElement.selectNodes("//@*[nodeName() >= 'xmlns']");

            for (ni = 0; ni < rNSDeclarations.length; ni++)
            {
                declaration = rNSDeclarations(ni);
                ListLine(results, declaration.text, "black", tabsize, linesize);
                linesize += 4;
                rQualElements =
                    parser.documentElement.selectNodes("//*[nodeName() >= '"
                                                  + declaration.basename + ":']");
                if (rQualElements.length > 0)
                    tabsize += 12;
                for (nj = 0; nj < rQualElements.length; nj++)
                {
                    element = rQualElements(nj);
                    if (element.prefix == declaration.basename)
                    {
                        ListLine(results, element.basename, "blue", tabsize, linesize);
                        linesize += 4;
                    }
                }

                if (rQualElements.length > 0)
                    tabsize -= 12;

                rQualAttributes =
                    parser.documentElement.selectNodes("//@*[nodeName() >= '"
                      + declaration.basename + ":']");
                if (rQualAttributes.length > 0)
                    tabsize += 12;
```

```
                    for (nk = 0; nk < rQualAttributes.length; nk++)
                    {
                        attribute = rQualAttributes(nk);
                        if (attribute.prefix == declaration.basename)
                        {
                            ListLine(results, attribute.basename, "red", tabsize, linesize);
                            linesize += 4;
                        }
                    }
                    if (rQualAttributes.length > 0)
                        tabsize -= 12;
                }
            }
        else
            alert("Parser error:" + parser.parseError.reason);
    }
}
```

Next we move on from namespaces to turn our attention to true metadata.

# Resource Description Framework

The Resource Description Framework (RDF) is certainly the most ambitious of all the metadata efforts from the W3C Metadata Activity, it became a W3C Recommendation on the 22nd February 1999. RDF is a syntax for describing **resources**. Resources are defined as anything that can be designated by a URI. RDF does not specify a vocabulary for describing resources. Rather, it provides the means for vocabulary authors to build up descriptions and facts about some topic of interest. It was influenced by the W3C experience with PICS, but it attempts to break out of the narrow model of PICS by providing a generalized model for describing resources.

RDF is a model for defining statements about resources. Each resource possesses one or more properties, each of which has a value. The model provides a means of defining classes of resources and properties. These classes are used to build statements which assert facts about the resource. RDF defines a syntax for writing a schema for a resource. A schema is analogous to a DTD, but is much more expressive. The schema uses the model defined for some vocabulary to express the structure of a document in the vocabulary. The statements in the model place constraints on the statements that can be made in a document conforming to the schema.

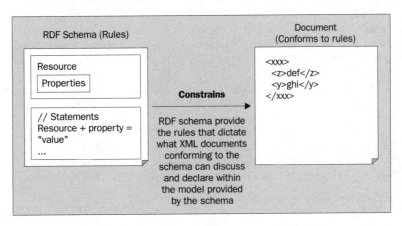

# RDF Model

The basic RDF model is built from three types of objects:

❑ Resources – anything that can be named with a URI
❑ Properties – a specific, meaningful attribute of a resource
❑ Statements – a combination of a resource, a property of the resource, and the value of the property

## Resources

Resources can be almost anything: a document, a collection of documents, a site, even a specific portion of a document. This allows RDF to describe almost anything that can be placed online.

## Properties

Properties have well-defined meanings. This means that constraints are placed on a property to define the types of resources to which it can be applied, the range and types of values it can take on, and how it relates to other properties. These constraints are a major reason why RDF is so expressive – the constraints give meaning to the properties, and hence to the resources they describe.

## Statements

Statements are triplets consisting of a **subject** resource, a **predicate** property, and an **object** value. Objects can be literal values or resources, making complex statements possible. Consider the natural language statement:

The topic of urn:this-book is designing distributed applications.

The subject resource is urn:this-book. The property is topic, and the object is designing distributed applications.

> *Strictly speaking, properties are a subtype of resources. This is important from a theoretical perspective, but it is simpler for our introductory purposes to think of them as entirely separate entities. Our common sense view of them as separate items will make it easier to conceptualize the RDF model.*

One property defined in the basic RDF model is type. This gives RDF a way to assign types to resources. Resources and properties use a class typing mechanism, so a given resource may be said to be a subtype of another class type. The RDF namespace has names for the class of resources and the subClassOf a property. By successively defining new classes of resources and properties, a vocabulary builder can develop RDF statements of arbitrary complexity and meaning.

Constraints are a specialized type of property. They are further refined in the range and domain of the property. Where typing gives us specialized properties, constraints bound a property, thereby giving it definition and meaning.

RDF also defines a variety of containers and collection classes. As we have seen in the previous chapter, it is often necessary to discuss collections of objects. RDF's container classes are much more sophisticated than ours. They define a variety of ordering and containment models.

> *An examination of RDF container classes is outside the scope of this book. The full W3C RDF Recommendation can be found at http://www.w3.org/TR/REC-rdf-syntax/*

## RDF Schema

RDF would be of little more than theoretical value if it did not include a format for transmitting data models. The creators of RDF chose to define an XML vocabulary for this task. This vocabulary defines resources and properties in a typed system similar to object oriented languages like C++ and Java.

The terminology of RDF can be overly theoretical in places. A few words on terminology for those of us who are not set theorists is therefore in order. RDF is a model for talking about things. Those things we can discuss, use, or otherwise refer to in an RDF schema are called **resources**. Both classes and properties are kinds of resources in the RDF model. Each property has a **range** – the set of values it can talk on – and a **domain** – the class to which the property applies.

Let's illustrate these concepts with a very simple RDF schema. Suppose we wish to talk about our retail customers. For generality, we'd like to say that retail customers are a specialized type of some customer class. This is done with the following lines:

```
<rdfs:Class rdf:ID="Customer">
    <rdfs:comment>Generic class for describing customers</rdfs:comment>
    <rdfs:subClassOf
        rdf:resource="http://www.w3.org/TR/WD-rdf-schema#Resource"/>
</rdfs:Class>

<rdfs:Class rdf:ID="RetailCustomer">
    <rdfs:comment>Derived class for describing retail customers</rdfs:comment>
    <rdfs:subClassOf rdf:resource="#Customer"/>
</rdfs:Class>
```

The `rdf` and `rdfs` namespaces are part of the RDF proposal and are declared elsewhere in our schema document. Our class named `Customer` is a subclass of the RDF-defined class `resource`. `RetailCustomer`, then, is a subclass of `Customer`. Now let's give our customer a way to pay for his purchases. `RetailCustomer` should have a property that will take on one of the names of a set of credit cards. That is accomplished with this property definition:

```
<rdf:Property ID="paymentType">
    <rdfs:range rdf:resource="#CreditCards"/>
    <rdfs:domain rdf:resource="#RetailCustomer"/>
</rdf:Property>
```

Our property is named `paymentType`. It takes on a value from the class `CreditCards`, which we shall define shortly. The property's domain – the class to which it can apply – is the class `RetailCustomer`. We know that the values for this property will be a limited number of strings naming the major credit card types. First we define a class of literals.

```
<rdfs:Class rdf:ID="CreditCards"/>
```

Next we define some literal values of this type:

```
<CreditCards rdf:ID="MasterCard"/>
<CreditCards rdf:ID="AmericanExpress"/>
<CreditCards rdf:ID="Visa"/>
<CreditCards rdf:ID="OtherCredit"/>
```

Perhaps we are interested in keeping track of who referred this customer to us. This should be a property whose value is a resource of the type `Customer`. This allows us to have any sort of customer derived class as a value for this property. That way, we could have referrals from `RetailCustomer` instances or as-yet undefined `WholesaleCustomer` instances without having to enumerate these specific derived classes. Similarly, if we derive more classes from `Customer`, the referrer can participate in these relationships without modifying the range declaration.

```
<rdf:Property ID="referrer">
   <rdfs:range rdf:resource="#Customer"/>
   <rdfs:domain rdf:resource="#RetailCustomer"/>
</rdf:Property>
```

Our property is called `referrer`, it can be applied to the `RetailCustomer` class, and its value must be a resource of the `Customer` class. Since we have previously defined that class, no further specification is necessary. Here's the full text of our simple RDF schema:

```
<rdf:RDF xmlns:rdf="http://www.w3.org/TR/WD-rdf-syntax#"
xmlns:rdfs="http://www.w3.org/TR/WD-rdf-schema#">

   <rdfs:Class rdf:ID="Customer">
      <rdfs:comment>Generic class for describing customers</rdfs:comment>
      <rdfs:subClassOf rdf:resource=
                              "http://www.w3.org/TR/WD-rdf-schema#Resource"/>
   </rdfs:Class>

   <rdfs:Class rdf:ID="RetailCustomer">
      <rdfs:comment>Derived class for describing retail customers</rdfs:comment>
      <rdfs:subClassOf rdf:resource="#Customer"/>
   </rdfs:Class>

   <rdf:Property ID="paymentType">
      <rdfs:range rdf:resource="#CreditCards"/>
      <rdfs:domain rdf:resource="#RetailCustomer"/>
   </rdf:Property>

   <rdf:Property ID="referrer">
      <rdfs:range rdf:resource="#Customer"/>
      <rdfs:domain rdf:resource="#RetailCustomer"/>
   </rdf:Property>

   <rdfs:Class rdf:ID="CreditCards"/>

   <CreditCards rdf:ID="MasterCard"/>
   <CreditCards rdf:ID="AmericanExpress"/>
   <CreditCards rdf:ID="Visa"/>
   <CreditCards rdf:ID="OtherCredit"/>

</rdf:RDF>
```

## RDF and Our Philosophy

RDF, quite simply, is far too ambitious for our purposes. Many of its assignments are nothing more than names. A complicated system of mappings between names and resources is needed to discern meaning. More advanced features, e.g., ranges, domains, and container classes, are needed to communicate metadata regarding the topic under discussion. These features, however, are a bit too much for the simple kinds of automated metadata applications we are likely to support in the immediate future. If RDF can be supported, it is a powerful mechanism for communicating intellectual models. Our needs, however, are somewhat simpler.

Indeed, both XML and our development philosophy share the belief that simple features that can be readily implemented are more useful than complex features that can be implemented only with great difficulty. Given some XML vocabulary, we'd like to be able to discover the proper structure for a document that conforms to that vocabulary. This is far simpler to implement. We really need a better way of encoding a DTD. This is what the remaining proposals aim to achieve.

# Meta Content Framework Using XML

The Meta Content Framework (MCF) is similar to RDF, although it doesn't seem to have influenced quite so many later efforts as has RDF. Like RDF (and, indeed, most of the metadata proposals), the MCF uses a directed graph model of nodes and edges to build conceptual models. Objects are the nodes and property values are the edges. An XML vocabulary is provided for encoding MCF models. Subclassing and inheritance is permitted. Like RDF, a core set of property and object types are used to describe more complicated types, and so forth until the complete metadata model is described. An interesting property of MCF is that its authors anticipated using MCF to define componentized blocks of metadata. These blocks would then be combined through the XML linking specification to compose complete metadata models. In this way, MCF blocks found to be useful to particular problems could be reused by other vocabulary authors working on related problems. The following illustration shows a simple MCF schema for this book. The book object is derived from the category (MCF's term for class) `Book`, which in turn derives from `Document`. The book has chapters (i.e., the book is the domain of the `Chapter` category) which takes their values from the category `English_Prose`. That category is derived from the category `text`. Note that `typeof`, `domain`, and `range` are properties of their respective objects.

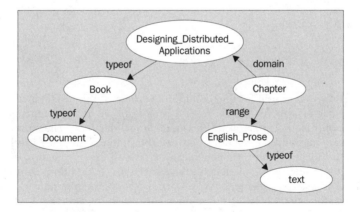

Here's the XML document that captures the information in the illustration above:

```
<xml-mcf>
  <Category id="Designing_Distributed_Applications">
    <name>Designing_Distributed_Applications</name>
    <superType unit="Book"/>
    <description>The category whose sole member is this book</description>
  </Category>

  <Category id="Book">
    <name>Book</name>
    <superType unit="Document"/>
    <description>The notion of a bound book</description>
  </Category>
```

```
<!-- The supertype, Page, is a category from MCF itself. -->
<Category id="Document">
   <name>Document</name>
   <superType unit="Page"/>
   <description>A generalized document</description>
</Category>

<Category id="Chapter">
   <name>Chapter</name>
   <superType unit="Page"/>
   <description>The notion of an organized sequence of pages</description>
   <domain unit="Designing_Distributed_Applications"/>
   <range unit="English_Prose"/>
</Category>

 <Category id="English_Prose">
   <name>English_Prose</name>
   <superType unit="text"/>
   <description>The notion of prose written in English</description>
</Category>

 <Category id="text">
   <name>text</name>
   <superType unit="Page"/>
   <description>The notion of some organized natural language</description>
</Category>
</xml-mcf>
```

*The W3C MCF Note can be found at* `http://www.w3.org/TR/NOTE-MCF-XML/`.

# XML Data

XML Data is an ambitious proposal for the definition of schemas. Like RDF, it can express both conceptual and syntactic models. To clarify, a DTD is an example of a syntactic model – it specifies the allowable syntax of some vocabulary, whereas a relational database schema is a conceptual model, as it describes things and the relations between things in the model. XML Data also uses an XML vocabulary as its documentation format. It can express all the information of a conventional XML DTD, but it adds strong typing of elements and attributes. In addition, constraints may be placed on the value and use of an element. XML Data also supports inheritance of types, which allows us to conveniently extend existing definitions. Further aiding authors of schemas is the ability to use a defined element type as a complex structure. Hence, our `RetailCustomer` from the RDF discussion may be used as a basic type in later schemas.

Unlike a DTD, an XML Data schema allows you to declare a model open. In an open model, the syntactic rules laid down in the schema do not preclude the inclusion of content not covered in the schema. This might be useful in cases when we wish to precisely define some content but are indifferent to other content that might be added to documents. If the model is declared closed, an XML Data schema specifies content in the same formal manner as a DTD. In which case, all content must be explicitly described in the schema to be permitted in a document conforming to the model. In order to embrace conceptual models such as relational database schemas, XML Data introduces relations, a concept in which an element acts as a reference to another. This is like the notion of primary and foreign keys in a database; an element contained in one item of content establishes a relationship with another item of content. The element in question is a key or index into the other content. Aliases are also permitted. This allows us to establish subtle concepts. An element can have an alias, or **correlative** in XML Data's terminology, which establishes the context of a relationship. For example, we might have a STUDIED element with the correlative STUDENT. This establishes that STUDIED is an alias for STUDENT, in the context of the student's relation to the topic she studies.

We will not discuss XML Data and the related proposal that follows, XML Document Content Description, in great depth because a partial implementation is included with the version of MSXML that ships with Internet Explorer 5.0. This partial implementation, intended as a technology preview, is termed XML Schema. We will discuss its implementation at length and develop some prototype code using it later in this chapter.

For further information on XML Data see the W3C Note on their Web site at
http://www.w3.org/TR/1998/NOTE-XML-data/

# XML Document Content Description

The XML Document Content Description (DCD) proposal is an attempt to extract the subset of XML Data's features that permit the encoding of a DTD in XML. It is thus a simplification of XML Data that addresses a pressing need in a valuable way. Its authors modified the syntax of XML Data so that DCD would be more closely aligned with RDF.

DCD also offers a few features that cannot be expressed in an XML 1.0 DTD. The first, and perhaps most important to the exchange of business data using XML, is the ability to specify the data type of elements and attributes. One criticism of XML is that it expresses all values as text, leaving the native data type in question. DCD identifies a host of native types drawn from common programming languages as well as the core tokenized types defined in XML 1.0.

DCD explored two additional features in appendices to the main submission. The first is the ability to nest element type definitions within other definitions in order to declare an element type with scope local to the containing element type definition. The second, of somewhat broader use, is the inheritance and subclassing mechanism. This borrows a powerful technique from the world of object oriented programming. Element and attribute type definitions can be extensions of simpler type definitions. When a type definition includes the keyword element <Extends Type="*some_type_definition*"/>, it inherits all the elements and properties previously defined for the class *some_type_definition*.

For further information on DCDs see the W3C Note on their Web site at
http://www.w3.org/TR/NOTE-dcd

# Metadata Support in Microsoft Internet Explorer

Internet Explorer 5.0 supports metadata in several ways. First, it uses the current draft of the namespaces specification. Second, it uses namespaces to provide an approach to typing of elements. This is coupled with Microsoft's extensions to the DOM so that a program can retrieve the value of an element in either text (i.e., as it appears in the document) or native binary data format (e.g., int, float). Finally, it offers a technology preview termed XML Schema. This is based on the XML Data proposal, but only supports the feature subset that is also part of the XML DCD proposal. These features may be used to explore the metadata in XML and suggest ways we could use it in our applications.

The various metadata efforts seen in this chapter cover a spectrum from the highly ambitious to the narrowly focused. Each minimally gives us a way to capture the same metadata about a vocabulary that a DTD expresses. Each goes further, however, adding more expressive techniques for describing data. That is what is interesting to us in terms of the third principle of developing cooperative network applications:

**3. Services shall be provided as self-describing data.**

The more descriptive our data can be, the better. An automated consumer of service data such as an agent may encounter an unfamiliar vocabulary. Unlike a human consumer, the robot needs a great deal of help in exploring the data. When the thicket of metadata efforts is cleared, service programmers will have a very powerful tool for providing that help. Since these efforts use XML for their own syntax, we have the added benefit of being able to reuse MSXML and other XML parsers with which we may be familiar.

## Defining Datatypes in XML

There are many occasions when the textual contents of an element represent a typed value other than text in the domain we are describing. This is most obvious in the case of numeric values. The integer 1234 requires two bytes of storage in its native form on a PC. In XML's default character encoding, it consumes four bytes. Worse, before we can use it in calculations, we must perform a conversion from the string to the numeric form. Beyond the issues of storage and conversion, if we simply use unadorned text the type of data is implicit knowledge. If we use the data type namespace, however, we can make the type explicit. This might be useful to us if we wanted to examine a document in an unknown format. For example, a graphing component might search a document for collections of numeric types. If found, these could be presented to the user for selection of what data to put in a graph. Use of the data type namespace also allows us to manipulate data in native form. For example, if I have this element

```
<VELOCITY dt:type="r8">1.5E5</VELOCITY>
```

I can retrieve it as either the string 1.5E5 or as an eight-byte floating point numeric value. The DOM extensions to support this consist of two properties of the Node class:

| Property | Description |
| --- | --- |
| nodeTypedValue | read-write; typed value of the node |
| dataType | read-write; the type of the node |

*Twenty-five types frequently encountered in programming languages are supported. Additionally, the XML 1.0 recommendation defines ten enumerated or tokenized types and these are supported as well. The definitive list of types supported is found at http://www.microsoft.com/workshop/xml/schema/reference/datatypes.asp.*

# XML Schema

This technology preview implements the core feature set of the XML DCD submission while using the element names of XML Data. While the two notes are similar in structure, there is some difference in keywords and the like. Note that the inheritance and subclassing features described in an appendix of the DCD note are not included in the preview implementation. Generally speaking, XML Schema loses relations, aliases, inheritance, and complex types as defined in XML Data.

*At the time of writing, we are referencing the DCD note of 31 July 1998 and the XML Data Note of 5 January 1998.*

The preview supports the following element types:

| Schema | Root element of a schema definition |
|---|---|
| `ElementType` | Defines a class of elements |
| `AttributeType` | Defines a class of attributes |
| `datatype` | Specifies the type of an `ElementType` or `AttributeType` element |
| `element` | Names a declared element class whose instances may appear in instances of the element class defined by an `ElementType` element |
| `attribute` | Names a declared attribute class whose instances may appear in instances of an `AttributeType` declaration |
| `description` | Provides textual documentation for `ElementType` and `AttributeType` elements |
| `group` | Defines a collection class |

We will now explore XML Schema by building a simple schema definition for documents describing employees. This will be a very simple schema, with the following DTD:

```
<!ELEMENT EMPLOYEE (NAME, HIREDATE, MANAGER, DEPARTMENT)>
<!ATTLIST EMPLOYEE employment-category (full | part |contract) #REQUIRED>

<!ELEMENT NAME #PCDATA>
<!ELEMENT HIREDATE #PCDATA>
<!ELEMENT MANAGER #PCDATA>
<!ELEMENT DEPARTMENT #PCDATA>
```

Here's a sample document in this vocabulary:

```
<?xml version="1.0"?>
<EMPLOYEE xmlns="http://myserver/HR/employeeschema.xml" employment-
category="full">
    <NAME>Phineas Armbuster</NAME>
    <HIREDATE>1990-01-02</HIREDATE>
    <MANAGER>B. G. Trouble</MANAGER>
    <DEPARTMENT>Finance_Collections</DEPARTMENT>
</EMPLOYEE>
```

## Defining a Schema

The `Schema` element is the root of any schema definition. It is used to declare the name of the schema and any namespaces required in the schema. It will typically declare the namespaces for schemas and datatypes. Thus, for our example, we have:

```
<Schema name="EMPLOYEE" xmlns="urn:schemas-microsoft-com:xml-data"
    xmlns:dt="urn:schemas-microsoft-com:datatypes">
```

## Elements

Element types are declared using the `ElementType` element. This element has one required attribute and four optional attributes:

| Attribute | Description |
|-----------|-------------|
| name | required; name of the element |
| content | optional an enumeration of empty, textOnly (i.e., PCDATA), eltOnly (i.e., elements), and mixed (i.e., elements and PCDATA) |
| dt:type | optional; data type of the element |
| model | optional; an enumeration of open (can contain content not defined in the schema) and closed (can only include content defined in the schema) |
| order | optional; an enumeration of one (i.e., only of a set of options, analogous to the \| DTD operator), seq (i.e., the specified elements must appear in the specified order), and many (i.e., permits any of the named elements to appear zero or more times in any order) |

Take the definition of the NAME element:

```
<ElementType name="NAME" content="textOnly"/>
```

We've defined an element NAME that contains text, i.e., PCDATA. Let's look at a more challenging example, the EMPLOYEE element.

```
<ElementType name="EMPLOYEE" content="eltOnly" model="closed" order="seq">
    <attribute type="employment-category"/>
    <element type="NAME"/>
    <element type="HIREDATE"/>
    <element type="MANAGER"/>
    <element type="DEPARTMENT"/>
</ElementType>
```

We've said `EMPLOYEE` can only contain other elements (`content="eltOnly"`) and only those elements we've specified in our schema (`model="closed"`). Moreover, the elements must all appear in the order listed (`order="seq"`). From there, we go on to provide a list of the attributes (in this case, `employment-category`) and elements (`NAME`, `HIREDATE`, `MANAGER`, and `DEPARTMENT`) that are contained in an `EMPLOYEE` element.

## Attributes

The `EMPLOYEE` definition included an attribute element. Clearly, we have to be able to declare attributes in a manner similar to the way we define elements. Not surprisingly, the `AttributeType` element exists to do just that. This element has the following attributes:

| Attribute | Description |
|---|---|
| name | required; name of the attribute being defined |
| dt:type | optional; data type of the attribute |
| dt:values | optional; when `dt:type` has the value `enumeration`, this attribute provides the permissible values |
| default | optional; default value for the attribute. If `dt:type` appears, the value of this attribute must be legal for that type. |
| required | optional; either of the enumerated values `yes` or `no`. Denotes whether the attribute is required to appear on an element. |

The definition for the `employment-category` attribute looks like this:

```
<AttributeType name="employment-category" required="yes" dt:type="enumeration"
        dt:values="full part contract"/>
```

We can see that this attribute is required to appear in any element – like `EMPLOYEE` – that uses the attribute. It is an enumerated type with the permissible values `full`, `part`, and `contract`.

## The Complete EMPLOYEE Schema

At this point, it is worthwhile to present the entire schema for our simple document type. We've managed to do a few things here that we couldn't do in the DTD version of this document model. We pulled in foreign namespaces to allow us to talk about schemas and data types. We've strongly typed our elements and attributes, making life somewhat simpler for our application programmers. The content and model information was elevated to an explicit statement through the use of attributes. In the DTD, you had to parse the line:

```
<!ELEMENT EMPLOYEE (NAME, HIREDATE, MANAGER, DEPARTMENT)>
```

to realize the EMPLOYEE element has sequential order and can contain only elements. Here, we've said so explicitly. Moreover, the model attribute lets us open up our model if our applications require us to do so, whereas DTDs are closed by definition.

```
<Schema name="EMPLOYEE" xmlns="urn:schemas-microsoft-com:xml-data"
    xmlns:dt="urn:schemas-microsoft-com:datatypes">

    <ElementType name="NAME" content="textOnly"/>
    <ElementType name="HIREDATE" dt:type="date" content="textOnly"/>
    <ElementType name="MANAGER" content="textOnly"/>
    <ElementType name="DEPARTMENT" content="textonly"/>

    <AttributeType name="employment-category" required="yes" dt:type="enumeration"
        dt:values="full part contract"/>

    <ElementType name="EMPLOYEE" content="eltOnly" model="closed" order="seq">
        <description>Simple element for describing employees</description>
        <attribute type="employment-category"/>
        <element type="NAME"/>
        <element type="HIREDATE"/>
        <element type="MANAGER"/>
        <element type="DEPARTMENT"/>
    </ElementType>

</Schema>
```

## Other XML Schema Elements

Our little example omitted two schema elements supported in the technology preview: datatype and group. The datatype element is an extension of the dt:type and dt:values attributes for ElementType and AttributeType elements. The datatype element allows us to specify not only the type of an element or attribute, but also minimum and maximum values. It has the following attributes:

| Attribute | Description |
|---|---|
| dt:type | optional; specifies the type of the element or attribute |
| dt:values | optional; when dt:type has the value enumeration, this attribute allows us to specify the permissible values |
| dt:max | optional; maximum value inclusive of the given value |
| dt:maxExclusive | optional; maximum value exclusive of the given value |
| dt:min | optional; minimum value inclusive of the given value |
| dt:minExclusive | optional; minimum value exclusive of the given value |
| dt:maxlength | optional; allows us to limit the length of certain data types |

Let's apply this to HIREDATE. Suppose our company came into existence on July 20, 1969 and will be disbanded when the founder retires on December 31, 1999 – no Y2K worries for us then! The definition becomes:

```
<ElementType name="HIREDATE" content="textonly">
    <datatype dt:type="date" dt:min="1969-07-20" dt:max="1999-12-31"/>
</ElementType>
```

The group element organizes content into a sequence. It specifies which elements appear, how often, and in what sequence. The permissible attributes are:

| Attribute | Description |
| --- | --- |
| maxoccurs | optional; the enumerated values 1 and * (at most one or many occurrences) |
| minoccurs | optional; the enumerated values 0 or 1 (a minimum of zero or one) |
| order | required; one of the enumerated values one, seq, many |

The attributes minoccurs and maxoccurs specify the minimum and maximum number of times the group can occur. The order attribute specifies the sequence and content of the group. The literal one means exactly one of the elements of the group may occur. This is like the | (OR) operator in DTDs. The seq attribute value means the elements in the group all appear, and appear in the specified order. The value many means that any of the elements may appear (or not) and in any order.

If we wanted to modify our EMPLOYEE element so that an employee could belong to multiple departments with a supervisor in each, e.g., the employee belongs to multiple teams, we would say:

```
<ElementType name="EMPLOYEE" content="eltOnly" model="closed" order="seq">
    <description>Simple element for describing employees</description>
    <attribute type="employment-category"/>
    <element type="NAME"/>
    <element type="HIREDATE"/>
    <group order="seq" minoccurs="1" maxoccurs="*">
        <element type="MANAGER"/>
        <element type="DEPARTMENT"/>
    </group>
</ElementType>
```

This would be a valid document under the revised schema:

```
<?xml version="1.0"?>
<EMPLOYEE xmlns="http://myserver/HR/employeeschema.xml" employment-
category="full">
    <NAME>Phineas Armbuster</NAME>
    <HIREDATE>1990-01-02</HIREDATE>
    <MANAGER>B. G. Trouble</MANAGER>
    <DEPARTMENT>Finance_Collections</DEPARTMENT>
    <MANAGER>G. Marconi</MANAGER>
    <DEPARTMENT>Engineering</DEPARTMENT>
</EMPLOYEE>
```

# Metadata in Network Applications

We've hinted at some of the uses of metadata as they might apply to our philosophy. When we discussed namespaces, we used the appearance of names from foreign namespaces as a clue to the meaning of an unknown XML vocabulary. Let's take a direct look at some of the specific ways we can use metadata to improve our cooperative applications.

# Validating Documents

First and foremost, we can validate documents using schemas. This is a mixed blessing. Validation let's us enforce the rules of a vocabulary rigorously. Sometimes though, we can improve the reliability of our applications by relaxing unimportant syntactic rules. If XML Data or XML DCD come to be recommendations of the W3C, we might be able to do both. An open model as defined by XML Data or XML DCD would allow us to enforce the rules that are important to us while admitting other content in a flexible way. Each metadata effort offers some interesting features that, if adopted as both a recommendation and as an implemented feature in a parser component, could help us apply our five principles. The XML metadata world is full of tantalizing possibilities and short on fulfillment. However, at the time of writing a working group of the W3C was producing a schema for XML using an XML syntax: more information was at
`http://www.w3.org/XML/Activity#schema-wg`.

# Searching for Useful Data

Strong typing of data and content organizing features, like the `group` element's `order` attribute in the XML Schema preview, help client applications search XML documents written in an unfamiliar vocabulary for data on which they can operate. A client that operates on text strings knows to skip numeric types. A calculation-oriented application would seek out numeric types. Groups indicate some association between elements, so a client would logically view such elements as part of a whole – a data series, a group of alternatives, properties of the containing parent. A client application working with metadata can make useful suggestions to a human user. If the application requires some numeric inputs, the application would present those types found in the document to the user. Based on the `order` attribute, the user interface could be reconfigured: a single selection list box for `one`, a group of mandatory inputs for `seq`, or a multiple selection list box for `many`. For example, in the XML Schema experiment at the end of this chapter, we will encounter a schema intended for building SQL queries. The schema will use the value `seq` with the `order` attribute and the enumerated values `"GT GE LT LE EQ"` to represent the operators `" >, >=, <, <=, = "` used in SQL `WHERE` clauses.

XML is a great advance over native data formats because it explicitly tags and labels each item of content. Metadata extends this by providing information about the structure, types, and relationships of the marked-up data. We've assumed that software clients will increasingly encounter unfamiliar vocabularies as networks grow decentralized. Once an XML metadata standard reaches recommendation status, client applications will find parsing the schema document as useful as parsing the data document.

# Learning Vocabulary Structure

A validating parser will only tell us when the data we use violates the rules of the vocabulary in question. The ability to parse a metadata document and discover the structure of the vocabulary enables us to avoid errors in the first place. Generally speaking, the metadata proposals we have seen in this chapter do not result in schema documents that proceed in a top-down fashion like our typical XML data document. In fact, since we usually like to define the component parts of larger structures before defining the overall structure, schema documents will usually be organized bottom-up. Once we have a root element definition, however, we can use the metadata definition to find its components. We can then either walk the parse tree or use the XSL pattern matching syntax to extract each of those components in turn. While this may not be terribly efficient from a programming point of view, keep in mind we're learning the structure that will be applied to all documents written to the vocabulary specified in the schema.

A certain amount of digging to learn the structure of the vocabulary will mean we can operate on data in a format we've never seen before. If we are using the specialization scheme presented in the last chapter, a client receiving a vocabulary more specialized than it desired can discover the structure of the specialized parts of the new vocabulary. This is a very powerful capability.

# Building Queries

A common task in our network experience will be composing queries to select data. We established the convention of using directory entries to indicate the vocabulary of our services back in Chapter Two. It is likely that the vocabulary for the queries will contain elements drawn from the response vocabulary. If, for example, we were searching for a person we would expect to provide a name for which to search. The name would certainly be part of the XML sent in response to the query. An application that understands the name element – and we are assuming a client understands the vocabulary it requires – could reasonably request input from the user for this element. The application, however, might not understand the vocabulary used to query the service. That vocabulary might change based on the SQL query used to implement the search. Some services might permit the submission of batches of unrelated queries while others would only accept one query based on one alternative at a time, e.g., searching by name or by age, but not both in one request.

Once a metadata recommendation is released by the W3C, we might reasonably extend our directory schema to include an entry for specifying the URL of the query schema for a particular service. A client searching for a given data vocabulary would locate a server, as we do now, but first retrieve and parse the query schema for that schema. With that in hand, a user or programmatic interface (for human and software agents, respectively) could be created dynamically. The client application would package the input data according to the query schema and transmit that in its request. This would give us considerably more flexibility than we presently have. Right now, we assume knowledge of both the response and query vocabularies. With a metadata capability, we could loosen our requirement for knowledge of the query vocabulary considerably. As we saw in the preceding section, we could also loosen the requirement to understand the response vocabulary to some extent. The degree to which we could loosen the requirement would of course depend on how much metadata is included in the schema. RDF and XML Data are at one extremely flexible end of the spectrum, with more limited proposals like XML DCD at the other.

| RDF          MCF | XML Data | DCD | XML DTD's |
|---|---|---|---|
| Descriptive; able to deal with deep relationships and concepts | Expresses simple relationships and syntax | | Syntax only |

# Experiments in Metadata

It is now time to get to work and try some experiments. Using the technology preview in MSXML, let's see what we can implement. We'll first see how XML Schema can be used to validate a document, then develop the ability to extract metadata from a schema, and finally try to build a dynamic query builder at the proof of concept level.

*It is well worth repeating that the metadata capabilities we're going to use are based on notes submitted to the W3C, not published recommendations. We are exploring, hoping to find the scope of future capabilities. It seems fairly certain that we will eventually see a metadata recommendation; it **is** certain that the syntax and capabilities of components implementing that recommendation will be a dramatic change from what we present here. Nevertheless, these experiments have value. Not only do they show us a path forward into a future in which we can communicate more effectively between clients and services, but the final metadata standards that are implemented in commercial parsers will likely be similar in spirit to what we will see here.*

# Validating a Document

We can control whether the parser performs validation with the `validateOnParse` property. If this property is `true`, which is the default value, the parser will perform validation when it parses a document. Errors, as we know, turn up in the `parseError` object property.

Using a DTD, we need to declare a `DOCTYPE` element declaring the DTD for the document. The technology preview, however, also allows MSXML to validate a document using an XML Schema. The `xmlns` name on an attribute declaring a namespace is treated specially. The parser will download the resource named by the attribute value unless the URI bears the `urn` prefix or a `DOCTYPE` element has been declared for the document. So, the resource named by this attribute must be an XML Schema file.

# Retrieving Metadata from an XML Schema

Having a schema encoded as an XML document means we can use our existing tools and experience to pick the schema apart and discover its structure and content constraints. This will usually be used to guide the construction of a document written according to an unfamiliar schema. It could also be used to look for overlapping structures in two schemas. For example, if we suspect two schemas are talking about the same topic, we might compare their structures. Two group elements composed of the same number and types of elements, regardless of name, would strongly suggest similarity of the encoded content. Similar constraints found in datatype schema elements would also be clues. Of course, the `dt:type` attributes would be of additional assistance to us in comparing two schemas.

We're about to embark on an experiment. It is not an uncommon task to format a query for a service as an XML document. The service extracts search criteria from the query document, performs a database query, and returns the results as an XML document written in the vocabulary specified in the directory. So far, we've assumed that the users of a vocabulary would understand it and also understand the required query vocabulary. Is it possible though, to parse a query vocabulary schema document and dynamically generate a query document builder? That is precisely what we shall try in our experiment.

# The Query Interface Experiment

Suppose we have a service that generates documents in the EMPLOYEE vocabulary in response to queries from clients. It might be the front end to a database of employee information. The queries are documents written to an XML schema. We'll assume the client application has obtained the URL for this schema document from the directory. For our purposes, we'll allow ourselves to directly input the URL in a Web page. When the user presses a button labeled **Create Form**, we want the script in the page to dynamically generate a user interface for composing a query for the service. The user interface should present us with the structure from the schema and allow us to input search criteria in the appropriate places. Once the user has finished entering values, he can click another button: **Complete Query**. The button handler script will compose a query according to the schema using the input parameters from the form and show us the XML in an alert box. This is our experimental page before anything is generated:

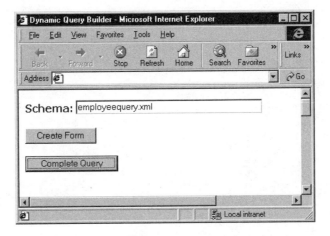

*The source code for the experiment is found in the file* QueryBuilder.html. *It can be downloaded from our site* http://www.wrox.com/ *or run from* http://webdev.wrox.co.uk/books/2270/.

## Query Schema

We need a schema for queries against the Employee service. We'll follow a couple of loose conventions. Since schemas can contain any number of top level element definitions, we need some way of specifying the root element name in our query vocabulary. Let's follow the DTD practice of naming the schema for the root node. This convention is solely for the purposes of our experiment. If this were a production application, we could store the name of the root in the directory or ask the client application to supply it. We could also adopt a convention of simply appending the word Query to the name of the response vocabulary. A more important convention is to use the names of elements in the response vocabulary to name elements in the query vocabulary. For example, if we wish to search by the employee's name, we shall have to supply a name against which to search. The element supplying this should be called NAME since that is the matching element name in the Employee vocabulary.

For reasons of simplicity we shall go into later, let's allow batched queries. That is, we will allow the user to provide parameters for searches by name, by hire date, by manager, and by department in a single request document. If all parameters were provided, multiple queries would be generated. Here is the schema we shall use.

```
<Schema name="EMPLOYEEQUERY" xmlns="urn:schemas-microsoft-com:xml-data"
   xmlns:dt="urn:schemas-microsoft-com:datatypes">

   <ElementType name="NAME" content="textOnly"/>
   <ElementType name="BYNAME" content="eltOnly">
      <description>Search by employee name</description>
      <element type="NAME"/>
   </ElementType>

   <ElementType name="HIREDATE" content="textOnly" dt:type="date"/>
   <ElementType name="OPERATOR" content="textOnly" dt:type="enumeration"
         dt:values="GT GE LT LE EQ">
      <description>Comparision operator for search</description>
   </ElementType>
   <ElementType name="BYHIRE" content="eltOnly">
      <description>Search with respect to hire date specified</description>
      <element type="HIREDATE"/>
      <element type="OPERATOR"/>
   </ElementType>

   <ElementType name="MANAGER" content="textOnly" />
   <ElementType name="BYMANAGER" content="eltOnly">
      <description>Search by employee's manager's name</description>
      <element type="MANAGER"/>
   </ElementType>

   <ElementType name="DEPARTMENT" content="textOnly"/>
   <ElementType name="BYDEPARTMENT" content="eltOnly">
      <element type="DEPARTMENT"/>
   </ElementType>

   <ElementType name="EMPLOYEEQUERY" content="eltOnly">
      <description>Query for Employee Service</description>
      <group order="many">
         <element type="BYNAME"/>
         <element type="BYHIRE"/>
         <element type="BYMANAGER"/>
         <element type="BYDEPARTMENT"/>
      </group>
   </ElementType>
</Schema>
```

This slightly formidable schema simply says that a document rooted with the EMPLOYEEQUERY element can contain any mix of BYNAME, BYHIRE, BYMANAGER, and BYDEPARTMENT elements. Each of these provides the parameters for an appropriate search. For every search type except BYHIRE, we simply provide the string for which to search. Searching by hire date requires the additional specification of an operator to tell us whether the search should look before or after the input date.

## User Interface Concerns

This schema is not what one would normally expect. One would normally specify an `order` attribute of `one` on the group so that the user would be asked to select which type of search he wished to perform. This would, however, add a substantial degree of complexity to our query form builder. In a production system, we would have to compose multiple pages or replace the form on our page as the user selected a search type. Since this is a proof of concept, we'll make the simplifying assumption of allowing any or all of the search types to be specified at once. That way, our query builder can simply generate a user input form that captures the entire structure. Note, however, this isn't exactly what `many` means. While the form matching this query schema will have one section for BYNAME, one for BYHIRE, and so forth, a document could have more than one of these types and be valid. Again, since we are simply exploring the feasibility of this concept, we'll leave the fine points for later work.

Given that, how shall we map schema element definitions to form elements?

## Retrieving the Structure

The core of our query builder is the ability to traverse a schema document so that we start with the root element of the vocabulary and recursively retrieve the definitions of its contained elements. In this way, we learn the structure of the vocabulary from the top down. Since the definitions can be in any order, we should use the `selectSingleNode()` method to search the parse tree for the definitions we require. First, let's get the `ElementType` element corresponding to the root element of our query vocabulary – in our example, EMPLOYEEQUERY:

```
var nameNode = schema.documentElement.attributes.getNamedItem("name");
if (nameNode != null)
{
   queryRootName = nameNode.nodeValue;
   var rootDef = schema.documentElement.selectSingleNode("//ElementType[@name='"
                                          + queryRootName + "']");

   if (rootDef != null)
      TraverseSchema(schema, rootDef, query, null, qform);
   else
      alert("ElementType named " + queryRootName + " not found.  Requires
         root element name.");
}
else
   alert("Name not set -- cannot determine root element");
```

The root element of the schema file is, of course, `<SCHEMA>`. In the informal convention we established, the `name` attribute should provide the name of the root element in our query vocabulary. If the `name` attribute is not found, our convention definitely isn't being observed, so we fail with an error message. If it is found, the line

```
queryRootName = nameNode.nodeValue;
```

will give us the name of the root node, which in this case will be EMPLOYEEQUERY. Now we use the parser to search for the `ElementType` element whose `name` attribute matches the name we just retrieved. Since each element type definition appears exactly once, we can use `selectSingleNode`. If the search turns up empty, the convention isn't being followed – the author of the schema provided a name that does not match an `ElementType` definition. However, if it returns a node, we can begin to descend through the schema parse tree.

To do this, we use the recursive `TraverseSchema()` function:

```
function TraverseSchema(schemaParser, schemaNode, docParser, docNode, qform)
{
    var currentNode;

    switch (schemaNode.nodeName)
    {
        case "ElementType":
            BuildQuery(schemaParser, docParser, schemaNode, docNode, qform);
            currentNode = BuildDoc(docParser, schemaNode, docNode);
            for (var nk = 0; nk < schemaNode.childNodes.length; nk++)
                TraverseSchema(schemaParser, schemaNode.childNodes(nk), docParser,
                               currentNode, qform);
            break;
        case "group":
            var orderType = schemaNode.attributes.getNamedItem("order");
            if (orderType == null || orderType.text == "many" ||
                    orderType.text == "seq")
            {
                for (var nj = 0; nj < schemaNode.childNodes.length; nj++)
                    TraverseSchema(schemaParser, schemaNode.childNodes.item(nj),
                                   docParser, docNode, qform);
            }

            break;
        case "attribute":
            break;
        case "datatype":
            break;
        case "description":
            BuildQuery(schemaParser, docParser, schemaNode, docNode, qform);
            break;
        case "element":
            var elementDef =
                schemaParser.documentElement.selectSingleNode(
                    "//ElementType[@name='" +
                    schemaNode.attributes.getNamedItem("type").nodeValue + "']");
            if (elementDef != null)
                TraverseSchema(schemaParser, elementDef, docParser, docNode, qform);
            break;
        case "AttributeType":
            nInputItemCount++;
            BuildQuery(schemaParser, docParser, schemaNode, null, qform);
            BuildDoc(docParser, schemaNode, docNode);
            break;
    }
}
```

The `switch` statement provides the appropriate processing for each type of schema element we will encounter (recall we're inside the one and only `Schema` element). `ElementType`, `group`, and `element` schema elements are the only elements that provide structural information. The `datatype`, `attribute`, and `AttributeType` elements may provide attribute and constraint information, but that is not of interest to us at the moment.

An `ElementType` element will either define `PCDATA` or will contain element content. For this reason, we call `TraverseSchema()` on each child element. The same is true of `group`. An `<element>` tag's type attribute refers to a corresponding `ElementType` element, so we need to do a search for that element to find its definition. The name we need to search for is specified in the current node's `type` attribute and will be found in the target's `name` attribute:

```
var elementDef =
            schemaParser.documentElement.selectSingleNode("//ElementType[@name='" +
            schemaNode.attributes.getNamedItem("type").nodeValue + "']");
```

If it is not found, there is a problem and we will be unable to go deeper into that particular subtree. Normally, however, we should find a match, in which case we submit it to `TraverseSchema()` to continue processing.

If you run this code in a debugger using our example schema, you will see that we properly traverse the schema. Of course, we haven't generated any output. The output we are looking for is an HTML form for eliciting user input, so let's add some code to `TraverseSchema()` to generate that form.

## User Interface Issues

Some items are going to require input from the user. Specifically, we will need inputs whenever an element can have text or mixed content, and when an attribute is defined other than the `datatype` namespace attributes, e.g., `dt:type`. We will make some simplifying assumptions to keep the example from becoming unwieldy. We will generate an input element in the page when we encounter text and mixed content elements. If we detect an enumeration datatype, we will create a single selection listbox and populate it with the individual items in the `dt:values` attribute.

There is another, critical simplifying assumption. Groups present no problem if the order is `seq`. If the order is `many`, we can present a form with all the grouped elements, i.e., as if the order had been `seq`. This will generate a document that obeys the schema, but we cannot generate all the combinations permitted under the `many` order attribute value. Similarly, `one` presents some difficulty. To resolve these situations, we would require some input from the user. We could obtain this with dialog boxes if we implemented the query builder as a Java applet or as an ActiveX control. For our purposes, it is enough to handle `seq` and `many` the same way and omit support for `one`.

We are also going to omit support for `AttributeType`. We could handle this in a manner similar to how we will handle `ElementType`, so we're going to leave this as an exercise for production. The `datatype` element will be supported to the extent of assigning the proper `dt:type` attribute to elements when the definition occurs in a `datatype` element. The other attributes could be used in a production system to support field level validation.

Now that we've decided what we won't do, let's decide how we're going to generate the user interface for our supported elements. We've built the essential navigational features in the preceding section. We will again traverse the schema in a top-down approach, but we will create the required user input form elements and the shell of an XML document that follows the schema as we go. The shell consists of the tags for the finished query document, but not the text values that the user will provide. The shell document then becomes our guide when it comes time to retrieve user inputs. We will traverse the shell document and fill each tag with a value from a similarly named HTML input element. Here's what the finished page looks like after generating a page for the `EMPLOYEEQUERY` schema:

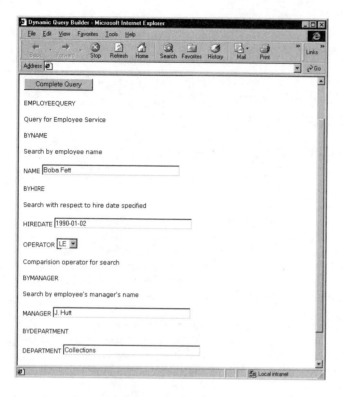

This isn't the nicest user interface page we've ever seen, but remember that it was built entirely without manual interference. The contents of this form derive entirely from the schema. If we provided the URL for a different XML schema, the form would change. Let's see how we got from simply traversing the schema document to generating an HTML form.

## Generating the User Interface

This necessitates some changes to the button handler for creating the form:

```
var nameNode = schema.documentElement.attributes.getNamedItem("name");
if (nameNode != null)
{
    queryRootName = nameNode.nodeValue;
    var rootDef = schema.documentElement.selectSingleNode("//ElementType[@name='" +
            queryRootName + "']");

    if (rootDef != null)
        TraverseSchema(schema, rootDef, query, null, qform);
    else
        alert("ElementType named " + queryRootName + " not found.  Requires root
            element name.");
}
else
        alert("Name not set -- cannot determine root element");
```

Notice that we have some new parameters in TraverseSchema. We pass in an instance of MSXML (in the schema variable) for use in building the shell document – query – and parameters for the current shell document node (null at the moment) as well as a <DIV> where we will be generating the user interface, qform. Now we turn our attention to TraverseSchema(). The actions on ElementType are typical. In addition to the schema traversal issues, we have issues related to creating HTML form elements and issues related to building the shell document. We handle these in the functions BuildQuery() and BuildDoc(), respectively.

```
case "ElementType":
        BuildQuery(schemaParser, docParser, schemaNode, docNode, qform);
        currentNode = BuildDoc(docParser, schemaNode, docNode);
        for (var nk = 0; nk < schemaNode.childNodes.length; nk++)
            TraverseSchema(schemaParser, schemaNode.childNodes(nk), docParser,
                            currentNode, qform);
        break;
```

`BuildQuery()` doesn't change anything in terms of the way we traverse the schema. `BuildDoc()`, however, is going to create new nodes in the shell document, so we will want to keep track of the current node in the shell document processing. This is handled with the `currentNode` variable. `BuildQuery()` takes both parsers, the current schema node, the current shell document node, and the `<DIV>` as parameters.

```
function BuildQuery(parserSchema, parserDoc, nodeSchema, nodeDoc, qform)
{
    var str, eltType, oEnums;

    switch (nodeSchema.nodeName)
    {
        case "ElementType":
            var eltName = nodeSchema.attributes.getNamedItem("name").nodeValue;
            qform.insertAdjacentHTML("beforeEnd", eltName);
            var contentType = nodeSchema.attributes.getNamedItem("content").text;
            switch (contentType)
            {
                case "empty":
                case "eltOnly":
                case "eltonly":
                    qform.insertAdjacentHTML("beforeEnd", "<p/>");
                    break;

                case "textOnly":
                case "textonly":
                case "mixed":
                    eltType = nodeSchema.attributes.getNamedItem("dt:type");
                    if (eltType != null && eltType.text == "enumeration")
                    {
                        oEnums = nodeSchema.attributes.getNamedItem("dt:values");
                        if (oEnums != null)
                            PopulateEnumeration(eltName + nInputItemCount, oEnums.text,
                                        qform);
                    }
                    else
                    {
                        str = " <input size='40' name ='" + eltName +
                                nInputItemCount + "'><p/>";
                        qform.insertAdjacentHTML("beforeEnd", str);
                    }
                    nInputItemCount++;
                    break;
            }
            break;

        case "description":
            qform.insertAdjacentHTML("beforeEnd", nodeSchema.text + "<p/>");
            break;
    }
}
```

In all cases, we are going to write out the name of the element as a label for the user:

```
var eltName = nodeSchema.attributes.getNamedItem("name").nodeValue;
qform.insertAdjacentHTML("beforeEnd", eltName);
var contentType = nodeSchema.attributes.getNamedItem("content").text;
```

If the element is empty or contains only element content, we simply write out a paragraph HTML element to provide some formatting. Things get interesting when we reach mixed and text content elements, however. We need to provide an input element and concern ourselves with whether this is a free or an enumerated value:

```
case "textOnly":
case "textonly":
case "mixed":
    eltType = nodeSchema.attributes.getNamedItem("dt:type");
    if (eltType != null && eltType.text == "enumeration")
    {
        oEnums = nodeSchema.attributes.getNamedItem("dt:values");
        if (oEnums != null)
            PopulateEnumeration(eltName + nInputItemCount, oEnums.text, qform);
    }
    else
    {
        str = " <input size='40' name ='" + eltName +
            nInputItemCount + "'><p/>";
        qform.insertAdjacentHTML("beforeEnd", str);
    }
    nInputItemCount++;
    break;
```

Note the global variable nInputItemCount. We need to generate unique identifiers for all the form elements we generate. We'll need to recreate these when we go back and pick up the user's inputs, so we've come up with the following rule:

> **A form element's name is the name of the element with the value of nInputItemCount appended.**

As long as we increment this variable when traversing the shell in the same order as when we traversed the schema, we'll be able to retrieve the values of the form elements we generate. Here's how PopulateEnumeration() works:

```
function PopulateEnumeration(sName, sVals, qform)
{
    var nStart, nFinish, nValsLength, sOptVal;

    // Write out the start of the list box
    str = " <select type='select-one' id='" + sName + "'>";

    if (sVals != null)
```

```
    {
        nValsLength = sVals.length;
        nStart = 0;
        nFinish = sVals.indexOf(" ");

        while (nStart < nValsLength && nFinish != -1)
        {
            sOptVal = sVals.substring(nStart, nFinish);
            str += "<OPTION value='" + sOptVal + "'>" + sOptVal + "</OPTION>";
            nStart = nFinish + 1;
            nFinish = sVals.indexOf(" ", nStart);
        }
        if (nStart < nValsLength)
        {
            sOptVal = sVals.substring(nStart, nValsLength);
            str += "<OPTION value='" + sOptVal + "'>" + sOptVal + "</OPTION>";
        }
    }
    str += "</SELECT><p/>";
    qform.insertAdjacentHTML("beforeEnd", str);
}
```

We always generate a single selection listbox – `type="select-one"`. Parsing the enumeration values creates the `<OPTION>` elements. We know these are delimited by spaces, so the parsing can be accomplished with the JavaScript `String.indexOf()` and `String.substring()` methods.

That takes care of handling the form building side of `ElementType` schema nodes. `TraverseSchema()` also takes care of building the shell document:

```
currentNode = BuildDoc(docParser, schemaNode, docNode);
```

`BuildDoc()` looks like this:

```
function BuildDoc(docParser, schNode, docNode)
{
    var newNode;

    switch (schNode.nodeName)
    {
        case "ElementType":
            var eltName = schNode.attributes.getNamedItem("name").nodeValue;
            newNode = docParser.createElement(eltName);
            if (docNode == null)
                docParser.documentElement = newNode;
            else
                docNode.appendChild(newNode);

            var contentType = schNode.attributes.getNamedItem("content").text;
            if (contentType == "mixed" || contentType == "textonly" ||
                contentType == "textOnly")
            {
                newNode.appendChild(docParser.createTextNode(""));
            }

            var eltType = schNode.attributes.getNamedItem("dt:type");
            if (eltType != null)
```

```
            {
                var newAttr = docParser.createAttribute("dt:type");
                newAttr.nodeValue = eltType.nodeValue;
                newNode.attributes.setNamedItem(newAttr);
            }
            break;

        case "AttributeType":
            break;
    }

    return newNode;
}
```

Whenever we encounter an `ElementType` node in the schema, we want to create an element in the shell document that takes its `name` from the name attribute of the `ElementType` element in the schema. If the current document node is `null`, we have an empty document. In that case, the newly created document is the `documentElement` in the DOM tree. Otherwise, the new node is appended as a child of the current node.

It is important to insert a placeholder for the user's inputs while we are generating the shell document. If we waited until later, the new `PCDATA` elements would continually change the number of child nodes which the mixed content nodes have. Also, if we insert the placeholder in its parent tag now, we can use this as a guide when it comes time to retrieve the user's inputs. Since both mixed content and text nodes require PCDATA at some point, we create a text node and append it to the current node without changing the current node:

```
newNode.appendChild(docParser.createTextNode(""));
```

While processing an `ElementType` schema element, we may also encounter a `dt:type` attribute. We want to add this to our shell document element to facilitate typed processing by the service that receives the query we are building.

```
var eltType = schNode.attributes.getNamedItem("dt:type");
if (eltType != null)
{
    var newAttr = docParser.createAttribute("dt:type");
    newAttr.nodeValue = eltType.nodeValue;
    newNode.attributes.setNamedItem(newAttr);
}
```

That's the entire picture for `TraverseSchema()` and `ElementType` schema elements. There is one other small change to `TraverseSchema()` from the simple traversal case, and that is our support for description elements. Our labels are the element names. We hope that the schema author chose descriptive names, but we will provide one more bit of assistance to our users. By writing out the contents of the description element, the user will have a bit of text to help her try and figure out what the schema element means:

```
case "description":
    BuildQuery(schemaParser, docParser, schemaNode, docNode, qform);
    break;
```

In `BuildQuery()` we saw these lines:

```
case "description":
    qform.insertAdjacentHTML("beforeEnd", nodeSchema.text + "<p/>");
    break;
```

Simply put, `BuildQuery()` retrieves the text the schema author entered and places it on a line of its own.

## Generating a Query in the Vocabulary

After our user has clicked on the **Create Form** button, he has a user interface for providing element values, and we have a shell query document. When the user clicks the **Complete Query** button, we want to complete the shell document with PCDATA values we retrieve from the user interface. Our button handler simply resets the `nInputItemCount` variable and calls a document traversal function. After traversing the document, it displays the finished XML document in an alert box.

```
function OnComplete()
{
    var root = query.documentElement;
    nInputItemCount = 0;

    // Depends on having built a shell query document via the form builder
    if (root != null)
    {
        // Recurse through the tree populating inputs, then display XML
        TraverseForm(root);
        alert(query.xml);
    }
    else
        alert("You must have built a form prior to selecting this option.");
}
```

The traversal function has but two functions to perform. First, when a text element is encountered in the shell, it must go out to the user interface and retrieve the value of the corresponding HTML form element. Next, regardless of the node type encountered, it must keep the recursion going to complete the document traversal, which it does by calling itself with each child node of the current node.

```
function TraverseForm(node)
{
    switch (node.nodeType)
    {
        case PCDATA:
            var str = node.parentNode.nodeName + nInputItemCount++;
            node.nodeValue = document.all(str).value;
            break;
    }
    for (var ni = 0; ni < node.childNodes.length; ni++)
        TraverseForm(node.childNodes(ni));
}
```

We can verify that this works by running the query builder against the schema found in employeequery.xml and providing the form inputs seen in the user interface illustration:

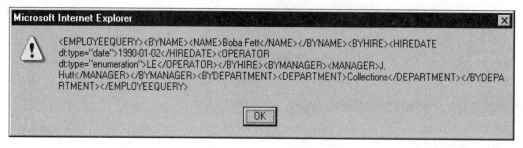

It isn't pretty, but it's all there.

## Further Work

This proof of concept clearly omits some features that are mandatory for a production system. AttributeType schema elements must be supported, and all the attributes of datatype elements need to be handled. Some sort of mechanism for handling the order attribute of group elements should be provided. Ideally this would come in two forms: a dialog-based mechanism for interaction with human users and a programmatic approach for software clients. Better formatting of form elements would be nice. It would be useful to have some mechanism for showing human users a comparison of the known (e.g., EMPLOYEE) schema for the desired service and the unknown (e.g., EMPLOYEEQUERY) schema in order to assist them in determining what to input into the various form elements.

Some of these items will be influenced by the specific nature of the client application. Others will stem from the syntax of whatever metadata proposal reaches W3C Recommendation status. An appreciation of the issues of traversing an XML schema and mapping it into something useful to a user without manual intervention is what is important at this stage in the evolution of XML metadata.

# What We Should Do Now

Metadata clearly has great potential for cooperative applications roaming a wide and loosely knit network. Metadata does the following for XML and its use in implementing our principles:

- ❑ It makes service data self-descriptive in a rich way
- ❑ It explains extensions to data by clarifying and describing what is in the extensions
- ❑ It helps our services support degradation by identifying overlapping and generalized elements

Of course, as has been noted, all the proposals, save namespaces and RDF, we saw and worked with in this chapter are still W3C Notes, not finished recommendations. For this reason, we shouldn't be too quick to adopt metadata techniques into our toolkit. As we finish this chapter, it is appropriate to reflect on what we know, where metadata is going, and what we should do now to prepare our applications for its eventual inclusion. After all, our fifth principle said in part that services should support extension. Metadata not only supports this, it will *be* an extension of what we can do now! Here are the things we should be doing:

- ❑ Encourage vocabulary authors to develop and document formal metadata for their work
- ❑ Consider how you might use metadata in your organization
- ❑ Keep abreast of metadata developmens at the W3C and software vendors

First, you should encourage vocabulary authors in your organization to develop and document formal metadata for their work. This can be in DTD or other schema form, but the important thing is to capture this knowledge while it is still explicit. Additionally, the effort will force authors to think through the ramifications of their vocabularies. This will result in better, more descriptive vocabularies. When a metadata recommendation is available, the documentation in hand can be translated into models according to the published recommendation. In the meantime, DTDs or XML syntax schemas can be used during development to validate test documents. Failing to do this may result in unintended changes to the vocabulary that will have to be supported as legacy features.

Next consider how you might use metadata in your organization. A closed intranet will have less need for metadata than an application based on an extranet or the public Internet. At most, a query building capability will be needed. Vocabulary discovery is less likely to be required; you should be able to obtain metadata information internally for important service vocabularies. Developers of applications and components that will work in a wider environment will want to consider their metadata discovery needs. A component builder will want to consider searching for useful information in unknown vocabularies. An extranet application might need to learn the structure of specialized vocabularies or search for overlap by examining the structure and content of element and attribute definitions.

Finally, architects of network applications and systems should keep abreast of developments in the W3C Metadata Activity and XML parser vendors. You will want to know the syntax and capabilities of whichever metadata model shapes the final recommendation (or recommendations; there is no guarantee the W3C won't support several in order to address various needs, and vendors may pick and choose what they will implement). You will also want to be ready with a parser or metadata tool that supports the final recommendation.

> *The reader is reminded to check http://www.w3.org/TR/ frequently to obtain the latest status of W3C efforts.*

# Summary

In this chapter we completed our examination of XML as a data transmission format by taking up the topic of XML metadata. We defined metadata as "data about data". We considered the current state of metadata by considering XML Namespaces, a working draft tangentially related to metadata proper. We looked at the future of metadata in the Web development world by examining the major submissions before the W3C Metadata Activity. These are:

- ❑ Resource Description Format (RDF)
- ❑ Meta Content Format (MCF)
- ❑ XML Data
- ❑ XML Document Content Description (DCD)

We then considered some future uses for metadata in the context of our development philosophy. Having done so, we demonstrated a prototype query builder. To do this we had to learn the syntax supported in Microsoft's XML Schema technology preview.

Metadata offers enormous power and flexibility that will help make networked applications more cooperative and robust in the face of unexpected data formats. It is a natural continuation of our use of tagged data – XML – for capturing our service data.

**6**

# Platform Services Combining the Old and the New

We've taken a purist approach to our development philosophy up to this point. We're using component software on each platform and passing XML vocabularies between the platforms. These platforms are a combination of computers and operating system software. While our examples have all used Microsoft Windows, our third principle – the use of XML to exchange service data – ensures our ability to communicate between dissimilar platforms. Any platform-specific services have been applied in accordance with our five principles. We've used the platform to support the future.

Frequently, however, practicing programmers are forced to compromise and adjust their futuristic approach to the requirements of legacy applications or platform services. This need not be a bad thing. In this chapter, we are going to look at the current state of the Windows platform and see how we can compromise with it. Specifically, when the platform currently provides a useful and widely known technique for performing some task, we shall question whether we should relax our principles to gain organizational acceptance? If so, in what way, and by how much?

We will focus on two avenues of development:

- ❑ Relational database access
- ❑ System utilities for transmitting data using HTTP

## Relational Database Access

Admittedly, we will be using state of the art platform features. Nevertheless, relational data technology is a longstanding, firmly entrenched programming approach. We can expect to find many programmers and managers who understand relational approaches, and legacy applications that are designed primarily to view relational data. By looking at ways of bending our XML exchange to the relational format will make our philosophy more palatable to many decision-makers.

### Transferring Data via HTTP

HTTP is our normal means of transmitting data between servers and clients for the many reasons we have discussed. In this case, we're going to use existing utilities and platform support to make our transmission more effective. In particular, we're going to revisit the HTTP POST problem we first discussed in Chapter 3 and arrive at a better solution.

We will deal with a variety of platform-specific techniques and tie up outstanding loose ends from earlier chapters. You will learn the following in the course of this chapter:

- ❏ Microsoft's architecture for data access on the Windows platform
- ❏ How to directly link XML elements to DHTML user interface elements
- ❏ An ASP technique for performing HTTP POST operations involving XML documents
- ❏ Two component-based techniques for POSTing XML documents

# The Merits of Compromise

We have gone to great lengths to articulate The 5 Principles of Cooperative Network Application Development in this book. The creation of these foundations for our development strategy has been inspired by forward-looking systems and uses several cutting edge technologies. So why would we suddenly want to compromise and expose data in the vernacular of standard operating system services? After you have spent time writing software for anyone other than yourself, you come to the humbling realization that software development does not take place in a pristine world of the future. Projects usually have a specific set of goals to meet and a budget of time and money in which to do it. Our principles are intended to help meet these goals and should not work at cross-purposes to them. The truth is, however, that programming techniques are not always chosen on their technical merits. An organization has an investment in staff skills, project experience, and legacy software. This will tend to reflect the system services of the organization's computing platform.

Compromising to the extent of using familiar system services may help sell your approach to those in a position to influence the project. It will certainly help protect your strategic decision to use key principles of the philosophy for the core of a proposed system. Staff and managers may be more willing to accept component software and XML-encoded data for the underpinnings of a system or application if they are able to work with familiar techniques at the margins.

One of the most familiar technologies is relational data access. Almost every system uses a database at some point. As a consequence, staff programmers will be familiar with the state of the art for relational data access on their platform. Their managers will also understand and appreciate the need for database technology. So while we have gone to some lengths to hide the particulars of data storage within the modules residing on the server, exposing our returned data through relational mechanisms will be beneficial. The access mechanisms will be familiar to programmers not grounded in our 5 principles. They will be able to do useful programming employing existing techniques while also getting to grips with the approaches we are advocating.

The use of platform services is not solely about selling stodgy managers on new technology or working with existing staff resources, however. Any popular computing platform provides numerous utilities to increase programming productivity. Many of the problems we encounter in the course of implementing new systems do not require new approaches, but are instead mundane little problems best solved with existing utilities. Instead of automatically building a new tool, the wise programmer knows when to reach for the familiar.

This juxtaposition of the new and the old is what this chapter is about. Finding a balance comes only from experience. Having relied so fully on the new in the preceding chapters, we now take time out to see what has been going on in Windows while we were out trying to build our brave new world.

# Microsoft Data Access Components

Not so long ago, programmers had to resort to vendor-specific libraries when they wanted access to databases. ODBC brought a high degree of abstraction to relational data access for Windows programmers. Given the importance of COM to the Windows operating system, it is not surprising that Microsoft would offer a set of COM interfaces to supercede ODBC. Rather than simply putting a component wrapper around relational data access, a new layer of abstraction was introduced. The goal of these interfaces is to provide a single approach to accessing any body of persistent data that can be expressed as tables of rows and columns. Comma-delimited text, XML, Excel spreadsheets, and relational databases can all be expressed in this way. This family of interfaces, appropriately named the **Microsoft Data Access Components** (MDAC), provides robust data access services to COM-aware applications. MDAC is sometimes known in marketing literature as Universal Data Access (UDA).

Although comparatively new, MDAC are the designated successor to ODBC. Although MDAC provides a driver for ODBC sources, database vendors are beginning to provide native COM drivers in order to support MDAC. If you do database programming on Windows, you have probably heard of ADO. ActiveX Data Objects (ADO) provide the client side of MDAC. Data binding, long a feature of the Microsoft Foundation Classes and lately a feature of Microsoft's implementation of DHTML, is a popular technique now built on top of MDAC.

You may be using MDAC without realizing it. MDAC, then, is inexorably becoming the Windows standard for data access. For this reason, any use we can make of MDAC will soon be considered a mainstream approach.

# The Big Picture

MDAC specifies a family of interfaces that allow different types of components to cooperate in the process of accessing structured data. These components are classified according to where they fit in the overall MDAC scheme. At the lowest level are **data source objects** (DSO). These are analogous to ODBC drivers. They provide a low-level COM interface to the underlying, proprietary store of data. The highest level of MDAC consists of **data consumers**. These are components that require data. For example, they may be complicated components or DHTML elements that we desire to bind to a DSO. If a single source of data meets the needs of a consumer, it is entirely appropriate for that component to work directly with the DSO offering access to that data store rather than through an intermediary.

The picture becomes more interesting when we need to combine sources or perform some post-processing on the data. In short, we require some **data service** to be performed by some component on behalf of the consumer. Like a three-tier architecture, the consumer communicates with the service and the service, in turn, communicates with the data source. In fact, a service may use the interfaces of several DSOs to obtain the data it needs in order to provide its service.

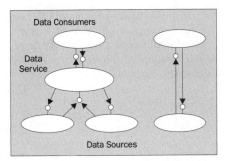

201

Whether they work through services or directly with a DSO, consumers receive data in the form of **rowsets**. The client components that support rowsets are known as **recordsets** for historical reasons. These are abstract collections of uniformly structured **rows** of data. Each row is composed of **columns**, each of which corresponds to some property stored by the DSO. This is directly applicable to relational data, because relational databases store columns of data. When a query is issued, the collection of data matching the query is returned as rows of data, each of which has the same columns. Other forms of data can also easily be represented by rowsets. Spreadsheets already use a row and column metaphor. Delimited text also fits this model, with each line comprising a row and each delimited value a column. Hierarchical stores like XML documents, however, are a harder fit. They can only be made to fit the rowset scheme if each column is permitted to take on multiple values. In such a case, the top-level child elements of the document root are the rows and their child elements are the columns. If there is structure below this level, the child elements are the multiple values of the columns. Multiple values are handled through collection objects.

# Data Sources

As we noted, DSOs represent a single type of data store. They expose interfaces permitting consumers and services to query the source's capabilities and contents. For example, an application may wish to inquire whether it can obtain dynamic access to the source or whether it will receive a static rowset capturing the state of the store at the time the rowset was created. The DSO, in turn, enforces security for the data store.

DSOs also provide functionality that will be familiar to relational database programmers. Consumers establish a session with a DSO and execute commands against it. Although these commands are typically SQL, MDAC makes no assumptions about the syntax of commands. In fact, one of the interfaces defined for MDAC permits the creation of different sorts of command interpreters to support different stores and application domains. In the past, users had to adapt their native queries to SQL in order to access relational stores. With MDAC, we can access a DSO for a specialized domain with a command language oriented to that domain by creating the appropriate command-interpreting component.We might want to use LDAP commands with a DSO for a directory, for example.

# Service Providers

Service providers combine the features offered by one or more DSOs with their own features to provide rich functionality to data consumers. Relational databases aren't always the most effective store for certain kinds of data. For example, frequent samples of data over time can be more efficiently retrieved by stores that are not relational. If our system includes such time series data as well as relational data, we might use a service component to combine the relational and time series DSOs into one artificial service to consumers.

Of specific importance to Web page developers are service providers, that can be an effective intermediary, mapping DSO rowsets to the elements on a page. Bits of data from a single rowset may be repeated in different places on the page. Changes to the rowset must be reflected in the consumers on the page. Mapping, repetition, and synchronization are important data services we shall use later in this chapter.

# Remote Data Service

One very important service for Web developers is the **Remote Data Service** (**RDS**). Although all client-server data access is inherently remote, Web applications give new meaning to the term 'remote'. HTTP is inherently stateless, yet data access requires stateful information – the status of the rowset, the access permissions of the session, and so forth. Just as ASP (and other, similar, implementations of server-side HTTP applications) have to build an elaborate framework for maintaining state across stateless page requests, RDS must also provide a mechanism for synchronizing state between the browser and the server.

Network administrators put great effort into the integrity of their firewalls. These measures typically preclude access to server resources over ports other than that used for HTTP. This normally blocks database access using traditional client-server libraries. RDS offers an efficient means of establishing access and transmitting the requested data over HTTP.

We should also note that, traditional client-server access occurs over a local area network in whic data is typically transmitted at high data rates. Access over the Internet is much slower, and Web servers may act as gateways to greater numbers of clients. So we need to minimize roundtrips to the server. RDS uses proxies on the client and the server to maintain a data cache on the client and keep it synchronized with the DSO on the server. The services layer of MDAC proves to be an essential aspect of offering rowset data over the Internet. Without RDS, we could not offer dynamic access to rowsets in an efficient manner.

> *For more information on RDS, check out* Professional ADO RDS Programming with ASP *from Wrox Press, ISBN 1-86001-64-9*

# Data Binding

One of the prime uses of rowset-structured data is to provide a visual representation of the data to users. As the user navigates through the rowset using some sequence of operations, the visual representation reflects the position of the recordset cursor. Even when a visual interface is not required, we want the rowset to faithfully reflect the state of the data in the underlying native store. This is accomplished through data binding. Data binding provides a data service interposed between data source objects and data consumers. This service is one of synchronization. Data binding is provided by MSHTML.DLL, which is a library providing two components known as the **binding** and **repetition** agents.

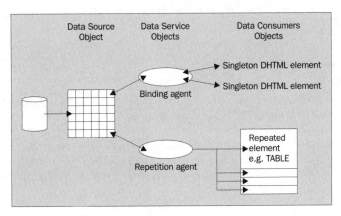

A page designer embeds one or more DSOs in an HTML page, then links them to DHTML page elements by adding `dataSrc` and `dataFld` attributes. The `dataSrc` attribute value is the name of the DSO with the prefix #. The `dataFld` attribute specifies which column of the rowset provided by the DSO should be bound to the page element. Here's an example of displaying the `Name` column of a rowset by binding an HTML `INPUT` element to a DSO called `myQuery`:

```
<INPUT dataSrc="#myQuery" dataFld="Name"...>
```

In this case, the binding agent uses the data source interfaces of the DSO to obtain the data it pushes to the `INPUT` element. As scripts manipulate the DSO, the binding agent keeps the `INPUT` element (and any other elements bound to the same source) synchronized with the data. Reissuing the SQL query that builds it refreshes the DSO rowset; the bound elements automatically reflect the change.

The repetition agent makes life easier for page designers. When we wish to present multiple rows, we can embed a `TABLE` element in the page and bind it to a data source. In particular, we provide a single table row (`<TR>`), providing the template for displaying each row of the recordset. Each cell in the table is bound to a particular column. The repetition agent takes care of repeating the table rows as many times as needed to display all the rows in the rowset. For example, suppose we want to display the results of a SQL query in an HTML table. Each row of the result set – and consequently the table – contains the columns `FirstName`, `LastName`, and `SSN`. Assuming the data source is named `peopleSource`, the appropriate data bound HTML is:

```
<TABLE dataSrc="#peopleSource">
    <TR>
        <TD><SPAN dataFld="FirstName"></SPAN></TD>
        <TD><SPAN dataFld="LastName"></SPAN></TD>
        <TD><SPAN dataFld="SSN"></SPAN></TD>
    </TR>
</TABLE>
```

Note that while you've provided only a single row, the table displayed to the user will have as many rows as there are rows in the query result set returned from the database, courtesy of the repetition agent.

The binding service provider components offer page designers the means by which to quickly and efficiently link data sources to data consumers. The complicated details of data synchronization with visual elements are hidden from us. This is one way in which the Windows platform offers a useful standard implementation of an MDAC service. In doing so, the promise of MDAC is realized for HTML designers by offering a common method for using disparate data stores. We shall make extensive use of this service through the XML data source object.

# XML DSO

One of the tenets of Uniform Data Access is the ability to provide access to data without respect to their underlying native storage format. The XML Data Source Object is a prime demonstration of this. The XML DSO was a Java applet in the earliest implementation of XML support in Windows. In the latest version, the DSO is a COM object closely integrated with Internet Explorer. The DSO exposes XML encoded text not only as data rowsets, but also as XML DOM parse trees. The choice of which to pick is ours; we are able to use whichever model best suits our programming needs.

## What the DSO Does

The DSO can be exposed to the programmer through XML data islands. Like some DHTML elements, data islands either have their content specified in place or referred to through a link to outside content. When a data island is loaded with a page, Internet Explorer transparently loads the data into a parse tree and offers several COM interfaces for our use. The standard DSO interfaces allow XML elements to participate in data binding as if the data were coming from a database. In addition, the familiar XML DOM interfaces are available as well. This is not surprising, as MSXML is the component that implements the XML DSO. The DSO parses the XML content and keeps bound elements synchronized with the content. As the user navigates through the rowset, the DSO will navigate through the parse tree, exposing each top-level child in turn as a 'row' of data. When the content is replaced, either through rewriting the internal structure of the data island or through refreshing the content pointed to through a link, the DSO keeps bound elements synchronized with the new content. The effect is the same as if a DSO providing access to a relational database had reissued a SQL query and obtained a new recordset.

## Using the DSO

We can embed an XML data island in a page by adding an `<XML>` tag and giving a name, like so:

```
<XML id="XMLdata"></XML>
```

Now we have a data island we can refer to through the name `XMLdata`. As it stands, this data island isn't particularly interesting, however we can give it content in one of two ways. The first and simplest is to simply place the XML content within the boundaries of the XML tag:

```
<XML id="XMLdata">
   <SomeXMLData>
      <Item>
         <Content>Some content for item 1</Content>
      </Item>
      <Item>
         <Content>Content for item 2></Content>
      </Item>
   </SomeXMLData>
</XML>
```

The top-level tag `<SomeXMLData>` is analogous to the recordset. It contains, in this example, two 'rows' named `Item` which contain one column each, named `Content`. Directly listing XML content in a data island is a simple yet effective approach for small quantities of data.

The other technique is to specify a source for the content through the `src` attribute. This greatly simplifies the data island and allows us to provide content through an external source such as an ASP script. For example:

```
<XML id="XMLdata" src="XMLGenerator.asp"></XML>
```

Here, the page written by some hypothetical ASP named `XMLGenerator.asp` becomes the contents of the data island. This is particularly useful to us, since our services are ASPs that write XML documents back to their clients. Consequently, we can bind to our services.

You may be wondering; "How do we access the dual nature of a data island?" The MDAC aspect is exposed through a `recordset` property. All the properties and methods of an ADO recordset are accessible through the data island's `recordset` property. In our example, we would move the internal cursor of the DSO to the next row of the recordset with the code fragment

```
XMLdata.recordset.moveNext()
```

The data island is also an XML DOM document exposing a `documentElement` property. We could find out how many top-level child nodes are in the data island through this simple code fragment:

```
XMLdata.documentElement.childNodes.length
```

Once again, all the properties and methods to which we have become accustomed in this book are accessible through the data island's `documentElement` property.

## Collection Binding Example

Let's apply the XML DSO. Assume we have an XML data island and we want to display it one row at a time. We'll borrow our `Customer` vocabulary from Chapter 3:

```
<Collection>
    <Customer>
        <LongName>Horace Greeley</LongName>
        <Address>123 Home Lane Greeley, CO</Address>
        <Phone>123-555-5555</Phone>
    </Customer>
    <Customer>
        <LongName>Grover Cleveland</LongName>
        . . .
</Collection>
```

This structure certainly fits well with the rows and columns model of MDAC. The `Collection` document is analogous to the entire table subset returned by a query. Each `Customer` element represents a row in the cursor, while `LongName`, `Address`, and `Phone` are the columns.

We'll bind this data to a page designed to display the data one customer at a time. We'll use ordinary HTML form elements placed in an HTML table for formatting. More importantly, we'll provide buttons allowing the user to move back and forth at will through the data.

Here's what the page will look like:

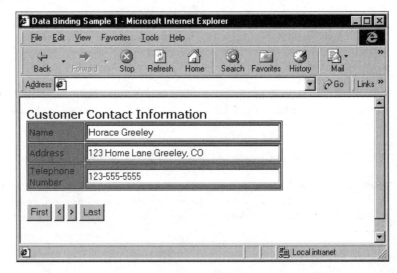

## Basic XML Data Binding

The `Customer` vocabulary fits neatly into the flat, rows and columns view of database tables. First we need to get the XML from a file into a data island. As we saw before, this is how it is done:

```
<XML id="xmlData" src = "Customers.xml"></XML>
```

The island is `xmlData` and the source of the data is the file `Customers.xml`. When the page loads, Internet Explorer will read the data from this file into an instance of the XML DSO. When the page is loaded, we'll have a complete XML parse tree and an ADO recordset built on it. Now that we have the data, we need to bind it to the HTML `INPUT` elements. We can do this with design time binding. We specify `dataFld` and `dataSrc` attributes for the `INPUT` elements like so:

```
<TABLE border="1" borderColor="maroon" cellPadding="1" cellSpacing="1"
width="75%">
  <TR bgColor="#999999">
    <TD><FONT color="maroon" size="2">Name</FONT></TD>
    <TD>
      <INPUT dataFld="LongName" dataSrc="#xmlData" style="HEIGHT: 22px; WIDTH:
                286px">
    </TD>
  </TR>
  <TR bgColor="#999999">
    <TD><FONT color="maroon" size="2">Address</FONT></TD>
    <TD>
      <INPUT dataFld="Address" dataSrc="#xmlData"
            style="HEIGHT: 22px; WIDTH: 286px">
    </TD>
  </TR>
  <TR bgColor="#999999">
    <TD><FONT color="darkred" size="2">Telephone Number</FONT></TD>
    <TD>
      <INPUT dataFld="Phone" dataSrc="#xmlData" style="HEIGHT: 22px; WIDTH:
                286px">
    </TD>
  </TR>
</TABLE>
```

That's all we need to bind our data to the user interface elements. Of course, when the page loads, we'll be looking at the first `Customer` element from our XML file. So we need to give the user some way to move through the data. Recall that the DSO provides both an XML parse tree and an ADO recordset. We'll use the latter to manipulate our XML just as if it came from a database. Here is the HTML for the buttons at the bottom of our page:

```
<INPUT id="button1" name="button1" onclick="xmlData.recordset.moveFirst()"
                type="button" value="First">
<INPUT id="button2" name="button2" type="button" value="&lt;" onClick="if
                            (xmlData.recordset.absoluteposition > 1)
                                xmlData.recordset.movePrevious()">
<INPUT id="button3" name="button3" type="button" value="&gt;" onClick="if
                        (xmlData.recordset.absoluteposition <
                                xmlData.recordset.recordcount)
                                xmlData.recordset.moveNext()">
<INPUT id="button4" name="button4" type="button" value="Last"
                    onClick="xmlData.recordset.moveLast()">
```

The key is the in the inline JavaScript fragments we provide to handle the `onClick` event. Take the handler for moving ahead one row:

```
if (xmlData.recordset.absoluteposition < xmlData.recordset.recordcount)
                              xmlData.recordset.moveNext()
```

Note that the data island has an ADO recordset object as a child. The `absoluteposition` property tells us what row the cursor is on. In this handler, if the cursor isn't on the last row of the recordset, we tell it to advance to the next row. When this happens, the DSO keeps the `INPUT` elements synchronized with the recordset, and the user sees the values for the next `Customer` element. That's it. We don't need parse tree manipulation scripts like those to which we've become accustomed.

## Hierarchical XML Data Binding

Of course, not every vocabulary fits so neatly into a flat, rows-and-columns view. XML is inherently hierarchical. This is particularly apparent when we deal with a derived vocabulary. Recall that we went on to develop the `Svc_customer` vocabulary from `Customer` in order to model the additional customer data maintained by the customer service department:

```
<Collection>
   <Svc_Customer>
      <Customer>
         <LongName>Horace Greeley</LongName>
         <Address>123 Home Lane Greeley, CO</Address>
         <Phone>123-555-5555</Phone>
      </Customer>
      <Svc_Plan>Gold-Plated</Svc_Plan>
      <Purchase_List>
         <Product>Master Widget</Product>
      </Purchase_List>
   </Svc_Customer>
   <Svc_Customer>
      <Customer>
         <LongName>Grover Cleveland</LongName>
   . . .
</Collection>
```

Now, our rows correspond to the `Svc_Customer` elements, and `Customer` elements are the columns. Unfortunately, `Customer` elements contain child elements. Suppose we want to continue using the user interface from the previous example. This might be the case when someone in another department wishes to view data maintained by the customer service department. Since they are unfamiliar with the `Svc_Customer` vocabulary, the additional elements are meaningless to them. To put this in the context of our 5 principles, they queried the directory for a server offering the `Customer` vocabulary. A server in the customer service department offers that as a secondary vocabulary: `Scv_Customer`. Our application therefore needs to be able to dive into each `Svc_Customer` element and extract the `Customer` data within.

Fortunately, the XML DSO is able to handle hierarchical structure. The technique is to bind the enclosing table to the `Customer` column within each row through its `dataFld` attribute, then bind the `INPUT` elements contained within the table to the child elements. We've done this in `SvcCustDataBindDSO.html`:

```
<TABLE border="1" borderColor="maroon" cellPadding="1" cellSpacing="1" width="75%"
         dataFld="Customer" datasrc="#xmlData">
   <TR bgColor="#999999">
     <TD><FONT color="maroon" size="2">Name</FONT></TD>
     <TD>
       <INPUT dataFld="LongName" dataSrc="#xmlData" style="HEIGHT: 22px; WIDTH:
             286px">
     </TD>
   </TR>
   <TR bgColor="#999999">
     <TD><FONT color="maroon" size="2">Address</FONT></TD>
     <TD>
       <INPUT dataFld="Address" dataSrc="#xmlData" style="HEIGHT: 22px; WIDTH:
             286px">
     </TD>
   </TR>
   <TR bgColor="#999999">
     <TD><FONT color="darkred" size="2">Telephone Number</FONT></TD>
     <TD>
       <INPUT dataFld="Phone" dataSrc="#xmlData" style="HEIGHT: 22px; WIDTH:
             286px">
     </TD>
   </TR>
</TABLE>
```

Another method is to specify the child elements using a qualified dot notation:

```
<INPUT dataFld="Customer.Phone" dataSrc="#xmlData" style="HEIGHT: 22px; WIDTH:
             286px">
```

## Data Binding and the XML Parse Tree

Of course, the preceding approach to hierarchical binding only works if you know the vocabulary's DTD (or schema) and therefore can anticipate the structure of the data rows to which you are binding. In an evolving network that probably won't always be the case, as in the example we set forth in the preceding section in which we bound to a document from the Svc_Customer vocabulary to provide additional detail. If you are getting XML from a server application whose primary format isn't the vocabulary you requested, you may not be familiar with the vocabulary you receive. By combining two of the techniques we have already met, however, we can overcome this hurdle. First, the DSO exposes the XML DOM parse tree. We are familiar with navigating this structure. Second, we addressed the problem of inheritance in Chapter 4. We can use DataSplicer on the unknown vocabulary, extract a collection of elements in the vocabulary we understand, and insert that into the data island. The steps we need to follow are these:

❑ Load the XML document in the unknown vocabulary into an instance of MSXML

❑ Use DataSplicer to obtain a collection of elements in the desired vocabulary

❑ Use the DOM parse tree of a placeholder data island to insert the nodes from the collection just obtained

❑ Use the recordset exposed by the data island to move through the data

Here's the first step as implemented in the file SvcCustDataBindXML.html to load the XML document using an unknown vocabulary into an instance of MSXML:

```
var xmlDoc = new ActiveXObject("microsoft.xmlDOM");
xmlDoc.async = false;
xmlDoc.load("svc_customer.xml");
```

Those lines could have been taken directly from Chapter 3. Next, we resort to `DataSplicer`, which we've embedded elsewhere on the page under the identifier `splicer`:

```
var rChildren = splicer.ExtractAll(xmlDoc, "Customer",
                                         xmlDoc.documentElement);
```

The parameters, as you may recall, are the MSXML instance (`xmlDoc`), the name of the vocabulary to extract (`Customer`), and the root of the subtree to search, which in this case is the entire document parse tree (`xmlDoc.documentElement`). The return value, `rChildren`, is a `Collection` element containing one or more `Customer` elements which make up the vocabulary.

You might be tempted to write the following line for the next step:

```
xmlData.documentElement = rChildren;
```

In this case, our data island is named `xmlData`. If you wrote that line, you'd run foul of one of the little quirks of the DSO. If the XML data island is empty, no recordset is created – after all, the 'database query' returned no data. Also, for the same reason, there isn't a `documentElement`. In that case, the data binding would fail and we'd never see anything in our table. To avoid this, our page contains the following shell data island:

```
<XML id="xmlData">
    <Collection>
        <Customer>
            <LongName>A</LongName>
            <Address>A</Address>
            <Phone>A</Phone>
        </Customer>
    </Collection>
</XML>
```

Consequently, we have a `documentElement`: `<Collection>`. The DSO doesn't appreciate having the contents of the recordset yanked out from under it while it is trying to bind, so swapping the existing `documentElement` with `rChildren` will cause the binding to fail. We can, however, add each node to the parse tree in turn. Of course, that would leave us with the placeholder `Customer` element. We can remove it, but we must wait until we've added some more nodes so that we don't empty the recordset data. That would – you guessed it – cause the data binding to fail. Here's how the code should be written:

```
if (rChildren != null)
{
    for (var ni = 0; ni < rChildren.childNodes.length; ni++)
        xmlData.documentElement.appendChild(
                                    rChildren.childNodes(ni).cloneNode(true));
    xmlData.documentElement.removeChild(xmlData.documentElement.childNodes(0));
    xmlData.recordset.moveFirst();
}
```

Remember that we've already removed all the old nodes but one so that the DSO has something to hold on to. The `for` loop adds all the new nodes to which we want to bind. Once they are in place, there is no longer a need for the node left over from the old data. We left it in the first position of the `childNodes` collection, so the call to `removeChild()` specifying the very first child node removes it for us. To make sure we are positioned on the first node of the new data, we call the `moveFirst()` method of the recordset owned by the DSO. We made copies of the new nodes when we were appending them to the DSO, so we should now reclaim the resources held by `rChildren` by setting that object to `null`, allowing the memory half for the tree to be freed. We've already moved on to the next step -- using ADO method calls to manipulate the recordset -- and we use the same button handlers from our previous example to allow the user to move freely through the recordset.

This may seem like a slightly tedious approach to dealing with unknown, derived vocabularies, but it illustrates something important. Since the DSO exposes the parse tree, we can use DOM methods to perform post-processing on the data. In addition to viewing the data, we might use the data typing namespace and MSXML's support for it to perform calculations using the returned data. We might even use the results of the calculations to alter the data we put into the data island. Suppose our data binding example above had provided a single numerical data value for each element instead of hierarchical strings, say the cost of some items. Thus:

```
<XML id="xmlData">
    <Collection>
        <Productprices>
            <CostBasic dt:dt="fixed.14.4">10.95</CostBasic>
            <CostDeluxe dt:dt="fixed.14.4">18.95</CostDeluxe>
        </ProductPrices>
    </Collection>
</XML>
```

If we wanted to display the cost with a ten percent markup, we could do so this way:

```
if (rChildren != null)
{
    for (var ni = 0; ni < rChildren.childNodes.length; ni++)
    {
        markupNode = rChildren.childNodes(ni).cloneNode(false);
        markupNode.text = markupNode.nodeTypedValue * 1.1
        xmlData.documentElement.appendChild(markupNode);
    xmlData.documentElement.removeChild(xmlData.documentElement.childNodes(0));
    xmlData.recordset.moveFirst();
}
```

Note that the lines including the variable `markupNode` get a copy of the retrieved node, then change it's XML text value to reflect the new price. It is this value that will appear in the data bound user interface.

The point is that the XML DSO gives us two metaphors – the DOM and the ADO recordset – which we can use as appropriate to perform whatever task is at hand.

# Transmission Services

So far we've bent our philosophy to the service of the computing platform, trying to present our data through tools widely in use by Windows programmers. Now it is time to put the platform at our service.

Let's see what tools exist to help us with a problem that has plagued us since Chapter 3: getting large amounts of XML data to the server without running afoul of HTTP request length limitations. We observed that some servers have a limit on the length of data that can be transmitted in an HTTP GET operation. For IIS, this is around 2K. If we expect to have very long documents to send to the server for any reason, we need another way to send them. We readily identified the answer as an HTTP POST operation, but had to resort to a work-around for getting the request POSTed when the response had to be returned to MSXML. It is time to see if Windows and ASP can offer a better approach.

We'll start by refining our work-around from Chapter 3 with more advanced aspects of HTML and ASP. As script programmers, though, our real desire is to find a component that provides a ready-made solution. In fact, we shall find two such components.

## HTTP POST the ASP Way

Jamming XML into a <DIV> under the guise of HTML isn't particularly elegant. It will work on most platforms, but that is about the only advantage of using this approach. The XML data island extension to HTML, while proprietary, offers a cleaner approach. We can accept an XML-encoded response as XML. The data binding tools available to us take care of getting the data into the parser. Since the <XML> tag is a peer of the other HTML tags, we can use some advanced HTML techniques to perform some clever user interface tasks, we'll look at these shortly. First, though, let's work through an example and see how the basic concept works in practice. After that, we'll add some features to improve the user experience in certain situations.

## A Simple POST Using an XML Data Island

As we saw in Chapter 3, we can overcome the limitations of the HTTP GET operation by using a POST. Unfortunately, MSXML uses a GET in its load() method. If we want to return data in XML form, we need some intermediate storage. In Chapter 3, the alternative we used was a hidden DIV element. This was definitely less than ideal as we were treating XML as HTML. Data islands, obviously, offer a better approach. Let's see how we can use data islands with the POST operation to obtain data more efficiently.

Here's a simple application. An HTML page presents the user with a form. The user inputs are used to build an XML document specifying some person to be added to a database. The details are then POSTed, in XML to the server, where an ASP enters the information into a database and sends a confirmation in XML to the submitting client. The XML confirmation will be returned to the client as a data island. Here's what the PersonForm.html submission page looks like:

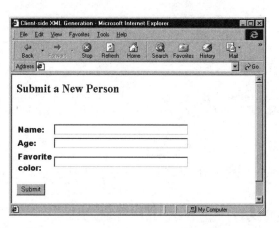

The user interface elements are ordinary HTML INPUT elements such as we've seen before. They reside in an HTML table strictly for formatting. They are not part of an HTML form.

We do, however, have a hidden form on the page. It contains a single INPUT element where we will place the completed XML document with our person submission. Here is the HTML for the hidden form:

```
<form method="post" action="XMLPersonHandler.asp" name="PersonForm">
  <INPUT name="XMLValue" style="DISPLAY: none">
```

The form is associated with XMLPersonHandler.asp, which is the page that will develop the reply XML document for us. Note that the button labeled Submit is not part of the form. We will access the form and force the submit through script. This happens in the button handler function, OnClick.

The OnClick function has to retrieve the user entries, compose some XML, place it in the hidden form, and then submit the form. We start by retrieving the data entered by the user:

```
sName = document.all("NameText").value;
sAge = document.all("AgeText").value;
sColor = document.all("ColorText").value;
```

Next, we compose our XML:

```
sXML = "<PERSON><NAME>" + sName + "</NAME><AGE>" + sAge + "</AGE>";
sXML += '<FAVORITE_COLOR>' + sColor + '</FAVORITE_COLOR></PERSON>';
```

Now we copy the text from our string, sXML, into the INPUT element in the hidden form. We've previously obtained a reference to the form and put it in a variable named oForm.

```
oForm.elements("XMLValue").value = sXML;
```

Finally, we force the form to submit its request with a POST:

```
oForm.submit();
```

Now let's turn our attention to XMLPersonHandler.asp. In an actual application, we'd do some work and return a new XML document which is distinct from what the client submitted. We are focusing on the mechanics of creating a data element in conjunction with a POST, however, so we'll simply echo the POSTed XML back to the client in a data island. A production application would also perform error checking and database operations in its script and build its document based on the results of those operations. Here's the critical portion of the BODY element created by this page:

```
<BODY>
<H2>Test Page: Receiving XML from a POST Operation</H2><P>
<XML id="xmlReply">

<% //Rem Echo the XML POSTed from the client
   var sXML;
   sXML = Request.Form("XMLValue").item(1);

   //Rem Echo the XML to the client IN A DATA ISLAND!

   Response.Write(sXML);
%>
</XML>
```

We use the stock Request object to receive the POSTed XML document. Inline ASP script is used to write it back between the opening and closing `<XML>` tags. In the remainder of the page that is returned to the client, we provide a button, an `OnClick` event handler function, and a `<DIV>`. The `<DIV>` holds the XML document created by the server. The `OnClick` event handler uses the DOM parse tree exposed by the data island to traverse the tree and display the contents using the `ProcessNode` function we developed in Chapter 3:

```
ProcessNode(xmlReply.documentElement);
```

This is a bit cleaner than the approach we used in Chapter 3 for dealing with the POST operation. We are, however, left with having to backtrack if we want to return to the person submission page. The page from the server replaces the HTML page that included the submission form. Let's see if we can support multiple user POSTs without leaving the submission page.

# Single Page Query Interface Example

Data entry functions, like the preceding example, aren't the only sort of application that would benefit from allowing the user to perform multiple roundtrips to the server without leaving the starting page. A search application could use this approach to good effect. The user might need to perform multiple queries until she found the right answer. Here's the user interface we're going to develop:

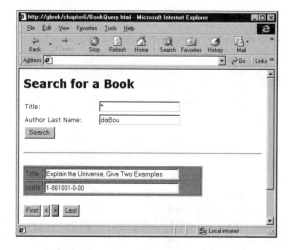

The interface elements above the horizontal rule allow our user to specify search criteria regarding the title of a book and the author's last name. Since some searches – such as the one above in which a wildcard is used for the title – can return multiple books, we use a data bound table in the lower part of the page. Of course, under our development philosophy, we aren't sure how the server stores book information. It might be a text file, a database, or some other store. We will use XML vocabularies, then, for submitting the search criteria and returning a collection of books in response to the query. We'll use POST to get the data to the server. Although this isn't strictly necessary in this case, unless the title or author name submitted is inordinately long, the general principle of using POST to remove the request length limit applies. Complicated search criteria developed from many input elements might need a POST rather than a GET operation. For convenience (and because we covered the topic at length earlier in this chapter), we'll use XML data binding to simplify the task of displaying the search results.

## Holding on to the Query Page: Theory

How are we going to POST our search criteria to an ASP and receive data without leaving this page? After all, in the previous example, the request fetched a new page that replaced the submission page. The key is to incorporate a hidden `IFRAME` element, which is not displayed, within our search page. The ASP that performs the search provides the contents of this frame. The frame will always have two data islands whether we have performed a search or not: one containing the shell of our search request XML document, and one for the search results. The frame also includes a `FORM` containing a hidden `INPUT` element, just as in the preceding example. We build our search XML using the shell data island, then stuff the resulting XML string into the `INPUT` element. The `FORM`'s `ACTION` is to request the search ASP, which it does via a POST.

Our page's `IFRAME` has two states. The initial state occurs when the page, `BookQuery.html`, loads. The `IFRAME` specifies the search page, `BookSearch.asp`, as its source. `BookSearch.asp` is requested as a consequence of loading `BookQuery.html`. Since we haven't submitted the form, `BookSearch.asp`, receives no request parameters. It should return the shell XML data island and a placeholder results data island in this case. It will also return the form whose action POSTs a request for `BookSearch.asp` and which contains the `INPUT` element we'll use to contain the query document.

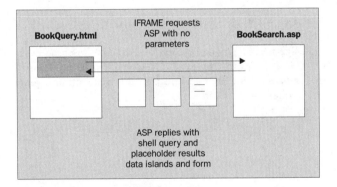

The other state occurs when the user clicks on the Search button. The button handler composes an XML document using the shell data island. This document is POSTed to the server. The search page should return the data island in its original, empty form – to prepare for the next search – and a data island containing the results of the search. It should also return the same `FORM` it returned under the conditions of the first, original state.

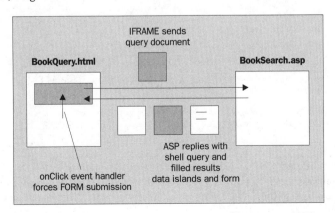

Because the INPUT elements at the bottom of the page are bound to the results data island, this sequence of events causes the results to be displayed on the page. So we can make new requests of the search page as many times as we wish, displaying new data each time, without leaving the query page.

There are a few details we shall have to overcome related to data binding, but these are best dealt with as we develop the actual code. We'll proceed to that right now.

## Holding on to the Query Page: Practice

Our example has three key pieces. The first consists of the crucial HTML elements in the query page that make this mechanism possible. Next is the script in the search page that returns results and populates the IFRAME. The final piece, without which these other two could not function, is the script in the query page that formats a request, triggers a POST, and makes the data binding work.

### Key Structures in the Query Page

Let's take a look at BookQuery.asp, the ASP that serves as the target of the IFRAME in BookQuery.html. The hidden IFRAME element is the heart of the scheme we're working on. It looks like this:

```
<IFRAME id="HiddenArea" src="BookSearch.asp" style="DISPLAY: none"></IFRAME>
```

This certainly doesn't look like much. The only thing we learn is the name – HiddenArea – and the src attribute which links this element to whatever BookSearch.asp returns. Let's see what the BookSearch.asp script returns under the conditions of the first state (no request parameters). It should return a shell for the query document:

```
<BookQuery>
    <BookTitle/>
    <AuthorLName/>
</BookQuery>
```

The ASP should also generate a placeholder consisting of an XML data island for the results vocabulary. We can't have an empty island, as we learned while discussing data binding, otherwise the binding will fail under those circumstances. We need a shell for that, too. Here's the shell:

```
<Results>
    <Book>
        <BookTitle/>
        <ISBN/>
    </Book>
</Results>
```

It also has to return the FORM we use to initiate a request for data. That HTML looks like this:

```
<FORM NAME=QueryPost METHOD=POST ACTION="BookSearch.asp">
    <INPUT TYPE=HIDDEN NAME=QueryString>
</FORM>
```

We see attributes directing a POST as well as the target of the request, BookSearch.asp. The hidden INPUT element, QueryString, is where we shall place the XML query document. When the FORM is POSTed, the value of the INPUT element, our document, will be sent as the value of the QueryString request parameter.

### Generating a Reply

Under the second state (a request generated by the client), we return the FORM, the shell data island, and a data island containing the results of the search. It isn't necessary to implement database retrieval for the purposes of this topic, so we'll simply send the contents of an XML file as an example of what would be the result of a real search. Here's the full script for `BookSearch.asp`:

```
<%@LANGUAGE=JavaScript%>
<HTML>
<BODY>
<FORM NAME=QueryPost METHOD=POST ACTION="BookSearch.asp">
<INPUT TYPE=HIDDEN NAME=QueryString>
</FORM>
<XML ID="xmlQuery">
    <BookQuery>
        <BookTitle/>
        <AuthorLName/>
    </BookQuery>
</XML>
<XML ID="xmlSearchResults">
<%
    if (Request.Form("QueryString").Item != "") %>
        <!-- #include file="Books.xml" -->
<% else
        Response.Write("<Results><Book><BookTitle/><ISBN/></Book></Results>"); %>

</XML>
</BODY>
</HTML>
```

*Readers who are interested in seeing data retrieval code for a similar problem may refer to Chapter 10 of XML Applications (Wrox Press, ISBN 1-861001-5-25).*

### Triggering the FORM Submission

One final piece remains. From the diagram depicting the second state, a request bearing search parameters, we see that the query page forces the HTML form submission, thereby triggering the retrieval. Several things happen in the `onClick` event handler. The shell XML query must be populated with the values entered by the user. We use the methods of MSXML to accomplish that:

```
var xmlQueryDoc = HiddenArea.xmlQuery.documentElement;
xmlQueryDoc.childNodes.item(0).text = title.value;
xmlQueryDoc.childNodes.item(1).text = author.value;
```

Note that we have to reach into the IFRAME named HiddenArea to obtain access to the data island, xmlQuery. Once we have a reference to the root of the parse tree, it is a simple matter to set the values of the nodes to the values taken from the HTML form elements elsewhere in BookQuery.html. Of course, this presupposes that we are familiar with the structure of the XML vocabulary we are using for the search. This will usually be the case. A server application should generally accept any vocabulary pertaining to requests for any of the vocabularies it supports. If metadata information is available, we can make use of techniques similar to the one we used in Chapter 5 to generate a user interface without prior knowledge of the underlying vocabulary.

Now that the query data island is populated with the request parameters, we need to send the XML to the server. The HTML FORM in the IFRAME contains an INPUT element expressly for this purpose. The value of this element will be sent to the server when the form is submitted. We use the xml method of MSXML to write out the XML, and the submit method of the HTML form to send it on its way:

```
var xmlString = xmlQueryDoc.xml;
HiddenArea.QueryPost.QueryString.value = xmlString;
HiddenArea.QueryPost.submit();
```

### Making Data Binding Work

At this point, we will receive the data obtained from BookSearch.asp. We might think that data binding would take care of the rest, but there are a few problems. We have to give data binding a little help.

The problem stems from the fact that the data binding will not work across the IFRAME boundary. Try as we might, we cannot get the HTML input elements outside the hidden IFRAME to bind to the results data island in the IFRAME. The fact that an XML data island exposes both MDAC and XML DOM methods and properties comes to our rescue. We will simply assign the value of the parse tree to an XML data island outside the IFRAME, then dynamically bind to that:

```
LocalCache.documentElement = HiddenArea.xmlSearchResults.documentElement;
TitleText.dataSrc = "#LocalCache";
TitleText.dataFld = "BookTitle";
ISBNText.dataSrc = "#LocalCache";
ISBNText.dataFld = "ISBN";
```

LocalCache is the name of the data island outside the IFRAME. We do a simple assignment to the documentElement, and the same XML document root object is referred to in two places: the data island returned from BookSearch.asp, and our data island outside the IFRAME. Since the remainder of the parse tree is contained as child properties of the documentElement, this one assignment has the effect of giving us access to the entire tree.

Dynamically binding the HTML INPUT elements TitleText and ISBNText is simply a matter of setting their dataSrc and dataFld properties using the syntax we previously used to statically bind elements. At this point, the user sees the first record returned and has the ability to navigate through the recordset.

# Components

The ASP approach will work well for many applications. It is especially useful for data binding applications, as we have just seen. However, there will be times when we want to have greater control over the transmission of our data. We may want to control when the data is sent and with what HTTP header information. We will also certainly want greater control over the XML that is returned. It would be convenient if the XML were kept in some object other than an HTML page element. Server-side applications, for example, won't be able to use the ASP approach. If the return value is strictly XML, we'd like to be able to bring it directly into an MSXML instance so that we can manipulate it without having to first retrieve it from some other location. In fact, this is what motivated our exploration of different HTTP POST techniques in the first place. Other times, as with data islands, we will want to be able to bring back arbitrary content via an HTTP POST operation. A solution that is consistent with our development principles is to find existing components that support HTTP POST operations, thereby turning our scripts into miniature browsers.

A look at the Windows platform turns up two candidates, both accessible through COM. Starting simply, we find our first candidate to be an old friend.

## MSXML Extension Interface

I've repeatedly said that MSXML's load() method uses a GET. This is true, and if you stick with the standard W3C DOM interfaces, this is all you can access through MSXML. Fortunately, MSXML supports several proprietary extension interfaces. Of particular interest is one called IXMLHTTPRequest.

This interface is provided expressly for the purpose of giving programmers greater control over how MSXML goes about getting its data for parsing. It provides general purpose HTTP request support, as one might suppose from the interface name. The following table lists the properties of the IXMLHttpRequest interface:

| Property | Meaning |
| --- | --- |
| readyState | Read-only; indicates the state of the request. The value of this four-byte integer is taken from the following enumeration:<br><br>UNINITIALIZED (0)   open has not been called<br><br>LOADING (1)   send has not been called<br><br>LOADED (2)   send has been called, the status and headers are available, but the response is not available<br><br>INTERACTIVE (3)   partial data has been received<br><br>COMPLETED (4)   all data has been received |
| responseBody | Read-only; the response as an array of unsigned bytes |
| responseStream | Read-only; the response as an IStream interface |
| responseText | Read-only; the response as a text string |
| responseXML | Read-only; the response as an XMLDOM parser instance |
| status | Read-only; the HTTP status code for the operation |
| statusText | Read-only; the HTTP status of the operation as a text string |
| onreadystatechange | Write-only; allows you to register a readyStateChange event handler |

It is important to remember the structure of an HTTP request. Every request contains an HTTP header. This is a group of variables, one to a line, and their values. Taken together, they describe the nature of the request. One such variable of relevance to the POST operation is Content-Type. We need to tell the server that the request is encoded as data from an HTML FORM in order for ASP's Request object to see the request data in its Forms collection. When a POST is performed, the data returned from the server is available from several properties. The prize from our point of view, however, is responseXML.

Once the response has been received – provided the server is configured with the correct MIME type for XML – `responseXML` holds an XML DOM parse tree.

Here are the methods of `IXMLHTTPRequest`:

| Method | Meaning |
|---|---|
| `abort` | Terminates an asynchronous request |
| `getAllResponseHeaders()` | Retrieves all the HTTP headers and their values following a successful call to send. Each pair is delimited by a carriage return-linefeed character |
| `getResponseHeader(sHeaderName)` | Retrieves the string value of the HTTP header named by `sHeaderName` |
| `open(method, URL, bAsync, UID, Pwd)` | Initializes the request |
| | `method`    HTTP method to use, e.g., "POST" |
| | `URL`    absolute URL of the request |
| | `bAsync`    optional; `true` for an asynchronous request (default value; open returns immediately) or `false` for a synchronous request (returns when response is completed) |
| | `UID`    optional; user name for servers requiring login |
| | `Pwd`    optional; user password for servers requiring login |
| `send(vBody)` | Sends the request and receives a response |
| | `vBody`    the body of the request. May be one of four types: a string, an array of unsigned bytes, an XMLDOM object, or an IStream interface |
| `setRequestHeader(sHeader, sValue)` | Sets an HTTP request header |
| | `sHeader`    the name of the HTTP header to set |
| | `sValue`    string form of the value of the header |

`Open()` is crucial to everything else. It requires two parameters, one for the request method – in our case the string `"POST"` – and one for the URL of the requested document. In addition, `Open()` can also take a user identifier and password as parameters when trying to retrieve documents from a secured server, and an optional parameter indicating whether the operation should be executed in an asynchronous manner.

`Send()` actually transmits the request. The order of use runs like this. First, establish a connection using the `open()` method. Next, configure the header of the request with `setRequestHeader()`. Most commonly, you will want to set the `Content-Type` header variable to the value `application/x-www-form-urlencoded` to indicate that you are sending data as if it were encoded and sent from an HTML form. Finally, use `Send` to transmit the body of the request. Let's write some brief code to illustrate this. We'll write an HTML page with a button on it. The `onClick` event handler will get an instance of `IXMLHTTPRequest` and send some XML to an ASP that simply echoes the XML back to the component. Here is the event handler, found in the file `HTTPXML.html`:

```
function OnClickXML()
{
    var requestor = new ActiveXObject("Microsoft.XMLHTTP");
    if (requestor != null)
    {
        requestor.Open("POST", "http://mymachine/chapter6/echo.asp", false);

        requestor.setRequestHeader("Content-Type",
                                   "application/x-www-form-urlencoded");

        requestor.Send("query=<Open>Something</Open>");

        requestor=null;
    }
    else
        alert("Unable to obtain a component for POSTing and parsing.");
}
```

Notice the new progid: `Microsoft.XMLHTTP`. If you examine the registry, you will see that this is implemented by `MSXML.DLL`, but it is an interface distinct from the ones we have been using such as DOM Document and DOM Node.

```
var requestor = new ActiveXObject("Microsoft.XMLHTTP");
```

Assuming we have a good component instance, we call `Open()`, specifying POST as our method and giving a URL for the ASP. Note that this URL must be absolute, not relative. No message is sent at the time `Open()` is called.

```
requestor.Open ("POST", "http://mymachine/chapter6/echo.asp");
```

To make HTTP believe we are submitting a form, it is necessary to set the header variable `Content-Type`. We give it the standard value denoting an HTML form encoding.

```
requestor.SetHeader("Content-Type",
                    "application/x-www-form- urlencoded");
```

With the request fully specified, we call `Send()`, providing the XML we want to forward to the server.

```
requestor.Send("query=<Open>Something</Open>"););
```

Upon receipt, the ASP extracts the value of the `query` element and writes it back to the response stream:

```
<% Response.Write(Request.Form("query")); %>
```

When the reply is received by the client, the `Send()` method returns. At this point, `responseXML` contains an XML document in tree form. How did IXMLHTTP know that the reply from the server was an XML document in need of parsing? The key is in the mime type set on the server. Here is the entire source code of our simple ASP, `echo.asp`:

```
<%@ Language=Javascript %>
<%
   Response.ContentType="text/xml";
   Response.Write(Request.Form("query"));
%>
```

The first line does the trick. Prior to sending anything back through the Response object, we set the mime type in the response header to the type `text/xml`. For this to work, we must also have configured our server to recognize this as a valid type. In IIS, we can set this under the **Mime Map** section of the server's property page. Just enter the type `text/xml` and the file extension `.xml`. When IXMLHTTP sees this header, it attempts to parse the response. If we had failed to set the header, we would have had to call `loadXML()` with the value of `responseText` as its parameter to manually trigger parsing.

For most of the tasks in this book, `IXMLHTTPRequest` is the only solution we will need to give us fine-grained control over the request and receipt of XML data. Let's take a brief look at another option available to us in case we want a more general solution.

## Internet Transfer Control

We would like to have a component that provides general access to HTTP operations. Instead of automatically pulling the response into MSXML, the component should hold the response in a buffer so we can manipulate it according to the programming task at hand. We might be working with a specialized problem in which we do not expect to receive XML – say, when we are working with a server that predates the adoption of our five principles. The Win32 API provides a subset of functions called the WinInet API. These offer fine control over HTTP operations, but they hardly fit into our five principles. These are low-level, detail oriented functions. They are intended for C and C++ programmers and are anything but component oriented. In fact, other components, including MSXML and the IXMLHTTP interface, are built on top of the WinInet functions to provide a simpler package for application programmers. Fortunately, other programmers have noticed this problem, and Microsoft ships a control that provides a component wrapper for WinInet as one of the stock components in Visual Basic 5.0 and later called the **Internet Transfer Control**.

Of course, this control isn't strictly a part of the Windows platform. While Visual Basic programmers may freely redistribute it with their programs, it does not come packaged with the operating system. Nevertheless, the popularity of Visual Basic as a development tool means that this control will be found in many environments we program for. If this is the case for in your environment, the Internet Transfer Control (`MSINET.OCX`) is a viable solution for the problem of general purpose access to HTTP in general and the POST operation in particular.

*Early versions of the control possessed a bug related to the problem at hand. This has been fixed in Visual Studio Service Pack 2. Programmers should obtain the service pack before using this control in production development.*

Just as with the IXMLHTTPRequest interface to MSXML, we need to specify some parameters of the request, before the request itself. The initial steps are just like those in IXMLHTTP:

- ❏ Establish a connection
- ❏ Specify the content type
- ❏ Execute the POST operation

The difference comes after we have our data. The control maintains the data in a buffer and makes no assumptions about the content. In particular, there is no expectation that you are dealing with XML that needs to be parsed. Instead, you keep reading data from the buffer into an application-specific buffer of your choosing until the control indicates that no more data is available. Let's see this in a practical example.

Returning to `HTTPXML.html`, we see an `onClick` event handler for a button labeled WinInet:

```
function OnClickHTTP()
{
    var sURL = "http://myserver/echo.asp";
    var sFormData = "query=<Open>Something</Open>";
    var sContentType = "Content-Type: application/x-www-form-urlencoded";
    xfer.Execute(sURL, "POST", sFormData, sContentType);
}
```

The first three lines should be familiar to you. We specify the document to request, the data in our FORM, and the fact that our request body will be encoded as form data. This is where things change. The Internet Transfer Control, which is embedded on our page with the identifier `xfer`, uses a method called `Execute()` to send the request (we will see how to embed it in the page shortly). It is here that we indicate our desire for a POST. More importantly, the control performs its work asynchronously. Although the interface we are using supports a property called `StillExecuting`, we expect to respond to the `StateChanged` event.

Gaining access to this event is why we had to embed the control in the page instead of creating it in the body of the script. Here is the tag we used to embed the control:

```
<OBJECT classid=clsid:48E59293-9880-11CF-9754-00AA00C00908 id=xfer name=xfer
    style="HEIGHT: 0px; WIDTH: 0px">
    <PARAM NAME="RequestTimeout" VALUE="60">
</OBJECT>
```

The `classid` is fixed and uniquely identifies this control. We provide the value `xfer` as the identifier by which we will refer to the control in our scripts. The `RequestTimeout` parameter sets an upper limit, in seconds, that the control will wait for a response before aborting the operation.

Internet Explorer gives us a mechanism for attaching event handlers to arbitrary events of controls on the page, but it requires design time knowledge of the control and its identifier. We need to attach a handler to process the `StateChanged` event. We attach our script to the `StateChanged` event with the following line:

```
<SCRIPT LANGUAGE=javascript FOR=xfer EVENT="StateChanged(state)">
```

This is the normal <SCRIPT> tag familiar to client-side programmers with the addition of the FOR and EVENT attributes. The FOR attribute specifies the name of the control, that in turn provides the event which we want to respond to. The EVENT attribute allows us to name the event fired by xfer that we will handle. Note how we've specified the event parameter state. This information comes from the control's type library. By providing it in the <SCRIPT> tag, we will have access to this parameter in our script. If we fail to provide it here, the event handler function will be called, but we will not have access to the specific state of the control. As we will shortly see, this is very important to us.

> *Visual Studio includes a programming tool call OLE View that permits us to inspect controls and type libraries. Although this tool is primarily intended for control developers, it permits script programmers to learn about the methods, properties, and enumerated values of controls they will be scripting. If you have any doubt about the accuracy of documentation, particularly in the case of beta software, the information provided by OLE View or a similar tool is the definitive source. It is reading the same source of information that the COM subsystem will use at runtime.*

The StateChanged event is fired by the control for a number of reasons. We are only interested in errors and successful completion of a transfer. The type library tells us that these states bear the enumerated values 11 and 12, respectively. Here is the event handler:

```
<SCRIPT LANGUAGE=javascript FOR=xfer EVENT="StateChanged(state)">
<!--
    switch (state)
    {
        case 11: // error
            alert("error on receipt");
            break;

        case 12: // response complete
                var sData = "";
                var sChunk;
                var bDone = false;
                sChunk = xfer.GetChunk(1024, 0);
                while (!bDone)
                {
                    sData += sChunk;
                    sChunk = xfer.GetChunk(1024, 0);
                    if (sChunk.length == 0)
                        bDone = true;
                }
                alert(sData);
                break;
    }
//-->
```

Since the Internet Transfer Control provides access to the response data through a buffer of arbitrary data, we do not explicitly know the start and end of the data. We shall have to read it much as we would read from an open file, asking for chunks and continuing until the control tells us there is no more data to be had. This is what the GetChunk() method allows us to do.

```
sChunk = xfer.GetChunk(1024, 0);
```

It takes two parameters: the first is the maximum amount of data to be returned by the method, and the second is a value specifying the type of data to be read. The latter parameter takes one of two values. Arbitrary byte streams are denoted by the value 1, while text is denoted by the value 0. Since we know that our requested ASP returns XML, we have specified text. GetChunk() returns data up to the length specified in the first parameter. An internal pointer is moved to the character following the last one read, so we can pick up where we left off with another call to GetChunk(). If no more data is to be had, a null value is returned. When the length of data returned is zero, we know we have the complete response and we terminate the loop. For the purposes of demonstration, we simply display the resulting data in a dialog box.

The Internet Transfer Control provides a COM interface to HTTP and a number of other services of the WinInet API. Programmers who need general access to Internet functions and who have licensed copies of the control (by virtue of having a licensed copy of Visual Basic) may find it an attractive solution to the problem we have presented here.

*Programmers who do not work in a Visual Basic environment, who need freeware, or simply want a more broadly accessible solution can try their hand at Java development. Classes in the core java.net package provide similar functionality. This should not be surprising, as HTTP is an open standard; all implementations will need to perform similar steps. This approach is more complicated than the simple scriptable components we have dealt with to date. You are developing the component through the use of core packages, not just using an existing, off the shelf component, and the Java approach will require intimate familiarity with several cooperating classes from java.net and java.io. In particular, you will get involved with Java's URL class and its derivations, as well as IO streams.*

# Summary

We paused on our road to the future and considered the state of the Windows operating system. The need to fit new approaches into existing practices suggests that we might find some benefit in using platform services to make the data we exchange readily accessible using non-XML techniques. The MDAC technology on Windows, while still emerging, is becoming the dominant data access technique for Windows programmers. It is the anointed successor to ODBC, and so programmers dealing with relational data on Windows are quickly adopting it. The ease of data binding in particular promotes MDAC in Windows-based organizations. Consequently, we explored extensions that marry MDAC and XML. We explored the XML DSO and XML data islands in some depth. We saw how the simplicity of the technique (and familiarity for database programmers) makes it an attractive one for making our XML data available in certain situations.

Moving on, we looked to Windows to solve a problem we left open at the end of Chapter 3: how to transmit potentially large quantities of XML to the server without encountering HTTP restrictions. We first used XML data islands to provide a solution. This technique enabled us to make any number of roundtrips to the server without leaving the page issuing the requests. We then refined our solution by exploring component options. First we saw an extension interface offered by MSXML supports HTTP POST operations wholly within the component. Then we looked at the Microsoft Internet Transfer Control, which, while not a part of the operating system, provides a general purpose, component-based solution to fine-grained HTTP transfers.

This chapter explored both sides of the line where the operating system and our development philosophy meet. A modest compromise on our side can win support and bring the advantages of our approach to more traditional techniques. Conventional utilities offered by the computing platform, in turn, offer solutions to problems we have encountered. As so often happens when theory is translated into practice, we learned that neither old nor new practices provide the appropriate solution; rather, a balance must be struck in which the new improves the old. The MDAC approach to XML, binding DHTML elements to the XML DSO, is far removed from our five principles, but is likely to be a familiar technique in Windows shops. Experienced ASP programmers may be more comfortable with the hidden IFRAME technique than with MSXML's IXMLHTTP interface. An experienced Visual Basic programmer may find the Internet Transfer Control more familiar than other techniques – it is similar, after all, to low level file IO functions. In all these cases, we should be willing to sacrifice pure XML DOM approaches, specifically IXMLHTTP, in order to gain a hearing for the broader principles we advocate. Allowing skeptical programmers a small victory – retaining familiar, working techniques – in order to get a bigger win with the five principles is a very effective, pragmatic approach.

# 7

# Communications

We've been using communications all along without really thinking about it. Somehow, HTTP has been getting our requests to the server and our data back to the client. On the server, we've made calls to databases and somehow the queries and record sets get where they need to go. Similarly, we've retrieved XML from the server without considering how it gets to MSXML and what that means for our application.

The protocols and timing of our communications can impose limits on our applications. Conversely, we can make these factors work for us by selecting the right communications mechanism for the task at hand. In this chapter, we'll start by looking at what it means to communicate in an intranet. We'll proceed to look at asynchronous messaging, which is a means of sending messages without blocking the flow of our applications. We'll also see some business cases where messaging makes sense.

Our sample application will be built using **Microsoft Message Queue** (MSMQ), the messaging solution for the Windows platform. We'll review the architecture and high-level features of MSMQ, then get an introduction to the COM object model that we'll be using in our application. Next, we'll extend our toolkit with four new components. These scriptlets will be the client and server-side versions of two components that allow us to send and receive messages in MSMQ without a detailed knowledge of the MSMQ object model. Finally, we'll apply these components to a simplified Web commerce order entry page.

## How Do We Communicate?

We can think of communications in terms of messages. A party wants some information or service from another party. To get it, they have to notify the other party and provide some information specifying exactly what it is they want. Regardless of how distributed applications are implemented, we can describe them in terms of messages. RPCs, Distributed COM, Java RMI, sockets – all are an exchange of discrete data. We've formalized our message passing in terms of structured XML-encoded documents. These lend themselves well to treatment as messages.

# Protocols

We're developing our applications with open Web protocols. These are based on socket communications. If you look at the low-level details of HTTP or FTP, you will see clients and servers passing messages back and forth. When we ask a browser to download a Web page, the browser sends a message to the server, then waits while the server retrieves some data and returns it. One look at a modern browser, however, suggests that matters are slightly more complicated.

Consider a page with some graphics on it. We get the page itself and the text starts to display. Meanwhile, the browser has gone back to the server to request the graphics files linked to the page. In a modern (multi-threaded) browser we may see text and graphics popping up on the page seemingly in no order. So we need a way to order our thinking about message passing.

# Time: Synchronous versus Asynchronous

There are two ways to exchange messages. They are classified according to their semantics in terms of time. The first and most common is **synchronous** communications. The sender and receiver wait for one another. There is no overlap in messages, and nothing happens in parallel. This is similar to what happens in a function call. The calling function makes a request of the called function, sending it the parameters required. The calling function **blocks**, suspending execution until the called function returns ("replies"). The called function doesn't do anything until it is called, and does nothing after it returns control to the caller.

> *COM and Java developers will raise an objection at this point. It is possible to write multi-threaded applications that overlap in terms of their execution. More importantly, it is possible to write truly parallel programs in which multiple instructions are actually carried out at the same time. Most components you will develop or use with scripted Web pages will be synchronous, although components intended for asynchronous downloads are a notable exception.*

**Synchronous** communication has the clear advantage of simplicity; it is easy to program. The code following a request can assume completion of the request because the program blocks awaiting a response. We have to deal with responses that include error information, but we don't have to worry about incomplete messages. Nor do we have to worry about when the response will come back or what we are allowed– under the logic of our application– to do in the meantime. Unfortunately, this isn't very efficient. Sometimes, we can continue working while we await a lengthy reply. In the case of a Web application, a popular site may take an extremely long time to reply to our request because it is overloaded with clients. If the application requires the services of a server application or resource that is currently off-line, the entire application will break.

**Asynchronous** communication answers these difficulties. We make a request; the server replies at some later point in time. We will make no assumptions about the timing of the reply. Instead, we will write our application so that it is event driven. This clearly involves some additional complexity. We need event handlers. We need a way to match requests with replies. Our program logic needs to check and see what information it has and whether it is able to continue any particular task. In return for this complexity, though, we gain the ability to handle intermittently available resources and slow servers.

# Synchronous XML

So far our use of MSXML to process structured data messages has forced our applications into synchronous communications. The script blocked on the load() or loadXML() methods, and processing resumed with a complete document after the component returned from the method call. In the sample applications we've developed so far, this worked perfectly well. Our applications retrieved structured data and displayed it. There was nothing that could be done in the meantime, and our documents were small and therefore quickly parsed.

We're going to take a quick look at asynchronous downloads for large documents, but then we'll revisit the problem of asynchronous messages later to see how we might make use of such loosely linked communications in terms of promoting the flow of an application.

# Asynchronous XML Downloads

If our only concern is preventing the download of a lengthy document from blocking our application, MSXML offers us an easy way out. In our code so far, we've had the following line:

```
docParser.async = false;
```

MSXML can perform asynchronous downloads. The line above disables that. If we omit that line, MSXML will download asynchronously by default. Let's see what a simple demonstration function looks like. We'll take an XML file URL in a text box, download the document, and display the results.

```
function OnLoad()
{
   var docURL;

   textArea = document.all("results");
   statusArea = document.all("status");

   textArea.innerHTML = "";
   statusArea.innerHTML = "";

   docParser.onreadystatechange = StateChangeHandler
   docParser.ondataavailable = DataAvailHandler

   docURL = FileURL.value;

   if (docURL != "")
      docParser.load(docURL);
   else
      alert("Please enter the URL of a file containing XML.");
}
```

Since we're used to synchronous downloads, the function looks bare following the call to MSXML's load() method. In fact, there's nothing there. The secret is telling the parser what functions should be called as event handlers. We've set up the parser to respond to the onreadystatechange and ondataavailable events fired by the parser by passing it references to our event handler functions. The former is called whenever the state of the parser changes – in fact, our handler will get called as soon as we try to download a document. The ondataavailable function gets called when some document data is available from the parser. Note that MSXML is not guaranteeing a complete document. We'll respond to the ondataavailable event by counting the number of nodes the parser can see from the document root:

```
function DataAvailHandler()
{
   var nodeCount = docParser.childNodes.length;
   var docRoot = docParser.documentElement;

   if (docRoot != null)
   {
      nodeCount += docRoot.childNodes.length;
   }

   document.all("status").innerHTML = nodeCount + _
                                " XML nodes loaded so far";
}
```

The first assignment of a value to `nodeCount` gives us the count of attributes off the root. The second assignment adds the number of child elements belonging to the document root. Of course, we're really more interested in seeing the entire document. We can do this in the state change handler by responding to the `COMPLETE` state:

```
function StateChangeHandler()
{
   if (docParser.readystate == COMPLETE)
   {
      if (docParser.parseError.reason == "")
      {
         oDisplayArea = document.all("results");
         TraverseTree(docParser);
      }
      else
         document.all("status").innerHTML = "Error: " +
                                      docParser.parseError.reason;
   }
}
```

When MSXML indicates completion, we look to see if any errors were detected. If so, we display them in the status `<DIV>`. If not, we pass the parse tree off to our usual functions for displaying an XML document.

MSXML made it easy for us to handle the event driven nature of an asynchronous download by making use of COM's event mechanism. We were able to ignore the problem of matching requests and replies because each instance of MSXML handles only one document. An asynchronous download, then, allows our script to realize the benefits of asynchronous communication but doesn't help MSXML itself. MSXML must still wait while the download takes place, but other script in our page can execute while MSXML is waiting.

While asynchronous communication isn't an explicit part of our five principles, it is in line with our view of networked applications. You can't predict what will take place between your client and someone else's server. Asynchronous communications keep your client from being held hostage by an ill-behaved network or server. So long as you can structure your application so that it can do useful work while some operation takes place in the background, asynchronous communications are well worth a look.

# Messaging

I've been very loose in using the term "message" so far in this chapter. That was deliberate, because it was important to think of messages in the context of technologies that aren't messaging applications, as the term is understood in the software industry. There is, however, a class of products that are formally known as messaging applications. The data exchanged between client and server is formally detached from the implementing technology. Whether the data goes by sockets or DCOM, the data is a structure handled independently from the using application. **Messaging middleware** handles the transfer and storage of arbitrarily structured data.

## General Characteristics of Messaging

Messaging is an established technology in the software industry. There are a number of messaging products on the market today. All have some general features in common, however. Each offers some sort of API for use with application software. The messaging product receives variable length data and instructions on "who" should receive the data. "Who" is a store – typically a queue – of messages on a named machine. Applications that expect to receive messages use the messaging API to check their queue and retrieve the data. The internal structure of the data is application specific. The only structure imposed by the messaging software is that required for message delivery.

This lends itself well to asynchronous communication between programs. The messaging software stores data until the receiving application retrieves it. Since there can be multiple messages in a queue at any given time, the messaging implementation must have some mechanism for differentiating between messages. An application can make use of this mechanism to associate requests and replies. Since structure is application-independent, we can use our XML-based approach without modification.

## Business Cases

Messaging middleware is widely used in high-volume applications and there is a reason for its widespread adoption. Asynchronous communication, as we will shortly see, allows us to build highly scalable applications efficiently. Since there is reduced concern for the amount of time needed to process a message, we can allow messages to back up in the queue during peak periods and clear the backlog as traffic eases off. As a result, we can deploy server resources based on the expected average volume of client requests, removing the need to buy hardware capable of handling the peak expected traffic. Enterprise-scale mainframe applications made use of messaging for this purpose. Clients could submit requests to the server and go about their tasks without waiting for a reply. The mainframe could process the messages in batch mode or continuously as it got to them. Peak loads simply filled the queue and computing resources could be scaled to the average load.

More recently, the automation of tasks traditionally handled in a manual fashion has led to the concept of **workflow applications**. These are applications that mix automated processes with manual, human-driven tasks. Processing is structured around a flow of tasks; as each task is accomplished, processing moves to the next step. Since some of these tasks are manual, there is no way of predicting the response time except to say that it will be long from a computer's point of view. Workflow applications (by definition) require asynchronous messaging for implementation.

Let's examine two hypothetical business cases to gain a better appreciation of the role of asynchronous messaging. The first is a high-volume e-commerce site accepting orders over the Web. The second will be a customer service order tracking application that follows the progress of an order through manufacturing and delivery.

## High-Volume Order Entry

Receiving large volumes of orders is a typical situation on e-commerce sites as well as being similar to many high-volume back-office applications. A large and variable number of client requests will be presented to a Web server. Satisfying the request is a matter of invoking some application that translates the request parameters into some action. This application is hosted on a server other than the one hosting the HTTP server. If the hand-off between the Web server and the back-end process is synchronous, then the HTTP server must block until the back-end process has completed processing. This imposes a delay on both the client and the Web server. Admittedly, virtually all HTTP servers are multi-threaded so other requests can be accommodated during this delay. Nevertheless, server resources may be tied up, and the client will certainly be blocked.

To avoid these problems, the HTTP server must be sized to handle the peak number of concurrent requests. This number will be higher than might otherwise be the case because client sessions will be extended due to the delay. The back-end application server must be able to process the peak number of expected requests within the desired maximum response time. The server issues can be dealt with provided we are willing to spend money on resources that will normally be underutilized. Unfortunately, improving the client experience is another matter. Either we lower the maximum response time, thereby increasing the burden on the servers, or we structure our client application in such a way as to be useful to the user during the wait for request satisfaction. This is not always possible.

A synchronous response is seldom required, however – e-commerce applications seldom return the service electronically and instantly. While you will always receive a receipt electronically, physical goods must travel conventionally. Instead, the client should be notified that an order has been securely placed. Delivery of the goods or services and other activities such as e-mail notification can follow seconds, hours, or days later.

This is where asynchronous communications can be useful. Consider this illustration of application architecture :

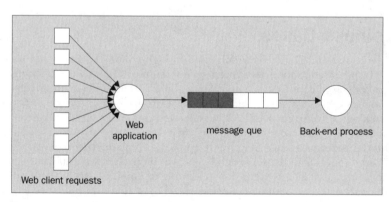

The client requests are submitted to the Web application. Rather than submit requests synchronously, the Web application posts the request as a message to a queue. The Web application returns to the client as soon as the message is submitted. The client can be notified whether the request was submitted successfully. The queue acts as a buffer for the back-end process. The application actually processing the requests, for example the part that generates orders for whatever our site is selling and places them in a database, retrieving messages as it can process them. It is built to accommodate the average expected traffic. During periods of peak demand, messages awaiting service back up in the queue. So long as the queue is big enough nothing will be lost. The back-end application drains the queue when demand drops. While the calculations can be difficult, the proper size for a queue expected to handle a certain demand profile with a specified reliability can be determined.

## Work Flow

The problem in this case is not excessive demand, but rather one of disconnects in the business process. The defined workflow usually involves some mix of manual and automated processes. The manual processes may take hours or days to occur, and the resources involved in the automated processing may not always be available. Message queues act as holding areas for workflow messages, allowing resources to be used efficiently and ensuring that workflow is not disrupted when resources are not immediately available.

The next illustration depicts a very simple manufacturing company that makes products on a just-in-time basis. Orders arrive through a call center and travelling sales agents. Managers may intervene to correct order errors or to change priorities and prices. An automated process verifies customer information and product compatibility before placing the order in the database. The appropriate information is passed on to manufacturing, where the actual fabrication of the goods may be scheduled for optimal efficiency. The actual manufacturing is a mix of automated and manual processes, which together take several hours. Once finished, the goods are delivered to the shipping area together with the appropriate customer shipping instructions. At any time in the process, customer service representatives may submit changes from the customer or check on the status of an order.

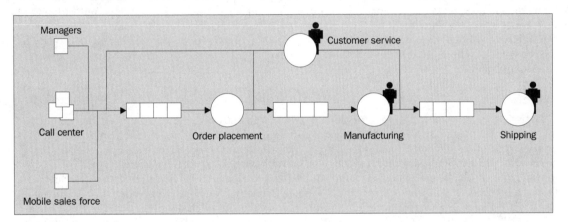

The message queue between the order placing entities (the managers, call center and sales force above) acts like the buffer in the order entry example we just examined. There is one additional benefit, however. The mobile salesmen submit orders while they are speaking to their customers. Their software cannot send the message to the order placement queue because the salesmen are disconnected from the company network. Instead, the messaging middleware client software places messages in a local queue for eventual delivery when the salesmen connect their computers to the company LAN at some later time.

The order placement process is entirely automated. It verifies customer information, validates billing instructions, and submits the order to a database. These tasks could be entirely synchronous. Unfortunately, the order is not satisfied immediately. Manufacturing and shipping can take days because they have manual components. The queues between order placement and manufacturing (and between manufacturing and shipping) therefore act to smooth out discontinuities in time. A message may be ready when the automated process is not. A process may go off-line for a period of time.

A database could be used to handle the time delay, but it would force us to transmit information in tightly defined structures. Our messages would have to fit a rigid table schema. As we've seen in earlier chapters, loosely structured XML can address a wide variety of issues that a strictly enforced database schema cannot. Messaging middleware handles the problem without imposing a rigid structure on the workflow.

# Microsoft Message Queue

It's time we got a practical, hands-on look at messaging middleware. There are many products on the market, but a recent offering, Microsoft Message Queue (MSMQ), is especially attractive to us because it is exposed through a series of COM component interfaces. This makes it easy to use in ASP scripts and client-side scripts under Microsoft Internet Explorer. MSMQ's features are typical of the general nature of messaging middleware. MSMQ also offers some features attractive to network administrators.

# Store and Forward Architecture

MSMQ uses a **store and forward** architecture. Messages are placed in queues for transmission, then **forwarded** to queues on the destination machine. Since messages are stored, sending applications can post a message even when the receiver is not available. Additionally, messages may be forwarded through several hops when breaks in the network topology preclude message transmission directly to the receiving machine. To understand MSMQ, we have to understand the different types of servers, clients, and queues.

## Servers

Messaging topologies in MSMQ are organized around an **enterprise**, which comprises the whole of the topology managed by a single organization, and a number of sites linked to the enterprise. An entire large firm would constitute an enterprise. Such an organization might have a number of geographically distinct locations. Each location would have a single LAN, or campus of internetworked LANs, such that communication within the location is all at high data rates. Such a location is termed a **site**. The enterprise has a single **Primary Enterprise Controller** (PEC), and each site has a **Primary Site Controller** (PSC). Additionally, each site (including that with the PEC) has a **Backup Site Controller** (BSC) in the event the PSC goes offline. All MSMQ servers must be running Windows NT Server.

The purpose of these servers is to maintain the **Message Queue Information Store** (MQIS). This is a SQL Server 6.5 database installed and managed by Message Queue that contains information describing the messaging network topology, server names, queue information, and other administrative details. MQIS allows MSMQ to perform **smart routing** to ensure messages are sent by the most direct route possible or are sent around a break in the topology. Clients use MQIS to discover the location and nature of queues.

The PEC, PSCs, and BSCs each maintain their own local copy of the MQIS. Primary controllers (PEC and PSCs) house read-write copies of the MQIS. Administrative changes made on one controller are replicated to the rest. Backup controllers hold a read-only copy.

In addition to controllers, MSMQ networks may also have **routing servers**. Routing servers perform smart routing and may act as intermediate queues when a message must go through more than one server or delivery to its ultimate destination. Controllers also act as routing servers, so dedicated routing servers may not be required. Dedicated routing servers are typically used for additional redundancy or for message interchange between computers running different network protocols.

## Clients

A client is any machine with MSMQ-aware software installed. Typically, this will consist of the MSMQ COM components and applications built to use them for messaging. There are two kinds of clients, independent and dependent.

**Independent clients** can persistently store messages in a local queue until they are able to forward them to the rest of the network. This provides protection in the event of network topology breaks. It is also useful for providing service to mobile users. These users can utilize messaging applications while disconnected from the messaging network, then forward the accumulated messages when a connection is established.

**Dependent clients**, on the other hand, use a server for their queues. This allows a client with minimal resources to use MSMQ, but it imposes a burden on the server in terms of storage. As we shall see in the next section, all queues come out of a fixed capacity on the server. All queues for a dependent client come out of this capacity on the server, so network administrators must be careful not to make too many clients dependent on a single server. Independent clients suit our vision of networks since they rely less on resources they can't control. Some situations, however, will require the use of dependent clients, so you can't be dogmatic about this issue.

## Queues

Under Windows 95/98, client queues can store almost two gigabytes of messages. Windows NT independent clients and servers can store almost four gigabytes of messages until they can be forwarded.

There is more to queues than capacity, however. Queues manage messages by priority, with high priority messages going ahead of lower priority messages in the queue. Queues are given names, which are unique within the machine. This allows us to set up multiple queues on a single client or server much as a post office has multiple mailboxes. Each application can work with one queue on the sending machine and one on the receiving machine, or messages may be spread across a set of queues. This is independent of MSMQ and is strictly for the convenience and logical organization of our applications. We can manually create the queues we need or dynamically create them through the MSMQ API.

Something that is of great interest to us is the privacy of messages. Each queue can be configured according to the privacy status of the messages it can receive. A message is considered private if the message body is encrypted and public if it is clear text.

> *MSMQ handles the encryption and decryption of messages. MSMQ administrators make some choices about algorithms and such, but users of the MSMQ interfaces simply state whether a message should be public or private.*

Queues may be marked to accept only private messages, only public messages, or they may accept a mix of the two (and be indifferent to message privacy). Again, this is a matter of application organization. What is important to us is that the sender of a message must match the privacy status of a message to be sent with the privacy status of the receiving queue to avoid an error on transmission. Clear-text messages cannot be sent to queues designated private, while encrypted messages cannot be sent to a queue that will only accept clear-text messages.

## *Messages*

We have seen how servers manage a messaging network. We have seen how clients interact with the messaging system. We have seen how queues store messages. One question remains: what is a message? For our purposes, a message is simply an arbitrary block of data up to four megabytes in length. The internal structure and format is entirely up to the application; MSMQ doesn't care. We will be using text to transmit XML documents, but we could use binary representations of a native format if we so chose.

Messages may be either **express** or **recoverable**. In some networks, loss of connectivity will be extremely rare, and resource utilization will be a higher priority. In such a case, clients may wish to use express messaging. Under this approach, messages are queued in memory rather than on disk. Obviously, this means any messages that are in a machine's queue will be lost if it crashes. If the messages are not individually important, or crashes are expected to be rare, however, express messaging is much faster since no disk access is required (note that queuing to disk requires two disk operations: once to write, and a second to read the message for forwarding). Recoverable messages, by contrast, are always saved to disk in the MQIS. If the machine fails, but the disk is intact when it is recovered, the queued messages may be recovered and forwarded.

# Transacted Messaging

An attractive feature of MSMQ is its ability to use transactions with messages. For example, an application designer might want to make delivery of a message dependent on the successful completion of a database operation, and vice versa. In this case, the message and the database operation would be executed within the body of a transaction. If the database operation fails, the message is removed from the queue. If the message transmission fails, the database operation is rolled back.

Transactions may be applied solely to messages to achieve some useful results. If it is important that a sequence of messages arrive at their destination exactly in the order in which they were sent, we can accomplish this with transacted messages. The dynamic nature of a messaging network can lead to a message being sent more than once. This could happen when breaks in the messaging topology are repaired or when a crashed server or client is recovered. If the message represents a critical event in our system, we don't want to respond more than once. Again, transactions are the answer. We can ensure a transacted message is delivered to its destination exactly once. Finally, we can use transactions to notify the sender that a message was successfully received.

# Integration with Other Systems

MSMQ is a relatively new messaging product. When it is used in conjunction with established mission-critical systems, it will frequently be necessary to integrate MSMQ applications with legacy messaging systems. These have been used with mainframe systems for some time. Level 8 Systems provides products that allow MSMQ to exchange messages with a variety of older messaging middleware systems, you can find out more about these at http://www.level8.com/. We can build a system that spans platforms using XML and the appropriate integration software. We will use the tools – scripting and components – that are common to our platform, while programmers on other platforms may use the messaging middleware and software construction techniques with which they are most familiar.

# MSMQ Object Model

As with most subsystems of the Windows platform, MSMQ is exposed to programmers through a series of COM interfaces. We shall deal with the three most important: queue information structures, queues, and messages.

## MSMQQueueInfo

This interface represents the MQIS to the programmer. We tell MQIS what queue we are interested in by setting the path of an MSMQQueueInfo object. The path is a combination of a machine name and a queue name. We can obtain a variety of interesting facts from this object, but its most important use is to obtain access to a queue. Calling the `Open()` method of an MSMQQueueInfo structure yields an MSMQQueue object.

## MSMQQueue

The first thing you want to do with a valid MSMQQueue object is to call its `Refresh()` method. The information contained in the MQIS may be stale due to delays in replication, but `Refresh` goes to the queue to obtain the current state of the queue. Despite the fact that you obtained the queue object through a call to the `Open()` method of an MSMQQueueInfo object, the queue may not actually be accessible in the mode (read-write etc.) that you desire, so you might not be able to send messages to it. `IsOpen` tells you if you have access. Finally, when you wish to send a message, we send the message object an `MSMQQueue` object as a parameter of its `Send()` method.

On the receiving end, however, MSMQQueue has three methods of special importance to us. Each queue, once open, has an internal pointer that governs how messages are accessed. `PeekCurrent()` and `PeekNext()` allow us to inspect the messages currently pointed to and its successor respectively, without removing messages from the queue. `PeekNext()` advances the internal pointer. `ReceiveCurrent()` physically removes the current message. Although the internal pointer hasn't been moved, it points to the succeeding message by virtue of the fact that the remaining messages are moved down to fill the hole let by removing the message in question.

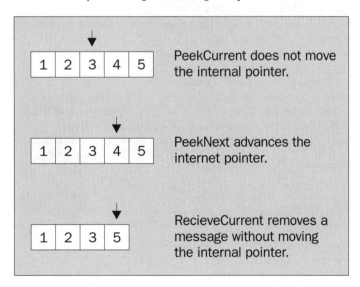

| 1 | 2 | 3 | 4 | 5 |

PeekCurrent does not move the internal pointer.

| 1 | 2 | 3 | 4 | 5 |

PeekNext advances the internet pointer.

| 1 | 2 | 3 | 5 |

RecieveCurrent removes a message without moving the internal pointer.

### MSMQMessage

Messages are the whole reason for using MSMQ. Every other object discussed so far exists to support the MSMQMessage object. It has properties for the label, body, and privacy type (encrypted or cleartext) of the message: `Label`, `Body`, and `PrivLevel`, respectively. After we have set up our message, we call MSMQMessage's `Send()` method. This method takes a single parameter, which is the MSMQQueue object representing the queue to which we wish to send the message.

The basic procedures involved with sending and receiving messages in MSMQ will become clear as we work through specific examples. Before building a messaging application, however, let's detour and build a few more components for our intranet toolkit.

# Messaging Components

The details of asynchronous messaging using MSMQ are simple but tedious for basic messaging operations. MSMQ provides many more features than we have explored so far. Even if we stick to the basic set, we won't want to repeat the code and maintain it throughout our applications. We should add some components to our toolkit that will abstract basic MSMQ operations and allow our intranet developers to focus on the business problem they are trying to solve. If you decide to stick with the MSMQ objects in your development, the exercise of building these components will be a good introduction to the basics of using MSMQ objects.

# The Task

What are our asynchronous needs in intranet development? Put simply, we want to send and receive messages and let the messaging middleware perform its magic for us with minimal intervention on our part. We need to focus on two operations: sending and receiving messages. We might also think of message reception as message pickup, but I'll stick with the term receive. We cannot shield the client programmer from knowledge of machine names and queues, nor can we hide whether a message is public or private. We'll leave aside transactions and priorities for teaching purposes. It is reasonable, however, to hide the particulars of message queue information structures as well as the process of opening queues for reading and writing. With this in mind, let's build two components: `Sender`, to send messages, and `Receiver`, to pick them up. `Sender` will allow a programmer to set the machine, queue, and privacy status for a message. `Receiver` will take a machine and a queue, and retrieve messages with a specified label. In this way, we can use labels to differentiate between classes of messages going to the same queue (orders and order inquiries for example) and use `Receiver` to retrieve only those messages relevant to the particular task at hand. In a practical setting, you will want to spend some time deciding how to manage different types of messages. You can segregate them according to queue, by message label, or some combination of the two.

# Sender

We start by defining a JavaScript object:

```
var public_description = new Sender;

function Sender()
{
    this.get_Machine = get_Machine;
    this.put_Machine = put_Machine;
    this.get_Queue = get_Queue;
    this.put_Queue = put_Queue;
    this.get_Private = get_Private;
    this.put_Private = put_Private;
    this.Send = Send;
}

var Machine;
var Queue;
var Private = false;
```

This gives us properties for the machine name hosting a queue (`Machine`), the queue itself (`Queue`), and the desired privacy level of the message (`Private`). `Private` is initially set to `false`, meaning messages will be sent clear text by default. Our property accessor functions do no validity checking; you may wish to modify this to fit your specific set-up. The functions for `Machine` are typical:

```
function get_Machine()
{
    return Machine;
}

function put_Machine(newValue)
{
    Machine = newValue;
}
```

The heart of this component, of course, is the `Send()` method. The client of this component provides two strings, one for the message label and the other for the body of the message itself. It assumes the machine and queue to which the message is being sent were previously set using the accessors methods. We start by creating a queue information object for the desired queue:

```
function Send(strLabel, strMsg)
{
    var mqInfo, mqQueue, mqMessage;

    mqInfo = new ActiveXObject("MSMQ.MSMQQueueInfo");
    if (mqInfo != null)
    {
        mqInfo.PathName = Machine + "\\" + Queue;

        mqQueue = mqInfo.Open(SEND, 0);
        mqQueue.Refresh;
```

Provided we have a valid message queue information object, we compose the path to the queue, open it for sending, and call the object's `Refresh()` method. This ensures the object has current information regarding the status of the queue. Provided the queue is open, we'll prepare our message:

```
        if (mqQueue != null && mqQueue.IsOpen == true)
        {
            mqMessage = new ActiveXObject("MSMQ.MSMQMessage");
            if (mqMessage != null)
            {
                mqMessage.Body = strMsg;
                mqMessage.Label = SafeLabel(strLabel);
```

To send a message, we need to create an MSMQ message object. Once we have that, we set the label and body properties of the object. We've provided a utility function to truncate the label provided to fit the maximum label size of Message Queue messages:

```
function SafeLabel(strLabelText)
{
    if (strLabelText.length <= MAX_LABEL)
        return strLabelText;
    else
        return strLabelText.slice(0, MAX_LABEL - 1);
}
```

Returning to the body of the `Send()` method, we have one final check to make before sending the message. Recall that Message Queue is particular about the privacy state of messages. A queue may be set up to require privacy, be indifferent to privacy status, or require clear-text messages only. We'll compare the `Private` property with the message queue information object and either proceed or return an error code denoting what has to be done to make the message compatible with the queue:

```
            nPrivacy = PrivacyCheck(Private, mqQueue.PrivLevel);
            if (nPrivacy != PRIV_OK)
                return nPrivacy;

            if (Private == true)
                mqMessage.PrivLevel = MSG_PRIVATE;
            else
                mqMessage.PrivLevel = MSG_PUBLIC;
            mqMessage.Send(mqQueue);
```

The `PrivacyCheck()` function illustrates the possible conflicts of message and queue privacy states:

```
function PrivacyCheck(bPrivate, nQueuePrivLvl)
{
    if (bPrivate == false && nQueuePrivLvl == Q_PVT_ONLY)
        return UPGRADE;

    if (bPrivate == true && nQueuePrivLvl == Q_PUBLIC_ONLY)
        return DOWNGRADE;

    return PRIV_OK;
}
```

Of all possible combinations, only two prevent sending a message to a specified queue. If a queue requires privacy and the message is marked for clear-text transmission, the privacy state of the message must be upgraded. If the queue bars private messages and the message is marked for privacy, the message's privacy level must be downgraded.

Once we've sent the message, we perform normal resource recovery. Here is the complete body of the `Send()` method:

```
function Send(strLabel, strMsg)
{
    var mqInfo, mqQueue, mqMessage;

    // Prepare queue path and privacy level
    mqInfo = new ActiveXObject("MSMQ.MSMQQueueInfo");
    if (mqInfo != null)
    {
        mqInfo.PathName = Machine + "\\" + Queue;

        // Open the queue for sending
        mqQueue = mqInfo.Open(SEND, DENY_NONE);
        mqQueue.Refresh;

        if (mqQueue != null && mqQueue.IsOpen == true)
        {
            // Compose a test message
            mqMessage = new ActiveXObject("MSMQ.MSMQMessage");
            if (mqMessage != null)
            {
                mqMessage.Body = strMsg;
                mqMessage.Label = SafeLabel(strLabel);

                nPrivacy = PrivacyCheck(Private, mqQueue.PrivLevel);
                if (nPrivacy != PRIV_OK)
                    return nPrivacy;

                if (Private == true)
                    mqMessage.PrivLevel = MSG_PRIVATE;
                else
                    mqMessage.PrivLevel = MSG_PUBLIC;
                mqMessage.Send(mqQueue);

                // Clean up resources
                mqMessage = null;
                mqQueue.Close();
                mqQueue = null;
                mqInfo = null;
                return SENT;
            }
            else
            {
                // No message object, clean up resources
                mqQueue.Close();
                mqQueue = null;
                mqInfo = null;
                return FAILED;
            }
        }
        else
        {
            // No queue object, clean up resources
            mqInfo = null;
            return FAILED;
        }
    }
    else
        return FAILED;
}
```

# Receiver

Now let's define a simple JavaScript object for retrieving messages from a queue:

```
var public_description = new Receiver;

function Receiver()
{
   this.get_Machine = get_Machine;
   this.put_Machine = put_Machine;
   this.get_Queue = get_Queue;
   this.put_Queue = put_Queue;

   this.Receive = Receive;
}
```

As with `Sender`, we have properties for the machine name and queue, and a single method for receiving messages. Since receiving really means retrieving messages from the queue, we'll ask the component's client to specify what to look for and how many messages to retrieve at maximum, `nMaxMsgs`. The client will receive an array of zero to `nMaxMsgs` messages. If the array contains the maximum number of messages, the queue may have more messages bearing the specified label. In that case, the client should continue retrieval until the array is returned empty. Having an array protects our clients from being overwhelmed in the event the queue contains a great number of messages. The client can tailor the maximum size of the returned array to fit its needs.

As with `Sender`, we proceed to create a message queue information object and open the desired queue appropriately. This time, we'll be opening for message reception in a non-exclusive mode – our use of the queue does not block anyone else from opening it:

```
function Receive(strLabel, nMaxMsgs)
{
   var mqInfo, mqQueue, mqMsg;
   var rMsgs = null;
   var nMsgsPulled;

   mqInfo = new ActiveXObject("MSMQ.MSMQQueueInfo");
   mqInfo.PathName = Machine + "\\" + Queue;

   // Open for reading
   mqQueue = mqInfo.Open(RECV, DENY_NONE);
```

Since we are searching a potentially large queue of messages for any messages that bear a particular label, we need to be able to look at message labels without disturbing the queue. The MSMQ Queue object's `PeekCurrent()` method will retrieve a copy of messages. When we reach the end of the queue, the method returns a null object. Our other stopping condition is the client-specified maximum, `nMaxMsgs`:

```
   if (mqQueue != null && mqQueue.IsOpen)
   {
      rMsgs = new Array();

      mqMsg = mqQueue.PeekCurrent(false, false, TIME_OUT);

      nMsgsPulled = 0;
      while (mqMsg != null && nMsgsPulled < nMaxMsgs)
      {
```

If the message we've copied isn't one with the label we're looking for, we simply call `PeekNext()`, which, as you might expect, looks at the next message in the queue. Things are slightly more complicated if we find a message with the desired label. To start, we want to extract the message from the queue and place it in our array. This changes the queue. Message Queue fills the hole with the succeeding messages in the queue. Our queue pointer now refers to the next message to look at even though we haven't moved it (like we would have with a `PeekNext()` call for example). We therefore call `PeekCurrent()` to keep our loop going properly:

```
        if (mqMsg.Label == strLabel)
        {
            rMsgs[nMsgsPulled++] = mqQueue.ReceiveCurrent(NO_TRANSACT,
                                   false, true, TIME_OUT);
            mqMsg = mqQueue.PeekCurrent(false, false, TIME_OUT);
        }
        else
            mqMsg = mqQueue.PeekNext(false, false, TIME_OUT);
    }
```

When we are finished, we close the queue and return the array of messages. Here's the complete code to `Receive()`:

```
function Receive(strLabel, nMaxMsgs)
{
    var mqInfo, mqQueue, mqMsg;
    var rMsgs = null;
    var nMsgsPulled;

    mqInfo = new ActiveXObject("MSMQ.MSMQQueueInfo");
    mqInfo.PathName = Machine + "\\" + Queue;

    // Open for reading
    mqQueue = mqInfo.Open(RECV, DENY_NONE);

    if (mqQueue != null && mqQueue.IsOpen)
    {
        rMsgs = new Array();

        mqMsg = mqQueue.PeekCurrent(false, false, TIME_OUT);

        // Iterate through the entire queue looking at labels
        // and extracting any messages that match the label.

        nMsgsPulled = 0;
        while (mqMsg != null && nMsgsPulled < nMaxMsgs)
        {
            if (mqMsg.Label == strLabel)
            {
                rMsgs[nMsgsPulled++] = mqQueue.ReceiveCurrent(NO_TRANSACT,
                                       false, true, TIME_OUT);

                // Queue fills the hole, so the "next" msg is now current
                mqMsg = mqQueue.PeekCurrent(false, false, TIME_OUT);
            }
            else
                mqMsg = mqQueue.PeekNext(false, false, TIME_OUT);
        }
        mqQueue.Close();
    }
    return rMsgs;
}
```

# Server-Side Versions

The DHTML scriptlets we've built so far are intended for use in client-side scripts. There are many occasions when we want to process messages in server-side scripts. This is especially important when dealing with applications exposed to the public Internet. Our messaging topology won't generally be publicly available, so we'll have to send our messages from server pages. There is a simple solution to this requirement. Let's take a few moments to recast our existing toolkit components for the server.

## Server Scriptlets

Component scriptlets on the server need to behave like "real" COM objects. We don't want to embed them as tags. We need to be able to instantiate them and use them from script just like any other COM object. Microsoft responded with an evolved variation on the DHTML scriptlets to which we've become accustomed. This technology, known simply as scriptlets, is implemented with some operating system support.

Microsoft provides a DLL named SCROBJ.DLL that acts as an intermediary between our scripts and the COM runtime system. We implement our scriptlets as files with the extension .sct. Instead of creating a JavaScript object, scriptlet files provide a bit of XML that tells SCROBJ.DLL how to map functions to the methods of the object (or objects) in the scriptlet file. This will become clear when we look at the implementation of our server-side messaging components.

When the scriptlet file is registered, the registry gets a key that maps the program ID to SCROBJ.DLL with the scriptlet file name as a parameter. Consequently, when an application tries to create an instance of our scriptlet, the COM runtime system loads SCROBJ.DLL. This component reads the XML in the scriptlet file and executes the script as needed to respond to property and method invocations.

> *A new version of REGSVR32.EXE is installed with the scripting package. It allows you to register a scriptlet file from the command line or from a context sensitive menu within the Windows Explorer. If you are using the older version of REGSVR32.EXE, you may register a scriptlet with the command line REGSVR32 scrobj.dll /n/i:URL/scriptletname. For example: REGSVR32 scrobj.dll /n/i:file://serversender.sct*

Let's examine our messaging components to see how this is implemented in practice.

## ServerSender

The surprising truth is that there is nothing in the Sender() script that needs to be changed to work on the server. All we need to do is build a scriptlet file with the proper mapping XML and add our existing source code.

> *We could write this XML by hand, but it is far easier to use the Microsoft Scriptlet Wizard, available from http:/msdn.microsoft.com/scripting/scriptlets/scp10en.exe. This self-extracting executable contains the scriptlet runtime SCROBJ.DLL, the Scriptlet Wizard, and documentation. Not only does the Scriptlet Wizard generate the needed XML, but it will generate a globally unique identifier (GUID) for the COM class ID. Otherwise, we'd need to do a few more steps ourselves. These steps are well known to long-time COM programmers (defined as anyone working before Visual Studio added COM wizards), but awkward for most script writers.*

Here's the structure of the XML we need. It's in the implementation file `ServerSender.sct`:

```
<scriptlet>
<Registration ... attributes to register a COM component here ... />
<public>
    ... XML elements mapping functions to methods here ...
</public>
<script language=Javascript> // or VBScript
<![CDATA[
    ... script code here
]]>
</script>
</scriptlet>
```

*One quirk of the Scriptlet Wizard beta users should be aware of is that Automation support is assumed. The beta 2 scriptlet wizard will generate an `<implements>` element that is assumed by `scrobj.dll`. This element is used to declare COM interfaces other than the one used for scripting. If the `<interfaces>` element is removed, the scriptlet will work properly.*

We tell `SCROBJ.DLL` we're defining a scriptlet, then we provide the information needed when we want to register the component. The mapping between the script and the methods and properties of the component is contained within the `<public>` element. The source itself is held in the usual `<script>` element. It is buried within a `CDATA` XML element to make the source code opaque to XML and preserve XML 1.0 compliance.

Here's how it works out for `ServerSender`, our server-side message sending component:

```
<?XML version="1.0"?>
<scriptlet>

<registration
    description="ServerSender"
    progid="ServerSender.Scriptlet"
    version="1.00"
    classid="{caa64010-b9e5-11d2-a51b-004005407f69}"
>
</registration>

<public>
    <property name="Private">
        <get/>
        <put/>
    </property>
    <property name="Machine">
        <get/>
        <put/>
    </property>
    <property name="Queue">
        <get/>
        <put/>
    </property>
    <method name="Send">
        <PARAMETER name="strLabel"/>
        <PARAMETER name="strMsg"/>
    </method>
</public>
```

#### Chapter 7

We started to create this through the following dialog in the Scriptlet Wizard:

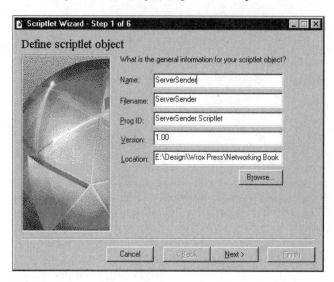

The `progid` for this component is `ServerSender.Scriptlet`; we'll need this identifier when we want to create an instance of the component in a script. The `classid` is generated by the Wizard. If you are not using the Wizard but are writing a component by hand, you will need to use some other tool (such as `GUIDGEN.EXE`, from Visual Studio) to generate this number.

Next, we select an implementation language and some options. Note that you do not need to check **Support Active Server Pages** to use your scriptlet with ASP. The support that option refers to allows you to get access to ASP's stock objects like `Request` and `Response`.

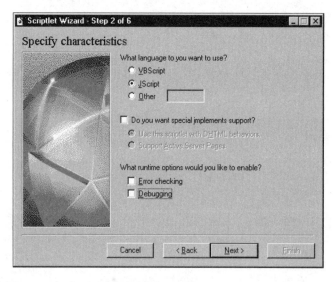

Now we need to define our methods and properties:

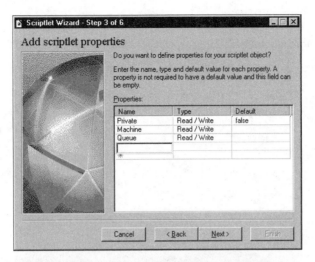

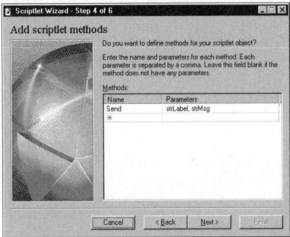

Our `Private`, `Machine`, and `Queue` properties are mapped to `get_xxx()` and `put_xxx()` methods as in the client-side DHTML scriptlet version. Our `Send()` method is defined by a `<method>` element whose name attribute provides the name of the method. We could provide an alias here if we wanted to have one name for the implementing function name and another for the publicly programmable interface. This is done like so:

```
<method name=Send internalName=MyAwfulInternalNameIDontWantToExpose>
```

where `internalName` is an attribute whose value is the name of the implementing function. If `internalName` does not appear, the value of `name` is used.

The next dialog in the Scriptlet Wizard allows you to specify events for your component, which is not important to this particular scriptlet. The final dialog summarizes what you have specified for your interface. Once you click Finish, the interface declarations in XML are generated. You finish the implementation by filling in the code for the properties and methods, which I did by copying it from the DHTML scriptlet version.

### *ServerReceiver*

The registration and interface mapping XML for the server-side version of `Receiver`, `ServerReceiver.sct`, is:

```
<?XML version="1.0"?>
<scriptlet>

<registration
    description="ServerReceiver"
    progid="ServerReceiver.Scriptlet"
    version="1.00"
    classid="{08e38020-b9e6-11d2-a51b-004005407f69}"
>
</registration>

<public>
    <property name="Machine">
        <get/>
        <put/>
    </property>
    <property name="Queue">
        <get/>
        <put/>
    </property>
    <method name="Receive">
        <PARAMETER name="strLabel"/>
        <PARAMETER name="nMaxMsgs"/>
    </method>
</public>
```

# Toy Ordering Sample Application

Let's put our components to use. We're going to build a very simple order entry page for an exciting new product line, the Mega-Trouble Toys. Customer orders will be placed into a message queue by an ASP script that uses the `ServerSender` component. Since we won't be building the entire business, we'll develop a page that uses `Receiver` to view all customer orders in the queue. This is loosely analogous to an internal management application.

Observe the flow within our miniature application. We've isolated messaging software within the organization so we don't have to expose our queues to public access. Depending on the needs of a real-world application, we might make the queues public or expose them selectively to trusted customers and vendors. For our application, we assume we are going to deal with the general public. We want to protect our queues and make the application available to clients that haven't installed our components and the MSMQ COM components.

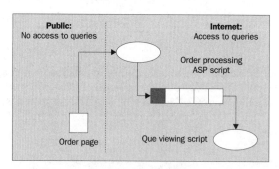

## Sending Toy Order Messages

The following screen shot shows our order entry page. It is a simple HTML forms-based page. There are no scripts; we simply send the order parameters to the order processing script, `OrderEntry.asp`, with a `POST`:

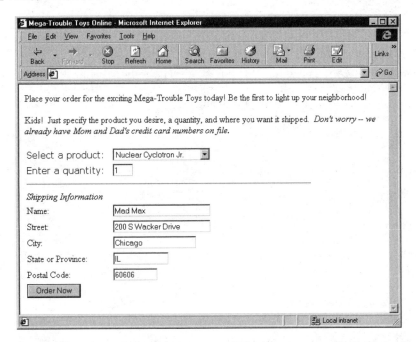

```
<FORM ACTION="OrderEntry.asp" METHOD="post">
<TABLE PADDING = 1 width="80%">

<tr>
    <td WIDTH="30%" STYLE="FONT-FAMILY: Verdana; align: left">
    Select a product:
    </td>
    ...
</tr>
</TABLE>
</FORM>
```

When the order reaches the server, we want to convert the form field values into XML, then submit the resulting document as a message to the toy order queue. The first task is to create a `ServerSender` component. Recall that this is a scriptlet, so we perform this task just as we would for any COM object:

```
MailBox = Server.CreateObject("ServerSender.Scriptlet");
if (MailBox != null)
{
    ...
```

Once we have a message-sending component, we compose our message. We get at the form field values through the usual calls to the ASP built-in method `Request()`. Since our XML is fairly simple for this example, we can build it "manually" rather than resorting to the XML DOM methods in MSXML.

```
strMsg += "<Order><Requestor><Name>" + Request.Form("shipname") +
        "</Name>";
strMsg += "<ShipTo>" + Request.Form("shipstreet") + " " +
        Request.Form("shipcity") + " ";
strMsg += Request.Form("shipstate") + " " + Request.Form("shipzip") +
        "</ShipTo></Requestor>";
strMsg += "<Product>" + Request.Form("productlist") + "</Product>";
strMsg += "<Quantity>" + Request.Form("quantity") + "</Quantity></Order>";
```

Sending the message is simply a matter of specifying the `Machine` and `Queue` properties to the name of the receiving machine and queue we've set up for our application, then calling the `Send()` method. If everything is successful, `Send()` returns the value `SENT`. Otherwise, one of a variety of error codes will be returned indicating the problem.

```
MailBox.Machine = "philly";
MailBox.Queue = "orders";

if (MailBox.Send("Toy order", strMsg) == SENT)
{
    ... // Congratulatory text here
```

Here's the full text of the order placing script in `OrderEntry.asp`:

```
var MailBox;
var strMsg = "";
var SENT = 1;

MailBox = Server.CreateObject("ServerSender.Scriptlet");
if (MailBox != null)
{
    strMsg += "<Order><Requestor><Name>" + Request.Form("shipname") +
            "</Name>";
    strMsg += "<ShipTo>" + Request.Form("shipstreet") + " " +
            Request.Form("shipcity");
    strMsg += Request.Form("shipstate") + " " + Request.Form("shipzip") +
            "</ShipTo></Requestor>";
    strMsg += "<Product>" + Request.Form("productlist") + "</Product>";
    strMsg += "<Quantity>" + Request.Form("quantity") +
            "</Quantity></Order>";

    MailBox.Machine = "philly";
    MailBox.Queue = "orders";

    if (MailBox.Send("Toy order", strMsg) == SENT)
    {
        Response.Write("Thank you for ordering a Mega-Trouble Toy!  ");
        Response.Write("We will send the following product:<p/><B>");
        Response.Write(Request.Form("productlist") + " (<em>quantity " +
                Request.Form("quantity") + "</em>)<p/>");
        Response.Write("</B>to<p/><B>");
        Response.Write(Request.Form("shipname") + "<p/>" +
                Request.Form("shipstreet") + "<p/>");
        Response.Write(Request.Form("shipcity") + ", " +
                Request.Form("shipstate") + " " +
                Request.Form("shipzip") + "</B>");
    }
}
```

```
        else
            Response.Write("We are experiencing difficulty entering your order
                            into our fulfillment system. No order has been taken.
                            Please try again soon.");

        MailBox = null;

    }
    else
        Response.Write("We are temporarily unable to process your request. Please
                        try again soon.");
```

For the values shown in the screen shot above, the message body would be:

```
<Order>
    <Requestor>
        <Name>Mad Max</Name>
        <ShipTo>200 S Wacker Drive Chicago IL 60606</ShipTo>
    </Requestor>
    <Product>Nuclear Cyclotron Jr.</Product>
    <Quantity>1</Quantity>
</Order>
```

This isn't a terribly robust vocabulary, but it is enough to give us a message to send to the order queue.

## Retrieving Toy Order Messages

Let's take a look at what's in the queue. We know we're looking for all messages with a label of `"Toy order"`. Since we're going to execute the code on a page within the boundaries of our message queuing topology, we'll use a simple HTML page with client-side script. That means we can embed an instance of the client-side `Receiver` component (DHTML scriptlet) on our page:

```
<OBJECT id="MailBox" style="HEIGHT: 0px; LEFT: 0px; TOP: 0px; WIDTH: 0px"
        type=text/x-scriptlet VIEWASTEXT>
    <PARAM NAME="Scrollbar" VALUE="0">
    <PARAM NAME="URL" VALUE="Receiver.html">
</OBJECT>
```

Since this DHTML scriptlet has no visible interface, we give it a value of zero for both dimensions. In case we decide to change the message label in the future, we'll provide the user with a form field for specifying the label. Remember, our intended user is someone inside the toy vendor's organization reviewing order status, so they'll know what label to look for. When the user clicks on a button, we want to retrieve the message label, then grab some messages from the queue. We'll grab up to four messages at a time. This is entirely arbitrary, and chosen largely for purposes of displaying the message bodies in a manageable window. We could make this user-definable in a real application or provide an interactive mechanism for working through the queue until all desired messages are found. This is completely independent of `Receiver`. It's `Receive()` method takes a maximum value without regard to how it was chosen.

We need to specify the `Machine` and `Queue` properties as we did when we sent the message, then call `Receive()` with the label value. Recall our DHTML scriptlet is named `MailBox`, and the form field containing the message label is named `SearchLabel`:

```
MailBox.Machine = "philly";
MailBox.Queue = "orders";
rMsgs = MailBox.Receive(document.all("SearchLabel").value, 4);
```

After that, we're just going to dump the message text into a `<DIV>` element on the page for viewing, adding a `<P/>` element after each one to place each message on a separate line.

```
for (var ni = 0; ni < rMsgs.length; ni++)
{
    oDiv.insertAdjacentHTML("beforeEnd", rMsgs[ni].Label + ": " +
                            rMsgs[ni].Body + "<p/>");
}
rMsgs = null;
```

We set the array variable to null to ensure proper clean up of resources. `MailBox` created the array object, but it is up to the client to release it. Here's the entire source for the button click handler:

```
function OnClick()
{
   var rMsgs, oDiv;

   MailBox.Machine = "philly";
   MailBox.Queue = "orders";
   rMsgs = MailBox.Receive(document.all("SearchLabel").value, 4);

   if (rMsgs != null)
   {
      oDiv = document.all("Msgs");
      oDiv.innerHTML = "";

      for (var ni = 0; ni < rMsgs.length; ni++)
      {
         oDiv.insertAdjacentHTML("beforeEnd", rMsgs[ni].Label + ": " +
                            rMsgs[ni].Body + "<p/>");
      }
      rMsgs = null;
   }
   else
      alert("Error in processing or no messages returned");
}
```

Here's what the page looks like for some sample toy orders. Note that while our message bodies are in XML, Internet Explorer doesn't know that and therefore won't recognize and render the markup even though we're using version 5. All we see is the PCDATA content:

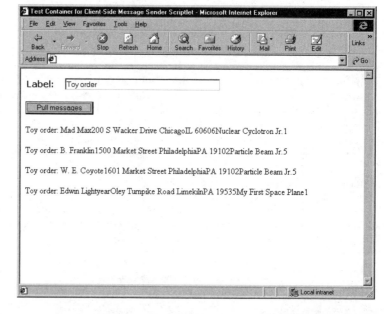

# Summary

In this chapter, we departed from our practice of synchronous communications to see how asynchronous communications could provide benefits in certain situations. Breaking the time dependencies between sender and receiver actions, which is at the heart of this style of communications, brings three kinds of benefits:

- ❑ Greater client responsiveness during lengthy waits
- ❑ Lesser requirements for servers under exceptional loads
- ❑ Ability to handle applications where the work spans long periods of time or has gaps in processing and resource availability

We started by exploring the asynchronous features of MSXML. We saw how to free the client to handle user input while waiting for lengthy XML document downloads. After that, we got to the heart of asynchronous communications with a general look at messaging middleware. We looked at Microsoft Message Queue as a specific, component-based example of messaging middleware. We built DHTML scriptlets to abstract the basic features of MSMQ, then used scriptlets (as opposed to DHTML scriptlets) to recast these components for server-side use. With these components in hand, we proceeded to build a lightweight application that illustrates the use of MSMQ in an e-commerce setting.

Although this chapter didn't extend our intranet development philosophy, it brought familiarity with a crucial aspect of intranet, and Internet, development. No matter what our development techniques, asynchronous messaging technology is required to make some classes of applications possible and scalable with internetworking approaches.

If you've been working through all the chapters of the book so far, you'll now have a good view of our 5 Principles of Cooperative Network Application Development. You've seen tools that make it easier to implement distributed intranet applications following the principles. However, you may be wondering how well the theory translates into practice. The next three chapters will answer your questions as we embark on three case studies using our tools and principles. You'll get to apply what you have learned and see how following the five principles can benefit you in practice.

# 8

# Wrox Blocks: Customer Service

Up until now we've spent our time developing our philosophy for building cooperative network applications. We defined the core principles, then introduced the techniques and technology needed to make them work. The remaining chapters of this book will be given over to the application of our philosophy. We'll build three small applications, each building on some portion of its predecessors.

Our examples are, of course, completely contrived. However, the design decisions may reflect the kinds of choices that actually get made in building software for corporations. Along the way, we'll purposely make some decisions that aren't optimal from the perspective of our extended example. In a real organization, managers and programmers cannot see the future. They must make decisions that minimize the risks they can anticipate. The purpose of making some decisions this way is to show how our techniques permit us to incorporate change without major disruption.

To start our case study, we introduce the fictional Wrox Blocks manufacturing company. Eager to convert to the idea of intranets, Wrox Blocks has decided to try out our philosophy in a small pilot project. The customer service department wants to be able to track calls to their customer service center. Customer service representatives will be able to enter new call incidents and review old ones.

## The Business Case

Wrox Blocks maintains a customer service call center. Customers who have problems or questions call representatives at this center. Providing good customer service requires that the representatives be able to retrieve the customer's history of calls. The Wrox Blocks call center is vast, with many customer service representatives. During peak buying periods, Wrox Blocks expands its customer service capability by press-ganging employees outside the call center into service as customer representatives. Consequently, the call tracking application must be inexpensive to deploy and require only a bare minimum of training to use. Client computer requirements must be minimal. Outside the call center we have no guarantee as to what computers will be available. Within the center, we wish to use the least expensive system we can in order to be able to equip the entire call center at a reasonable cost.

An intranet application seems ideal. Any system equipped with the company-standard browser (which for our purposes we are assuming is MS Internet Explorer 5.0) will be able to run the application. Presuming every Wrox Blocks employee knows how to use a browser, training will be limited to explaining the features specific to this application. If the user interface is well designed, training requirements should be minimal. Any computer within the organization has access to all Web servers deployed company-wide, so expanding the call center during peak seasons is simply a matter of providing new representatives with the URL of the page that starts the application. Using our philosophy, the application will be built so that it queries the directory for the location of services it needs.

Wrox Blocks has decided to give our philosophy a try, but insists that it be done at minimal extra expense. Any code written specifically to support the philosophy must be identified and kept to a minimum cost. The customer service call tracking application is intended to be a pilot program: the finished application must meet the business requirements of the call center, but there is no guarantee that the philosophy will be extended to other projects. The project will be considered to be a success if the following criteria are met:

❑ Staff programmers must be able to use the techniques with minimal extra training
❑ Cost for the project should be similar to, or less than, the cost of implementing it with traditional development techniques (excluding pre-packaged solutions)
❑ The application should have lower maintenance costs than an application built with traditional techniques
❑ The project should create resources that can be used in future projects

# Application Design

The key to a successful user interface for this application is minimizing the number of pages the service representative must view. In the course of working with customers, the service representative will have to perform the following tasks:

❑ Query the system for customer information
❑ Add new customers and update existing customers
❑ Query the system for call incident history
❑ Enter a new call incident

We should be able to fit this onto one page, which we will split with a horizontal line. Above this line we will have a data-bound form displaying the information for one customer. Below the line we will have a call history table, displaying in each cell the date and time of calls received along with a text box containing the call details.

This is what the page will look like above the rule:

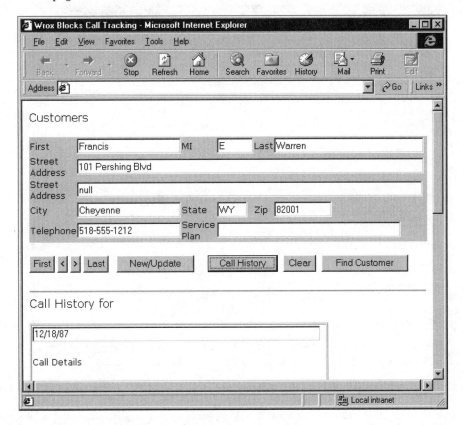

The four buttons in the lower left of the illustration perform the same functions as those we saw in the data binding examples of Chapter 6. They allow the user to display either the first or last customer in the bound collection, or move forward or backward one customer. The elements in the customer form will be bound to the XML returned from the server. In the event the server returns more than one customer in response to a search, we can use the buttons to move back and forth among those customers.

The remaining buttons allow us to perform the following functions:

- ❏  Enter new customers
- ❏  Edit existing customer information
- ❏  Retrieve the call history for a customer, to be displayed below the horizontal line on the page
- ❏  Clear the customer form in preparation for a search or new customer insertion
- ❏  Search for an existing customer

The lower portion of the page, shown in the following screen shot, allows a customer service representative to view the call history for a customer, or to insert new incident reports (new calls).

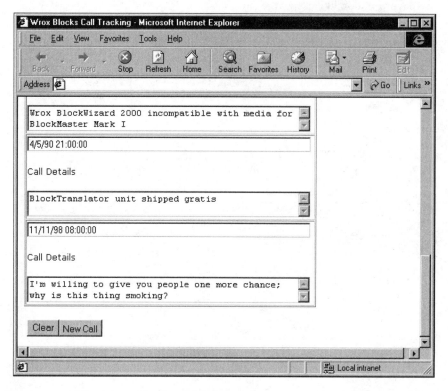

This application could be designed to bind directly to the database of customer information. Our principles, however, encourage us to hide the details of data storage from the application. Instead, we should bind the elements to customer and call tracking services. These services will operate directly with the database, but will exchange information with clients in the form of XML documents. This gives us freedom on the client-side to use methods other than data binding, as well as freedom on the server-side to change databases and database schemas.

> *If you wish to try out the application, you are encouraged to download the code and sample database from our Web site at* http://www.wrox/com. *The database includes customer and call entries for customers with the last names Greenleaf, Greeley, Mitty, Smith, Swift, and Warren.*

## How it All Fits Together

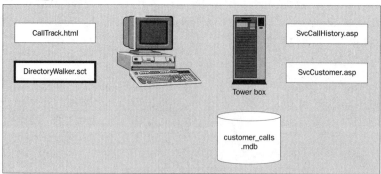

Here is the overall view of our application. We have a page, `CallTrack.html`, that will be downloaded to the client. As our user works with the elements in the page, scripts will execute locally. These scripts will use the DirectoryWalker scriptlet on the client to obtain the location of the services they require. These services are implemented on a Web server and are named `SvcCallHistory.asp` and `SvcCustomer.asp`. Each service parses the XML from the client to obtain search parameters. It then executes a SQL query against the database `customer_calls.mdb` and creates a new XML document based on the results. The client, meanwhile, receives the XML document created by the server in response to its request. Upon receipt, client-side scripts parse the document and display the contents in a data-bound DHTML form. Note that the server hides the details of data storage and retrieval from the client, while the client hides presentation issues from the server. Our principle of using XML to exchange data in a platform-neutral way preserves our independence and consequently improves the possibility of reuse. You could, for example, replace the client, `CallTrack.html`, with a software agent and nothing would need to be changed on the server.

# The Customer Service Client

The client side of the application, which we saw above, consists of a single HTML page. A customer service representative using the application need never leave this page. Nevertheless, there is a high degree of interactivity and communication with the server. The client queries each of two services to obtain data regarding customers and customer call history. This data is encoded in two XML data vocabularies. Each vocabulary is paired with a query vocabulary. The client takes values from the form, encodes an appropriate query, and submits it to the proper service. When the data is returned, the XML is bound to the form. When a customer service representative enters data on a new customer, or call information on an existing customer, the application formats this information in the data vocabulary and submits it to the server.

Our system uses two classes of objects: **Customers** and **Calls**. Customers in the customer service department's view are specialized from the general Wrox Blocks Customer class through the addition of a service plan property. Ideally, then, the programmers developing the service that manages Service Customers should write their server to handle both the Service Customer and Customer vocabularies. That way, the service can share the Customer subset of Service Customer information with any application that can process Customer information. This follows from principle 5, which calls in part for services to degrade gracefully. Call history is unique to the customer service department and their view of customers. Since call reports are unique to Service Customers it is useful to manage this data through another service rather than trying to fold it into the one handling customers.

Either way, the client is isolated from the server-side details of managing the data. As long as the client uses the techniques we developed in earlier chapters, we are free to use whatever database or file management techniques we wish. More importantly, everyone who has knowledge of the XML vocabularies we define can make use of the services we develop. Conversely, the servers are isolated from the techniques used by the client. Although we use data binding, the services are not required to support this. We could move the services to another operating system with no support for UDA and the application would continue to work.

# The Services

The services we develop are implemented with ASPs. Not surprisingly, these ASPs use ADO to access customer data in an Access database, which is by far the simplest technique for our purposes. We are developing the whole system from scratch, so we are free to use technology that is friendly to our platform and efficient in terms of the requirements of the system. Many real-life organizations, however, will have legacy data residing on mainframe systems. They could use messaging or some proprietary API to access the data.

Both services follow a similar format. They extract the values passed in a form element named `XMLRequest`, parsing the XML and determining what vocabulary is being submitted. Customers and call reports are packaged as collections. Even though our particular client will only submit one customer record or one call report at a time, it is reasonable to pass collections of customers and calls back and forth between clients and the service (in fact, this will be a common occurrence going from the server to the client). Once the server determines which vocabulary it is seeing it formats a SQL query, executes it, and returns data to the client as an XML document. In the case of a query, this will be a collection of zero or more Customers, Service Customers, or Call Reports. In the case of a submission from the client, it will be a positive or negative acknowledgement to the client.

The ASPs are pure script and return nothing but XML. They contain no `<HTML>`, `<HEAD>`, or `<BODY>` elements. They make liberal use of MSXML and objects from ADO, but these are created dynamically. Consequently, they are more like small program fragments than Web pages.

# Exchange Vocabularies

Our application will require four XML vocabularies for the exchange of data between the client and server. The client needs to be able to ask the server for customers matching some criteria and for calls from a particular client. The server, in turn, will need to respond with collections of customers matching a customer query, and collections of calls matching a call query. In addition, the client will use the customer and call collection vocabularies to push new customers and calls to the server for storage.

## Customer Query

We've decided to allow applications to query the `SvcCustomer` service by the customer's last name, zip code, and service plan name. The programming team recognizes that their notion of a customer is a specialized form of a 'basic' customer, the only difference being the service plan. Knowing this, they write their `SvcCustomerQuery` as being inherited from `CustomerQuery`, which they define at the same time. A valid query must contain a `CustomerQuery`. Additionally, `SvcCustomerQuery` will have a `SvcPlan` element. This vocabulary, in turn, must contain one or more of the following: a customer ID, customer last name, and zip code. Here is a shell for a complete `SvcCustomerQuery`:

```
<SvcCustomerQuery>
    <CustomerQuery>
        <CustomerID/>
        <LastName/>
        <PostalCode/>
    </CustomerQuery>
    <SvcPlan/>
</SvcCustomerQuery>
```

Although we won't be using a DTD to validate our documents, the shell is more formally defined thus:

```
<!ELEMENT    SvcCustomerQuery    (CustomerQuery, SvcPlan)>
<!ELEMENT    CustomerQuery       (CustomerID, LastName, PostalCode)>
<!ELEMENT    CustomerID          #PCDATA>
<!ELEMENT    LastName            #PCDATA>
<!ELEMENT    PostalCode          #PCDATA>
<!ELEMENT    SvcPlan             #PCDATA>
```

The Customer service maintains a unique customer ID. As a matter of course, Wrox Blocks does not expose this ID to its customers – the human touch and all that. Our client application, therefore, will not use the ID as part of its query, although the customer collection returned in response to a query will have this information. Similarly, when a new customer is entered we will allow the service to assign the ID.

## Call Query

It was reasonable to query for customers based on the customer's name and other parameters. This is the sort of information a customer service representative would receive over the telephone. This, of course, could result in multiple customer rows being returned to the client. Each will have a customer ID, so we can be more precise when searching for the call records for the customer. In fact, we need to be more precise to avoid mixing call records for several customers. Here is the shell for the SvcCallQuery:

```
<SvcCallQuery>
    <CustomerID/>
</SvcCallQuery>
```

This corresponds to the following DTD:

```
<!ELEMENT    SvcCallQuery    CustomerID>
<!ELEMENT    CustomerID      #PCDATA>
```

## Customer Response

Documents returned in response to a SvcCustomerQuery query will always consist of a Collection of one or more SvcCustomer elements. As noted previously, SvcCustomer is a specialization of Customer. A Customer element contains elements for the name, customer identifier, and contact information of the customer. The SvcCustomer element contains an element for the name of the service plan the customer purchased as well as the Customer element. All elements are mandatory. Here is a shell for a document containing one SvcCustomer element:

```
<Collection>
    <SvcCustomer>
        <Customer>
            <CustomerID/>
            <FirstName/>
            <MI/>
            <LastName/>
            <Street1/>
            <Street2/>
            <City/>
            <State/>
            <PostalCode/>
```

```
            <Telephone/>
        </Customer>
        <SvcPlan/>
    </SvcCustomer>
</Collection>
```

The DTD for this is a little unusual. We are going to use `Collection` as the document type. Strictly speaking, this should translate to one DTD, but we've been using `Collection` as a general purpose container. Purists would say we need to declare a namespace for each use of `Collection`, but we won't be that strict here:

```
<!ELEMENT    Collection    SvcCustomer*>
<!ELEMENT    SvcCustomer   (Customer, SvcPlan)>
<!ELEMENT    Customer      (CustomerID, FirstName, MI, LastName, Street1, Street2,
                            City, State, PostalCode, Telephone)>
<!ELEMENT    CustomerID    #PCDATA>
<!ELEMENT    FirstName     #PCDATA>
<!ELEMENT    MI            #PCDATA>
<!ELEMENT    LastName      #PCDATA>
<!ELEMENT    Street1       #PCDATA>
<!ELEMENT    Street2       #PCDATA>
<!ELEMENT    City          #PCDATA>
<!ELEMENT    State         #PCDATA>
<!ELEMENT    PostalCode    #PCDATA>
<!ELEMENT    Telephone     #PCDATA>
<!ELEMENT    SvcPlan       #PCDATA>
```

*If we stick with a document type of Collection, the internal structure would be set by the first use of Collection. Any subsequent use would be invalid because it didn't match the first use. For example, we could have a Collection of Customers and a Collection of Call Records. The two would have very different structures below the first child level. The pure approach would be to declare a Customer namespace and a Call Records namespace so that we could reuse the Collection element.*

## Call History Response

Call history response documents, like `SvcCustomer` documents, consist of collections of zero or more `CallReport` elements, each of which must contain elements for the date and time of the call, and an element containing the free-form textual details entered by a customer representative.

```
<Collection>
    <CallReport>
        <CustomerID/>
        <Date/>
        <CallDetails/>
    </CallReport>
</Collection>
```

Here is the variation of `Collection` that we are using:

```
<!ELEMENT    Collection    CallReport*>
<!ELEMENT    CallReport    (CustomerID, Date, CallDetails)>
<!ELEMENT    CustomerID    #PCDATA>
<!ELEMENT    Date          #PCDATA>
<!ELEMENT    CallDetails   #PCDATA>
```

# Implementation

The Wrox Blocks programming team familiarized themselves with our development philosophy before beginning. In addition to discerning the types of classes in the system and the XML vocabularies, the team latched onto the use of components. The team decided to use the MSXML DOM interfaces for parsing and manipulating the exchange data; the IXMLHTTP interface of MSXML to facilitate the transmission of XML without leaving the page; and the XML DSO (last seen in Chapter 6), again implemented by MSXML, for data binding. ADO is employed for the retrieval, insertion, and updating of relational data. The DirectoryWalker scriptlet we developed earlier in this book is being used to locate the services (in scriptlet, not DHTML scriptlet form).

Given the projected release date of Windows 2000, many of our readers will not be able to use the Active Directory when working through this chapter. Even after it becomes available, many of you will be working without a dedicated server. For this reason, I have provided a stub version of the DirectoryWalker scriptlet with the toolkit. This resource may be downloaded from our Web site at http://www.wrox.com/. Open the scriptlet in an editor and modify the value of the variable sLocation to reflect the virtual directory where you put the ASPs. The stub is identical to the live version in terms of its interface and usage.

Regardless of which version of the DirectoryWalker you use, be sure to register it as discussed in Chapter 7. In addition to the usual IIS steps to create a new virtual directory, you will need to set up an ODBC system DSN through the ODBC portion of the Control Panel. It should refer to ordertrack.mdb, use the Microsoft Access ODBC driver, and have no user ID and no password associated with it.

The programming team might also have made use of the DataSlicer scriptlet on the server to help build and breakdown SvcCustomer and Customer records. The team missed this possibility, but the impact is slight. The difference between the two vocabularies is minimal, so the DataSplicer offers only a small amount of assistance.

# Locating Services

We assume the network administrator configured Active Directory with information regarding the Customer, SvcCustomer, and CallReport vocabularies using the conventions in Chapter 2. HTTP is assumed as the transmission protocol, so the directory entry includes only the path and resource portions of the URL. Since this is a pilot project, the entries were made in the home domain of the Customer Service department. If it succeeds, the information can be migrated farther up on the directory tree to increase its visibility. The client page, CallTrack.html, contains a global instance of the DirectoryWalker scriptlet and a utility function using it:

```
var walker = new ActiveXObject("DirectoryWalker.Scriptlet");

function GetASP(svc)
{
    walker.User = "custsvcdept";
    walker.Pwd = "";
    return walker.SearchHome(svc);
}
```

When we need a service URL, we call GetASP() with the name of the needed vocabulary as its parameter. We add the prefix 'http://' to the value returned from GetASP() and use the result as the URL for the XMLHTTP component.

*If you use scriptlets with the most typical security settings in IE, you will likely be prompted to the effect that the components in the page may not be safe for scripting. In some configurations, the script may fail because you are not allowed to run unsafe components. There are several remedies for this. First, and simplest, you can set security to low. If you do not wish to be prompted, you can change the settings as follows: Go into the Security tab of the Internet Options... dialog under Tools and click on the Custom Level button. In the dialog box that appears, change the Initialize and Script ActiveX controls not marked as safe setting from Prompt to Enable.*

*More advanced readers may wish to modify the registry settings for the components we use to mark them safe for scripting. This involves the use of* RegEdt32 *to modify the registry at a low level, so it is not an approach to be taken lightly. In some cases, if the component you are using is tied to a DHTML element, creating a DHTML behavior might be more appropriate. Both of the latter approaches are advanced scripting and COMtopics. You may find more information regarding this on MSDN at* http://msdn.microsoft.com/scripting/.

It is understood that any service that supports a given data vocabulary, like SvcCustomer, also understands the complimentary query vocabulary, in our case SvcCustomerQuery. The query vocabularies are useless without their data vocabularies, and the data vocabularies are only useful without the query vocabularies when submitting data. With the understanding that query and data vocabularies are linked, we are free to ask for either when locating a service. Some programmers will find it natural to always ask for the data vocabulary, since that is what they are really interested in. Others will want to ask for whatever vocabulary they are about to send to the server, since that is what the service must process. The advantage to asking for the data vocabulary is that both parties are very clear on what will be returned to the client. Asking for the query vocabulary, however, ensures that the server can process what you are about to send up to the server. If there is any doubt that a particular query vocabulary is always paired with the data vocabulary, you should ask for the query vocabulary. Otherwise, clients should ask for the data vocabulary. This is a good place to keep things loose so that new applications can easily integrate older services.

# Managing the Data Binding

Data binding will get quite a work out in CallTrack.html. We use the technology to display both the customer records and the call report records in two forms on the page. The call report form is a table, so we are calling on data binding to replicate a single template row as many times as is needed to display the call history for a single customer. This is not done just once. A typical user session will have a customer service representative making multiple searches for customers and call histories, with insertions of customers and call reports interspersed. We have to take some care to make sure the binding is never broken.

To accomplish this, CallTrack.html contains two data islands, one for each form. These are empty shells within the <BODY> element of the page:

```
<XML id=xmlCustomers>
<Collection>
   <SvcCustomer>
      <Customer>
          <CustomerID></CustomerID>
          <FirstName></FirstName>
          <MI></MI>
```

```
            <LastName></LastName>
            <Street1></Street1>
            <Street2></Street2>
            <City></City>
            <State></State>
            <PostalCode></PostalCode>
            <Telephone></Telephone>
        </Customer>
        <SvcPlan></SvcPlan>
    </SvcCustomer>
</Collection>
</XML>

<XML id=xmlCalls>
<Collection>
    <CallReport>
        <Date></Date>
        <CallDetails></CallDetails>
    </CallReport>
</Collection>
</XML>
```

The form elements are bound at design time to the appropriate data island. This is the INPUT element for the first name on the customer form:

```
<INPUT dataFld=FirstName dataSrc=#xmlCustomers id=firstNameText
name=firstNameText>
```

Subsequently, we shall see that we need to manually manipulate the parse tree of the data islands and dynamically bind to the data, as we did in Chapter 6. With this in mind, let's proceed to the specifics of our functional implementation.

# Entering and Editing Customers

We'll start by examining what happens when we add a new customer into the database from the client. Starting from a blank form, the customer service representative fills in the information and clicks the button marked New/Update. Things begin to happen on the client side in the button click handler function, OnInsertClick(). The client begins to build a query document from the data provided by the user.

## Client Side

The client will perform exactly the same actions to build the query document whether we are entering a completely new customer record or modifying an old one. We want to format a Collection document containing a SvcCustomer element, which in turn contains the values of the fields in our form. There is one hidden INPUT element, custIDText, which makes all the difference. If we are entering a new customer, there is nothing in this field. If the server receives no text value in the CustomerID element, it assumes this document represents a new customer and assigns a value.

The client, however, is indifferent. `OnInsertClick()` begins by retrieving the form element values and plugging them into the proper places in an XML document:

```
function OnInsertClick()
{
   var sReq = "";

   sReq  = "<Collection><SvcCustomer><Customer><CustomerID>" +
           custIDText.value + "</CustomerID>";
   sReq += "<FirstName>" + firstNameText.value + "</FirstName><MI>" +
           miText.value + "</MI>";
   sReq += "<LastName>" + lnameText.value + "</LastName><Street1>" +
           street1.value + "</Street1>";
   sReq += "<Street2>" + street2.value + "</Street2><City>" + City.value +
           "</City>";
   sReq += "<State>" + state.value + "</State><PostalCode>" + zip.value +
           "</PostalCode>";
   sReq += "<Telephone>" + telephone.value + "</Telephone></Customer>";
   sReq += "<SvcPlan>" + svcPlanText.value +
           "</SvcPlan></SvcCustomer></Collection>";
```

Next we want to create an instance of the `IXMLHTTP` interface and use it to `POST` the document to a service supporting the `SvcCustomer` vocabulary. However, there's a small issue to contend with. For simplicity, we are using the mime encoding for an HTML form. That means the document we've just composed must have spaces converted to the literal `%20` before transmission. Other non-alphanumeric characters are affected as well. We use the JavaScript `String` object's `replace()` method to perform the conversion. This needs a regular expression parameter for the character we wish to find and replace. We create such a constant and call `replace`:

```
var regExp = / /g;
sReq = sReq.replace(regExp, "%20");
```

*I've omitted the conversion for other, atypical, characters in the interest of simplicity. The form encoding makes life easy for us on the server as the ASP Request object can retrieve the XML document in one piece given the name of the form element, in our case XMLRequest, whose value is the document. Some real-world problems may involve the frequent occurrence of non-alphanumeric characters. In that case, it might be easier to use another mime encoding. However, doing so means that we would have to retrieve the value in chunks, as we did in Chapter 6 with the Internet Transfer Control.*

So far, our client has no idea where to send the information. We query the directory using the `GetASP()` utility function we saw earlier. This encapsulates the calls to the `DirectoryWalker` component, returning the core of a URL naming the service. We've previously established two instances of the `XMLHTTP` component with global scope. We'll use one, `xmlCustomerd`, to process the posting of customer information. We complete the URL with the protocol identifier (`http://`) and use the steps we've seen before to cause a `POST` from `xmlCustomerd`:

```
var xmlCustomerd=new ActiveXObject("Microsoft.XMLHTTP");
var sServer = "http://" + GetASP("SvcCustomer");
xmlCustomerd.Open("POST", sServer, false);
xmlCustomerd.setRequestHeader("Content-Type",
                "application/x-www-form-urlencoded");
xmlCustomerd.Send("XMLRequest=" + sReq);
```

At this point, `xmlCustomerd` contains a parsed XML document from the server. If the customer insertion went well, this document should read `<ACK/>` (representing 'acknowledged'). If we receive any other indication, we inform the user of an error:

```
    if (xmlCustomerd.ResponseXML.documentElement.nodeName != "ACK")
        alert("Customer update was not accomplished due to a server problem.");
}
```

This anticlimactic finish hides all the activity that took place on the server following our POST.

# Server Side

Our service for the `SvcCustomer` vocabulary is an ASP, `SvcCustomer.asp`, that consists entirely of text. It begins by retrieving the root node of the document passed to it by the `XMLHTTP` component. Now, all the vocabularies it is prepared to deal with require some sort of database access, so we prepare an ADO connection and recordset objects:

```
<%@ Language=JavaScript %>
<%

var dbConn, dbRecordSet;

/* Create a parser object and retrieve the XML search request
   from the server's Request object. */

var parser = Server.CreateObject("microsoft.xmldom");
parser.loadXML(Request.Form("XMLRequest").Item);

// Configure the mime type to reflect XML
Response.ContentType="text/xml";

if (parser.readyState == 4 && parser.parseError == 0)
{
   // Establish a global connection
   dbConn = Server.CreateObject("ADODB.Connection");
   dbConn.Open("CustService", "", "");
   dbRecordSet = Server.CreateObject("ADODB.RecordSet");
```

## Determining What to Do

The service is prepared to respond to `SvcCustomerQuery`, `CustomerQuery`, and `Collection` vocabulary documents. In the latter case, we need to look inside and see if the collection consists of `SvcCustomer` or `Customer` objects. That's the case here:

```
switch (parser.documentElement.nodeName)
   {
      case "SvcCustomerQuery":
         ProcessSvcCustomerQuery(parser.documentElement);
         break;
      case "CustomerQuery":
         ProcessCustomerQuery(parser.documentElement);
         break;
      case "Collection":
         // Receiving an update to SvcCustomer
         switch (parser.documentElement.childNodes(0).nodeName)
```

```
        {
            case "SvcCustomer":
            case "Customer":
                // Only difference is SvcPlan, which can be null
                ProcessCustomerInsertion(parser.documentElement);
                break;
        }
        break;
    ...
```

## Putting Data into the Database

Whether we are adding a new customer or updating an existing one, the ASP will be receiving elements for all the columns of the customer table in the database. There are eleven of them. The first thing we want to do, then, is retrieve them and place them in an array of strings:

```
function ProcessCustomerInsertion(collectionNode)
{
    var rsFrags = new Array("", "", "", "", "", "", "", "", "", "", "");

    for (var ni = 0; ni < collectionNode.childNodes.length; ni++)
    {
        switch (collectionNode.childNodes(ni).nodeName)
        {
            case "SvcCustomer":
                // First child must be Customer
                var custNode = collectionNode.childNodes(ni).childNodes(0);
                for (var nk = 0; nk < custNode.childNodes.length; nk++)
                {
                    var sFragVal = custNode.childNodes(nk).text;
                    switch (custNode.childNodes(nk).nodeName)
                    {
                        case "CustomerID":
                            rsFrags[0] = sFragVal;
                            break;

                        case "FirstName":
                            rsFrags[1] = sFragVal;
                            break;
                        case "MI":
                            rsFrags[2] = sFragVal;
                            break;
                        ...
                    }
                } // end of Customer loop
                break; // SvcCustomer case
            case "SvcPlan":
                rsFrags[10] = collectionNode.childNodes(ni).text;
                break;
        } // end of master switch statement
    } // end of master for - next loop
```

*All the columns of our simple customer table are string values. We'll keep things basic, as far as database retrieval goes, simply composing our SQL query through string concatenation. If your data includes a variety of data types, you will want to use a SQL query containing parameter placeholders, then use the ADO Parameter object to compose things by data type. This topic is covered in ADO 2.0 Programmers Reference, Wrox Press (ISBN 1-861001-83-5). We'll be focusing on the XML aspects of our topic in this chapter.*

Recall our business rule regarding customer IDs. We'll assign a unique number for new customers. For this, we can use the `Autonumber` data type in Access. Once assigned, we do not permit the ID to be modified Consequently, the presence of a non-empty `CustomerID` element tells us we are updating an existing customer; its absence indicates a new customer. Each case requires a different SQL query. A new customer requires an `INSERT`, for example:

```
INSERT INTO customers (cust_first, cust_mi, cust_last, cust_street1, cust_street2,
cust_city, cust_state, cust_postalcode, cust_telephone, cust_plan) VALUES ("John",
"A", "Doe", ... , "Gold");
```

An existing customer change requires an `UPDATE` to an existing row:

```
UPDATE customers SET cust_first="Jerome", cust_mi="B", ..., cust_plan="Minimal"
WHERE cust_id = "157";
```

Returning to `ProcessCustomerInsertion()`, we check for the presence of a `CustomerID` value and prepare the appropriate SQL command text:

```
if (rsFrags[0] == "")
{
   sCore = "INSERT INTO customers (cust_first, cust_mi, cust_last,
            cust_street1, cust_street2, cust_city, cust_state,
            cust_postalcode, cust_telephone, cust_plan) VALUES (";
   sQuery = sCore + MakeCustValues(rsFrags) + ");";
   DoQuery(sQuery);
}
else
{
   sCore = "UPDATE customers SET ";
   var sConstraint = " WHERE cust_id = " + rsFrags[0];
   sQuery = sCore + MakeCustSets(rsFrags) + sConstraint + ";";
   DoQuery(sQuery);
}
```

The first array entry, `rsFrags[0]`, contains the value, if any, for the `CustomerID` element. `MakeCustValues()` and `MakeCustSets()` are utility functions that compose the column-based portion of their respective SQL commands using the values in `rsFrags`.

`DoQuery()` is a utility function we use to execute the SQL command:

```
function DoQuery(sQuery)
{
   try
   {
      dbConn.Execute(sQuery);
      if (dbConn.Errors.Count > 0)
```

```
            Response.Write("<NACK/>");
        else
            Response.Write("<ACK/>");
    }
    catch(e)
    {
        Response.Write("<NACK/>");
    }
}
```

We use a `try-catch` block in the above code to avoid critical stops due to exceptions thrown by ADO. The `Errors` collection of the connection object indicates the presence or absence of problems with the command. If no problems were encountered, we expect to return the rowset and simply write `<ACK/>` back to the client to indicate success. If any problem is found, we send the negative acknowledgement, `<NACK/>`.

That takes us back to the point where we left the client. The next sections show the collected code for the client and server portions.

# Complete Client Code for Customer Insertion

The task of inserting a customer took us through code that is highly representative of the rest of the application. It is worthwhile studying this code in some depth. For convenience, here is the complete source code for the client side of that task.

```
function OnInsertClick()
{
    var sReq = "";

    sReq  = "<Collection><SvcCustomer><Customer><CustomerID>" +
            custIDText.value + "</CustomerID>";
    sReq += "<FirstName>" + firstNameText.value + "</FirstName><MI>" +
            miText.value + "</MI>";
    sReq += "<LastName>" + lnameText.value + "</LastName><Street1>" +
            street1.value + "</Street1>";
    sReq += "<Street2>" + street2.value + "</Street2><City>" + City.value +
            "</City>";
    sReq += "<State>" + state.value + "</State><PostalCode>" + zip.value +
            "</PostalCode>";
    sReq += "<Telephone>" + telephone.value + "</Telephone></Customer>";
    sReq += "<SvcPlan>" + svcPlanText.value +
            "</SvcPlan></SvcCustomer></Collection>";

    var regExp = / /g;
    sReq = sReq.replace(regExp, "%20");
    var sServer = "http://" + GetASP("SvcCustomer");
    xmlCustomerd.Open("POST", sServer, false);
    xmlCustomerd.setRequestHeader("Content-Type",
                                  "application/x-www-form-urlencoded");
    xmlCustomerd.Send("XMLRequest=" + sReq);

    if (xmlCustomerd.responseXML.documentElement.nodeName != "ACK")
        alert("Customer update was not accomplished due to a server problem.");
}
```

# Complete Server Code for Customer Insertion

The main body of SvcCustomer.asp is shared by all the tasks using this service. Many of the things we accomplished implementing customer insertion will prove to be representative of the rest of this service. Here, then, is the complete server-side source code for customer insertion.

```javascript
<%@ Language=JavaScript %>
<%

var dbConn, dbRecordSet;

/* Create a parser object and retrieve the XML search request
   from the server's Request object. */

var parser = Server.CreateObject("microsoft.xmldom");
parser.loadXML(Request.Form("XMLRequest").Item);

// Configure the mime type to reflect XML
Response.ContentType="text/xml";

if (parser.readyState == 4 && parser.parseError == 0)
{
    // Establish a global connection
    dbConn = Server.CreateObject("ADODB.Connection");
    dbConn.Open("CustService", "", "");
    dbRecordSet = Server.CreateObject("ADODB.RecordSet");

    // Check for the primary and secondary supported vocabularies
    switch (parser.documentElement.nodeName)
    {
        case "SvcCustomerQuery":
            ProcessSvcCustomerQuery(parser.documentElement);
            break;
        case "CustomerQuery":
            ProcessCustomerQuery(parser.documentElement);
            break;
        case "Collection":
            // Receiving an update to SvcCustomer
            switch (parser.documentElement.childNodes(0).nodeName)
            {
                case "SvcCustomer":
                case "Customer":
                    // Only difference is SvcPlan, which can be null
                    ProcessCustomerInsertion(parser.documentElement);
                    break;
            }
            break;

        default:
            // Lack of ACK will signal db error,
            // empty collection doesn't spoil data binding
            Response.Write("<Collection></Collection>");
    }
    // Clean up resources
    try
    {
        dbRecordSet.Close();
        dbConn.Close();
        dbConn = null;
        dbRecordSet = null;
    }
```

```
      catch (e)
      {
      }
}
else
   Response.Write("<Collection></Collection>");

parser = null;

function ProcessCustomerInsertion(collectionNode)
{
   var rsFrags = new Array("", "", "", "", "", "", "", "", "", "", "");

   for (var ni = 0; ni < collectionNode.childNodes.length; ni++)
   {
      switch (collectionNode.childNodes(ni).nodeName)
      {
         case "SvcCustomer":
            // First child must be Customer
            var custNode = collectionNode.childNodes(ni).childNodes(0);
            for (var nk = 0; nk < custNode.childNodes.length; nk++)
            {
               var sFragVal = custNode.childNodes(nk).text
               switch (custNode.childNodes(nk).nodeName)
               {
                  case "CustomerID":
                     rsFrags[0] = sFragVal;
                     break;

                  case "FirstName":
                     rsFrags[1] = sFragVal;
                     break;

                  ... // other properties here

                  case "PostalCode":
                     rsFrags[8] = sFragVal;
                     break;
                  case "Telephone":
                     rsFrags[9] = sFragVal;
                     break;
               }
            } // end of Customer loop
            break; // SvcCustomer case
         case "SvcPlan":
            rsFrags[10] = collectionNode.childNodes(ni).text;
            break;
      } // end of master switch statement
   } // end of master for - next loop

   var sCore, sQuery;
   if (rsFrags[0] == "")
   {
      sCore = "INSERT INTO customers (cust_first, cust_mi, cust_last,
             cust_street1, cust_street2, cust_city, cust_state,
             cust_postalcode, cust_telephone, cust_plan) VALUES (";
      sQuery = sCore + MakeCustValues(rsFrags) + ");";
      DoQuery(sQuery);
   }
```

```
        else
        {
            sCore = "UPDATE customers SET ";
            var sConstraint = " WHERE cust_id = " + rsFrags[0];
            sQuery = sCore + MakeCustSets(rsFrags) + sConstraint + ";";
            DoQuery(sQuery);
        }
    }
```

# Searching for Customers

Our customer service representatives won't always be modifying customer records, of course. More typically, they'll receive calls from existing customers and have to retrieve records from the SvcCustomer service. This is started in CallTrack.html, with the button handler function OnFindClick.

## Client Side

We permit searches by some combination of customer ID, last name, and zip code using the SvcCustomerQuery vocabulary. We once again make use of the global XMLHTTP component, xmlCustomerd, to perform a POST of a query document:

```
function OnFindClick()
{
    var sReq = "";
    var sServer = "http://" + GetASP("SvcCustomerQuery");
    xmlCustomerd.Open("POST", sServer, false);

    // Compose a SvcCustomerQuery
    sReq =
        "XMLRequest=<SvcCustomerQuery><CustomerQuery><CustomerID/><LastName>";
    sReq += lnameText.value + "</LastName>";
    sReq += "<PostalCode>" + zip.value + "</PostalCode></CustomerQuery>";
    sReq += "<SvcPlan>" + svcPlanText.value +
                                "</SvcPlan></SvcCustomerQuery>";

    // Convert spaces for mime encoding
    var regExp = / /g;
    sReq = sReq.replace(regExp, "%20");
    xmlCustomerd.setRequestHeader("Content-Type",
                "application/x-www-form-urlencoded");
    xmlCustomerd.Send(sReq);
    // Fix up the binding
    FixCustBinding();
}
```

This is similar to what we did when sending a customer record to the server. We compose an XML document, perform the mime encoding, and execute a POST using the component. In this case, however, we expect to receive zero or more SvcCustomer objects in a Collection document.

We need to manage the data binding, which we do in `FixCustBinding()`:

```
function FixCustBinding()
{
   while (xmlCustomers.documentElement.childNodes.length > 1)
   {
      xmlCustomers.documentElement.removeChild(
         xmlCustomers.documentElement.childNodes(1));
   }

   for (var ni = 0;
            ni < xmlCustomerd.ResponseXML.documentElement.childNodes.length;
            ni++)
   {
      xmlCustomers.documentElement.appendChild(
         xmlCustomerd.ResponseXML.documentElement.childNodes(ni).cloneNode(true));
   }

   if (xmlCustomers.documentElement.childNodes.length > 1)
   {
      xmlCustomers.documentElement.removeChild(
         xmlCustomers.documentElement.childNodes(0));
   }

   xmlCustomers.recordset.moveFirst();

   custtable.dataFld="Customer";
   custtable.dataSrc="#xmlCustomers";
   firstNameText.dataFld="FirstName";
   firstNameText.dataSrc="#xmlCustomers";

   ... // the rest of the fields here

   custIDText.dataFld = "CustomerID";
   custIDText.dataSrc = "#xmlCustomers";
}
```

This follows the pattern we established in Chapter 6: delete all but the first child of the data island root node, append deep copies of the returned `SvcCustomer` elements, then delete the remaining node from the original tree in the data island. Failing to do this causes the binding to fail as we would otherwise be pulling the data out from under the DSO while it is in use. Once all that is done, we jog the data binding through code to set the `dataFld` and `dataSrc` attributes of each form element. At this point, the customer form displays the new values received from the service. Let's see what `SvcCustomer.asp` had to do to obtain those values.

# Server Side

We return to the main body of `SvcCustomer.asp` to see where we go in response to the received document:

```
if (parser.readystate == 4 && parser.parseError.reason == "")
{
   dbConn = Server.CreateObject("ADODB.Connection");
   ...
   switch (parser.documentElement.nodeName)
   {
      case "SvcCustomerQuery":
```

```
            ProcessSvcCustomerQuery(parser.documentElement);
            break;
        case "CustomerQuery":
            ProcessCustomerQuery(parser.documentElement);
            break;
        case "Collection":
            switch (parser.documentElement.childNodes(0).nodeName)
            {
                case "SvcCustomer":
                case "Customer":
                ...
            }
            break;

        default:
            Response.Write("<Collection></Collection>");
    }
```

## Retrieving Customers

In the case under consideration, the ASP is receiving a document formed according to the
SvcCustomerQuery vocabulary. Our programming team, however, realized they should support
the generalized vocabulary CustomerQuery and structured their code accordingly:

```
function ProcessSvcCustomerQuery(node)
{
    var sSelectCore = "SELECT cust_first, cust_mi, cust_last, cust_id,
                    cust_street1, cust_street2, cust_city, cust_state,
                    cust_postalcode, cust_telephone, cust_plan FROM CUSTOMERS";

    var sConstraint = "";

    sConstraint = MakeSvcCustomerConstraint(node);
    if (sConstraint != "")
        sConstraint = " WHERE " + sConstraint;

    var sQuery = sSelectCore + sConstraint + ';';
    dbRecordSet = dbConn.Execute(sQuery);

    if (!dbRecordSet.BOF)
        dbRecordSet.MoveFirst();

    if (dbRecordSet.EOF)
        Response.Write("<Collection></Collection>");

    // Write the collection root node and then the rest of the contents
    Response.Write("<Collection>");
    while (!dbRecordSet.EOF)
    {
        WriteSvcCustomerBody(dbRecordSet);
        dbRecordSet.MoveNext();
    }
    Response.Write("</Collection>");
}
```

We build a query, execute it, and then write out the resulting recordset values as XML. As with our
previous example, we use string concatenation rather than Parameter objects to build the query.

Here's an example of a completed SQL command corresponding to a `SvcCustomerQuery` document:

```
SELECT cust_first, cust_mi, cust_last, cust_id, cust_street1, cust_street2,
cust_city, cust_state, cust_postalcode, cust_telephone, cust_plan FROM CUSTOMERS
WHERE cust_last="Smith" AND cust_postalcode="19103";
```

*Our query vocabulary allows the inclusion of the customer's ID number for generality of use. In our application, the ID is never displayed or entered manually, so this can never appear in a query arising from our client. Nevertheless, the service was built without knowledge of any particular client, so we include the code to handle that search parameter when building our SQL query.*

### Returning XML to the Client

Now that we have the result set, we have to write the values back to the client as XML so that they can be displayed. This occurs in `WriteSvcCustomerBody()`, which takes as its sole parameter the recordset we just obtained:

```
function WriteSvcCustomerBody(rsSvcCustomers)
{
   Response.Write("<SvcCustomer>");
   WriteCustomerBody(rsSvcCustomers);
   Response.Write("<SvcPlan>" + rsSvcCustomers("cust_plan") + "</SvcPlan>");
   Response.Write("</SvcCustomer>");
}
```

The code in the function `WriteCustomerBody()` is written as a separate function to allow us to handle `CustomerQuery` documents, and it functions much the same way.

# Clearing the Customer Form

It is useful to have a button that clears all entries in the customer form, particularly when a new call comes in and the customer representative needs to quickly enter search parameters. The programming task is one of putting the data binding back to an empty `SvcCustomer` document. When the user clicks on the **Clear** button, we ask MSXML to load a document consisting entirely of elements with no textual contents, then perform our usual tree manipulation – deleting all but one child, appending the new elements, then deleting the last original node from the parse tree. This leaves the form elements bound to an XML document whose text elements are empty. As a result, nothing appears in the form.

```
function OnClearClick()
{
   var parser = new ActiveXObject("microsoft.xmldom");
   parser.loadXML("<Collection><SvcCustomer><Customer><CustomerID/>
                <FirstName/><MI/><LastName/><Street1/><Street2/><City/>
                <State/><PostalCode/><Telephone/></Customer><SvcPlan/>
                </SvcCustomer></Collection>");
   if (parser.readystate == 4 && parser.parseError == 0)
   {
      while (xmlCustomers.documentElement.childNodes.length > 1)
```

```
        {
            xmlCustomers.documentElement.removeChild(
                xmlCustomers.documentElement.childNodes(1));
        }

        for (var ni = 0; ni < parser.documentElement.childNodes.length; ni++)
        {
            xmlCustomers.documentElement.appendChild(
                parser.documentElement.childNodes(ni).cloneNode(true));
        }

        if (xmlCustomers.documentElement.childNodes.length > 1)
        {
            xmlCustomers.documentElement.removeChild(
                xmlCustomers.documentElement.childNodes(0));
        }

        xmlCustomers.recordset.moveFirst();
    }
    parser = null;
}
```

# Entering Customer Call History

Once we've created a new customer, we need to be able to enter brief reports about their calls to the customer service center. `CallTrack.html` performs this task from the button click handler function `OnInsertCall()`.

## Client Side

We start by enforcing an important business rule: call reports cannot exist without being tied to a customer. We enforce this by looking for a customer ID in the hidden `INPUT` element named `custIDText`. If it is not found, the form is either empty or a new customer has not been submitted to the service. Either way, we shouldn't submit the call report. If we pass this check, we want to compose a document in the `CallReport` vocabulary and submit it the way we submitted `SvcCustomer` documents. This vocabulary consists of a `Collection` containing one or more `CallReport` elements. Our client will only ever submit one call report at a time, but some clients might engage in batch transfers, so we've enabled the vocabulary to handle this. Let's have a look at `OnInsertCall()`:

```
function OnInsertCall()
{
    var sRequest;

    if (custIDText.value != "")
    {
        // Compose a CallReport collection
        sRequest  = "<Collection><CallReport><CustomerID>" + custIDText.value +
                    "</CustomerID>";
        sRequest += "<Date>" + callDate.value + "</Date><CallDetail>" +
                    callDetail.value;
        sRequest += "</CallDetail></CallReport></Collection>";
```

Notice our programming team violated the spirit of our development philosophy. They knew the service would enter the current time when it received the document, because they were programming both sides of the exchange. Strictly speaking, the code above should have submitted a value for the <Date> element just in case a service speaking the `CallReport` vocabulary didn't perform this utility function. This is not a fault on the part of the service programmers; indeed, enforcing the current time as the time of the call report is a reasonable business decision, intended to preserve data integrity. Omitting the timestamp from the client side is typical of the kind of thing that goes on in the real world, but which might cause a problem down the line. Let's proceed to the rest of `OnInsertCall()`:

```
        // Convert spaces for mime encoding
        var regExp = / /g;
        sRequest = sRequest.replace(regExp, "%20");
        var sServer = "http://" + GetASP("CallReport");
        xmlCalld.Open("POST", sServer, false);
        xmlCalld.setRequestHeader("Content-Type",
                "application/x-www-form-urlencoded");
        xmlCalld.Send("XMLRequest=" + sRequest);
        OnCallHistory();
    }
    else
        alert("We cannot add a service incident report without a customer.");
}
```

We've seen this before. It's virtually identical to the code we used to submit `SvcCustomer` and `SvcCustomerQuery` documents. What's that call to `OnCallHistory()` though? After submitting a call report, the easiest way to refresh the client is to retrieve the customer's entire call history. Even if this is the first call report for a new customer, we'll at least pick up the time stamp added on the server side. Call report retrieval is our next task. Before we get to that, however, let's wrap up this task by looking at what happens on the server.

# Server Side

A quick check with `DirectoryWalker` shows that the `CallReport` vocabulary is supported by an ASP named `SvcCallHistory.asp`. The main body of that script is nearly identical to `SvcCustomer.asp`. We retrieve the incoming document, set up some database resources, then switch according to the vocabulary of the incoming document. A `CallReport` document, as we saw above, is part of a `Collection`. Here's the relevant part of the switch statement in `SvcCallHistory.asp`'s main body:

```
    ...
    case "Collection":
       switch (parser.documentElement.childNodes(0).nodeName)
       {
          case "CallReport":
             ProcessCallReport(parser.documentElement);
             break;
          default:
             Response.Write("<Collection></Collection>");
             break;
       }
       break;
    ...
```

## Handling Call Reports

`ProcessCallReport()`, in turn, composes a SQL query and submits it to the database. Again, we've included the flexibility to handle more than one call report per `Collection` document:

```
function ProcessCallReport(collectionNode)
{
    var sDetails, sID;

    for (var ni = 0; ni < collectionNode.childNodes.length; ni++)
    {
        switch (collectionNode.childNodes(ni).nodeName)
        {
            case "CallReport":
                sDetails = collectionNode.childNodes(ni).childNodes(2).text;
                sID = collectionNode.childNodes(ni).childNodes(0).text;
                InsertCallReport(sDetails, sID);
                break;
        }
    }
}
```

We work through each child element of the `Collection` root. If it is a `CallReport` – and who knows what crazy information a bad client might send? – we extract the detail text and the customer ID and send it off to `InsertCallReport()`. That function compiles the SQL statement for one insertion and executes it.

## Database Details for a Call Report

We're not permitting customer service representatives to edit existing call reports – the temptation to cover up bad service would be too great! This has the happy effect of simplifying our programming. We don't have to worry about whether we need an `INSERT` or an `UPDATE`. All our commands related to the task of submitting call reports will be `INSERT`s. An example of the kind of SQL we need looks like this:

```
INSERT INTO cust_calls (call_date, cust_id, call_event) VALUES (NOW(),"157",
"Something bad happened to my new Wrox Blocks.");
```

`NOW()` is a function built into Access that returns the current date and time. With that in mind, the rest of the code for inserting a new call report should look familiar:

```
function InsertCallReport(sCall, sID)
{
    var sCore = "INSERT INTO cust_calls (call_date, cust_id, call_event)
                VALUES (NOW(), ";
    var sQuery = sCore + "'" + sID + "', '" + sCall + "');";
    dbConn.Execute(sQuery);
    if (dbConn.Errors.Count > 0)
        Response.Write("<NACK/>");
    else
        Response.Write("<ACK/>");
}
```

After building the SQL text, we execute the query and look for errors. If none are found, we return the very short XML document `<ACK/>`.

# Clearing the Call History Form

This task, performed in response to clicking on the Clear button under the call history form, is functionally identical to the process we went through to clear the customer form. We are resetting the parse tree for the data island named `xmlCalls` to a `Collection` document containing one `CallReport` element. The `CallReport` element and its children contain no textual values, only elements. Here is the source code to do this:

```
function OnClearCall()
{
    var parser = new ActiveXObject("microsoft.xmldom");
    parser.loadXML("<Collection><CallReport><Date/>
                <CallDetails/></CallReport></Collection>");
    if (parser.readystate == 4 && parser.parseError == 0)
    {
        while (xmlCalls.documentElement.childNodes.length > 1)
        {
            xmlCalls.documentElement.removeChild(
                xmlCalls.documentElement.childNodes(1));
        }

        for (var ni = 0; ni < parser.documentElement.childNodes.length; ni++)
        {
            xmlCalls.documentElement.appendChild(
                parser.documentElement.childNodes(ni).cloneNode(true));
        }

        if (xmlCalls.documentElement.childNodes.length > 1)
        {
            xmlCalls.documentElement.removeChild(
                xmlCalls.documentElement.childNodes(0));
        }

        xmlCalls.recordset.moveFirst();
    }
}
```

# Retrieving a Customer's Call History

There's just one feature left to implement and that is retrieving all the existing call reports for the customer displayed on the page. This occurs in `CallTrack.html` in the `OnCallHistory()` handler. In this case, we are POSTing a `SvcCallQuery` document to the server and receiving a `Collection` document containing zero or more `CallReport` elements. After receiving the document from the service, we fix up the data binding.

## Client Side

The job of composing the query document is fairly simple since we only need to send up the value of the `CustomerID` field:

```
function OnCallHistory()
{
    var sReq = "";
    if (custIDText.value != "")
```

```
        {
            var sServer = "http://" + GetASP("SvcCallQuery");
            xmlCalld.Open("POST", sServer, false);

            // Compose a SvcCallQuery
            sReq = "XMLRequest=<SvcCallQuery><CustomerID>" + custIDText.value +
                      "</CustomerID></SvcCallQuery>";

            xmlCalld.setRequestHeader("Content-Type",
                      "application/x-www-form-urlencoded");
            xmlCalld.Send(sReq);
            // Fix up the binding
            FixCallBinding();
        }
    }
```

FixCallBinding performs the dynamic fix-up we've seen several times in this chapter. The only novelty here is that we are binding to a repeating HTML element. Each row of our table is matched to a CallReport element by the XML DSO. CallTrack.html merely has to provide a template consisting of one row. This is the table as it exists at design time:

```
<TABLE border=1 cellPadding=1 cellSpacing=1 width="75%" id=callTable name =
callTable>      .
    <TR>
        <TD>
        <P>
            <INPUT id=callDate name=callDate style="HEIGHT: 22px; WIDTH:
                  422px"> 
        </P>
        <P>
            <FONT face=Verdana size=2 >Call Details</FONT></P>
        <P>
            <TEXTAREA id=callDetail name=callDetail style="HEIGHT: 38px;
                                      WIDTH:422px"></TEXTAREA>
        </P>
        </TD>
    </TR>
</TABLE>
```

The INPUT and TEXTAREA elements, callDate and callDetails, are bound dynamically when we retrieve any data. We remove all but the very first node from the existing document, leaving the first to prevent the binding from failing. Next, we append all the new nodes, then delete the remaining node from the old document:

```
function FixCallBinding()
{
    while (xmlCalls.documentElement.childNodes.length > 1)
    {
        xmlCalls.documentElement.removeChild(
                          xmlCalls.documentElement.childNodes(1));
    }

    for (var ni = 0; ni <
            xmlCalld.ResponseXML.documentElement.childNodes.length; ni++)
```

```
      {
         xmlCalls.documentElement.appendChild(
            xmlCallId.ResponseXML.documentElement.childNodes(ni).cloneNode(true));
      }

      if (xmlCalls.documentElement.childNodes.length > 1)
         xmlCalls.documentElement.removeChild(
                              xmlCalls.documentElement.childNodes(0));

      xmlCalls.recordset.moveFirst();

      callTable.dataSrc="#xmlCalls";
      callDate.dataFld="Date";
      callDetail.dataFld="CallDetails";
   }
```

# Server Side

Once `SvcCallHistory.asp` receives our query document, it switches on the root node:

```
         case "SvcCallQuery":
            ProcessSvcCallQuery(parser.documentElement);
            break;
```

`ProcessSvcCallQuery()` is responsible for converting our XML into a SQL SELECT statement. A sample SQL statement of this type would be:

```
   SELECT cust_id, call_date, call_event FROM CUST_CALLS WHERE cust_id="157";
```

`ProcessSvcCallQuery()` passes the bulk of the SQL text composition off to a function named `MakeCallConstraint()` (detailed below) before executing the query:

```
   function ProcessSvcCallQuery(callQNode)
   {
      var sSelectCore = "SELECT cust_id, call_date, call_event FROM CUST_CALLS";

      var sConstraint = "";

      sConstraint = MakeCallConstraint(callQNode);
      if (sConstraint != "")
         sConstraint = " WHERE " + sConstraint;

      var sQuery = sSelectCore + sConstraint + ';';
      dbRecordSet = dbConn.Execute(sQuery);
```

Once it has issued the query, it must step through the recordset's results and write each row out as a member of a `Collection` document:

```
      if (!dbRecordSet.BOF)
         dbRecordSet.MoveFirst();

      if (dbRecordSet.EOF)
         Response.Write("<Collection></Collection>");
```

```
    // Write the collection root node and then the rest of the contents
    Response.Write("<Collection>");
    while (!dbRecordSet.EOF)
    {
        WriteCallBody(dbRecordSet);
        dbRecordSet.MoveNext();
    }
    Response.Write("</Collection>");
}
```

Here are our two helper functions, MakeCallConstraint() and WriteCallBody(). MakeCallConstraint() extracts the customer ID passed in the query document and builds the heart of the SQL WHERE clause. WriteCallBody() is called from ProcessSvcCallQuery() to convert the results of the database query into the XML document that is sent to the client:

```
function MakeCallConstraint(node)
{
    var sClause = "";
    var sID = "";
    for (var ni = 0; ni < node.childNodes.length; ni++)
    {
        switch (node.childNodes(ni).nodeName)
        {
            case "CustomerID":
                if (node.childNodes(ni).text != "")
                    sID = "cust_id = " + node.childNodes(ni).text;
                break;
        }
    }
    sClause = sID;
    return sClause;
}

function WriteCallBody(rsCalls)
{
    Response.Write("<CallReport><CustomerID>");
    Response.Write(rsCalls("cust_id"));
    Response.Write("</CustomerID><Date>");
    Response.Write(rsCalls("call_date"));
    Response.Write("</Date><CallDetails>");
    Response.Write(rsCalls("call_event"));
    Response.Write("</CallDetails></CallReport>");
}
```

# Lessons Learned

Now that our hypothetical programming team has completed the pilot project for the Customer Service Department of Wrox Blocks, we should grade their work against the standards of our development philosophy. The application meets the functional requirements for the project:

- ❑ Staff programmers must be able to use the techniques with minimal extra training
- ❑ Cost for the project should be similar to, or less than, the cost of implementing it with traditional development techniques (excluding pre-packaged solutions)

- ❑ The application should have lower maintenance costs than an application built with traditional techniques
- ❑ The project should create resources that can be used in future projects

Whether they've met the goal of successfully applying the new techniques remains to be seen. More important to Wrox Blocks managers, it remains to be seen whether the new approach provides any value over older methods of software construction.

# Violations of the Development Philosophy

As we noted previously, the implementation of the call report insertion feature violated generality, in that the client team composed an incomplete CallReport element, in the knowledge that the server would provide a timestamp regardless of what they provided. This works for this project, but might break if a future service answering to this vocabulary changed the implementation. The programmers should always write complete documents as defined by the vocabulary.

Data binding forced our programmers into coupling the SvcCustomer vocabulary fairly tightly with the customer form, and the CallReport vocabulary with the call history table. We can't really call this a violation, at least in the absence of an accepted metadata standard. The use of data binding greatly simplified the programming task and gave us a compact user interface on the client. Nevertheless, changes to the vocabularies may break the client application. The programmers might have minimized this by using the versioning scheme proposed in Chapter 4.

# Components

Development was greatly aided by the use of MSXML and its related interfaces, the XML DSO and IXMLHTTP. Although this restricts us to Microsoft Internet Explorer 5.0 as the client browser, these components provided key functions that would have been expensive to replace with custom programming. The team, however, has missed something. They have not created any components of their own. Specifically, our development philosophy called for using components on each tier, with component data being translated into XML to survive passage between platforms. Where are the components that go with SvcCustomer and CallReport?

A SvcCustomer class could have been created in JavaScript as a pilot for a COM component. We might have used that for field validation or enforcing business rules. For example, there are databases and rules for determining valid zip codes and telephone area codes. Such a component would have been valuable on the server side of the application. This was impractical and unnecessary for the purposes of illustration, but in a real-world setting it would be important. As things stand, no other applications that make use of customers have anything they can reuse in terms of code except the scripts embedded in the client and server pages.

# Reuse Potential

There are, however, two great resources coming out of this project that can be reused in the future: the two services represented by SvcCallHistory.asp and SvcCustomer.asp. Their services are generalized and in accordance with our development philosophy, so any other application that needs these vocabularies will be able to call on them. That's the whole purpose of cooperative network applications. You develop services and publicize their availability through a directory listing. Client applications can use them because they are assured of a known interface.

In this case, the interfaces consist of our XML vocabularies. These vocabularies are themselves reusable resources, provided they faithfully model some useful part of the Wrox Blocks business. As we will see in the next two chapters, the 'Customer' we've defined will become the base for several variations.

`DirectoryWalker` proved to be about as useful as we intended it to be. Recasting it as a scriptlet (as opposed to DHTML scriptlet) streamlined its reuse in our application. Hopefully, we will find `DataSplicer` to be similarly useful in the next chapter. Had the programming team created a `Customer` class in JavaScript, we might be in a position to make that a scriptlet in our next project. Better still, if it proved sufficiently useful, we might rewrite it as a COM object in Java or C++ to improve performance. So far, though, nothing we've suggested for such an object requires that treatment. The performance of field validation methods, however, is more likely to be governed by database retrieval speed than implementation language.

# Summary

We created our first business application using the principles and tools of our software development philosophy. Our hypothetical programming team built an intranet-based customer service call tracking application. Our old friend MSXML did the lion's share of the work through the various interfaces it supports. In particular, we used it to do the following:

- ❑ Parse XML documents into DOM trees
- ❑ Execute HTTP POSTs for the transmission of data within an HTML page
- ❑ Perform data binding between XML data islands and HTML form elements

The following points of our philosophy saw service in this exercise:

- ❑ Use of components to jump-start development
- ❑ Use of XML for the exchange of object-oriented data
- ❑ Use of our specialization scheme in XML
- ❑ Use of the Active Directory for the location of services

Of course, the real proof of our philosophy will be in seeing whether the services we built in this chapter can provide benefit to the applications we shall build next. With that in mind, let's continue our saga of the intrepid programmers of the Wrox Blocks company.

# Wrox Blocks: Order Tracking

The true test of our philosophy is how it helps us to build new applications from existing services. In the last chapter, we built the basis for tracking customers of Wrox Blocks. Next we're going to expand our ability to serve our customers. Rather than cutting our existing application apart, however, we're going to build the new one without giving it any special access to the data controlled by the existing `customer` service which we built in the last chapter. While we're at it, we'll see how different programming choices can be supported by current systems. This case study illustrates the following points:

- ❑ Using and extending an existing service through specialization
- ❑ Hiding the details of data storage behind XML
- ❑ Use of the XML DOM to create XML documents
- ❑ Use of DHTML on the client to dynamically create content

In addition to using the `Customer` service, we're going to make use of `DirectoryWalker` and `DataSplicer`. The parser and DOM capabilities of MSXML will also be used, along with its `IXMLHTTP` interface. To keep things interesting, we'll also be taking a different approach to building XML documents, and generating HTML dynamically. In short, we're going to shake things up and see if our philosophy is still useful.

## The Business Case

Wrox Blocks management is sufficiently pleased with the Customer Service application to follow it up with another project. In particular, they like the idea that basic customer contact information is maintained in one place. Management would like to keep it that way, allowing individual departments to manage their own extensions to customer data while accessing the newly built `Customer` service for the core information.

A branch of the sales department has been recording customer orders and customer payment information. They want a simple intranet application to display a customer's order history, particularly the status of open orders. Starting the project, the application programming team realizes it is necessary to display customer contact information while viewing a customer's order history.

If there's a delay in fulfilling an order, they must be able to contact the customer to discuss matters. With management's desire to centralize core customer information under the control of the Customer Service department, Sales has no choice but to embrace the new development philosophy and learn to speak the `Customer` vocabulary.

The fact that the new programming team is independent of the original team makes matters difficult, but offers some freedom as well. The new team has no access to the customer database – in fact, the original programming team is seriously considering migrating the data to an LDAP compliant directory. Customer information changes infrequently, but is retrieved quite often, and it is almost always read the same way, i.e., there are no ad hoc queries. Customer information, moreover, is easy to organize in an hierarchical fashion – say, by organizing customers by geographic region or according to some sales category. These are tasks an LDAP directory performs well, so migrating from a relational database could improve performance. Whatever happens with the customer data, the programming team from Sales has no choice but to deal with it through the `Customer` service. Studying the new development philosophy, they realize the best approach is to build an `OrderCustomer` service that specializes the `Customer` vocabulary through the addition of payment information.

The team makes some different choices regarding the client end of the application. The information is currently available through a very limited terminal-based application. The team is attracted to the idea of using open standards for displaying data. Data binding, however, strikes them as too platform specific. Although they are committed to using Internet Explorer for the client interface, they want to move in the direction of the DOM and Dynamic HTML. Since the data is distinct from its presentation under our approach, they can do this without modifying the data returned by the `Customer` service. Coincidentally, they choose to build their XML using the DOM rather than building XML by concatenating strings in script code outside the parser. This wasn't a carefully considered decision, but rather the sort of arbitrary choice that often gets made in the course of implementing an application.

# Application Design

The application will consist of three sections: a client-side page permitting multiple searches without leaving the page, and two ASPs implementing services for the provision of specialized customer information and customer order history data. A user of the application will enter a customer ID number and receive the results in a series of dynamically populated HTML tables. The data will be obtained from two services created by the Sales team, but must also make use of the existing `Customer` service to obtain the core of the `OrderCustomer` vocabulary.

## How It All Fits Together

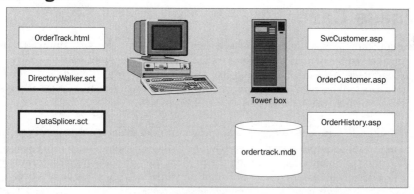

The application we see here is similar to the one we built in the last chapter. Our client application, `OrderTrack.html`, makes use of DirectoryWalker once again and adds DataSplicer to manipulate the data received from the server. Despite this, it is similar in spirit to `CallTrack.html` in that it relies on requesting and receiving platform-neutral XML documents for its implementation.

The server-side, meanwhile grows a bit more complicated. We have managed to reuse `SvcCustomer.asp` for core customer data, adding `OrderCustomer.asp` only to obtain the data added by the `OrderCustomer` vocabulary. `OrderHistory.asp` is added to provide order history documents. We are beginning to see the advantages of reuse promised by our principles – we've extended an existing service rather than re-implementing the functions in an application-specific form.

# The Client

Unlike their peers in the Customer Service department, Sales users are accustomed to dealing with customer ID numbers. This simplifies the user interface, which will be implemented in the page `OrderTrack.html`. A user of the application will enter the ID and click on a button. Having seen the Customer Service application, the Sales programming team is attracted to the notion of reusing the same page for multiple searches, but they have no interest in using data binding. In fact, never having dealt with MDAC before, data binding is just one more technology they would have to learn. Instead, they decide to present their results through standard HTML elements. Let's take a look at a screenshot of the client application they have in mind:

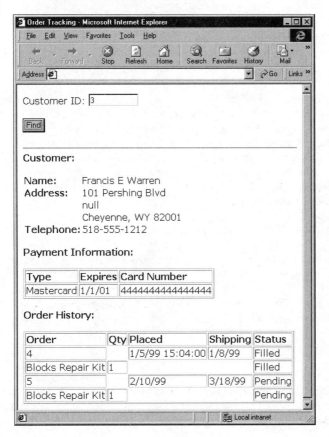

The information shown in this screenshot follows a search for the order history of the customer with ID number 3.

Customer contact information will be displayed in a form reminiscent of a mailing label. A customer's credit card information will appear as cells in a table. The customer's order history, a mix of order summary information and the individual line items comprising each order, must be mixed in a table to suggest a report. In particular, the first line of each order should include the order number, the date on which the order was placed, the projected or actual shipping date, and the status, Filled or Pending, of the order. An order consists of one or more individual products.

Following the summary line, then, will be one or more lines showing the product description, the quantity ordered, and the status of that part of the order. If the product has been drawn from inventory, the status will be Filled. If there is insufficient stock or the stock has not been drawn from inventory, the status will be Pending. Note that an order may be Pending even if each item has a status of Filled. In fact, this is a situation of particular interest to the Sales department because it may indicate a payment or shipping problem. This is why ready access to order tracking information is important to the department.

> *As always, the source code for this application is available from our Web site at* `http://www.wrox.com/`. *The accompanying database,* `ordertrack.mdb`, *contains payment information and order history for the customers defined in the previous chapter. These bear the customer IDs 1, 2, 3, 4, 10, and 12. Since we are not developing the order entry application, you will need to use Microsoft Access to manually enter new customers. If you do this, be sure to modify* `customer_calls.mdb` *at the same time, or use the Customer Service application to add the new customers.*

# The Services

The client utilizes two new services. These are `OrderCustomer` for the customer contact and payment information, and `OrderHistory` for the listing of order status. Following previous practice, each service is implemented with an ASP. `OrderCustomer` will draw on the `Customer` service for the generalized customer information. All information specific to the Sales department – payment information and order history – is stored in a Microsoft Access database. Clients need to be able to interrogate the services, so we shall define two new vocabularies for this purpose: `OrderCustomerQuery` and `OrderHistoryQuery`. The services will respond with documents in the vocabularies `OrderCustomer` and `OrderHistory`, respectively.

As we shall see, our query documents will always be very short, so we'll keep things simple and use an HTTP `GET` to interrogate the services. Our `CustomerQuery` documents will also be small. We are asking for one customer at a time, and we will only be transmitting the customer ID. Nevertheless, the `CustomerQuery` vocabulary can result in long documents, which is why the service required an HTTP `POST` in the first place. The Sales programming team must respect this as they have no influence over the Customer Service department's programming team and cannot ask them to make modifications to their service.

# Exchange Vocabularies

Before getting into the implementation details, let's take the time to formally define our vocabularies. These are the interfaces through which all clients must interact with our services. We'll be writing a client at the same time as the services, so we might be tempted to define the vocabularies as we go along.

The Customer Service department worked the same way, but now we are using their `CustomerQuery` vocabulary as an interface. Since the same thing can happen to our service, we should specify formal vocabularies and see how well they hold up in practice. If it doesn't work for us, we can always make changes before we release the interfaces to the rest of Wrox Blocks. Programming our client, then, is a test of the interface provided by the vocabulary definitions. If we have problems, future users will have problems too, but then we are in a position to fix the interface before we release it.

## Customer Query

Here is a shell document written in the `OrderCustomerQuery` vocabulary:

```
<OrderCustomerQuery>
    <CustomerID/>
</OrderCustomerQuery>
```

This is easy to define in a DTD:

```
<!ELEMENT   OrderCustomerQuery   CustomerID>
<!ELEMENT   CustomerID           #PCDATA>
```

That's it – a root element and exactly one element containing a single customer's ID.

## Order Customer Response

The reply to such a query is a good deal more complicated. Let's take a look at a sample:

```
<OrderCustomer>
    <Customer>
        <CustomerID>13</CustomerID>
        <FirstName>Buck</FirstName>
        <MI>Q</MI>
        <LastName>Rogers</LastName>
        <Street1>10E3 Galactic Lane</Street1>
        <Street2>Dimension 4</Street2>
        <City>Colorado Springs</City>
        <State>CO</State>
        <PostalCode>99999</PostalCode>
        <Telephone>999-999-9999</Telephone>
    </Customer>
    <PaymentOptions>
        <CreditCard>
            <Type>MasterCard</Type>
            <Number>444444444444444</Number>
            <ExpirationDate>12/1/2000</ExpirationDate>
        </CreditCard>
        <CreditCard>
            <Type>American Express</Type>
            <Number>444466666655555</Number>
            <ExpirationDate>3/4/2001</ExpirationDate>
        </CreditCard>
    </PaymentOptions>
</OrderCustomer>
```

The first thing we see is a `Customer` document embedded in our new document. This is exactly what we expect given the rules laid down in Chapter 4. We shall obtain this information from the `Customer` service without change. Next we see a `PaymentOptions` element containing one or more `CreditCard` elements. Each `CreditCard` element defines the type, card number, and expiration date of one credit card. Here's the formal definition:

```
<!ELEMENT    OrderCustomer      (Customer, PaymentOptions)>
<!ELEMENT    Customer           (CustomerID, FirstName, MI, LastName, Street1,
                                 Street2, City, State, PostalCode, Telephone)>
<!ELEMENT    CustomerID         #PCDATA>
<!ELEMENT    FirstName          #PCDATA>
<!ELEMENT    MI                 #PCDATA>
<!ELEMENT    LastName           #PCDATA>
<!ELEMENT    Street1            #PCDATA>
<!ELEMENT    Street2            #PCDATA>
<!ELEMENT    City               #PCDATA>
<!ELEMENT    State              #PCDATA>
<!ELEMENT    PostalCode         #PCDATA>
<!ELEMENT    Telephone          #PCDATA>
<!ELEMENT    SvcPlan            #PCDATA>

<!ELEMENT    PaymentOptions     CreditCard+>
<!ELEMENT    CreditCard         (Type, Number, ExpirationDate)>
<!ELEMENT    Type               #PCDATA>
<!ELEMENT    Number             #PCDATA>
<!ELEMENT    ExpirationDate     #PCDATA>
```

## Order History Query

Given the restriction of querying by a single customer ID at a time, the `OrderHistoryQuery` vocabulary is very short:

```
<OrderHistoryQuery>
    <CustomerID/>
</OrderHistoryQuery>
```

This is the DTD:

```
<!ELEMENT    OrderHistoryQuery    CustomerID>
<!ELEMENT    CustomerID           #PCDATA>
```

Looking at the two query vocabularies, you can see why a simple HTTP GET with the entire query document appended to the URL is a safe choice. We will never be up against the limits on URL request lengths.

## Order History Response

The `OrderHistory` vocabulary is the longest and most complicated vocabulary we have seen to date. It introduces a number of novel features. Here's a sample document:

```
<Collection xmlns:dt=urn:schemas-microsoft-com:datatypes">
    <OrderHistory>
        <CustomerID>1</CustomerID>
        <Order>
            <OrderNumber>4</OrderNumber>
```

```
            <Status>Filled</Status>
            <PlacementDate>7/20/1999 14:00</PlacementDate>
            <ShipDate>7/21/1999 08:00</ShipDate>
            <OrderProduct>
                <Quantity dt:dt="int">1</Quantity>
                <SubTotal dt:dt="fixed.14.4">$10.00</SubTotal>
                <Product>
                    <PartNumber>16</PartNumber>
                    <Name>Rocket Tube Liner Inspector</Name>
                </Product>
                <FillStatus>Filled</FillStatus>
            </OrderProduct>
        </Order>
        <Order>
            <OrderNumber>8</OrderNumber>
            <Status>Pending</Status>
            <PlacementDate>7/21/1999 14:00</PlacementDate>
            <ShipDate>7/24/1999 08:00</ShipDate>
            <OrderProduct>
                <Quantity dt:dt="int">1</Quantity>
                <SubTotal dt:dt="fixed.14.4">$10000.00</SubTotal>
                <Product>
                    <PartNumber>20</PartNumber>
                    <Name>Rocket Tube Liner</Name>
                </Product>
                <FillStatus>Filled</FillStatus>
            </OrderProduct>
            <OrderProduct>
                <Quantity dt:dt="int">1</Quantity>
                <SubTotal dt:dt="fixed.14.4">$1000.00</SubTotal>
                <Product>
                    <PartNumber>60</PartNumber>
                    <Name>Rocket Tube Liner Installer</Name>
                </Product>
                <FillStatus>Filled</FillStatus>
            </OrderProduct>
        </Order>
    </OrderHistory>
</Collection>
```

The document consists of a collection containing a single OrderHistory element. This element contains the CustomerID of the customer to which this history applies, and can also contain one or more orders. Each Order element contains summary information and one or more OrderProduct elements. In the context of order history, a product has two kinds of information. One is the information created by the order: the quantity ordered, the subtotal value for this product, and status of that particular part of the order (Filled or Pending). Note that the subtotal is not always equal to the arithmetic product of the quantity and unit price; special pricing and discounts may have been applied. The other type of information is that which belongs to the product simply by being maintained in the inventory: the part number and name of the product. We distinguish between these two types of information by encapsulating the intrinsic information within a Product element. Here's the DTD for this vocabulary:

```
<!ELEMENT    Collection       OrderHistory>
<!ATTLIST    Collection
             xmlns:dt         CDATA    #REQUIRED>
<!ELEMENT    OrderHistory     (CustomerID, Order+)>
<!ELEMENT    CustomerID       #PCDATA>
```

```
<!ELEMENT    Order              (OrderNumber, Status, PlacementDate, ShipDate,
                                 OrderProduct+)>
<!ELEMENT    OrderNumber        #PCDATA>
<!ELEMENT    Status             #PCDATA>
<!ELEMENT    PlacementDate      #PCDATA>
<!ELEMENT    ShipDate           #PCDATA>
<!ELEMENT    OrderProduct       (Quantity, SubTotal, Product, FillStatus)>
<!ELEMENT    Quantity           #PCDATA>
<!ATTLIST    Quantity
             dt:dt              CDATA    #REQUIRED>

<!ELEMENT    SubTotal           #PCDATA>
<!ATTLIST    SubTotal
             dt:dt              CDATA    #REQUIRED>

<!ELEMENT    Product            (PartNumber, Name)>
<!ELEMENT    PartNumber         #PCDATA>
<!ELEMENT    Name               #PCDATA>

<!ELEMENT    FillStatus         #PCDATA>
```

To begin with, we're using the **datatyping** namespace, implemented in MSXML, to allow us to indicate the numerical nature of the Quantity and SubTotal elements. This will permit clients to perform calculations using the data if they so desire.

> *The details of this namespace are explained in Appendix D. The definitive source for namespaces in XML is the W3C recommendation, found at* http://www.w3.org/TR/REC-xml-names.

Next, we have introduced structure that does not denote specialization of the vocabulary. We are using this structure to indicate subordinate bodies of information, compartmentalizing our data structure to indicate how properties are associated with one another. This is a judgement call – clients can treat this as an arbitrary distinction. The meaning is determined by the vocabulary designer and may or may not be meaningful to the client of the vocabulary.

> *We've taken a few shortcuts with this DTD to simplify it. We can do this because we aren't planning to use it for validation purposes. DTDs provide terrible support for namespaces. When we use an element or attribute from another namespace, we have to include its definition within our DTD. We've simply denoted the namespace declaration and datatype attributes as* PCDATA *to dispose of them. A rigorous DTD would be more particular. Similarly, we've defined the* FillStatus *element as* PCDATA *even though we've seen it can take on one of two enumerated values. Both namespaces and datatypes are easy to denote in a schema written in XML syntax and hard to do in a DTD.*

# Implementation

We previously alluded to the fact that the Sales department's programming team decided not to use data binding, preferring a DHTML approach instead. Both the client and the services will use the HTML DOM to build the tables displaying the results of a search. We will find two data islands in the client, but their data binding abilities will not be used. Instead, they appear simply as templates for the convenience of the programming team in creating query documents. The idea of templates also appears in the display of results. The tables are statically created with the labels. When results are returned, any old results are cleared, then the tables are dynamically modified through the programmatic addition of rows and cells.

The DOM approach is carried over into the implementation of the services. The programming team has elected to build their response documents entirely through the DOM methods of MSXML. Whereas previous applications built documents through the concatenation of string literals and database values, the services in this chapter will use MSXML to build the documents. In addition to introducing another way to build XML documents, this ensures we never forget to include an element's closing tag – MSXML takes care of it for us. The source code, however, will look a good deal different to that which we have become accustomed.

Components are used throughout this implementation. `DirectoryWalker` is back for the location of services and `DataSplicer` will be used to extract customer core information from a Customer document collection. MSXML will be used to assemble and parse documents, and its `IXMLHTTP` interface will be used to interrogate the `Customer` service.

# Locating Services

The client needs to locate several services. It needs to find the `OrderCustomer` and `OrderHistory` services. To fulfill the `OrderCustomer` request, we need to find the `Customer` service. We turn to `DirectoryWalker` for this task. To find the two services developed for this application, we simply call the `SearchHome()` method of `DirectoryWalker`. When it comes to locating the `Customer` service, however, we will call `SearchTree()`. The programming team knows that the services they develop will be deployed within their domain, but the Customer Service department is known to be in another domain within their tree of the directory. They do not know where the `Customer` service is deployed, but it seems likely that it will be outside their domain. To be safe, we'll search the entire tree for the `Customer` service.

# Displaying the Data with DHTML

The DHTML implementation in Internet Explorer uses a DOM similar to that used by MSXML. We're going to use this to put our results into the page. We have a `<DIV>` containing three HTML tables. In the first, the labels are in the first cell of each row. We have a known number of rows, so clearing the table is a matter of clearing the second cell in each row. Adding the new results is performed by setting the text value of the same cell.

The tables for payment and order history information are different. The labels comprise the first row of these tables, which will possess a variable number of rows. In fact, when the page is first loaded, there is only one row in each of the tables. Clearing the table, then, requires removing any rows after the first. Entering new information will require adding a row then filling it cell by cell.

# Searching for Order Customer Information

Let's begin the round trip. We'll be composing two queries, one for each service. Transmitting the resulting documents is easier than in the last chapter, since we can use MSXML's `load()` method to send a `GET` to the server. The reply then comes directly back to the parser. Once MSXML has a DOM tree ready for us, we clear the page of any old results, walk the tree, and use DHTML to push the results into the page.

## Composing a Request

`OrderTrack.html` contains two data islands when it is loaded:

```
<XML id=CustomerBlank>
    <OrderCustomerQuery>
        <CustomerID/>
    </OrderCustomerQuery>
</XML>
<XML id=OrderBlank>
    <OrderHistoryQuery>
        <CustomerID/>
    </OrderHistoryQuery>
</XML>
```

We're not going to use any of the exotic data binding features we got to know in the last chapter. All that the data islands do is give us a simple, well known template from which to construct our queries. We can address these templates by name through code and insert the customer ID the user has entered in the HTML `INPUT` element. Here's how it is done in the `OnFindClick()` function of `OrderTrack.html`:

```
CustomerBlank.documentElement.childNodes(0).text = CustIDText.value;
OrderBlank.documentElement.childNodes(0).text = CustIDText.value;
```

`CustIDText` is the named `INPUT` element. In each query document, the sole child node is the one we have to complete. Once we make the above assignments, we are ready to transmit our first request, the one for the `OrderCustomer` service:

```
parserCust.async = false;
parserCust.load("http://" + svcCustLocation + "?RequestXML=" +
                CustomerBlank.xml);
```

`parserCust` is an instance of MSXML, and `svcCustLocation` is a string containing the result of the `DirectoryWalker`'s `SearchHome()` call for `OrderCustomerQuery`. There are no non-alphanumeric characters in this document by design, so we don't have to do any preprocessing to replace white space with the hexadecimal equivalent. Let's take a look at what happens when the query document is received.

## The OrderCustomer Service

When the `OrderCustomer` service receives a request, it needs to retrieve the customer ID parameter. The `OrderCustomer` document is a composition of the result of a `Customer` search and a local database retrieval. Here's how this works in theory:

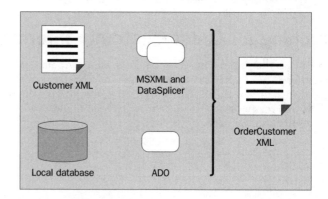

MSXML's IXMLHTTP interface can retrieve the Customer document. We know we're only going to have a single customer, so DataSplicer's Extract() method is perfect for getting this element for us. With this in hand, we turn to ADO components to go to the order database and get the information maintained by the Sales department. We can then use MSXML's DOM methods to piece together an OrderCustomer document and write it to the stream returning from the ASP.

### An Unfortunate Limitation

When we try to use IXMLHTTP from within OrderCustomer.asp, we quickly discover a problem. Everything works until we have to perform the POST with the Send() method. This method generates an error. We will be unable to use this component from the ASP. One approach would be to resort to building our own component using low level socket programming, but the programming team elects to compromise somewhat instead. Knowing that OrderCustomer builds on Customer, they write OrderCustomer.asp so that it returns the Sales specific portion of the OrderCustomer document, then use IXMLHTTP to retrieve the core Customer information from the client. This has the advantage of simplicity, but it compromises the OrderCustomer service. It isn't a matter of remaining true to some notion of object oriented programming; it renders OrderCustomer incapable of being reused unless the client is aware of the service's implementation. Successful reuse requires strict attention to the interface at all times. Our programming team gets their application working, but they have forgotten why we use interfaces in the first place. Leaving them to their folly for the moment, let's continue with the service's implementation.

### Fielding the Request

The service knows it will receive the query document as a parameter appended to the URL. It needs to strip this off and feed it to MSXML. Here's how it is done in OrderCustomer.asp:

```
var parser = Server.CreateObject("microsoft.xmldom");
var sSearchID;
var sLocation, sSvcQuery, sSQLQuery;

parser.loadXML(Request("RequestXML").Item);
Response.ContentType="text/xml";

if (parser.readyState == 4 && parser.parseError == 0)
{
    if (parser.documentElement.nodeName != "OrderCustomerQuery")
        Response.Write("<NACK/>");
    else
        sSearchID = parser.documentElement.childNodes(0).text;
}
else
    Response.Write("<NACK/>");
```

This should be familiar by now. We use the built-in Request object furnished by ASP to get our query document and feed it to the parser with the loadXML() method. This is done synchronously to streamline the code. After all, the document is known to be quite small, so asynchronous operation buys us nothing but complexity. If an error occurs, we write a negative acknowledgement document back to the client.

Now we need to proceed to the database retrieval. This is accomplished with two functions, one to compose the SQL command, and one to execute the command and compose a response document:

```
sSQLQuery = MakeLocalQuery(sSearchID);
MakeOrderCustomer(sSQLQuery);
```

Recall that sSearchID is the customer ID we just retrieved from the query document.

### Database Retrieval

Our order database is a bit more complicated than the call tracking database we saw in the last chapter. It contains four tables following a typical relational decomposition. Without going too deeply into the details of primary and foreign keys, we can see the basic relationships in the diagram below:

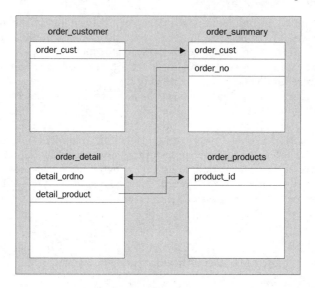

The table order_customer holds payment information for our customers. This is keyed according to the customer ID number created in the call tracking database, which after all is the primary repository for all things related to customers. This key also points into the order_summary table. This table captures an order at a high level. It contains the status, placement date, ship date, and order number of the order, but no information about the individual products that make it up. The order number is used as a foreign key into the order_detail table, which has that line-by-line information for each product ordered. This table keeps the subtotal value and quantity of each product ordered. It uses the part number as a foreign key into the order_products table. This final table is a lightweight inventory table. It contains the product's part number, product id, and a text description of each product Wrox Blocks stocks.

The SQL query used to complete the outer portion of an OrderCustomer document need only touch the order_customer table. The function MakeLocalQuery() does this for us:

```
function MakeLocalQuery(sID)
{
    return "SELECT order_cardtype, order_cardnum, order_expires FROM
            order_customer WHERE order_cust=" + sID;
}
```

The customer ID is a numeric value in the database, so we use the = operator rather than the LIKE operator used with string values.

This SQL query goes off to the function MakeOrderCustomer(). This function's first task is to perform the by now routine ADO tasks required to obtain a result set.

```
function MakeOrderCustomer(sQuery)
{
   var dbConn, dbRecordSet, oNode, oOpts, oCardNode;
   var parserOrderCust = Server.CreateObject("microsoft.xmldom");
   dbConn = Server.CreateObject("ADODB.Connection");
   dbConn.Open("OrderTrack", "", "");
   dbRecordSet = Server.CreateObject("ADODB.RecordSet");

   dbRecordSet = dbConn.Execute(sQuery);

   if (!dbRecordSet.BOF)
      dbRecordSet.MoveFirst();
```

We use the `Server.CreateObject()` method to allow ASP and IIS to properly manage object lifetimes, and create ADO `Connection` and `RecordSet` objects for our retrieval. The order database is represented by the system DSN `OrderTrack`, which uses neither user ID nor password.

> *This keeps things simple for the purposes of publication. Although I hope you are following better security procedures in your production efforts!*

After executing the query, we move the cursor to the first row, if any, in the recordset object. Now we are ready to start composing our response document.

## Composing the Reply

We create the outer element of our reply using MSXML's DOM methods:

```
oNode = parserOrderCust.createElement("OrderCustomer");
parserOrderCust.documentElement = oNode;

oNode = parserOrderCust.createElement("PaymentOptions");
parserOrderCust.documentElement.appendChild(oNode);
oOpts = oNode;

if (dbRecordSet.EOF)
   Response.Write("<NACK/>");
```

`parserOrderCust` is an initially empty instance of MSXML. We call `createElement()` to create the `OrderCustomer` element, then assign this object to the `documentElement` property of the document to provide a root node. We also know that we need a `PaymentOptions` node in the document. Although it won't be the first child of the root in the finished document, it is the first element the service is able to complete from local information. After we append it to the `childNodes` list of the root node, we also retain a reference to this node in the variable `oOpts`. This is strictly for convenience. We'll be referring to it frequently, and so it is worth avoiding the additional calls to the root's `childNodes` collection in order to improve performance.

If the record set is empty (meaning that no rows were returned by the query), the `EOF` property will have the value `rue`. If this is the case, we can't compose a useful document, so we send a negative acknowledgement back instead. Suppose, however, that we have one or more rows. Here's how we begin to fill out our document:

```
while (!dbRecordSet.EOF)
{
   // Create and fill nodes from the db for each credit card
   oCardNode = parserOrderCust.createElement("CreditCard");
```

```
        oNode = parserOrderCust.createElement("Type");
        oNode.text = dbRecordSet("order_cardtype").Value;
        oCardNode.appendChild(oNode);
        oNode = parserOrderCust.createElement("Number");
        oNode.text = dbRecordSet("order_cardnum").Value;
        oCardNode.appendChild(oNode);

        oNode = parserOrderCust.createElement("Expiration");
        oNode.text = dbRecordSet("order_expires").Value;
        oCardNode.appendChild(oNode);

        oOpts.appendChild(oCardNode);
        dbRecordSet.MoveNext();
    }
```

We start by creating a `CreditCard` element. Recall that this fragment is composed of elements for the type of credit card, card number, and expiration date:

```
...
<CreditCard>
    <Type>MasterCard</Type>
    <Number>4444444444444444</Number>
    <ExpirationDate>12/1/2000</ExpirationDate>
</CreditCard>
...
```

We follow a common pattern for each of these elements. First, we use the document object's `createElement()` method to create a named element in the variable `oNode`. Next, we assign a value from the recordset to the `text` property of the node. Finally, we append the node to the node representing the `CreditCard` element. The default collection for the recordset object is indexed by the names of the columns returned by the query. The object that is returned by this collection contains a number of properties. The `Value` property contains the data we need for our document.

With the document completed to the degree that it can be in this ASP, we write it out to the client using the `Response` object's `Write()` method:

```
Response.Write(parserOrderCust.xml);
```

We then reclaim resources by closing the connection and setting our object variables to `null`. This is wrapped in a `try...catch` block because ADO can throw exceptions in rare cases. None of these cases affect our client, so we just make sure they don't expose the error to the user.

```
    try
    {
        dbRecordSet.Close();
        dbConn.Close();
        dbConn = null;
        dbRecordSet = null;
    }
    catch (e)
    {
    }
    parserOrderCust = null;
}
```

## Getting Customer Data

Returning now to the client page, `OrderTrack.html`, we check MSXML to see whether we received an `OrderCustomer` document or a negative acknowledgment:

```
if (parserCust.readyState == 4 && parserCust.parseError == 0)
    if (parserCust.documentElement.nodeName == "OrderCustomer")
    {
        FixCustomer(parserCust, CustIDText.value);
```

The aptly named `FixCustomer()` function is going to perform the ugly task of retrieving a `Customer` document and patching our `OrderCustomer` document until it is complete. It takes the instance of MSXML containing the `OrderCustomer` partial document and the customer's ID number. The function begins with the basic preliminaries of creating components and locating the `Customer` service:

```
function FixCustomer(parser, sID)
{
    var xmlCustomerBase = new ActiveXObject("Microsoft.XMLHTTP");
    var walker = new ActiveXObject("DirectoryWalker.Scriptlet");
    walker.User = "orderdept";
    walker.Pwd = "";
    sLocation = "http://" + walker.SearchTree("Customer");
    walker = null;
```

Now we quickly compose a `CustomerQuery` document. We use the `IXMLHTTP` interface to open a connection to the service, set up the request, specify the mime type in the request header, and perform the `POST` using the `Send()` method of the interface:

```
xmlCustomerBase.Open("POST", sLocation, false);
sSvcQuery = "<CustomerQuery><CustomerID>" + sID + "</CustomerID>";
sSvcQuery += "<LastName/><PostalCode/></CustomerQuery>";
xmlCustomerBase.setRequestHeader("Content-Type",
                                 "application/x-www-form-urlencoded");
xmlCustomerBase.Send("XMLRequest=" + sSvcQuery);
xmlCustomerBase.responseXML.loadXML(xmlCustomerBase.responseText);
```

## Composing OrderCustomer Documents

The `Customer` vocabulary consists of a `Collection` element containing one or more `Customer` elements. We turn to the `DataSplicer` component to extract what we know will be a single `Customer` element. We then append it to the root node of the `OrderCustomer` document we received from the service. The document already has a child node, `PaymentOptions`, so we use the `insertBefore()` method to correctly position this element. That method requires an object denoting the element we wish to precede with the node we are inserting. This node is currently the first member of the `childNodes` collection for the document's root node.

```
    var splicer = new ActiveXObject("DataSplicer.scriptlet");
    var custTree = splicer.Extract("Customer",
                        xmlCustomerBase.ResponseXML.documentElement);

    parser.documentElement.insertBefore(custTree,
                        parser.documentElement.childNodes(0));
```

The document returned from the server contained the outer shell of the document, the `OrderCustomer` element, and the last part of the document, the `PaymentOptions` node. The client retrieved the `Customer` element itself and inserted the element into the first part of the `OrderCustomer` document. It's a work-around, but from here on the client can deal with a complete `OrderCustomer` document without knowing how it was patched together.

## Displaying the Results

We've elected to take a DHTML DOM approach to displaying results. We have a response document containing customer information and several tables that will receive the information for display. We will clear out any old data and rebuild the tables using the methods of the DHTML object model.

### Clearing Tables

It is now time to clear out the old information and insert the newly obtained `OrderCustomer` document. Here's what the client is doing in the button handler function for the Find button after it gets a reply from the service:

```
FixCustomer(parserCust, CustIDText.value);
ClearTable(PaymentTable);
ClearTable(OrderHistTable);
FillCustomer(parserCust);
```

Since this is the first step that changes what the user sees, it is important to clear not only the core customer table and the payment table, but the order history table as well. As noted previously, the last two tables are laid out a bit differently than the first. Here's what all the tables look like when the page is loaded:

```
<FONT face=Verdana>
<B>Customer:</B>
<P>
<TABLE id=CustTable cellPadding=1 cellSpacing=1>

    <TR>
        <TD><B>Name:</B></TD>
        <TD></TD></TR>
    <TR>
        <TD><B>Address:</B></TD>
        <TD></TD></TR>
    <TR>
        <TD></TD>
        <TD></TD></TR>
    <TR>
        <TD></TD>
        <TD></TD></TD>
    <TR>
        <TD><B>Telephone</B></TD>
        <TD></TD></TR>
</TABLE>
<P>
<B>Payment Information:</B>
<P>
<TABLE id=PaymentTable border=1>
    <TR>
        <TD><B>Type</B></TD>
        <TD><B>Expires</B></TD>
        <TD><B>Card Number</B></TD>
```

```
        </TR>
    </TABLE>
    <P>
    <B>Order History:</B>
    <P>
    <TABLE id=OrderHistTable border=1>
        <TR>
            <TD><B>Order</B></TD>
            <TD><B>Qty</B></TD>
            <TD><B>Placed</B></TD>
            <TD><B>Shipping</B></TD>
            <TD><B>Status</B></TD>
        </TR>
    </TABLE></FONT>
```

Note how `CustTable` has its labels in cells in the first column of a fixed length table, while `PaymentTable` and `OrderHistTable` have a single row with the labels. Additional rows are inserted by the functions that display search results. The function `ClearTable()` takes a `TABLE` object (in this case either `PaymentTable` or `OrderHistTable`) and deletes any rows following the first.

```
function ClearTable(table)
{
    var nRows;

    nRows = table.rows.length - 1;
    for (var ni = 0; ni < nRows; ni++)
        table.deleteRow(1);
}
```

The `deleteRow()` method of the DHTML `TABLE` object takes a zero-based index and deletes the corresponding row from the table's collection of rows. We determine how many rows the table has at the start, then repeatedly delete the second row. Each time this occurs the remaining rows fall down a level, allowing us to delete each of the rows in turn. This deletion is performed one time less than the initial number of rows. When the function completes, the referenced table has only a single row. In our usage, this is the row containing the labels.

When the two calls to `ClearTable()` complete, `CustTable()` may still have results in it. Since this table is unique, we'll take care of clearing it in `FillCustomer()`. Here's how that function starts:

```
function FillCustomer(CustDOMTree)
{
    var sConcat = "";
    var cardRow;
    var cardCell;

    // Clear old values
    for (var ni = 0; ni < CustTable.rows.length; ni++)
        CustTable.rows(ni).cells(1).innerText = "";
```

The number of rows in `CustTable` is fixed. We know that by definition, the second cell of each row is the one that receives data. This is denoted by `rows(ni).cells(1)`. Setting the `innerText` property to a zero-length string clears it.

## Customer Contact Information

We are finally ready to let the user see something useful. We start by displaying the core customer information. Since we'll be referring to child elements of the `Customer` element, it is useful to start by getting a reference to that node in the parse tree into a variable:

```
var custBase = CustDOMTree.documentElement.childNodes(0);
```

What follows takes a common pattern. We're going to assemble strings in a way that makes sense to the user instead of placing each atomic item into its own spot as we did in the data binding example of the last chapter. Consequently, we build our string using MSXML's DOM methods, then set the `innerText` property of the appropriate cell to the value of the string.

```
// Name
sConcat = custBase.childNodes(1).text;
sConcat += " " + custBase.childNodes(2).text;
sConcat += " " + custBase.childNodes(3).text;
CustTable.rows(0).cells(1).innerText = sConcat;

// Street1 and Street2
CustTable.rows(1).cells(1).innerText = custBase.childNodes(4).text;
CustTable.rows(2).cells(1).innerText = custBase.childNodes(5).text;

// City, State, Zip
sConcat = custBase.childNodes(6).text + ", " + custBase.childNodes(7).text;
sConcat += " " + custBase.childNodes(8).text;
CustTable.rows(3).cells(1).innerText = sConcat;

// Telephone
CustTable.rows(4).cells(1).innerText = custBase.childNodes(9).text;
```

## Payment Information

The pattern changes when we move on to the payment information table. Here, each cell contains one item of information, but these cells do not yet exist. We have to use DHTML methods to create the rows and cells before we fill them. We do this within a loop:

```
var payOpts = CustDOMTree.documentElement.childNodes(1);
for (var ni = 0; ni < payOpts.childNodes.length; ni++)
{
    // Create and fill a row for each credit card
    cardRow = PaymentTable.insertRow();
    cardCell = cardRow.insertCell();
    cardCell.innerText = payOpts.childNodes(ni).childNodes(0).text; // name
    cardCell = cardRow.insertCell();
    cardCell.innerText = payOpts.childNodes(ni).childNodes(2).text; // expires
    cardCell = cardRow.insertCell();
    cardCell.innerText = payOpts.childNodes(ni).childNodes(1).text; // card #
}
```

Each row is filled from the `PaymentOptions` element of the `OrderCustomer` document. We obtain a reference to this element's node in the parse tree, then go into a loop that fills one row for each `CreditCard` element under the `PaymentOptions` element.

Within the loop, we call the TABLE object's insertRow() method to append a new, empty row to the PaymentOptions table. Next, we call insertCell() on that row to create a cell. We then fill the cell with the value of the text property of the appropriate node in the parse tree. We do this once for each of the Type, ExpirationDate, and Number elements.

# Searching for Order History Information

At this point, we are back in the client, OrderTrack.html, and our users can see the customer's contact information and his options for paying for orders. The purpose of this application, however, is to obtain the customer's active order history. We haven't even requested this information yet. Let's press on and get this for our users.

## Requesting an OrderHistory Document

We're in the Find button handler function following receipt and display of the customer contact and payment information. We are about to request the customer's order history. Our OrderHistoryQuery vocabulary is constrained to produce very short documents, so we can once again use an HTTP GET operation to obtain our search results. Recall that we composed the query document at the very beginning of the button handler function:

```
OrderBlank.documentElement.childNodes(0).text = CustIDText.value;
```

Requesting a search consists of composing the proper URL and calling MSXML's load() method. The URL consists of the protocol identifier, the location of the service as returned by the DirectoryWalker, and a single parameter, RequestXML. The value of the parameter is our XML query document. The response to the request is the XML document generated by OrderHistory.asp that we wish to load into the parser:

```
parserOrders.async = false;
parserOrders.load("http://" + svcOrderLocation + "?RequestXML=" +
                OrderBlank.xml);
if (parserOrders.readyState == 4 && parserOrders.parseError == 0)
{
   // Display the results
   FillOrderHistory(parserOrders);
}
```

Before we dive into FillOrderHistory() to display our results, let's go over to the OrderHistory service to see what had to happen to obtain those results.

## The OrderHistory Service

The service is implemented in OrderHistory.asp. It follows the same pattern that we saw in it's sister service, OrderCustomer.asp. We receive a query document, check for errors, then perform a local database query and build a response document according to the response vocabulary of the service.

### Fielding the Request

We turn to ASP's Request object to obtain the value of the RequestXML parameter that was appended to the URL. If the parser has an error or we didn't receive the appropriate query document, we respond with a negative acknowledgement document. Otherwise, we extract the customer ID that we'll use in our search.

```
var parser = Server.CreateObject("microsoft.xmldom");
var sSearchID;
var sSQLQuery;

parser.loadXML(Request("RequestXML").Item);

if (parser.readyState == 4 && parser.parseError == 0)
{
    if (parser.documentElement.nodeName != "OrderHistoryQuery")
        Response.Write("<NACK/>");
    else
        sSearchID = parser.documentElement.childNodes(0).text;
}
else
    Response.Write("<NACK/>");
```

## Database Retrieval

The customer ID is the one piece of data we need to create our SQL query. We'll compose the query, then pass it off to the function `GetOrderHistory()` to execute the query and compose a response document:

```
sSQLQuery = MakeSQLQuery(sSearchID);
GetOrderHistory(sSQLQuery);
```

`MakeSQLQuery()` builds the query by concatenating strings until it has a complete query. Unlike the `OrderCustomer` query, this query is somewhat complicated. If you refer to the diagram we saw previously depicting the database structure, you'll see we have to perform a join across the tables `order_summary`, `order_detail`, and `order_products` to obtain the data needed. This involves following a trail of foreign keys that begins with the customer ID. That gets us into the proper spot in the `order_summary` table, where we obtain the proper order number. That leads us into the `order_detail` table, where we obtain the product part numbers. That takes us to the `order_products` table, where we collect the last item of information, the product's textual description. A complete SQL query for the customer whose ID is 4 looks like this:

```
SELECT s.order_cust, s.order_no, s.order_date, s.order_complete,
s.order_ship_date, d.detail_product, d.detail_subtotal, d.detail_filled,
d.detail_quantity, p.product_description
FROM order_summary as s, order_detail as d, order_products as p
WHERE s.order_cust=4 AND d.detail_ordno=s.order_no AND
p.product_id=d.detail_product
ORDER BY s.order_no";
```

We need to get our results in a sequence appropriate to the document we are going to build. Using the `ORDER BY` clause gives us a result set in which all the details for a given order appear sequentially. When the value of the `order_no` column in the recordset changes, we know we are starting a new order and have completed the preceding one.

Implementing this in `MakeSQLQuery()` is quite simple. Our code looks like this:

```
function MakeSQLQuery(sID)
{
    var sQuery;
```

```
        sQuery   = "SELECT s.order_cust, s.order_no, s.order_date, s.order_complete,";
        sQuery  += " s.order_ship_date, d.detail_product, d.detail_subtotal,
                 d.detail_filled, d.detail_quantity, ";
        sQuery  += " p.product_description from order_summary as s,
                 order_detail as d,";
        sQuery  += "order_products as p WHERE s.order_cust=" + sID;
        sQuery  += " AND d.detail_ordno=s.order_no AND p.product_id=d.detail_product ";
        sQuery  += " ORDER BY s.order_no";
        return sQuery;
    }
```

`GetOrderHistory()` begins with the familiar steps to execute a SQL query and check for errors:

```
    function GetOrderHistory(sQuery)
    {
        var dbConn, dbRecordSet, oNode, oOpts, oCardNode;
        var oAttr;
        var parserOrderHist = Server.CreateObject("microsoft.XMLDOM");

        dbConn = Server.CreateObject("ADODB.Connection");
        dbConn.Open("OrderTrack", "", "");
        dbRecordSet = new ActiveXObject("ADODB.RecordSet");

        dbRecordSet = dbConn.Execute(sQuery);

        if (!dbRecordSet.BOF)
            dbRecordSet.MoveFirst();

        if (dbRecordSet.EOF)
            Response.Write("<NACK/>");
        else
        {
```

We open the database using the DSN `OrderTrack`, call the `Connection` object's `Execute()` method, then position the recordset's pointer. If we have no results, we send back a negative acknowledgement to indicate that no order history was found. Now we'll begin to compose our response document. Given the novel features of the `OrderHistory` vocabulary, we can expect to learn a few new things.

### Composing the Reply Document

We learned a bit about using MSXML's DOM methods to build a document from scratch when we implemented the `OrderCustomer` service. `OrderHistory`, however, uses the data typing namespace implemented in Internet Explorer 5.0, so we need to learn how to create attributes. This starts with the `Collection` element itself, which requires a namespace declaration attribute.

```
        oNode = parserOrderHist.createElement("Collection");
        oAttr = parserOrderHist.createAttribute("xmlns:dt");
        oNode.setAttributeNode(oAttr);
        oNode.setAttribute("xmlns:dt", "urn:schemas-microsoft-com:datatypes");

        parserOrderHist.documentElement = oNode;
```

We create our `Collection` node using the `createElement()` method of the document object. Next, we create an attribute node using `createAttribute()`. We pass the namespace-qualified name of the attribute as a parameter.

We append this node to the `Collection` node's `attributes` collection using the `setAttributeNode()` method. We can't set the value of the node using the text property, since attributes don't have any `PCDATA` children, but there is a method named `setAttribute()` for just this purpose. Now that the `Collection` node is correctly configured, we make it the root of the document.

> *There is a bit of ambiguity in the MSXML documentation. At the time of writing (March 1999), the documentation says that* `createAttribute()` *won't correctly configure the namespace property of an element. While this may or may not be true in the general case of an arbitrary namespace, it works correctly for Microsoft's data typing namespace. You can verify this by examining the namespace property and calling the* `nodeTypedValue()` *method of the child nodes we'll create shortly from within the script debugger.*

Recall the start of the structure of an `OrderHistory` document:

```
<Collection xmlns:dt=urn:schemas-microsoft-com:datatypes">
    <OrderHistory>
        <CustomerID>1</CustomerID>
        <Order>
            <OrderNumber>4</OrderNumber>
            <Status>Filled</Status>
            <PlacementDate>7/20/1999 14:00</PlacementDate>
            <ShipDate>7/21/1999 08:00</ShipDate>
            ...
```

We've created the root node, so now we need to create an `OrderHistory` node and append one or more `Order` nodes to it:

```
        oNode = parserOrderHist.createElement("OrderHistory");
        parserOrderHist.documentElement.appendChild(oNode);

        oNode = parserOrderHist.createElement("CustomerID");
        oNode.text = dbRecordSet("order_cust").Value;
        parserOrderHist.documentElement.childNodes(0).appendChild(oNode);

        curOrdNo = dbRecordSet("order_no").Value;
        oOrderNode = CreateOrderNode(parserOrderHist, dbRecordSet);
        parserOrderHist.documentElement.childNodes(0).appendChild(oOrderNode);
```

We create and append the `OrderHistory` and `CustomerID` nodes to the document we've just created. After that, we prime the pump for our loop through the recordset by obtaining the first order number and creating our first `Order` element. Before we see how that's done, let's take a look at how we move through the recordset:

```
    while (!dbRecordSet.EOF)
    {
      if (dbRecordSet("order_no").Value != curOrdNo)
      {
        oOrderNode = CreateOrderNode(parserOrderHist, dbRecordSet);
        parserOrderHist.documentElement.childNodes(0).appendChild(oOrderNode);
        oProdNode = CreateProdNode(parserOrderHist, dbRecordSet);
        oOrderNode.appendChild(oProdNode);
      }
      else
```

```
        {
        oProdNode = CreateProdNode(parserOrderHist, dbRecordSet);
        oOrderNode.appendChild(oProdNode);
        }
        dbRecordSet.MoveNext();
        }
        ...
```

Each row of the result set can mean one of two things: either we are continuing with the detail information of the current order, or we are starting a new order. The latter condition is signaled when the value of the order_no column changes. If we are continuing with an existing order, we create a new Product node and append it. If we are starting a new order, we must create and append a new Order node, then create and append the first Product node of the new order. Since we created a new Order node before entering the loop, the first row of the resultset is seen as a continuation of an existing order and we follow the else clause. Now that we've built the overall structure, let's implement the details of creating Order and Product nodes, in the CreateOrderNode() and CreateProdNode() functions:

```
function CreateOrderNode(parser, dbRS)
{
    var oOrdNode = parser.createElement("Order");
    var oNode;

    oNode = parser.createElement("OrderNumber");
    oNode.text = dbRS("order_no").Value;
    oOrdNode.appendChild(oNode);

    oNode = parser.createElement("Status");
    if (dbRS("order_complete").Value == 1)
        oNode.text = "Filled";
    else
        oNode.text = "Pending";
    oOrdNode.appendChild(oNode);

    oNode = parser.createElement("PlacementDate");
    oNode.text = dbRS("order_date").Value;
    oOrdNode.appendChild(oNode);

    oNode = parser.createElement("ShipDate");
    oNode.text = dbRS("order_ship_date").Value;
    oOrdNode.appendChild(oNode);

    return oOrdNode;
}
```

The only novelty in CreateProdNode() relates to how the order status is represented in the database. The order_complete column is an Access Yes/No datatype, which the JavaScript interpreter sees as a 1 or 0. We look at the value and fill in the appropriate text for the user (Filled or Pending):

```
function CreateProdNode(parser, dbRS)
{
    var oProdNode, oNode, oDetailNode, oAttr;

    oProdNode = parser.createElement("OrderProduct");
```

```
oNode = parser.createElement("Quantity");
oAttr = parser.createAttribute("dt:dt");
oNode.setAttributeNode(oAttr);
oNode.setAttribute("dt:dt", "int");
oNode.text = dbRS("detail_quantity").Value;
oProdNode.appendChild(oNode);

oNode = parser.createElement("SubTotal");
oAttr = parser.createAttribute("dt:dt");
oNode.setAttributeNode(oAttr);
oNode.setAttribute("dt:dt","fixed.14.4");
oNode.text = dbRS("detail_subtotal").Value;
oProdNode.appendChild(oNode);

oNode = parser.createElement("Product");
oDetailNode = parser.createElement("PartNumber");
oDetailNode.text = dbRS("detail_product").Value;
oNode.appendChild(oDetailNode);

oDetailNode = parser.createElement("Name");
oDetailNode.text = dbRS("product_description").Value;
oNode.appendChild(oDetailNode);
oProdNode.appendChild(oNode);

oNode = parser.createElement("FillStatus");
if (dbRS("detail_filled").Value == 1)
    oNode.text = "Filled";
else
    oNode.text = "Pending";
oProdNode.appendChild(oNode);

return oProdNode;
}
```

CreateProdNode() uses the same method of indicating the status of an order line item that we used for the overall order status. In addition, we are using the data typing namespace to indicate numeric values for the SubTotal element, a fixed precision floating-point type, and the Quantity element, an integer.

So, when we leave the loop in GetOrderHistory() we have a complete OrderHistory document. We send it back to the client this way:

```
while (!dbRecordSet.EOF)
{
    ...
}
Response.Write(parserOrderHist.xml);
```

The xml property returns the text representation of the document, and Response.Write() places the string onto the stream returning to the client. The ASP's main script body ends with the usual code we use to close the database and reclaim resources.

## Displaying the Results

Now that the service is finished with its work, recall where we left the client. It had just made a request of the service from within the `load()` method of MSXML. Now the client needs to respond to the document it received from the service:

```
if (parserOrders.readyState == 4 && parserOrders.parseError.reason == 0)
{
    // Display the results
    FillOrderHistory(parserOrders);
}
```

### Displaying Orders

`FillOrderHistory()` is the function that will navigate through the response document and add rows to the TABLE object named `OrderHistTable`; it's in `OrderTrack.html`:

```
function FillOrderHistory(parser)
{
    var historyList;
    var order;
    var nOrders;
    var Row, Cell;

    if (parser.documentElement.nodeName == "Collection" &&
        parser.documentElement.childNodes(0).nodeName == "OrderHistory")
    {
        historyList = parser.documentElement.childNodes(0);
        nOrders = historyList.childNodes.length - 1; // account for the cust ID
        for (var ni = 1; ni <= nOrders; ni++)
        {
            order = historyList.childNodes(ni);
            Row = OrderHistTable.insertRow();
            Cell = Row.insertCell();
            Cell.innerText = order.childNodes(0).text;   // order number
            Cell = Row.insertCell();                     // blank cell
            Cell = Row.insertCell();
            Cell.innerText = order.childNodes(2).text;   // date placed
            Cell = Row.insertCell();
            Cell.innerText = order.childNodes(3).text;   // ship date
            Cell = Row.insertCell();
            Cell.innerText = order.childNodes(1).text;   // status

            for (var nj = 4; nj < order.childNodes.length; nj++)
                WriteProducts(order.childNodes(nj));
        }
    }
}
```

We start by checking the document to ensure that it is a Collection containing at least one OrderHistory element. If it isn't then we do nothing, and the user will see an empty order history table. If the document is the sort we are expecting, we navigate to the start of the OrderHistory (using `historyList = parser.documentElement.childNodes(0);`) and loop through the individual order elements.

## Displaying the Products Within an Order

For each `Order`, we insert a row and fill it with the summary information on the order. Next, we step through the `Product` elements that comprise the order's line items and build their rows in the utility function `WriteProducts()`:

```
function WriteProducts(product)
{
    var Row, Cell;

    Row = OrderHistTable.insertRow();
    Cell = Row.insertCell();
    Cell.innerText = product.childNodes(2).childNodes(1).text; // product name
    Cell = Row.insertCell();
    Cell.innerText = product.childNodes(0).text; // quantity
    Cell = Row.insertCell();
    Cell = Row.insertCell();
    Cell = Row.insertCell();
    Cell.innerText = product.childNodes(3).text;
}
```

## The Complete Client Main Body

We may be forgiven for being a bit unclear on the overall flow of the client by this time. We've twice broken off from studying it to pursue the services it calls. Here is the complete source code for the Find button handler function showing how the client works:

```
var walker = new ActiveXObject("DirectoryWalker.Scriptlet");
walker.User = "orderdept";
walker.Pwd = "";

function OnFindClick()
{
    var svcCustLocation = walker.SearchHome("OrderCustomerQuery");
    var svcOrderLocation = walker.SearchHome("OrderHistoryQuery");

    if (CustIDText.value != "")
    {
        // Set up our query documents with the customer ID value
        CustomerBlank.documentElement.childNodes(0).text = CustIDText.value;
        OrderBlank.documentElement.childNodes(0).text = CustIDText.value;

        // Load the customer document
        var parserCust = new ActiveXObject("microsoft.xmldom");
        var parserOrders = new ActiveXObject("microsoft.xmldom");
        parserCust.async = false;
        parserCust.load("http://" + svcCustLocation + "?RequestXML=" +
                    CustomerBlank.xml);
        if (parserCust.readyState == 4 && parserCust.parseError == 0)
            if (parserCust.documentElement.nodeName == "OrderCustomer")
            {
                FixCustomer(parserCust, CustIDText.value);

                ClearTable(PaymentTable);
                ClearTable(OrderHistTable);
                FillCustomer(parserCust);
            }

        parserOrders.async = false;
        parserOrders.load("http://" + svcOrderLocation + "?RequestXML=" +
                    OrderBlank.xml);
```

```
        if (parserOrders.readyState == 4 &&
                           parserOrders.parseError.reason == 0)
        {
            FillOrderHistory(parserOrders);
        }
    }
}
```

# Lessons Learned

The nice thing about case studies is that we have the luxury of criticizing a hypothetical programming team. We've set them up to make some mistakes for our education, and now it is time to collect. Most programmers enjoy critiquing someone else's code as much as they dislike having their code critiqued! Don't feel sorry for the Sales programming team, however. No living programmers were harmed in the creation of this case study.

# Interfaces

The programming team stumbled badly over the matter of creating interfaces. The first, most obvious failure was one we noted before: the failure to completely create the OrderCustomer document within a single service. Upon detecting the problem with IXMLHTTP, the programming team should have investigated other options. Their shortcut streamlined their development at the expense of everyone who comes after them. Distributed applications require careful attention to formal interfaces. This is especially true when trying to build cooperative distributed applications that facilitate reuse. As things stand, the OrderCustomer service is not reusable unless one has knowledge of the implementation.

A subtler mistake was committed in the design and implementation of the OrderHistory service. The vocabulary designer had the right idea in mind when he chose to make it a collection. Unfortunately, he had the details of the current application in the forefront of his mind and failed to allow the document to have more than one OrderHistory element in the collection. Instead of this DTD fragment:

```
<!ELEMENT    Collection        OrderHistory>
```

the designer might have written this:

```
<!ELEMENT    Collection        OrderHistory+>
```

By permitting more than one OrderHistory element, the designer would have stayed true to the intent of the Collection vocabulary and allowed other applications to obtain batches of OrderHistory documents on multiple customers. This would, of course, have necessitated a change to the OrderHistoryQuery DTD to permit a sequence of more than one CustomerID elements.

The lesson to take away from this mistake is one of divorcing analysis from the specific task of implementing the application at hand. Designers and analysts are better off talking to the business users within the organization in an effort to elicit the fundamentals of the business being modeled. If we create objects that faithfully model aspects of the business, reuse will naturally follow. After all, the same aspects turn up all over the business.

A baker will have to deal with ingredients and loaves of bread throughout the course of the business. If the analysts focus on a particular application problem instead, the FloatingPointFitsinADatabaseandDisplaysWell objects they create will be incapable of reuse. The mistake our designer made in this application is going to cause problems for the next programming team in Chapter 10.

# Components

The Sales department's programming team, like the one from the Customer Service department before them, was more a recipient of the benefits of component software than a facilitator. MSXML did yeoman's service once again in its various guises. Our toolkit saw a little more use. In addition to the DirectoryWalker, we brought the DataSplicer into the application, albeit in a very limited fashion. The team didn't create any objects of their own, however. Still, the idea may have been percolating just below the surface, when they designed the OrderHistory vocabulary. One reason the programming team in this chapter didn't bother to build any components was that the objects represented by the various vocabularies had no behavior of their own. They were static data structures intended for display and nothing more. There is little reason to wrap such structures inside script. We imagined software agents as consumers of services in Chapter 1. The services we have built in the last two chapters are ill-suited to such consumers.

The OrderHistory designer, however, decided to enable calculations using some of the data within exchange documents by preserving the data types of the SubTotal and Quantity elements. A future service consumer can retrieve the data in a strongly typed form and perform calculations. So, we can give the team slightly higher marks on components than they earned on interfaces.

# Reuse Potential

We've seen how the flaw in the OrderHistory vocabulary may restrict reuse of this resource. So long as any future application wants OrderHistory data on a one-at-a-time basis, the vocabulary will be just as useful as any other we have built. In general, however, this is an unlikely candidate for reuse. OrderCustomer, likewise, is a vocabulary that operates on a singleton basis. The Sales department team has been the beneficiary of reuse, but has done little to return the favor to other, future, programming teams.

Using data types is the sole exception. The current application has no use for it, but a design decision was made to retain as much intrinsic data as possible. This sort of gesture toward generality – preserving options wherever possible – helps to promote reuse and makes for cooperative applications.

# Summary

This chapter carries our development principles forward into a more difficult case. A service we built in the last chapter became a legacy application we had to reuse. This is always a challenge. We saw examples of the following:

- ❑ Specializing an existing service for reuse
- ❑ Hiding how we got our data behind an XML vocabulary
- ❑ Creation of an XML document using the DOM methods of MSXML
- ❑ Repeatedly creating new content within a single DHTML page

The Order Tracking application was the first real test of our development philosophy. The Customer Service application also specialized a vocabulary, but it did so at the same time that the generalized vocabulary was written and the application was implemented. We would expect the new vocabulary to work well. This application, however, drew on a pre-existing vocabulary for useful work. Our toolkit components are now in routine use. While our vocabulary designer made a critical mistake with one aspect of the `OrderHistory` vocabulary, he made a good choice in preserving the native data types of certain data properties.

In proving how a well-written service can be reused successfully, and a poorly written service can cause problems, this application provided a lesson in the importance of clean, well-written interfaces to distributed applications. These interfaces – the exchange vocabularies in our technique – are the only way for applications to interact with one another. If they track the rules of the business they serve, they are likely to promote reuse. If they are too tightly tied to a specific use, they will become orphans that serve only one client. Effort spent on design pays ample dividends and makes the entire organization's information system stronger.

This chapter illustrated another point regarding distributed applications. The implementation details of any single application should be invisible to the other applications in the system. We used completely different approaches to the composition of XML and the display of results than those used in the preceding chapter, but the standard we established for the transmission of data between processing tiers in our system worked for both.

The use of XML and location transparency in our philosophy is working well. We're in a position to completely change the location and implementation of our services without breaking the overall system. The use of component software is partially in place. We've derived tremendous benefit from the use of MSXML and ADO, and some utility from our toolkit components. We have yet to promote the creation of new and useful components by our programming teams, however. In addition, our applications are still human-centric. Humans are, of course, the most important users of our applications, but we are limiting the utility of our services if they do no more than fetch data for display on the screen without translation. With this in mind, let's proceed to the final chapter in the Wrox Blocks case studies.

# 10

# Wrox Blocks: Order Analysis

We noticed a troubling error in the `OrderHistory` implementation in the last chapter. The success of two projects so far has spread the story of our development philosophy through ever-wider circles within the Wrox Blocks company. In this chapter, we'll see how someone solving an isolated problem can benefit from the work that went before, and how the organization as a whole can easily accommodate change for the better.

We've spent two chapters wondering why no one has built any custom business components. Our wait is over. We'll be constructing a modest component to test our goal of isolating business rules in discrete components. We'll show how this prototype component can evolve without disturbing applications built upon its use. This component is distinct from the components we built for our tool kit. Those components were intended to be widely used utilities implementing some of the techniques we developed in earlier chapters. They were not specific to any one customer or organization. As such, they were only slightly less useful than the ADSI, ADO, and XML related components from Microsoft. The component we build in this chapter, by contrast, encapsulates some of the business wisdom of Wrox Blocks. It will be used, we hope, throughout that fictional organization, but never by outsiders.

This case study, then, addresses a number of issues that may crop up around our use of the five principles. In particular, our fictional programmers will have to deal with the following:

- ❑ Introducing an improved service implementation into an organization
- ❑ Capturing business logic in reusable components
- ❑ Putting an existing service to a new use without modifying the service's implementation

## The Business Case

Wrox Blocks is having an order fulfillment problem. A small number of orders remain pending even after all the products have been drawn from inventory and assigned to the order. Wrox Blocks management would like to know why and have assigned someone from outside the Sales department to track the problem down. It will be necessary to locate some of these problematic orders, so our hero begins by studying the Order Tracking system in use by the Sales department.

Order status at Wrox Blocks comes in two forms, as we saw in the last chapter. Each product is classified as Filled or Pending. The order as a whole is also classified as Filled or Pending. If all the line items and the overall order are Filled, the order is ready to ship. In a normal order, the overall order goes from Pending to Filled when the last line item goes to Filled. Wrox Block's shipping clerks devised the notion of internal status to reconcile the overall and line item statuses. The internal status is Open while any line item status is Pending, and Ready when all product items and the overall status are Filled.

Occasionally, an order is held up for reasons other than fulfilling the line items. An order can have an overall Pending status due to external problems, like shipping backlog, even though all the products in the order have been assembled. When this happens, the internal status is Problem. If an order is erroneously marked Filled while one or more line items is Pending, the internal status is Inconsistent. The full set of possibilities is shown in the table below:

| Overall order | All line items | Internal Status |
| --- | --- | --- |
| Filled | Filled | Ready |
| Filled | Pending | Inconsistent |
| Pending | Filled | Problem |
| Pending | Pending | Open |

Our analyst, then, needs to look for delayed orders with an internal status of either Problem or Inconsistent. The existing Order Tracking application is customer-centric, so using it to locate problematic orders would take far too long. The OrderHistory vocabulary, however, has all the required information. The analyst needs to ask a different question, but he would still like the answer in OrderHistory format. Specifically, he needs all the OrderHistory elements for some time period. Since he is looking for delayed orders, he designs his application to look for orders with shipping dates more than some user-specified number of days in the future. An ordinary order moves through the system fairly rapidly; an order with an extended shipping date either has a fulfillment problem or is an order with a troubling internal status. Once the application receives a collection of OrderHistory elements, it should apply the business rules regarding internal status and display those with a status of Problem or Inconsistent.

There is one further item in which the analyst should take an interest. Wrox Blocks wants to know how much revenue is at risk when an order is delayed. The company bills customers at the time of shipment, so a Problem order costs money. If the analyst has a list of problematic orders, he can focus his efforts on those with the highest dollar value. This is calculated as the sum of the subtotals for the individual items.

# Application Design

The application consists of a single client page, ProblemOrderHistory.html, a component for calculating order values and internal status, and a new implementation of the OrderHistory service. The client application requests a collection of OrderHistory elements matching a specified criterion, performs post-processing on the result using the business component, and displays the results.

Although this application uses the same exchange vocabulary for its results, the underlying semantics are a good deal different from the Order Tracking application. That system requested data on a single customer. This one asks for data that might well span many users. The Order Tracking information performed no calculations, but displayed detailed information about each order. This application performs calculations and processing according to the business rules of Wrox Blocks, then displays summary information.

### *How It All Fits Together*

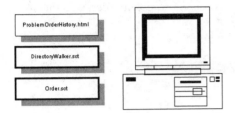

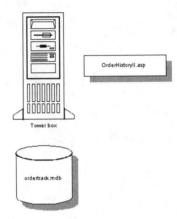

Both sides of this application – client and server – have gotten more complicated as we move into the final case study. On the server, we have replaced the `OrderHistory` implementation from the last chapter with an improved implementation, `OrderHistoryII.asp`. In all other respects, the flow remains the same as in the other case studies. The server receives a request in XML, extracts the parameters, issues a query, and builds a response XML document from the results.

It is the client that is especially interesting in this case study. We again have a client page, `ProblemOrderHistory.html`. It uses the DirectoryWalker to locate its source of `OrderHistory` documents. Once it receives such a response document, however, it creates uses the data to initialize an order validator scriptlet component. That component implements the business-specific logic of checking for problem orders and computing the total cost of the order. Scripts in `ProblemOrderHistory.html` are used to control and manipulate the Order component and to issue requests to the server.

# The Client

The client consists of a single page with a user interface not unlike that in the Order Tracking application. The user specifies an integral number of days from the current date. After the user clicks on the Search button, the client requests the order history for all orders whose projected shipping date is more than the user-specified number of days in the future. For example, if a user wishes to focus on all orders whose ship date is a week or more in the future, they would enter 7 in the input box.

In return, the client receives an XML document in `OrderHistory` format. It applies the internal status rules to each order and displays any order with **Problem** or **Inconsistent** status. The customer identifier is displayed, followed by one or more tables with summary information regarding the troubled order. The information displayed allows the user to perform the following tasks:

❑ Identify problematic orders requiring investigation
❑ Identify the revenue placed at risk by delayed orders
❑ Obtain information leading to customer contact information
❑ Obtain information leading to detailed order history information

The first two tasks are completely accomplished with this application. The customer ID is sufficient to obtain detailed contact and order history information using the Order Tracking application. Once the user has the customer's name, he can also view the customer's call history through the Customer Service application. The chief utility of this application is in identifying troubled orders and the at-risk revenue. If the user wants to delve further into the problem on-line, he can use the information in troubled orders as parameters for the applications we developed in the preceding chapters.

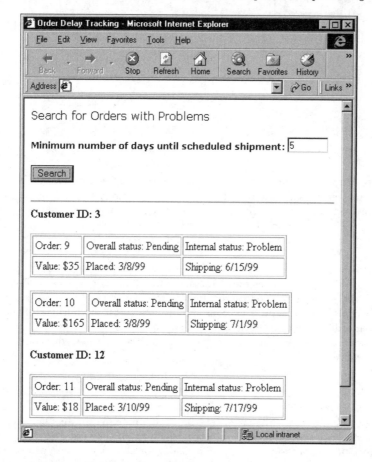

## The Order Validator Component

The main novelty in this application is the use of a software component to capture and use the business logic regarding orders and shipping. This component maintains properties corresponding to the information transmitted by `Order` elements in an `OrderHistory` document. In addition, it has methods for adding, editing, and deleting order line items, calculating the total value of an order, and checking the internal status of the order.

The component is oriented toward computation, not display. It simply tracks the various properties of an order and allows for the calculation of an order's value and internal status. In short, it is a utility component. It can be reused wherever we need to discuss orders in the Wrox Blocks company. Display tasks tend to be application specific, so we leave that to the application that makes use of this component.

Components like this are the complement to our exchange data. The server takes data from one specific form , a relational database, and writes it out in an application neutral format of our devising. Although the server doesn't use business components, we can conceive of situations where it might. The source of our data could be a real-time feed from an order call center. Such an application could use messaging to transmit orders (written in some hypothetical Order vocabulary) to a client. However the data originated, we have transmitted it in a neutral format. Now we are building an application that needs to do more than simply display the data it receives. It is natural, then, to create an object to represent the order. This object is capable of working with the data it receives using rules that define our business. This gets back to our original vision in Chapter 1. Each tier uses whatever object technology works best for its problem, and XML is used as a neutral exchange format for moving object-oriented data between tiers.

# Competing for Service

One of the first things our analyst notices when he tries to use the existing OrderHistory service for the task at hand is the deficiency we noted at the end of the last chapter. Despite the use of the Collection element and the fact that multiple OrderHistory elements are possible and useful, the programming team that implemented the service neglected to support that possibility. Their application didn't require multiple OrderHistory elements, so it never occurred to them to implement that feature.

This leaves our analyst with a dilemma. He has no leverage over the Sales department, so he cannot force them to fix what he sees is a deficiency. He will have to make his own implementation. This leaves the system administrator of the Wrox Blocks network with a problem. How can he accommodate another implementation?

## Options

This problem will become a familiar occurrence in a network of loosely coupled, distributed applications. This is especially true if the organization embraces rapid prototyping and development. In the rush to assemble prototypes using preexisting services, bugs will be found. There will be tremendous resistance to change if an existing service meets the requirements of the original application. You must have some sort of mechanism in place to avoid the proliferation of similar services that meet the needs of a single application. Let's look at four options for tackling the problem at hand: alternate service names, locality of service, versioning, and leveraging location transparency.

### Alternate Service Names

The easiest approach for our analyst is to change the name of the service. Substitute OrderDelays for OrderHistory and we have no naming conflict. Anyone who wants to obtain the history of orders with delays needs to be instructed to look for OrderDelays instead of OrderHistory. To some extent, we already have this. If clients are careful to look for the name of the query vocabulary, there will be no conflict. We've permitted clients to use either in the past. If too much information has to be communicated to client application developers, our network will become tightly coupled and we'll lose some of the advantages we seek. The use of alternate service names, then, creates some problems for us.

To start with, we're communicating more and more information to prospective client application developers. At some point, we might as well write a traditional client-server application. Services must be loosely coupled to be reusable in helpful ways. We are better served by deferring as much information as we can until runtime, retrieving it by querying the directory service. More importantly, if every programming team can work around problems by coining a new service name, it won't be long before every service written has a distinct name and there are no services that are globally useful. We will also lose the sense that everyone shares a common understanding of the business. OrderHistory captures the notion of a collection of orders over time. That idea is common to both the task in the last chapter and the current one. Each application is asking a different question, but speaking using the same concept. On balance we definitely want to avoid alternate service names.

## Locality of Services

Offering a service within a particular home domain is another option. The analyst presumably has some influence within his workgroup or department. Applications will generally search for services locally unless they have prior knowledge about a service's location. Consequently, if the analyst were to register his service within the home domain and not with the tree or forest, his service would not conflict with the one deployed by the Sales department.

This falls apart on two grounds. Firstly, we cannot always assume that conflicting requirements will occur along domain lines. The analyst might be part of the same domain as the Sales department. He might be a member of the Sales department, but unable to convince the team fielding the original service to change. Secondly, prospective clients outside the domain in which the service is deployed lose its benefits. If the new service is truly a better implementation of the semantics of the OrderHistory vocabulary, its use should expand until it supercedes the original one. Good ideas should bubble up through the organization and drive out lesser ideas. At best, keeping competing service implementations local is a temporary solution, one best used during development and beta testing.

## Versioning

Chapter 4 proposed a mechanism for versioning. In many cases, this is the proper solution. If the change in the implementation fits the versioning scheme – which happens when there is a distinct change in the schema – using versioning to introduce a new implementation is the perfect way to go. Unfortunately, this is not the case here. The only change is to allow multiple occurrences of the OrderHistory element within the Collection element. Collection is a mutable construct in our philosophy; although it is technically a vocabulary in its own right, we expect its contents to change with each service. A strict DTD for the Collection vocabulary would be so nebulous as to be useless. Within OrderHistory, there is nothing to change and we cannot use versioning. Although versioning is a useful tool, it does not bring any power to bear on the problem at hand.

## Location Transparency

Ultimately, our use of location transparency is the mechanism by which the new service will supplant the old. As we saw when examining locality of service, the new implementation can gain a foothold within the local domain without conflicting with implementations from other domains. There is also nothing wrong with deploying two implementations within the same domain. Active Directory permits us to have multiple values for the same service entry. Our examples so far have assumed a single entry because we know there will only be one entry – these are toy applications for teaching purposes and additional complexity for the sake of generality will only get in the way of understanding the key concepts. If, however, production applications look for multiple implementations, even across domain lines, they will increasingly discover how many options they have. If a client requiring multiple OrderHistory elements uses the original implementation, for example, it will quickly come to understand that the original service does not fully answer its questions.

If it knows about the other implementation, it can try that service and get better results.

The exact means by which a client tries different implementations of a service must vary with the nature of the network environment and the application's demands. A network with a rich selection of poorly understood service implementations must use and compare each implementation and draw conclusions about the quality of results achieved and the performance observed. Such features could require significant effort to attain. In a small network with few services and good communication between programming teams, a client with limited demands can take and use the first implementation it finds.

In our case, the analyst decides to begin by deploying his service within his home domain. Over time, the number of distinct applications that use his service will press the case to use his implementation. The network administrator may then choose to enter his implementation at higher levels of the directory, expanding the user base. Eventually, a consensus will be reached that this is a superior implementation and the entries for the old implementation will be removed. Since all clients have been querying the directory at runtime for the location of the service, none of them will notice the change. If the analyst is careful to write his implementation so that it can answer queries from the `OrderHistoryQuery` vocabulary as well as the query vocabulary for the new application, it will be able to assimilate and supercede the old implementation without disrupting service to any clients.

## Our Solution

Clearly, then, our analyst's decision is an easy one. He should structure his service so that it writes `OrderHistory` documents independently of the query used to retrieve the data. A particular SQL query is driven by the query vocabulary received by the service. We might, for example, look for the information but limit the search with different constraints. Since we are using a relational database, we can do this by having separate functions to compose the two SQL queries, then a common set of functions to execute the query and write the XML document. The same code can be used because the columns retrieved are the same; only the particular rows are different. In fact, some of the code to handle `OrderHistoryQuery` requests will look suspiciously familiar.

# Exchange Vocabularies

The application we are developing introduces a single new vocabulary, `OrderHistoryDelaysQuery`, and provides a new implementation of `OrderHistory`.

## OrderHistoryDelaysQuery

Like `OrderHistoryQuery` before it, `OrderHistoryDelaysQuery` is a very simple vocabulary. Here's a sample:

```
<OrderHistoryDelaysQuery>
    <DaysToShip>7<DaysToShip>
</OrderHistoryDelaysQuery>
```

This document simply says that the client wants to know what orders with shipping dates a week or more in the future are on file. `DaysToShip` is an element specifying the minimum number of days in the future needed to qualify an order for inclusion in the result set; there is no upper limit. Here's the DTD:

```
<!ELEMENT    OrderHistoryDelaysQuery    DaysToShip>
<!ELEMENT    DaysToShip                 #PCDATA>
```

**325**

Client programmers should also have the implicit understanding that DaysToShip must be an integer, and should be a positive, nonzero number, although we may not enforce the latter constraint in our code. This is difficult to specify in a DTD. Although other metadata schemes make this easier, we'll keep the example simple and leave this information as an informal constraint.

### OrderHistory Revisited

The DTD we developed in Chapter 9 for OrderHistory is valid in the context of the client application we developed in parallel with the service in that chapter. It met the client's requirements, so we cannot say it's totally wrong. The idea we have put forward in the present chapter (that multiple OrderHistory elements should be permitted with a Collection) document, is better because it allows a service implementing it to answer a wider variety of questions. So, the revised DTD requires just one simple change to the original; the addition of a + sign. This change is highlighted below (the rest of the DTD is the same as it was in Chapter 9):

```
<!ELEMENT   Collection        OrderHistory+>
<!ATTLIST   Collection
            xmlns:dt          CDATA    #REQUIRED>
<!ELEMENT   OrderHistory      (CustomerID, Order+)>
...
```

# Implementation

Our application is implemented with three new entities: the client page, ProblemOrderHistory.html, a scriptlet component used by the client, Order.sct, and an ASP-based service, OrderHistoryII.asp. In addition, we will be reusing DirectoryWalker as well as ADO components and MSXML in its various guises. Although the component is implemented as a scriptlet using JavaScript, we will see that this decision is completely irrelevant to the client, and may indeed change over time for a variety of reasons.

# Locating Service

When the user clicks on the **Search** button in ProblemOrderHistory.html the OnSearchClick() function is called. The client begins with the steps needed to locate a service within the home domain of the user. This service should be capable of answering queries from the OrderHistoryDelaysQuery vocabulary with documents from the OrderHistory vocabulary. Here's how the button handler function works:

```
function OnSearchClick()
{
    var ni, sDays, sQueryDays, sLocation, nCount, oHist;
    var oValidator;
    var walker = new ActiveXObject("DirectoryWalker.scriptlet");
    var xmlProblems = new ActiveXObject("microsoft.xmldom");

    walker.User = "orderdept";
    walker.Pwd = "";
    sLocation = walker.SearchHome("OrderHistoryDelaysQuery");
    walker = null;
```

We provide a user ID and password common to the user's department, call the SearchHome() method to query the home domain, then reclaim the resources consumed by the component by setting the variable walker to the value null.

# Performing the Search

Posing a question of the revised service will require a value for the `DaysToShip` element from the user, composing the XML query, and transmitting it to the service. The service, in response, must extract the value we passed, compose and execute a SQL query, then compose and return a reply according to the rules of the `OrderHistory` vocabulary.

## Composing a Query

`ProblemOrderHistory.html` contains an `INPUT` element bearing the name `daysDelayText`. When the user clicks on the Search button, we read the value of the element and perform some error checking. This comprises the next section of the `OnSearchClick()` handler function.

We use the generic `Math` object's `round()` method to obtain the nearest whole number value for the value entered by the user. If the user entered an integer value, this new value will be the same as the value he entered and we may proceed to building the query.

```
sDays = daysDelayText.value;
   if (Math.round(sDays) == sDays)
   {
       // Clear old data
       resultArea.innerHTML = "";

       // Build a query document and request an OrderHistoryResponse
       QueryBlank.documentElement.childNodes(0).text = daysDelayText.value;
       xmlProblems.async = false;
       xmlProblems.load("http://" + sLocation + "?RequestXML=" +
                   QueryBlank.xml);
       if (xmlProblems.readyState == 4 && xmlProblems.parseError == 0)
       {
           ...
```

The client page also includes a `DIV` element named `resultArea` where we will be dynamically inserting our results. In anticipation of obtaining new results, we clear the `DIV` element by setting its HTML contents to an empty string. This process will destroy any prior tables and text. We then use the technique we introduced in the last chapter to compose an XML request. When the client page loads, it contains a data island containing the shell for our query:

```
<XML id=QueryBlank>
<OrderHistoryDelaysQuery>
   <DaysToShip/>
</OrderHistoryDelaysQuery>
</XML>
```

`QueryBlank`'s one and only child node is `DaysToShip`, so we set up our query by setting the child node's textual value to the value obtained from the `INPUT` element (see the above code):

```
QueryBlank.documentElement.childNodes(0).text = daysDelayText.value;
```

With such a simple query vocabulary, we know our requests will always be short enough to transmit using an HTTP `GET`, so we make a synchronous request using MSXML's `load()` method. If there are no problems, we proceed to parse and display the results obtained from the service.

## A New OrderHistory Implementation

According to our design, our service implementation is to be an improved version of the one we saw in the last chapter. The code will be restructured slightly for generality, and we will fulfill requests from the `OrderHistory` and `OrderHistoryDelaysQuery` vocabularies.

### A Generalized Main Body

To open up the main body of our service, it is necessary to look at the query vocabulary and direct our efforts accordingly. Here's how the service (`OrderHistoryII.asp`) begins:

```
var queryParser = Server.CreateObject("microsoft.xmldom");
Response.ContentType = "text/xml";

queryParser.loadXML(Request("RequestXML").Item);
if (queryParser.readyState == 4 && queryParser.parseError == 0)
{
    if (queryParser.documentElement.childNodes.length > 0)
        sToken = queryParser.documentElement.childNodes(0).text;

    switch (queryParser.documentElement.nodeName)
    {
        case "OrderHistoryDelaysQuery":
            sQuery = BuildDelayQuery(sToken);
            break;
        case "OrderHistoryQuery":
            sQuery = BuildOHistQuery(sToken);
            break;
        default:
            sQuery = "";
            Response.Write("<NACK/>");
            break;
    }
}
```

We instantiate the MSXML parser and ask it to parse the query document. The document was passed as the value of the `GET` operation's `RequestXML` parameter. The string is loaded into the parser using the `loadXML()` method. After we determine that the parser is ready and experienced no errors, we proceed to look at what was sent to us. We know that the two query vocabularies we can handle have at least one child node, the outer element defining which query vocabulary was sent. If the root element – presumably the `Collection` element – has at least one child, we proceed. Both query vocabularies carry a single parameter in the value of the child node of the query element (`CustomerID` or `DaysToShip`). Next, we look at what we have and branch according to the name of the first child node.

If it is one of the query vocabularies, we call the appropriate function to build the SQL query, passing the value we obtained from the query document passed as a parameter to the function. If we do not recognize the query vocabulary, we immediately pass back a `<NACK/>` document to indicate an error.

### Query Generation

`BuildDelayQuery` is the function that composes the SQL query in response to an `OrderHistoryDelaysQuery` document. For the sample we saw earlier, in which the value 7 was passed in the `DaysToShip` element, the query we need would look like this:

```
SELECT s.order_cust, s.order_no, s.order_date, s.order_complete,
    s.order_ship_date, d.detail_product, d.detail_subtotal, d.detail_filled,
```

```
d.detail_quantity, p.product_description FROM order_summary AS s,
order_detail AS d, order_products AS p WHERE d.detail_ordno=s.order_no AND
p.product_id = d.detail_product AND (s.order_ship_date - NOW()) > 7 AND
s.order_complete = false ORDER BY s.order_no
```

We're requesting the same columns from the same tables as we did in the last chapter. This isn't so surprising; we're building the same kind of document. The first two constraints in the WHERE clause are identical, too. These are needed to perform the join between the various tables. The next one ((s.order_ship_date – NOW()) > 7) does the arithmetic to filter out any orders with ship dates earlier than the date the user provided. The final constraint (s.order_complete = false) limits the result set to those orders that have an overall status of **Pending**. This is in accordance with the business rules we established earlier. We are searching for orders that are having problems, not orders that are flowing smoothly. The function BuildDelayQuery() concatenates strings to build the query:

```
function BuildDelayQuery(sDays)
{
   var sQuery

   sQuery  = "SELECT s.order_cust, s.order_no, s.order_date,
              s.order_complete, ";

   sQuery += "s.order_ship_date, d.detail_product, d.detail_subtotal,
              d.detail_filled, ";
   sQuery += "d.detail_quantity, p.product_description FROM order_summary AS
              s, order_detail AS d, ";
   sQuery += "order_products AS p WHERE d.detail_ordno=s.order_no AND
              p.product_id = d.detail_product AND ";
   sQuery += "(s.order_ship_date - NOW()) > " + sDays + " ";
   sQuery += "AND s.order_complete = false ORDER BY s.order_no";

   return sQuery;
}
```

The NOW() function is specific to Microsoft Access. Other RDBMS's provide different built-in functions to determine the current date.

BuildOHistQuery(), the function that builds the SQL query in response to an OrderHistory query, is taken from the implementation we built in the last chapter and renamed:

```
function BuildOHistQuery(sID)
{
   var sQuery;

   sQuery  = "SELECT s.order_cust, s.order_no, s.order_date,
               s.order_complete, ";
   sQuery += "s.order_ship_date, d.detail_product, d.detail_subtotal,
               d.detail_filled, d.detail_quantity, ";
   sQuery += "p.product_description from order_summary as s, order_detail as
               d, ";
   sQuery += "order_products as p WHERE s.order_cust=" + sID;
   sQuery += " AND d.detail_ordno=s.order_no AND
               p.product_id=d.detail_product ";
   sQuery += "ORDER BY s.order_no";
   return sQuery;
}
```

## Data Retrieval

Emerging from the switch statement, the string variable `sQuery` will have the text of a useful SQL query if the service recognizes the query vocabulary, or else will be an empty string. In the former case, we want to execute the query and build an appropriate `Collection` document containing one or more `OrderHistory` elements. The query vocabulary is irrelevant to the script in `OrderHistoryII.asp` from this point forward.

```
if (sQuery != "")
{
   dbConn = Server.CreateObject("ADODB.Connection");
   dbConn.Open("OrderTrack", "", "");
   dbRecordSet = Server.CreateObject("ADODB.RecordSet");

   dbRecordSet = dbConn.Execute(sQuery);

   if (!dbRecordSet.BOF)
      dbRecordSet.MoveFirst();

   if (dbRecordSet.EOF)
      Response.Write("<Collection/>");
   else
      WriteOrderHistory(dbRecordSet);
```

We open an ADO connection to the `OrderTrack` database (which we created in the preceding chapter) and create a recordset object by executing the query formed during the `switch` statement. We can still encounter a situation that prevents us from writing a useful document. If the query returns no rows – as in the case where no orders are pending past the cutoff the user provided – we write an empty `Collection` element. Otherwise, we turn to the function `WriteOrderHistory()` to compose a `Collection` of `OrderHistory` elements from our recordset.

*The version of the* `OrderTack` *database included with the source code for this chapter has been augmented with rows for problematic orders. These bear shipping dates for July 1999. Depending on when you read this, you may need to go into Access, open the database, and modify the shipping dates for orders nine, ten, and eleven.*

## Composing a Reply

`WriteOrderHistory()` is slightly different from the function we built for the original implementation of the `OrderHistory` service. After all, we have to accommodate multiple `OrderHistory` elements. As before, though, we create the `Collection` element and give it the data typing namespace declaration as an attribute:

```
function WriteOrderHistory(dbRecordSet)
{
   var oNode, oOpts, oCardNode, oOrderNode, oProdNode, oHistNode;
   var oAttr, curCust, nCustID;
   var parserOrderHist = Server.CreateObject("microsoft.xmldom");

   oNode = parserOrderHist.createElement("Collection");
   oAttr = parserOrderHist.createAttribute("xmlns:dt");
   oNode.setAttributeNode(oAttr);
   oNode.setAttribute("xmlns:dt", "urn:schemas-microsoft-com:datatypes");
```

Next, we want to initialize the MSXML parser instance and set up some local variables that we will use to determine when customer IDs and order numbers change. Since each customer has his own `OrderHistory` element, a changed customer ID indicates the need to begin a new element. Similarly, a changed order ID indicates the need to begin a new `Order` element. Since these values are primary keys within the `OrderTrack` database, we know they will never have the value zero (Access assigns nonzero values to `AutoNumber` values). We shall initialize our variables to zero, so we'll begin with new `OrderHistory` and `Order` elements.

```
parserOrderHist.documentElement = oNode;
curCust = 0;
curOrdNo = 0;
```

Now we want to step through each row of the recordset. Each row corresponds to a product line item in an order. Each row also includes customer and order information. First of all, we look at the customer ID. If it changes, we create an `OrderHistory` element and append it to the `Collection` element's `childNodes` collection. We also create a `CustomerID` element and append it to the `OrderHistory` element.

```
while (!dbRecordSet.EOF)
{
    nCustID = dbRecordSet ("order_cust").Value;

    // If the ID changes, we need to write a new OrderHistory element
    if (nCustID != curCust)
    {
        curCust = nCustID;
        oHistNode = parserOrderHist.createElement("OrderHistory");
        parserOrderHist.documentElement.appendChild(oHistNode);

        oCustNode = parserOrderHist.createElement("CustomerID");
        oCustNode.text = nCustID;
        oHistNode.appendChild(oCustNode);
    }
```

Now consider what happens when the order number changes. We need to create a new `Order` element and add it to the `OrderHistory` element in progress.

```
    if (dbRecordSet("order_no").Value != curOrdNo)
    {
        curOrdNo = dbRecordSet("order_no").Value;
        oOrderNode = CreateOrderNode(parserOrderHist, dbRecordSet);
        oHistNode.appendChild(oOrderNode);
        oProdNode = CreateProdNode(parserOrderHist, dbRecordSet);
        oOrderNode.appendChild(oProdNode);
    }
    else
    {
        // Always create one OrderProduct element per row
        oProdNode = CreateProdNode(parserOrderHist, dbRecordSet);
        oOrderNode.appendChild(oProdNode);
    }
    dbRecordSet.MoveNext();
```

We create the `Order` element and add it to the `OrderHistory` element. Next, we create and add an `OrderProduct` element to the `Order` element. If the order number hasn't changed from the preceding row, the most common situation, we just create and add an `OrderProduct` element to the `Order` element.

The real work of creating `Order` and `OrderProduct` elements is passed off to the functions `CreateOrderNode()` and `CreateProdNode()`, respectively. We saw these before in the original implementation:

```
function CreateOrderNode(parser, dbRS)
{
    var oOrdNode = parser.createElement("Order");
    var oNode;

    oNode = parser.createElement("OrderNumber");
    oNode.text = dbRS("order_no").Value;
    oOrdNode.appendChild(oNode);

    oNode = parser.createElement("Status");
    if (dbRS("order_complete").Value == 1)
        oNode.text = "Filled";
    else
        oNode.text = "Pending";
    oOrdNode.appendChild(oNode);

    oNode = parser.createElement("PlacementDate");
    oNode.text = dbRS("order_date").Value;
    oOrdNode.appendChild(oNode);

    oNode = parser.createElement("ShipDate");
    oNode.text = dbRS("order_ship_date").Value;
    oOrdNode.appendChild(oNode);

    return oOrdNode;
}

function CreateProdNode(parser, dbRS)
{
    var oProdNode, oNode, oDetailNode, oAttr;

    oProdNode = parser.createElement("OrderProduct");

    oNode = parser.createElement("Quantity");
    oAttr = parser.createAttribute("dt:dt");
    oNode.setAttributeNode(oAttr);
    oNode.setAttribute("dt:dt", "int");
    oNode.text = dbRS("detail_quantity").Value;
    oProdNode.appendChild(oNode);

    oNode = parser.createElement("SubTotal");
    oAttr = parser.createAttribute("dt:dt");
    oNode.setAttributeNode(oAttr);
    oNode.setAttribute("dt:dt","fixed.14.4");
    oNode.text = dbRS("detail_subtotal").Value;
    oProdNode.appendChild(oNode);

    oNode = parser.createElement("Product");
    oDetailNode = parser.createElement("PartNumber");
    oDetailNode.text = dbRS("detail_product").Value;
    oNode.appendChild(oDetailNode);
```

```
        oDetailNode = parser.createElement("Name");
        oDetailNode.text = dbRS("product_description").Value;
        oNode.appendChild(oDetailNode);
        oProdNode.appendChild(oNode);

        oNode = parser.createElement("FillStatus");
        if (dbRS("detail_filled").Value == 1)
           oNode.text = "Filled";
        else
           oNode.text = "Pending";
        oProdNode.appendChild(oNode);

        return oProdNode;
}
```

After we've created the response document in `parserOrderHist`, we can write it out to the client with the following line:

```
        Response.Write(parserOrderHist.xml);
```

Here, then, is the complete main body of the service ASP, `OrderHistII.asp`:

```
var sQuery, dbConn, dbRecordSet;
var sDays;
var queryParser = Server.CreateObject("microsoft.xmldom");

queryParser.loadXML(Request("RequestXML").Item);
if (queryParser.readystate == 4 && queryParser.parseError.reason == 0)
{
    if (queryParser.documentElement.childNodes.length > 0)
        sToken = queryParser.documentElement.childNodes(0).text;

    switch (queryParser.documentElement.nodeName)
    {
        case "OrderHistoryDelaysQuery":
            sQuery = BuildDelayQuery(sToken);
            break;
        case "OrderHistoryQuery":
            sQuery = BuildOHistQuery(sToken);
            break;
        default:
            sQuery = "";
            Response.Write("<NACK/>");
            break;
    }

    if (sQuery != "")
    {
        //Perform the query
        dbConn = Server.CreateObject("ADODB.Connection");
        dbConn.Open("OrderTrack", "", "");
        dbRecordSet = Server.CreateObject("ADODB.RecordSet");

        dbRecordSet = dbConn.Execute(sQuery);

        if (!dbRecordSet.BOF)
            dbRecordSet.MoveFirst();
```

```
          // Check for problems; if okay, write out the document
      if (dbRecordSet.EOF)
          Response.Write("<Collection/>");
      else
          WriteOrderHistory(dbRecordSet);

      try
      {
          /* Reclaim resources; some ADO conditions can lead to
             exceptions that we've dealt with previously. */

          dbRecordSet.Close();
          dbConn.Close();
          dbConn = null;
          dbRecordSet = null;
      }
      catch (e)
      {
      }
   }
}
else
   Response.Write("<NACK>ParserError</NACK>");

queryParser = null;
```

The `try...catch` clause handles exceptions such as when we try to close an empty recordset object. Although the use of an empty catch block may seem like sloppy programming, we've already detected and handled this condition. We wrote out the empty `Collection` object in response. This technique saves us the trouble of checking for all the different conditions that could occur when we are no longer interested in the state of the ADO objects. All we are trying to do at this point is clean up our resources.

# Validating Orders

Let's step back and consider where we are at this point. The client, `ProblemOrderHistory.html`, has sent a request to the service and received an `OrderHistory` collection in response. MSXML has parsed the document and constructed a DOM tree for it. In previous examples we would be ready to display the results. This is where this application gets interesting. We still have some processing to do. The document we received shows us all the Pending orders whose anticipated shipping date falls after the cutoff the user supplied. While these might be interesting just from the standpoint of revealing a sluggish shipping department, our fictional analyst is after more serious problems. We need to check the internal status so we can display only those orders that have a status of Problem or Inconsistent. Rather than build this into the client, we're going to segregate this logic into a component in the hopes that we will be able to reuse it elsewhere.

## Why a Scriptlet?

This will be a COM component. We need to consider what language to use to implement it. At some point, we'll need to consider performance. If this component is used heavily, we'll want to write it using a compiled language like C++ or Java and use the services provided by Microsoft Transaction Server to get the best combination of speed and resource utilization. That's a bit much for the application at hand. Our purposes will be well-served by writing another scriptlet as a prototype. If the component proves useful, we can port it to one of the other languages and add MTS support.

In fact, if we use JavaScript, the effort to port it to Java will be minimal. Since the interface remains the same, client applications won't notice the change when we port the component. Since it is a COM component, we'll be able to reuse the business logic in all sorts of applications written in a variety of languages. Component-based software is ideal for rapid prototyping and development.

## The Interface

The first and most important task is to design our interface. This component is intended to be a work horse that operates behind the scenes. We won't need any interface-oriented, resource consuming properties like the human-friendly product names, but we will need the status codes and identifiers so using applications can find this information for themselves. Here are the properties the component should have:

| Property | Meaning and Usage |
| --- | --- |
| CustomerID | read-write; customer ID taken from the database |
| OrderNumber | read-write; order number taken from the database |
| SummaryStatus | read-write; overall status taken from the database |
| LineCount | read-only; number of product line items in the order |
| DatePlaced | read-write; the date the order was placed |
| DateToShip | read-write; the anticipated shipping date |

Note that the property LineCount is actually a calculated value. We'll have a collection of line items for our products. This property will check the count of items in the collection at the time it is called and return that value. Now consider the methods for our component:

| Method | Meaning and Usage |
| --- | --- |
| CheckInternalStatus() | Applies the internal status rules we developed and returns a status code. |
| AddLineItem(partNum, subtotal, quantity, isFilled) | Adds a line item entry to the component to represent this line item product. |
| DeleteLineItem(partNum) | Deletes the line item if found. Returns true if the product line item is found and deleted, false otherwise. |
| ChangeLineItem(partNum, subtotal, quantity, isFilled) | Replaces the last three values with the passed values if partNum is already part of the order. |
| ClearOrder() | Empties the line item collection, sets the CustomerID to zero, the SummaryStatus to empty, and the date properties to null strings. |
| ComputeTotalCost() | Returns the sum of the line item subtotal values for the order. |

ClearOrder() is important to us because it allows us to create a single component instance and use it for every order in the response document. We call ClearOrder() to remove the data from the preceding order, then set the properties and add line items to create a representation of the current order. We will use CheckInternalStatus() to determine whether we want to display the current order. ComputeTotalCost() gives us the total revenue placed at risk by a troubled order.

> *There's one final thing to consider in terms of an interface. The Scriptlet Wizard generates a* progid *that ends with* .scriptlet. *Since we expect to port this to a more powerful language at a later date, we should manually change this* progid *to* Order.Validator *in the registration element of the scriptlet. The registration element is used by the scriptlet runtime to add the proper registry entries when the component is registered. If we replace* .scriptlet *with something less specific, the component registration won't be misleading when the implementation language changes.*

```
<registration
    description="Order"
    progid="Order.Validator"
    version="1.00"
    classid="{1683b0b0-d58e-11d2-a53e-004005407f69}">
</registration>
```

> *The Scriptlet Wizard automatically generates the* classid. *If you write a scriptlet manually, use should use* GUIDGEN.EXE *from Visual Studio to create a unique* classid.

## Implementation

The first implementation decision we face is what sort of data structure to use to represent the product line items. An array is easy to use, but not very efficient. We don't know how many items we'll have when we start an order, and sequential access to line items won't work well for us. Sequential access would serve for CheckInternalStatus() and ComputeTotalCost() since we will have to iterate through the entire collection, but what about ChangeLineItem() and DeleteLineItem()? We need an efficient way to find a line item given its part number. The stock Dictionary scripting object is useful for this task, provided we use the part number as the key. In the class constructor function, then, in addition to the assignment of function names to property and method names, we need a line to instantiate a Dictionary object, which we will call rLineItems:

```
function Order()
{
    this.get_CustomerID = get_CustomerID;
    this.put_CustomerID = put_CustomerID;

    ... // remaining assingments here

    rLineItems = new ActiveXObject("Scripting.Dictionary");
}
```

We also declare global variables to represent the various summary and internal status states in our model. These go outside the functions comprising the component:

```
var EMPTY = 0;
var PENDING = 1;
var FILLED = 2;
```

```
var INCONSISTENT = 4;
var OPEN = 5;
var READY = 6;
var PROBLEM = 7;
```

### Maintaining the Line Item Collection

It's worth spending a few moments looking at the implementation of `AddLineItem()`, `ChangeLineItem()`, and `DeleteLineItem()` to get an understanding of the `Dictionary` object. Since line items don't have a meaningful existence outside the `Order` component, it isn't worth creating a component to represent them. Instead, we'll take advantage of the polymorphic nature of JavaScript arrays to represent these items. Each product line item will consist of a four element array containing the part number, line item subtotal, quantity, and fill status in that order. The product part number does double duty as the key by which we index this entry. The `Dictionary`'s `Add()` method will take the key and the array object, and insert the array into the collection. We'll add a final nuance. If the part number already exists as a line item, we want to add the subtotal and quantity to the existing line item representation, and replace its fill status with the one passed in the method call:

```
function AddLineItem(partNum, Subtotal, Quantity, Filled)
{
   var newItem = new Array(4);
   if (this.rLineItems.Exists(partNum))
   {
      var oItem = this.rLineItems.Item(partNum);
      oItem[1] += Subtotal;
      oItem[2] += Quantity;
      oItem[3] = Filled;
      return true;
   }
   else
   {
      newItem[0] = partNum;
      newItem[1] = Subtotal;
      newItem[2] = Quantity;
      newItem[3] = Filled;
      this.rLineItems.Add(partNum, newItem);
      return false;
   }
   return true;
}
```

The `Dictionary`'s `Exists()` method allows us to determine whether a line item already exists for the given part number.

Now that we know about the `Exists()` method, we use it and the `Item()` method to implement `ChangeLineItem()`. The `Item()` method takes a key and returns the corresponding object, or `null` if the key is not found.

```
function ChangeLineItem(partNum, SubTotal, Quantity, Filled)
{
   if (this.rLineItems.Exists(partNum))
   {
      var oItem = this.rLineItems.Item(partNum);
      oItem[1] = SubTotal;
      oItem[2] = Quantity;
```

```
        oItem[3] = Filled;
     }
   else
      return false;
}
```

We need to use one more method in the `Dictionary` interface: `Remove()`. Not surprisingly, it takes a key and removes the referenced object from the collection. Here's how `DeleteLineItem()` is implemented:

```
function DeleteLineItem(partNum)
{
   if (this.rLineItems.Exists(partNum))
   {
      this.rLineItems.Remove(partNum);
      return true;
   }
   else
      return false;
}
```

### Business Rules

The whole point of the `Order.Validator` component, of course, is to capture the business logic of Wrox Blocks shipping. Determining the internal status of an order is a matter of comparing the overall status to the aggregate status of the product line items. The `SummaryStatus` property gives us the overall status, but we need to iterate through the collection to determine the aggregate status of the line items. If one or more line items have the status `Pending`, the aggregate status will also be Pending. Here's the source code for the `CheckInternalStatus()` method:

```
function CheckInternalStatus()
{
   /* Implements a matrix of possibilities
      by dynamically checking the status of the
      order and the individual line items. */
   var rItems, oItem;
   var bItemsFilled = true;

   if (get_SummaryStatus() == EMPTY)
      return EMPTY;

   rItems = (new VBArray(rLineItems.Items())).toArray();
   for (ni in rItems)
   {
      if (rItems[ni][3] == false)
         bItemsFilled = false;
   }

   if (bItemsFilled)
   {
      if (get_SummaryStatus() == FILLED)
         return READY;
      else
         return PROBLEM;
   }
   else
```

```
    {
        if (this.get_SummaryStatus() == FILLED)
            return INCONSISTENT;
        else
            return OPEN;
    }
    return INCONSISTENT;
}
```

If the `SummaryStatus` property is `EMPTY`, we need go no further. Generally, however, we'll need to proceed to look at each of the line items in the collection. `Dictionary` has a method called `Items()` that returns the contents of the collection as an array. If we didn't have this, we would have to enumerate all the keys in the collection, then retrieve them using `Item()`. The documentation on `Items()` is a bit misleading, however. It doesn't give us a JavaScript array with properties like length. We need to jump through a few hoops to get the kind of array to which we're accustomed. The function class `VBArray` provides a COM style enumerator. We'll convert the Items collection to a JavaScript array, then create a `VBArray` instance from that. Hence the following line:

```
rItems = (new VBArray (rLineItems.Items())).toArray();
```

This creates a VBScript style array, complete with enumerator, and converts it to a JavaScript array. This fairly opaque line is worth the trouble, because it makes the collection enumeration much simpler, as we see in the lines that follow that one. Once we have the aggregate status, we perform a few Boolean comparisons to yield the internal status according to the matrix we presented in the business case for this application.

Calculating the total value of the order follows directly, once we understand how to iterate through the `Dictionary` collection. Here's the code our analyst writes to implement the `ComputeTotalCost()` method:

```
function ComputeTotalCost()
{
    var fTotal = 0.0;
    var oItem;

    var rItems = (new VBArray(rLineItems.Items())).toArray();
    for (ni in rItems)
    {
        oItem = rItems[ni];
        fTotal += oItem[1];
    }

    return fTotal;
}
```

This is where the use of strong typing through the data types namespace pays off. Because our vocabulary designer decided to retain the knowledge of data types implicit in `Order`, MSXML is able to provide us with the desired native type. We could do the conversion ourselves, but then the information about the element's type would be implicit. This way, anyone – human reader or automated agent – can tell what data type is intended at a glance.

### Some Thoughts on Future Performance

We have enough to proceed with our client application's task. Let's ponder the problems that programmers may encounter when they port our component to a language supposedly offering higher performance. While the runtime efficiency of the implementation language helps, it is neither the only factor effecting performance, nor even the most important. How a component manages the resources it draws on, and how well it allows an application server to manage it are far more important.

This component uses no external resources other than memory for the `Dictionary` component. This simplifies matters somewhat. The component itself, however, consumes memory. It should work in harmony with MTS to allow MTS to control the efficient allocation of resources to various clients. Most components, this one included, will be idle most of the time. If the client holds a component instance for long periods of time, then, memory will be wasted that could be given to another client for use with its components. Ideally, components that will be managed by MTS should be stateless. This allows MTS to free the component's resources between method calls, or assign the component to another client for use. A poorly designed component holds information for long periods of time and requires clients to hold it in memory for the life of the application. Our component falls between the two extremes. The calculations made by `ComputeTotalCost()` and `CheckInternalStatus()` do not add any persistent information that must be maintained between method invocations. They are, however, dependent upon the state of the order product line items. It will be important for clients using a future version of the component intended for high performance environments to group line item assignments and calculations together, and tell MTS when it is safe to release the component's resources. We will see a partial example of this in `ProblemOrderStatus.html`. We defer creating the component instance until we need it, group our calculations together, then release the component as soon as possible. That ensures the state does not change in the midst of a group of calculations. If necessary, we can perform the calculations inside a transaction. While this is hardly the final word in efficient component usage, it is the sort of thing programmers should strive for when they begin to build large-scale applications.

### Using the Order Validator Component

Let's return to the client. We have the response document parsed into a tree structure. Now it's time to iterate through the `OrderHistory` elements and look for problematic orders. Here is the remainder of the button handler function:

```
if (xmlProblems.readyState == 4 && xmlProblems.parseError == 0)
{
   if (xmlProblems.documentElement.nodeName == "Collection")
   {
      nCount = xmlProblems.documentElement.childNodes.length;
      oValidator = new ActiveXObject("Order.Validator");
      for (ni = 0; ni < nCount; ni++)
      {
         oHist = xmlProblems.documentElement.childNodes(ni);
         if (oHist.nodeName == "OrderHistory")
            ProcessHistory(oHist, oValidator);
      }
      oValidator = null;
   }
   else
      alert("Please ask your network administrator to check the
            configuration for the OrderHistoryDelaysQuery service.");
}
```

```
        else
            alert("An error was encountered processing the data
                    returned from the service.");
    }
    else
        alert("You must enter an integer number of days.");

    xmlProblems = null;
}
```

We look at each child element under the `Collection` root element. If it has the node name `OrderHistory` we send it off to `ProcessHistory()` together with an instance of the order validator component. As soon as we emerge from the loop iterating over the `OrderHistory` elements, we release the component instance. The rest of the function is error handling.

Obviously, `ProcessHistory()` must be where the interesting work takes place. Here's the code for that function:

```
function ProcessHistory(oHistoryNode, oValidator)
{
    var nStatus, ni, bWroteCustomer, oOrderNode

    bWroteCustomer = false;
    // For each Order node... length = # orders + cust id
    for (ni = 1; ni < oHistoryNode.childNodes.length; ni++)
    {
        oValidator.ClearOrder();
        oValidator.CustomerID = oHistoryNode.childNodes(0).text;

        oOrderNode = oHistoryNode.childNodes(ni);
        LoadValidator(oOrderNode, oValidator);
        nStatus = oValidator.CheckInternalStatus();

        // Only output problem orders
        if (nStatus == INCONSISTENT || nStatus == PROBLEM)
        {
            // See if we need to write the customer ID
            if (!bWroteCustomer)
            {
                bWroteCustomer = true;
                resultArea.insertAdjacentHTML("beforeEnd", "<B>Customer ID: " +
                                        oValidator.CustomerID + "</B><P/>");
            }
            WriteOrder(oValidator);
        }
    }
}
```

The first child element of the `OrderHistory` element is the `CustomerID` element. The rest are `Order` elements. We hand `Order` nodes and the validator off to a function named `LoadValidator()`. That function extracts data from the `Order` node and loads it into the properties of the validator component. When the function returns, we have a validator object that faithfully reflects the data passed in the `Order` element.

Let's pause for a moment to see how the XML-encoded data enters the order validation component. Here is the `LoadValidator()` function:

```
function LoadValidator(oONode, oValid)
{
  var oOProductNode;
  var ni;

  oValid.OrderNumber = oONode.childNodes(0).text;
  if (oONode.childNodes(1).text == "Filled")
     oValid.SummaryStatus = FILLED;
  else
     oValid.SummaryStatus = PENDING;
  oValid.DatePlaced = oONode.childNodes(2).text;
  oValid.DateToShip = oONode.childNodes(3).text;

  for (ni = 4; ni < oONode.childNodes.length; ni++)
  {
     oOProductNode = oONode.childNodes(ni);
     nQuantity = oOProductNode.childNodes(0).nodeTypedValue;
     fSubTotal = oOProductNode.childNodes(1).nodeTypedValue;
     sPartNum  = oOProductNode.childNodes(2).childNodes(0).text;
     if (oOProductNode.childNodes(3).text == "Filled")
        bStatus = true;
     else
        bStatus = false;

     oValid.AddLineItem(sPartNum, fSubTotal, nQuantity, bStatus);
  }
}
```

If you compare this with an `Order` element, you see we are looking at child nodes to find particular properties, and then initializing the component through its properties and methods. The most complicated part comes in the loop that begins:

```
for (ni = 4; ni < oONode.childNodes.length; ni++)
```

The fifth child of the `Order` element (recall MSXML's `childNodes` collection is zero-based) is where `OrderProduct` elements begin. For each one of these, we extract the four properties of a line item then call the component's `AddLineItem()` method to add a line item to the `Dictionary`. When the loop completes, the order validator contains a copy of the order's summary information and a representation of all the line items in the order.

# Displaying Results

Remember where we are in the calling routine:

```
for (ni = 1; ni < oHistoryNode.childNodes.length; ni++)
{
   oValidator.ClearOrder();
   oValidator.CustomerID = oHistoryNode.childNodes(0).text;

   oOrderNode = oHistoryNode.childNodes(ni);
   LoadValidator(oOrderNode, oValidator);
   nStatus = oValidator.CheckInternalStatus();

   if (nStatus == INCONSISTENT || nStatus == PROBLEM)
```

```
    {
        if (!bWroteCustomer)
        {
            bWroteCustomer = true;
            resultArea.insertAdjacentHTML("beforeEnd", "<B>Customer ID: " +
                                          oValidator.CustomerID + "</B><P/>");
        }
        WriteOrder(oValidator);
    }
```

We call `CheckInternalStatus()` to determine if this order is one in which we are interested. If it is, we check to see if we've displayed the customer's ID. A customer may have more than one order that is a problem, and we only want to show the ID once. After that task is accomplished for troubled orders, we call `WriteOrder()` to generate a table showing the information our analyst needs to prioritize and track down troubled orders. Here is the body of `WriteOrder()`:

```
function WriteOrder(oValid)
{
    var oTable, oRow, oCell, oBdrAttr;

    oTable = document.createElement("TABLE");
    oTable.border = 1;
    oTable.cellPadding = 4;
    resultArea.appendChild(oTable);
    oRow = oTable.insertRow();
    oCell = oRow.insertCell();
    oCell.innerText = "Order: " + oValid.OrderNumber;

    oCell = oRow.insertCell();
    if (oValid.SummaryStatus == FILLED)
        oCell.innerText = "Overall status: Filled";
    else
        oCell.innerText = "Overall status: Pending";

    oCell = oRow.insertCell();
    switch (oValid.CheckInternalStatus())
    {
        case EMPTY:
            sIStat = "Empty";
            break;
        case PENDING:
            sIStat = "Pending";
            break;
        case FILLED:
            sIStat = "Filled";
            break;
        case INCONSISTENT:
            sIStat = "Inconsistent";
            break;
        case OPEN:
            sIStat = "Open";
            break;
        case READY:
            sIStat = "Ready";
            break;
        case PROBLEM:
            sIStat = "Problem";
            break;
    }
```

```
        oCell.innerText = "Internal status: " + sIStat;

    oRow = oTable.insertRow();
    oCell = oRow.insertCell();
    oCell.innerText = "Value: $" + oValid.ComputeTotalCost();
    oCell = oRow.insertCell();
    oCell.innerText = "Placed: " + oValid.DatePlaced;
    oCell = oRow.insertCell();
    oCell.innerText = "Shipping: " + oValid.DateToShip;

    resultArea.insertAdjacentHTML("beforeEnd", "<P/>");
}
```

This is similar to the technique we used in the last chapter, except we don't have to worry about leaving the first row of the table intact. Each table represents an order. Each has a fixed number of rows (two) per table, and three cells per row. We create these tables entirely from scratch. We set the border and cell padding attributes so that the table is nicely formatted. The only frills here are assembling user-friendly content strings for each cell and the generality of the switch statement. This function will only be called for orders whose internal status is `Problem` or `Inconsistent`. We've written code to handle all the possible states just in case we ever want to use this function in another client. If that ever happens, we may have forgotten the fine points of the business logic, so it is good to take care of them now. Although our development philosophy stresses reuse through components, as experienced programmers we know better than to turn up our noses at the prospect of source code reuse. A little extra effort now may help someone else at a later date.

Since we interrupted our study of the main client button handler function, we'll repeat the function in its entirety to help in understanding the flow of our client application:

```
function OnSearchClick()
{
    var ni, sDays, sQueryDays, sLocation, nCount, oHist;
    var oValidator;
    var walker = new ActiveXObject("DirectoryWalker.scriptlet");
    var xmlProblems = new ActiveXObject("microsoft.xmldom");

    walker.User = "orderdept";
    walker.Pwd = "";
    sLocation = walker.SearchHome("OrderHistoryDelaysQuery");
    walker = null;
    sDays = daysDelayText.value;
    if (Math.round(sDays) == sDays)
    {
        resultArea.innerHTML = "";

        QueryBlank.documentElement.childNodes(0).text = daysDelayText.value;
        xmlProblems.async = false;
        xmlProblems.load("http://" + sLocation + "?RequestXML=" +
                QueryBlank.xml);
        if (xmlProblems.readyState == 4 && xmlProblems.parseError == 0)
        {
            if (xmlProblems.documentElement.nodeName == "Collection")
            {
                nCount = xmlProblems.documentElement.childNodes.length;
                oValidator = new ActiveXObject("Order.Validator");
                for (ni = 0; ni < nCount; ni++)
```

```
            {
                oHist = xmlProblems.documentElement.childNodes(ni);
                if (oHist.nodeName == "OrderHistory")
                    ProcessHistory(oHist, oValidator);
            }
            oValidator = null;
        }
        else
            alert("Please ask your network administrator to check the
                    configuration for the OrderHistoryDelaysQuery service.");
    }
    else
        alert("An error was encountered processing the data returned from the
                service.");
    }
    else
        alert("You must enter an integer number of days.");

    xmlProblems = null;
}
```

# Lessons Learned

This brings us to the conclusion of the Wrox Blocks saga. What have we learned in this chapter? What do these case studies tell us about the practical application of our development philosophy?

## Change and Decentralized Development

The biggest problem we overcame in this chapter was a managerial one: how to gracefully introduce an improved implementation into an organization without high-handed action from above. We saw that the decentralized nature of development worked to the organization's advantage in this case. Our analyst brought a fresh view to the problem of constructing OrderHistory documents and saw how to improve the implementation. Since our clients are loosely coupled to services whose location they discover at runtime, the simple act of changing directory settings allows the use of the improved version to spread through the organization as it becomes accepted – no clients need to be rewritten. No instructions need to be sent out directing a client configuration change at a particular time on a particular date. Things can just happen as consensus grows around the new implementation.

## Components

We finally – finally! – saw how applications benefit from custom components encapsulating local business logic. We could be forgiven for thinking that only general-purpose components from a third-party vendor are capable of reuse. This application saw us pull together some business rules into a nice COM component and test it out in one client application. If other programming teams see value in it, they will be able to reuse our business logic as easily as we used MSXML and the toolkit components.

We used JavaScript and Microsoft's scriptlet implementation to rapidly build and test our component. If, as we expect, other teams see value in this component, we can port the code to another implementation for better performance. With some attention to how the component is used, we can even bring it under the administration of MTS for better management of system resources.

# Reuse Potential

The improved implementation of the `OrderHistory` service is our best candidate for reuse. This construct has turned up in two different applications, and there is no reason to think it won't apply to other problems as well. It is quite likely a key concept in the Wrox Blocks business. By making the implementation more flexible, and capable of handling a wider view of the concept, we improve its chances of reuse. It is worth pouring extra effort into the design and construction of services as they are the foundation of our system's computing resources. They are more likely to be of high quality and fidelity to the business that they are intended to represent because they are centrally deployed and managed. Problems will surface sooner and reach resolution more quickly because of this. The flexibility of the location transparency approach is an added benefit.

The order validating component is another candidate for reuse. Our analyst captured one aspect of the Wrox Blocks company's business domain knowledge and packaged it in a form that is easy to reuse. The fact that it was packaged will help advertise the existence of this knowledge, and its availability. Since it is packaged "black box" fashion, it is more likely to be reused than if each programming team that wished to make use of it had to seek out and copy the source code.

Components can be tested independently of the applications that use them. If the team that develops a component neglects this task, the use of a component in a new application with new assumptions will bring problems to light sooner rather than later.

Finally, little touches like handling all possible states in the `WriteOrder()` function instead of the minimum needed facilitate reuse. Its not so much that we expect much source code reuse in the future, but that we promote quality in the expectation of future enhancements. There is no substitute for robust code if we want to avoid future bugs. Keeping bugs to a minimum lets our applications live longer on the network. Services that have not been shown to contain bugs are more likely to be used by future clients than those with a long history of bug fixes. This is a matter of a programmer's style and his approach to writing code.

# Final Thoughts on The 5 Principles of Cooperative Network Application Development

In the end, a programmer's philosophy of writing distributed applications is what our development philosophy is all about. The objectives and practices of our 5 Principles of Cooperative Network Application Development do not lend themselves to cookbook style application. A lazy programmer cannot follow the steps by rote because there are no rote steps to follow. It must become a matter of taking the lessons we have learned to heart. A good system designer strives for improvement, not only in the mechanics of his code, but in its elegance and style.

Hopefully, the case studies have shown you the value of developing applications according to our 5 Principles of Cooperative Network Application Development. Such short, contrived applications cannot answer all possible objections to the approach promoted in this book. They set up some common problems experienced in real-world development and showed how to overcome them using the techniques and goals we set out in the very first chapter. They repeatedly demonstrated how to apply the most common techniques – XML-based exchange formats and component software – in the context of intranet application development. If nothing else, we hope this book has given you a hint of the many exciting technologies available to intranet developers for the construction of distributed applications. Chosen wisely, and for their relevance to your specific problems, these technologies form a robust platform on which to build powerful, flexible, and long-lived applications and services.

# Summary

This chapter tackled some practical problems that come up when we apply the five principles. Rather than illustrating problems with the principles themselves, though, this case study demonstrated the flexibility our principles introduce. The main problems we solved in this chapter were the following:

❑   Fixing a flawed service implementation and introducing the change into the network environment
❑   Putting proprietary business logic into components for reuse in other applications
❑   Using an existing service to solve a new problem

In this chapter, we returned to the problem of the flawed `OrderHistory` implementation and showed how an improved version can be brought into use within the organization with a minimum of managerial intrusion and disruption of client applications. We devised yet another scriptlet to aid our programming efforts, slightly different from the ones we have used so far. This scriptlet focused squarely on a small piece of the knowledge that makes up the Wrox Blocks company. Although it will never be as widely used as MSXML or even our toolkit components, this component will be very useful to Wrox Blocks programmers. Using script code for its implementation is an inexpensive way to test an idea. Once a component proves itself, more resources will become available to improve and refine the implementation. We took a brief look at the issues involved with scaling such a component up to the level needed for high-performance, enterprise scale use. This case study completed our look at the hypothetical Wrox Blocks company. It also completed our illustration of the most common techniques needed to put our 5 Principles of Cooperative Network Application Development into practice. Actually putting the philosophy into common practice is the on-going task of you the programmer, from the trenches of business application development.

# Toolkit Reference

We built four script-based COM components in the course of this book to support common tasks in our development philosophy. They should provide intranet programmers with a useful starting point, although they are certainly not the last word in their respective implementations. Most importantly, I hope they will prove thought provoking as programmers debate the interfaces and argue over their implementations. Take some time, study the code, and use it to seed you own component toolkit.

Although the components were completely discussed in the chapters that introduced them, it may prove useful to programmers to have a concise reference to the usage and interfaces offered by each component. As always, the full source code is available on our Web site at http://www.wrox.com/ The DHTML scriptlet versions will run in any installation of Internet Explorer 4.0 or later. The scriptlet versions of the components require Internet Explorer 5.0 for client-side use and the Microsoft scripting technology beta. The latter package is available for download at http://msdn.microsoft.com/scripting/

The reference material for each component includes script samples for using the component. Client-side examples consist of the HTML needed to embed a DHTML scriptlet on an HTML page and load it with the proper scriptlet file. Relative URL references are used, although the technology supports absolute URL references. Server-side usage consists of a JavaScript code fragment needed to instantiate the component. The server-side usage may also be used within client-side script functions.

DHTML scriptlets require no registration prior to use. Internet Explorer registers a COM component that loads the HTML files containing the script code. Scriptlets, however, are another matter. These must be registered like any other COM component. If you have the scriptlet technology beta installed, you may simply right-click on the mouse for the implementation file and select Register. Otherwise, you will need to use regsvr32 from the command line.

Now let's turn to each of the four components: DirectoryWalker, Receiver, Sender and DataSplicer.

# DirectoryWalker

This component is designed for use with the Active Directory technology provided with Windows NT 5.0. It assumes the conventions for naming the location of services we provided in Chapter 2. `DirectoryWalker` uses the Microsoft ADSI COM components for its implementation. It is a generic simplification of the steps needed to use ADSI components to retrieve service location information from the directory.

## Implementation Files

The DHTML version is implemented in the file `DirectoryWalker.html`. The scriptlet version is implemented in `DirectoryWalker.sct`.

## Client-Side Usage

To embed an instance of the component on a client page at load-time:

```
<OBJECT id=walker style="HEIGHT: 0px; LEFT: 0px; TOP: 0px; WIDTH: 0px"
                   type=text/x-scriptlet>
    <PARAM NAME="URL" VALUE="DirectoryWalker.html">
</OBJECT>
```

*The DHTML scriptlet version requires Microsoft ADSI components and access to a computer running Microsoft Windows NT Server 5.0 with ActiveDirectory. You must specify a user ID and password that pertain to a valid user of the directory.*

## Server-Side Usage

From within an ASP script executing on the server:

```
var walker = Server.CreateObject("DirectoryWalker.Scriptlet");
. . . // use component here
walker = null;   // free resources
```

Alternately, from within a client-side script dynamically creating the object:

```
var walker = new ActiveXObject("DirectoryWalker.Scriptlet");
. . . // use component here
walker = null;   // free resources
```

*The scriptlet version is a stub version designed for programmers who do not have access to an Active Directory installation. It makes the assumption that all services reside in the same directory. To update the component to work with your particular installation, edit* `DirectoryWalker.sct` *so that the variable* `sLocation` *refers to the directory containing your services. If you change the name of the ASPs, you will also need to make the appropriate changes within the* `SearchHome`, `SearchTree`, *and* `SearchDirectory` *implementations.*

# Interface

`DirectoryWalker` offers an interface to connect to the Active Directory and query for a service using our conventions. The search may be limited in scope to the home domain, the user's Tree, or the entire directory structure.

## Properties

| Property Name | Meaning and Usage |
|---|---|
| User | Read-write; the user ID of a valid user of the directory |
| Pwd | Read-write; the password for the user ID provided in the User property |
| HomeDomain | Read-only; retrieves the name of the user's home domain |
| TreeRootDomain | Read-only; retrieves the name of the domain that is the root of the user's Tree |

## Methods

| Method Name | Meaning and Usage |
|---|---|
| SearchHome() | Takes a string containing the name of the desired XML service vocabulary and returns the URL, sans protocol, of the page implementing the service within the user's home domain. A new connection is made and released in the course of the method call using the User and Pwd values. |
| SearchTree() | Performs the same function as SearchHome, except that the user's entire Tree within the directory is searched. |
| SearchDirectory() | Performs the same function as SearchHome, except the entire directory is searched for the desired service. |

## Example

The following example creates a new instance of the component, then searches the home directory for a user whose ID is MyUID and whose password is MyPassWord.

```
var walker = new ActiveXObject("DirectoryWalker.Scriptlet");
Walker.User = "MyUID";
Walker.Pwd = "MyPassWord";
Walker.SearchHome("OrderHistory");
Walker = null;
```

# DataSplicer

The DataSplicer is a utility component designed to support the use of specialization, collections, and versioning as developed in Chapter 4. The speciailization-specific methods are also useful for finding a particular subtree within a given XML document.

## Implementation Files

The DHTML scriptlet is implemented in DataSplicer.html. The scriptlet is found in DataSplicer.sct.

## Client-Side Usage

To embed an instance of the component on a client page at load-time:

```
<OBJECT id=splicer name=splicer
     style="BORDER-LEFT: medium none; HEIGHT: 0px; LEFT: 0px; TOP: 0px;
           WIDTH: 0px"
     type=text/x-scriptlet VIEWASTEXT>
     <PARAM NAME="URL" VALUE="DataSplicer.html">
</OBJECT>
```

## Server-Side Usage

From within an ASP script executing on the server:

```
var splicer = Server.CreateObject("Datasplicer.scriptlet");
```

Alternately, from within a client-side script dynamically creating the object:

```
var splicer = new ActiveXObject("Datasplicer.scriptlet");
```

# Interface

The DataSplicer scripting interface provides a series of utility functions to the using client. These permit the extraction of generalized types from a specialized XML document, the creation of collections and reporting on the attributes of collections, and the reconciliation of versioned XML documents. The conventions used by DataSplicer are described at length in Chapter 4. DataSplicer maintains no state information, nor does it create instances of MSXML. When such an instance is required, e.g., for the creation of new nodes, the method will take an existing instance as a parameter.

### Properties

DataSplicer has no native properties.

## *Methods*

| Method Name | Meaning and Usage |
| --- | --- |
| MakeCollection() | Creates a `Collection` node and sets the attributes specified by our convention. It takes the following parameters:<br><br>`Parser` – an instance of the MSXML document interface<br><br>`ObjectType` – a string denoting the type of contained objects<br><br>`OrderType` – a string from the enumeration {`sequential`, `ascending`, `descending`}; defaults to `ascending`<br><br>`ColName` – a string naming the collection; defaults to the string composed of the `objectType` and the letter `s`<br><br>The method returns a reference to the new Collection node. |
| FindNamedCollection() | Searches recursively through a subtree for a `Collection` element with the `colName` attribute specified. It takes the following parameters:<br><br>`Name` – a string specifying the value of `colName` for which we are searching<br><br>`Node` – an MSXML DOM node anchoring the subtree to search for the collection<br><br>The method returns a reference to the `Collection` node if found or `null`. |
| FindTypedCollection() | Searches recursively through a subtree for a `Collection` element whose `objectType` attribute bears the value specified. It takes the following parameters:<br><br>`ObjectType` – a string naming the desired search value<br><br>`Node` – an MSXML DOM node anchoring the search subtree<br><br>The method returns a reference to the Collection node if found or `null`. |
| CollectionOrder() | This method returns the value of a `Collection` elements `Order` attribute. It takes the parameter:<br><br>`Node` – an MSXML node denoting a `Collection` element<br><br>It returns the string value of the attribute or the string `"Error: Node is not a collection"` if the parameter is not a `Collection` node, or an empty string if the attribute does not appear. |

*Table Continued on Following Page*

| Method Name | Meaning and Usage |
| --- | --- |
| CollectionName() | Returns the string value of a collection's Name attribute. It takes the parameter: |
| | Node – an MSXML node denoting a Collection element |
| | It returns the attribute value as a string or the string "Error: Node is not a collection" if the parameter is not a Collection node, or an empty string if the attribute does not appear. |
| TypesInCollection() | Returns the string value of a collection's ObjectType attribute. It takes the following parameter: |
| | Node – an MSXML node denoting a Collection element |
| | It returns the attribute value as a string or the string "Error: Node is not a collection" if the parameter is not a Collection node, or an empty string if the attribute does not appear. |
| Extract() | Finds a given node within a given subtree and returns a reference to it. Its purpose is to locate the general type within a specialized XML type. This method takes the following parameters: |
| | toExtract – a string naming the element to find |
| | StartNode – an MSXML DOM node anchoring the subtree to search |
| | It returns a reference to the node whose nodeName is equal to toExtract or null if not found. |
| ExtractAll() | Finds all occurrences of a particular generalized element within a subtree. This method is useful for finding all the generalized types within a collection of specialized elements. This method takes the following parameters: |
| | Parser – an instance of the MSXML document interface |
| | toExtract – a string naming the element to find |
| | StartNode – an MSXML DOM node anchoring the subtree to search |
| | This method returns a new Collection element node containing all instances of toExtract found within the subtree anchored by startNode. The collection may be empty if no instances are found. |

| Method Name | Meaning and Usage |
|---|---|
| `CollapseVersion()` | This method performs version reconciliation on a versioned XML document as described in Chapter 4. It takes the following parameters: |
| | `parser` – an instance of the MSXML document interface |
| | `ObjectNode` – the root node of the document to reconcile |
| | `sVersion` – a string specifying the latest version to which to reconcile the document. |
| | The method returns a new node which, with its child nodes, represents the reconciled document. This node is not an MSXML document interface. The original document or subtree represented in `objectNode` is unchanged. |

### Example

The following call locates a `Customer` element with the XML document contained in `xmlCustomerBase` and returns a reference to the `Customer` node.

```
custTree = splicer.Extract("Customer",
xmlCustomerBase.ResponseXML.documentElement);
```

# Sender

The Sender component is an encapsulation of the basic procedure for sending a simple message under Microsoft MessageQueue. It utilizes the MSMQ COM components to perform its work, but it simplifies the interface. Scripts that use it are able to specify the machine and queue names to which the message is to be sent. In addition, programs that use it can specify whether the body of the message should be encrypted using the default settings in effect on their system. There are no provisions for sender notification.

## Implementation Files

The DHTML version is found in `Sender.html`. The scriptlet version is in `ServerSender.sct`.

## Client-Side Usage

Use the following to embed an instance of the component on a client page when it loads:

```
<OBJECT id=MailBox style="HEIGHT: 0px; LEFT: 0px; TOP: 0px; WIDTH: 0px"
    type=text/x-scriptlet VIEWASTEXT>
    <PARAM NAME="URL" VALUE="Sender.html">
</OBJECT>
```

# Server-Side Usage

To dynamically create an instance from within a server-side ASP script:

```
MailBox = Server.CreateObject("ServerSender.Scriptlet");
```

To dynamically create an instance from client-side code:

```
MailBox = new ActiveXObject("ServerSender.Scriptlet");
```

# Interface

The scripting interface of the component allows script code to establish where and how the message should be sent. A single method is provided to accept the text of the message and actually send the message. The interface is intended for teaching purposes or to implement the most basic Message Queue features.

## Properties

| Property | Meaning and Usage |
| --- | --- |
| Private | A boolean value that takes true if the message should be sent with encryption, or false for plain text. The default value is false. |
| Machine | A string specifying the name of the machine to which to send the message. |
| Queue | A string specifying the queue on Machine to which to send the message. |

## Methods

| Method | Meaning and Usage |
| --- | --- |
| Send() | Sends the given message text to Queue on Machine using the privacy option specified in Private. This method takes the following parameters: StrLabel – user specified text for a message label StrMsg – the message body text The method will return one of the following enumerated values: SENT (1) – the method was successful FAILED (0) – a critical error occurred and the message could not be sent UPGRADE (3) – the message could not be sent because the specified queue requires privacy and Private was set to false DOWNGRADE (4) – the message could not be sent because the specified queue accepts only clear-text messages and Private was set to true |

### Example

The following example sends a simple XML message to the queue `AQueue` on the computer `MyFriend`.

```
strMsg = "<Body>This is the message I wish to send</Body>";
MailBox.Machine = "MyFriend";
MailBox.Queue = "AQueue";
MailBox.Send("Test", strMsg);
```

# Receiver

This component illustrates the basic procedure for retrieving messages from a queue using Microsoft Message Queue. It allows a script to go to a specific queue on a particular machine and retrieve messages with a specified label. Messages are taken from the queue up to a limit specified in a method call parameter. This permits the programmer to manage the retrieval of messages from queues that may potentially contain very large quantities of messages with the specified label.

## Implementation Files

The DHTML scriptlet version is found in `Receiver.html`, while the scriptlet version is found in `ServerReceiver.sct`.

## Client-Side Usage

Use the following `<OBJECT>` tag to embed an instance of the component on an HTML page when it loads:

```
<OBJECT id=MailBox style="HEIGHT: 0px; LEFT: 0px; TOP: 0px; WIDTH: 0px"
    type=text/x-scriptlet VIEWASTEXT>
    <PARAM NAME="URL" VALUE="Receiver.html">
</OBJECT>
```

## Server-Side Usage

The following line of script code creates an instance of the component from within an ASP script on the Web server:

```
MailMan = Server.CreateObject("ServerReceiver.Scriptlet");
```

To create an instance from within a client-side script, use the following line of JavaScript:

```
MailMan = new ActiveXObject("ServerReceiver.Scriptlet");
```

# Interface

The component presents a simple scripting interface intended to illustrate the basic method of retrieving messages from a queue. The only embellishment is that the quantity of messages retrieved is specified in the method call. Messages retrieved are removed from the queue.

## *Properties*

| Property | Meaning and Usage |
|----------|-------------------|
| Machine | Name of the computer hosting the target queue |
| Queue | Name of the queue on Machine from which to retrieve messages |

## *Methods*

| Property | Meaning and Usage |
|----------|-------------------|
| Receive | Looks for messages with a particular label and removes them from the queue on the machine specified in the component's properties. This method takes the following parameters: <br><br> strLabel – text of the label to look for in the queue <br><br> nMaxMsgs – maximum number of messages to retrieve in one method call <br><br> The method returns a newly created JavaScript array. The consuming script should check the array's length property to determine how many messages were actually found and removed. |

## *Example*

The following example looks for messages with the Label Warning! In the Consumer queue on the computer named MyHost:

```
MailMan.Machine = "MyHost";
MailMan.Queue = "Consumer";
RMsgs = MailMan.Receive("Warning!", 5);
If (rMsgs.length < 5)
{
    // denotes no more messages are available
```

# Resources and References

## Future Systems

Windows DNA is an ongoing part of the Windows platform. The DNA homesite is found at
`http://www.microsoft.com/dna/`.

Millennium is an effort of Microsoft Research. The Millennium home site can be found at
`http://www.research.microsoft.com/sn/Millennium/`.

Java Jini comes from Sun Microsystems. The Jini home site is found at
`http://www.sun.com/jini/index.html`. Note especially the Jini specifications at
`http://www.sun.com/jini/specs/`.

## XML

There is a wealth of XML related material on the Web. Two rich XML introductory sources are the
Micrsoft XML site at `http://developer.microsoft.com/xml` and XML.com at
`http://www.xml.com`. A newsgroup of special interest to users of MSXML is
`microsoft.public.xml` on the news server `msnews.microsoft.com`. The definitive source, of
course, is the W3C. In general, you should always refer to `http://www.w3.org/TR/` to determine
the latest status of documents. The following table lists the status of documents mentioned in the text
as of the time of publication:

| Standard | Status | URL |
|---|---|---|
| Extensible Markup Language (XML) | W3C Recommendation *10-February-1998* | `http://www.w3.org/TR/1998/REC-xml` |
| Document Object Model Level 1 (DOM) | W3C Recommendation *1- October-1998* | `http://www.w3.org/TR/REC-DOM-Level-1/` |
| Document Object Model Level 2 | W3C Working Draft *4-March-1999* | `http://www.w3.org/TR/WD-DOM-Level-2/` |
| Extensible Style Language | W3C Working Draft *16-December-1998* | `http://www.w3.org/TR/WD-xsl` |
| Namespaces in XML | W3C Recommendation *14-January-1999* | `http://www.w3.org/TR/REC-xml-names/` |
| XML Schema Requirements | Note *15-February-1999* | `http://www.w3.org/TR/NOTE-xml-schema-req` |
| XML Data | Note *17-December-1997* | `http://www.w3.org/Submission/1997/18/Overview.html` |
| Document Content Description | Note *31-July-1998* | `http://www.w3.org/TR/NOTE-dcd` |
| Resource Description Framework | W3C Recommendation *22-February-1999* | `http://www.w3.org/TR/REC-rdf-syntax/` |

# XML-Dev

XML-Dev is a mailing list for XML developers. It is a list for people actively involved in developing resources for XML. While it is not restricted to members of the working group (WG) many subscribers to XML-Dev are actively working on implementing some part of the spec. XML-Dev is an informal unmoderated list to support those who are interested in the implementation and development of XML. You can subscribe by sending an email to

majordomo@ic.ac.uk

you only need to enter the following message:

subscribe xml-dev

As this can be quite a busy mailing list, you may prefer to subscribe to the digests, which contain the major threads of the discussions in one daily email, rather than filling your inbox with lots of messages. To subscribe to the digest enter the following message instead (mailed to the same address):

subscribe xml-dev-digest

An archive of the mailing list is maintained at:

`http://www.lists.ic.ac.uk/hypermail/xml-dev/`

They have the following to say regarding what is discussed on the mailing list:

---

Examples of what might be discussed:
- ❑ the detailed implementation of the spec
- ❑ resources such as documentation, test data, test results
- ❑ XMLification of components (DTDS, entity sets, catalogs, etc.)
- ❑ APIs for software developers
- ❑ problems in implementation, and queries for XML-related resources
- ❑ the use of existing SGML tools in creating XML resources

It is NOT appropriate to:
- ❑ request general information on XML (use the FAQ)
- ❑ discuss non-XML topics in SGML (use comp.text.sgml)
- ❑ discuss revision of the spec (use the WG)

---

The XML FAQ is maintained by Peter Flynn, and can be viewed at: `http://www.ucc.ie/xml/`

# Message Queuing

Level 8 Systems produce a range of components for accessing proprietary message queues on other systems such as IBM MVS, MQ, CICS, OS/2 and AS400 platforms; Sun Solaris, HP-UNIX, and AIX UNIX their homepage is `http://www.level8.com`

Microsoft also provide their own MSMQ pages at `http://www.microsoft.com/msmq/`

# IE5 XML Document Object Model

This section contains a complete reference to the **Document Object Model** that is supported in Internet Explorer 5.0. This includes full support for the W3C version 1.0 DOM Recommendations, plus extensions specific to IE5. It is divided into four sections:

- ❑ **The Base DOM Objects**
- ❑ **The High-level DOM Objects**
- ❑ **IE5-Specific Parser Objects**
- ❑ **The DOM NodeTypes**

## The Base DOM Objects

In IE5, all the nodes that appear in an XML document, with a couple of minor exceptions, are based on the IXMLDOMNode object. This represents the base Node object from which the specialist node objects, such as Element, Attribute, Comment, etc, inherit. There are three other base objects as well. The full list is:

- ❑ Node (the IXMLDOMNode object)
- ❑ NodeList (the IXMLDOMNodeList object)
- ❑ NamedNodeMap (the IXMLDOMNamedNodeMap object)

## Node — the IXMLDOMNode Object

The IE5 IXMLDOMNode object extends the W3C DOM recommendations (which Microsoft implement as the IDOMNode object) by adding support for data types, namespaces, DTDs, and XML schemas. In the following tables, •indicates properties and methods that are extensions to the base W3C object model.

## Node Properties

| Name | Description |
|------|-------------|
| attributes | Returns a collection of the `Attribute` (or `Attr`) objects for this node as a `NamedNodeMap` object. |
| baseName | Returns the node name with any namespace removed. For example, in a node declared as `<nspace:elemname>` it returns the `"elemname"` part. |
| childNodes | Returns a `NodeList` containing all the child nodes of this node, for nodes that can have child nodes. |
| dataType | Sets or returns the data type for this node. |
| definition | For `EntityReference` nodes, returns the entry in the DTD or schema containing the definition for the entity, i.e. `"<!ENTITY entityname 'entity value'>"`. For other nodes, returns `null`. |
| firstChild | Returns a reference to the first child node of this node. |
| lastChild | Returns a reference to the last child node of this node. |
| namespaceURI | Returns the URI for the namespace as a string. For example, in the namespace declaration `xmlns:name="uri"` it returns the `"uri"` part. |
| nextSibling | Returns a reference to the next sibling node of this node, i.e. the next node in the source data file at the same level of the hierarchy. |
| nodeName | Returns the name of the node, which will depend on the node type. See the list of Node Types at the end of this appendix for more details. |
| nodeType String | Returns the node type as a string. See the list of Node Types at the end of this appendix for more details. |
| nodeType | Returns the node type as a number. See the list of Node Types at the end of this appendix for more details. |
| nodeTyped Value | Sets or returns the strongly typed value of the node, expressed in its defined data type. If no data type has been defined for the node, its `nodeValue` is returned. |
| nodeValue | Sets or returns the value of the node as plain text. |
| ownerDocument | Returns the root node of the document that contains the node. |
| parentNode | Returns the parent node of this node, for nodes that can have parents. |
| parsed | Returns `true` if this node and all its descendants have been parsed and instantiated. |
| prefix | Returns the element namespace prefix as a string. For example, in a node declared as `<nspace:elemname>` it returns the `"nspace"` part. |
| previous Sibling | Returns a reference to the previous sibling node of this node, i.e. the previous node in the source file at the same level of the hierarchy. |

| Name | Description |
|---|---|
| • specified | Indicates whether the node value is explicitly specified or derived from a default value in the DTD or schema. Normally only used with attribute nodes. |
| • text | Sets or returns the entire text content of this node and all its descendent nodes. |
| • xml | Returns the entire XML content of this node and all its descendent nodes. |

## Node Methods

| Name | Description |
|---|---|
| appendChild(new_node) | Appends the node object new_node to the end of the list of child nodes for this node. |
| cloneNode( recurse_children) | Creates a new node object that is an exact clone of this node, including all descendent nodes of this node if recurse_children is set to true. |
| hasChildNodes() | Returns true if this node has any child nodes. |
| insertBefore(new_node, this_node) | Inserts a new node object new_node into the list of child nodes for this node, to the left of the node object this_node or at the end of the list if this_node is omitted. |
| removeChild(this_node) | Removes the child node this_node from the list of child nodes for this node, and returns it. |
| replaceChild(new_node, old_node) | Replaces the child node old_node with the new child node object new_node, and returns the old child node. |
| • selectNodes(pattern) | Applies a specified pattern to this node's context and returns a node list object containing matching nodes. The string pattern specifies the XSL pattern-matching operation to be used. |
| • selectSingleNode (pattern) | Applies a specified pattern to this node's context and returns just the first node object that matches. The string pattern specifies the XSL pattern-matching operation to be used. |
| • transformNode (stylesheet) | Processes this node and its children using an XSL style sheet specified in the stylesheet argument, and returns the resulting transformation. The style sheet must be either a Document node object, in which case the document is assumed to be an XSL style sheet, or a Node object in the xsl namespace, in which case this node is treated as a standalone style sheet fragment. |

# NodeList — the IXMLDOMNodeList Object

This object represents a collection (or list) of Node objects. The object list is 'live', meaning that changes to the document are mirrored in the list immediately. The IE5 extensions support iteration through the list in addition to indexed access. In the following tables, •indicates properties and methods that are extensions to the base W3C object model. The base NodeList object is implemented in IE5 as IDOMNodeList.

## NodeList Property

| Name | Description |
| --- | --- |
| length | Returns the number of nodes in the node list. |

## NodeList Methods

| | Name | Description |
| --- | --- | --- |
| | item(index) | Returns the node at position index in the node list, where the first node is indexed zero. |
| • | nextNode() | Returns the next node object in the node list, or null if there are no more nodes. |
| • | reset() | Resets the internal pointer to the point before the first node in the node list. Prepares the list for iteration with the nextNode() method. |

# NamedNodeMap — the IXMLDOMNamedNodeMap Object

This object provides a collection of Node objects that allows access by name as well as by index. This collection is typically used with attribute objects rather than element or other node types, and is 'live' like the NodeList object. The IE5 extensions add support for namespaces, and iteration through the collection of attribute nodes. In the following tables, •indicates properties and methods that are extensions to the base W3C object model. This base object is implemented as IDOMNamedNodeMap by Microsoft.

## NamedNodeMap Property

| Name | Description |
| --- | --- |
| length | Returns the number of nodes in the named node map. |

## NamedNodeMap Methods

| | Name | Description |
| --- | --- | --- |
| | getNamedItem(name) | Retrieves the node object with the specified name. Typically used to retrieve attributes from an element. |
| • | getQualifiedItem( base_name, namespace_uri) | Returns the node object with the specified base_name and namespace_uri values. |

| Name | Description |
|------|-------------|
| `item(index)` | Returns the node at position index in the named node map, where the first node is indexed zero. |
| `nextNode()` | Returns the next node object in the named node map, or `null` if there are no more nodes. |
| `removeNamedItem(name)` | Removes the node object with the specified name from the named node map. Typically used to remove attributes from an element. |
| `removeQualifiedItem(`<br>`base_name,`<br>`namespace_uri)` | Removes the node object with the specified `base_name` and `namespace_uri` values from the named node map. |
| `reset()` | Resets the internal pointer to the point before the first node in the node list. Prepares the list for iteration with the `nextNode()` method. |
| `setNamedItem(new_node)` | Inserts the node object `new_node` into the named node map, updating the XML document. Any existing node with the same name is replaced with the new node. Typically used to update attribute values for an element. |

# The High-level DOM Objects

Because each type of node in an XML document differs in both obvious and subtle ways, specific objects are available for different types of nodes. Most inherit the properties and methods of the base `Node` (`IXMLDOMNode`) object, and add the specific properties and methods required for best tailoring the object to its purpose.

The specific objects are:

- ❑ `Document` (the `IXMLDOMDocument` object)
- ❑ `DocumentType` (the `IXMLDOMDocumentType` object)
- ❑ `DocumentFragment` (the `IXMLDOMDocumentFragment` object)
- ❑ `Element` (the `IXMLDOMElement` object)
- ❑ `Attribute` or `Attr` (the `IXMLDOMAttribute` object)
- ❑ `Entity` (the `IXMLDOMEntity` object)
- ❑ `EntityReference` (the `IXMLDOMEntityReference` object)
- ❑ `Notation` (the `IXMLDOMNotation` object)
- ❑ `CharacterData` (the `IXMLDOMCharacterData` object)

❑   CDATASection (the IXMLDOMCDATASection object)

❑   Text (the IXMLDOMText object)

❑   Comment (the IXMLDOMComment object)

❑   ProcessingInstruction (the IXMLDOMProcessingIntruction object)

❑   Implementation (the IXMLDOMImplementation object)

In addition to these, there are interfaces called IDOMDocument, IDOMDocumentType etc. which implement the W3C Recommendation, without the Microsoft extensions. These inherit from IDOMNode, which is the Microsoft implementation of the W3C Node object. The following tables repeat the base properties and methods, and add the node-specific ones. This provides a complete reference, with no need to check elsewhere which extra properties and methods the base objects provide in addition.

# Document — the IXMLDOMDocument

The Document object is the root object for an XML document. In IE5, it is the object that is instantiated by creating a new ActiveXObject with the identifier "Microsoft.XMLDOM".

The IE5 IXMLDOMDocument object extends to the base DOM document interface (implemented in IE5 by the IDOMDocument object) to include parser-specific functions. These include the ability to load documents asynchronously and control validation. The IXMKDocument object also provides access to other IE5-specific objects such as parseError. In the following tables, • indicates properties and methods that are extensions to the base W3C object model.

## Document Properties

| | Name | Description |
|---|---|---|
| • | async | Sets or returns whether asynchronous download of the XML data is permitted. Values are true (the default) or false. |
| | attributes | Returns a collection of the Attribute (or Attr) objects for this node as a NamedNodeMap object. |
| • | baseName | Returns the node name with any namespace removed. For example, in a node declared as <nspace:elemname> it returns the "elemname" part. |
| | childNodes | Returns a NodeList containing all the child nodes of this node, for nodes that can have child nodes. |
| • | dataType | Sets or returns the data type for this node. |
| • | definition | For EntityReference nodes, returns the entry in the DTD or schema containing the definition for the entity, i.e. "<!ENTITY entityname 'entity value'>". For other nodes, returns null. |
| | doctype | Returns a reference to the DocumentType node specifying the DTD or schema for this document. |

| Name | Description |
|------|-------------|
| documentElement | Returns a reference to the outermost element of the document. |
| firstChild | Returns a reference to the first child node of this node. |
| implementation | Returns a reference to the Implementation object for the document. This object provides methods that are application-specific and document object model implementation independent. |
| lastChild | Returns a reference to the last child node of this node. |
| • namespaceURI | Returns the URI for the namespace as a string. For example, in the namespace declaration xmlns:name="uri" it returns the "uri" part. |
| nextSibling | Returns a reference to the next sibling node of this node, i.e. the next node in the source data file at the same level of the hierarchy. |
| nodeName | Returns the name of the node, which will depend on the node type. See the list of Node Types at the end of this appendix for more details. |
| • nodeTypeString | Returns the node type as a string. See the list of Node Types at the end of this appendix for more details. |
| nodeType | Returns the node type as a number. See the list of Node Types at the end of this appendix for more details. |
| • nodeTypedValue | Sets or returns the strongly typed value of the node, expressed in its defined data type. If no data type has been defined for the node, its nodeValue is returned. |
| nodeValue | Sets or returns the value of the node as plain text. |
| ownerDocument | Returns the root node of the document that contains the node. |
| parentNode | Returns the parent node of this node, for nodes that can have parents. |
| • parsed | Returns true if this node and all its descendants have been parsed and instantiated. |
| • parseError | Returns a reference to the ParseError object that contains information about any errors encountered while parsing the document. |
| • prefix | Returns the element namespace prefix as a string. For example, in a node declared as <nspace:elemname> it returns the "nspace" part. |
| • preserveWhite Space | Specifies whether white space should be preserved. The default is false. |
| previousSibling | Returns a reference to the previous sibling node of this node, i.e. the previous node in the source file at the same level of the hierarchy. |

*Table Continued on Following Page*

| Name | Description |
|------|-------------|
| • readyState | Indicates the current state of the XML document: |
| | 0 ("UNINITIALIZED") — the object has been created but the load has not yet been executed. |
| | 1 ("LOADING") — the load() method is executing. |
| | 2 ("LOADED") — loading is complete and parsing is taking place. |
| | 3 ("INTERACTIVE") — some data has been read and parsed and the object model is now available. The data set is only partially retrieved and is read-only. |
| | 4 ("COMPLETED") — document has been completely loaded. If successful the data is available read/write, if not the error information is available. |
| • resolveExternals | Indicates whether external entities are resolved and the document is validated against external DTDs or schemas. The default is false. |
| • specified | Indicates whether the node value is explicitly specified or derived from a default value in the DTD or schema. Normally only used with attribute nodes. |
| • text | Sets or returns the entire text content of this node and all its descendent nodes. |
| • url | Returns the URL of the last successfully loaded document, or null if the document was built from scratch in memory. |
| • validateOnParse | Sets or returns whether the parser should validate the document. Takes the value true to validate or false (the default) to check only for 'well-formedness'. |
| • xml | Returns the entire XML content of this node and all its descendent nodes. |

## Document Methods

| Name | Description |
|------|-------------|
| • abort() | Aborts a currently executing asynchronous download. |
| appendChild(new_node) | Appends the node object new_node to the end of the list of child nodes for this node. |
| cloneNode( recurse_children) | Creates a new node object that is an exact clone of this node, including all descendent nodes of this node if recurse_children is set to true. |
| createAttribute( attr_name) | Creates an Attribute node with the specified name. |

| Name | Description |
| --- | --- |
| createCDATASection( text) | Creates a CDATASection node containing text. |
| createComment(text) | Creates a Comment node containing text as the comment between the <!-- and --> delimiters. |
| createDocumentFragment() | Creates an empty DocumentFragment node that can be used to build independent sections of a document. |
| createElement( tag_name) | Creates an Element node with the specified name. |
| createEntityReference( ref_name) | Creates an EntityReference node with the supplied name for the reference. |
| createNode (node_type, node_name, namespace_uri) | Creates any type of node using the specified node_type, node_name, and namespace_uri parameters. |
| createProcessing Instruction(target, text) | Creates a ProcessingInstruction node containing the specified target and data. |
| createTextNode( text_data) | Create a Text node containing the specified text data. |
| getElementsByTagName( tag_name) | Returns a NodeList of elements that have the specified tag name. If tag_name is "*" it returns all elements. |
| hasChildNodes() | Returns true if this node has any child nodes. |
| insertBefore(new_node, this_node) | Inserts a new node object new_node into the list of child nodes for this node, to the left of the node object this_node or at the end of the list if this_node is omitted. |
| load(url) | Loads an XML document from the location in url. |
| loadXML(string) | Loads a string that is a representation of an XML document. |
| nodeFromID(id_value) | Returns the node object whose ID attribute matches the supplied value. |
| removeChild(this_node) | Removes the child node this_node from the list of child nodes for this node, and returns it. |
| replaceChild(new_node, old_node) | Replaces the child node old_node with the new child node object new_node, and returns the old child node. |
| save(destination) | Saves the document to the specified destination, assuming the appropriate permissions are granted. |

*Table Continued on Following Page*

**373**

| Name | Description |
|------|-------------|
| • selectNodes( pattern) | Applies a specified pattern to this node's context and returns a node list object containing matching nodes. The string pattern specifies the XSL pattern-matching operation to be used. |
| • selectSingleNode( pattern) | Applies a specified pattern to this node's context and returns just the first node object that matches. The string pattern specifies the XSL pattern-matching operation to be used. |
| • transformNode( stylesheet) | Processes this node and its children using an XSL style sheet specified in the stylesheet argument, and returns the resulting transformation. The style sheet must be either a Document node object, in which case the document is assumed to be an XSL style sheet, or a Node object in the xsl namespace, in which case this node is treated as a standalone style sheet fragment. |

## Document Events

| Name | Description |
|------|-------------|
| • ondataavailable | The ondataavailable event occurs when data becomes available. When an asynchronous data load is in progress it allows processing in parallel with the download. The readyState property changes through several states to indicate the current status of the download. |
| • onreadystate change | The onreadystatechange event occurs when the value of the readyState property changes. This provides an alternative way to monitor the arrival of XML data when asynchronous loading is not used. |
| • ontransformnode | The ontransformnode event is fired when a node is transformed through the transformNode() method of the Node object using an XSL style sheet. |

# DocumentType — the IXMLDOMDocumentType Object

This object contains information about the document type declaration or schema for the document. It is the equivalent of the <!DOCTYPE> node. In the following tables, •indicates properties and methods that are extensions to the base W3C object model. IE5 implements this base object as IDOMDocumentType.

## DocumentType Properties

| Name | Description |
|------|-------------|
| attributes | Returns a collection of the Attribute (or Attr) objects for this node as a NamedNodeMap object. |
| • baseName | Returns the node name with any namespace removed. For example, in a node declared as <nspace:elemname> it returns the "elemname" part. |

| Name | Description |
|------|-------------|
| childNodes | Returns a `NodeList` containing all the child nodes of this node, for nodes that can have child nodes. |
| dataType | Sets or returns the data type for this node. |
| definition | For `EntityReference` nodes, returns the entry in the DTD or schema containing the definition for the entity, i.e. "`<!ENTITY entityname 'entity value'>`". For other nodes, returns `null`. |
| doctype | Returns a reference to the `DocumentType` node specifying the DTD or schema for this document. |
| documentElement | Returns a reference to the outermost element of the document. |
| entities | Returns a node list containing references to the `Entity` objects declared in the document type declaration. |
| firstChild | Returns a reference to the first child node of this node. |
| lastChild | Returns a reference to the last child node of this node. |
| name | Returns the name of the document type (`!DOCTYPE`) for this document. |
| namespaceURI | Returns the URI for the namespace as a string. For example, in the namespace declaration `xmlns:name="uri"` it returns the "`uri`" part. |
| nextSibling | Returns a reference to the next sibling node of this node, i.e. the next node in the source data file at the same level of the hierarchy. |
| nodeName | Returns the name of the node, which will depend on the node type. See the list of Node Types at the end of this appendix for more details. |
| nodeTypeString | Returns the node type as a string, depending on the node type. See the list of Node Types at the end of this appendix for more details. |
| nodeType | Returns the node type as a number. See the list of Node Types at the end of this appendix for more details. |
| nodeTypedValue | Sets or returns the strongly typed value of the node, expressed in its defined data type. If no data type has been defined for the node, its `nodeValue` is returned. |
| nodeValue | Sets or returns the value of the node as plain text. |
| notations | Returns a node list containing references to the `Notation` objects present in the document type declaration. |
| ownerDocument | Returns the root node of the document that contains the node. |
| parentNode | Returns the parent node of this node, for nodes that can have parents. |
| parsed | Returns `true` if this node and all its descendants have been parsed and instantiated. |

*Table Continued on Following Page*

| Name | Description |
|------|-------------|
| prefix | Returns the element namespace prefix as a string. For example, in a node declared as `<nspace:elemname>` it returns the "nspace" part. |
| previous Sibling | Returns a reference to the previous sibling node of this node, i.e. the previous node in the source file at the same level of the hierarchy. |
| specified | Indicates whether the node value is explicitly specified or derived from a default value in the DTD or schema. Normally only used with attribute nodes. |
| text | Sets or returns the entire text content of this node and all its descendent nodes. |
| xml | Returns the entire XML content of this node and all its descendent nodes. |

## DocumentType Methods

| Name | Description |
|------|-------------|
| appendChild (new_node) | Appends the node object `new_node` to the end of the list of child nodes for this node. |
| cloneNode( recurse_ children) | Creates a new node object that is an exact clone of this node, including all descendent nodes of this node if `recurse_children` is set to `true`. |
| hasChildNodes() | Returns `true` if this node has any child nodes. |
| insertBefore (new_node, this_node) | Inserts a new node object `new_node` into the list of child nodes for this node, to the left of the node object `this_node` or at the end of the list if `this_node` is omitted. |
| removeChild (this_node) | Removes the child node `this_node` from the list of child nodes for this node, and returns it. |
| replaceChild (new_node, old_node) | Replaces the child node `old_node` with the new child node object `new_node`, and returns the old child node. |
| selectNodes (pattern) | Applies a specified pattern to this node's context and returns a node list object containing matching nodes. The string `pattern` specifies the XSL pattern-matching operation to be used. |
| selectSingleNode( pattern) | Applies a specified pattern to this node's context and returns just the first node object that matches. The string `pattern` specifies the XSL pattern-matching operation to be used. |
| transformNode( stylesheet) | Processes this node and its children using an XSL style sheet specified in the `stylesheet` argument, and returns the resulting transformation. The style sheet must be either a `Document` node object, in which case the document is assumed to be an XSL style sheet, or a Node object in the `xsl` namespace, in which case this node is treated as a standalone style sheet fragment. |

# DocumentFragment — the IXMLDOMDocumentFragment Object

A document fragment is a lightweight object that is useful for tree insert operations. A new document fragment can be created and elements added to it, then the entire fragment can be added to an existing document. It is also useful for storing sections of a document temporarily, such as when cutting and pasting blocks of elements. This object adds no new methods or properties to the base `IXMLDOMNode` object. In the following tables, •indicates properties and methods that are extensions to the base W3C object model. The unextended object is implemented in IE5 by the `IDOMDocumentFragment` object.

## DocumentFragment Properties

| | Name | Description |
|---|---|---|
| | attributes | Returns a collection of the `Attribute` (or `Attr`) objects for this node as a `NamedNodeMap` object. |
| • | baseName | Returns the node name with any namespace removed. For example, in a node declared as `<nspace:elemname>` it returns the "elemname" part. |
| | childNodes | Returns a `NodeList` containing all the child nodes of this node, for nodes that can have child nodes. |
| • | dataType | Sets or returns the data type for this node. |
| • | definition | For `EntityReference` nodes, returns the entry in the DTD or schema containing the definition for the entity, i.e. "`<!ENTITY entityname 'entity value'>`". For other nodes, returns `null`. |
| | firstChild | Returns a reference to the first child node of this node. |
| | lastChild | Returns a reference to the last child node of this node. |
| • | namespaceURI | Returns the URI for the namespace as a string. For example, in the namespace declaration `xmlns:name="uri"` it returns the "uri" part. |
| | nextSibling | Returns a reference to the next sibling node of this node, i.e. the next node in the source data file at the same level of the hierarchy. |
| | nodeName | Returns the name of the node, which will depend on the node type. See the list of Node Types at the end of this appendix for more details. |
| • | nodeType String | Returns the node type as a string, depending on the node type. See the list of Node Types at the end of this appendix for more details. |
| | nodeType | Returns the node type as a number. See the list of Node Types at the end of this appendix for more details. |
| • | nodeTyped Value | Sets or returns the strongly typed value of the node, expressed in its defined data type. If no data type has been defined for the node, its `nodeValue` is returned. |
| | nodeValue | Sets or returns the value of the node as plain text. |
| | ownerDocument | Returns the root node of the document that contains the node. |

*Table Continued on Following Page*

| Name | Description |
|---|---|
| parentNode | Returns the parent node of this node, for nodes that can have parents. |
| parsed | Returns true if this node and all its descendants have been parsed and instantiated. |
| prefix | Returns the element namespace prefix as a string. For example, in a node declared as <nspace:elemname> it returns the "nspace" part. |
| previous Sibling | Returns a reference to the previous sibling node of this node, i.e. the previous node in the source file at the same level of the hierarchy. |
| specified | Indicates whether the node value is explicitly specified or derived from a default value in the DTD or schema. Normally only used with attribute nodes. |
| text | Sets or returns the entire text content of this node and all its descendent nodes. |
| xml | Returns the entire XML content of this node and all its descendent nodes. |

## DocumentFragment Methods

| Name | Description |
|---|---|
| appendChild(new_node) | Appends the node object new_node to the end of the list of child nodes for this node. |
| cloneNode( recurse_children) | Creates a new node object that is an exact clone of this node, including all descendent nodes of this node if recurse_children is set to true. |
| hasChildNodes() | Returns true if this node has any child nodes. |
| insertBefore(new_node, this_node) | Inserts a new node object new_node into the list of child nodes for this node, to the left of the node object this_node or at the end of the list if this_node is omitted. |
| removeChild(this_node) | Removes the child node this_node from the list of child nodes for this node, and returns it. |
| replaceChild(new_node, old_node) | Replaces the child node old_node with the new child node object new_node, and returns the old child node. |
| selectNodes(pattern) | Applies a specified pattern to this node's context and returns a node list object containing matching nodes. The string pattern specifies the XSL pattern-matching operation to be used. |
| selectSingleNode( pattern) | Applies a specified pattern to this node's context and returns just the first node object that matches. The string pattern specifies the XSL pattern-matching operation to be used. |

| Name | Description |
|------|-------------|
| transformNode(<br>  stylesheet) | Processes this node and its children using an XSL style sheet specified in the stylesheet argument, and returns the resulting transformation. The style sheet must be either a Document node object, in which case the document is assumed to be an XSL style sheet, or a Node object in the xsl namespace, in which case this node is treated as a standalone style sheet fragment. |

# Element — the IXMLDOMElement Object

This object represents the elements in the document, and together with the Attribute and Text nodes, is likely to be one of the most common. Note that the text content of an Element node is stored in a child Text node. An Element node always has a nodeValue of null. In the following tables, • indicates properties and methods that are extensions to the base W3C object model. IE5 implements the unextended object through the IDOMElement interface.

## Element Properties

| Name | Description |
|------|-------------|
| attributes | Returns a collection of the Attribute (or Attr) objects for this node as a NamedNodeMap object. |
| baseName | Returns the node name with any namespace removed. For example, in a node declared as <nspace:elemname> it returns the "elemname" part. |
| childNodes | Returns a NodeList containing all the child nodes of this node, for nodes that can have child nodes. |
| dataType | Sets or returns the data type for this node. |
| definition | For EntityReference nodes, returns the entry in the DTD or schema containing the definition for the entity, i.e. "<!ENTITY entityname 'entity value'>". For other nodes, returns null. |
| firstChild | Returns a reference to the first child node of this node. |
| lastChild | Returns a reference to the last child node of this node. |
| namespaceURI | Returns the URI for the namespace as a string. For example, in the namespace declaration xmlns:name="uri" it returns the "uri" part. |
| nextSibling | Returns a reference to the next sibling node of this node, i.e. the next node in the source data file at the same level of the hierarchy. |
| nodeName | Returns the name of the node, which will depend on the node type. See the list of Node Types at the end of this appendix for more details. |

*Table Continued on Following Page*

| Name | Description |
|------|-------------|
| nodeTypeString | Returns the node type as a string, depending on the node type. See the list of Node Types at the end of this appendix for more details. |
| nodeType | Returns the node type as a number. See the list of Node Types at the end of this appendix for more details. |
| nodeTypedValue | Sets or returns the strongly typed value of the node, expressed in its defined data type. If no data type has been defined for the node, its nodeValue is returned. |
| nodeValue | Sets or returns the value of the node as plain text. |
| ownerDocument | Returns the root node of the document that contains the node. |
| parentNode | Returns the parent node of this node, for nodes that can have parents. |
| parsed | Returns true if this node and all its descendants have been parsed and instantiated. |
| prefix | Returns the element namespace prefix as a string. For example, in a node declared as <nspace:elemname> it returns the "nspace" part. |
| previous Sibling | Returns a reference to the previous sibling node of this node, i.e. the previous node in the source file at the same level of the hierarchy. |
| specified | Indicates whether the node value is explicitly specified or derived from a default value in the DTD or schema. Normally only used with attribute nodes. |
| tagName | Sets or returns the name of the element node; i.e. the text name that appears within the tag. |
| text | Sets or returns the entire text content of this node and all its descendent nodes. |
| xml | Returns the entire XML content of this node and all its descendent nodes. |

## Element Methods

| Name | Description |
|------|-------------|
| appendChild(new_node) | Appends the node object new_node to the end of the list of child nodes for this node. |
| cloneNode( recurse_children) | Creates a new node object that is an exact clone of this node, including all descendent nodes of this node if recurse_children is set to true. |
| getAttribute( attr_name) | Returns the value of the attribute with the specified name. |
| getAttributeNode( attr_name) | Returns the attribute node with the specified name as an object. |

| Name | Description |
|------|-------------|
| getElementsByTagName( name) | Returns a node list of all descendant elements matching the specified name. |
| hasChildNodes() | Returns true if this node has any child nodes. |
| insertBefore(new_node, this_node) | Inserts a new node object new_node into the list of child nodes for this node, to the left of the node object this_node or at the end of the list if this_node is omitted. |
| normalize() | Combines all adjacent text nodes into one unified text node for all descendent element nodes. |
| removeAttribute( attr_name) | Removes the value of the attribute with the specified name, or replaces it with the default value. |
| removeAttributeNode( attr_node) | Removes the specified attribute node from the element and returns it. If the attribute has a default value in the DTD or schema, a new attribute node is automatically created with that default value and the specified property is updated. |
| removeChild(this_node) | Removes the child node this_node from the list of child nodes for this node, and returns it. |
| replaceChild(new_node, old_node) | Replaces the child node old_node with the new child node object new_node, and returns the old child node. |
| selectNodes(pattern) | Applies a specified pattern to this node's context and returns a node list object containing matching nodes. The string pattern specifies the XSL pattern-matching operation to be used. |
| selectSingleNode( pattern) | Applies a specified pattern to this node's context and returns just the first node object that matches. The string pattern specifies the XSL pattern-matching operation to be used. |
| setAttribute( attr_name, value) | Sets the value of the attribute with the specified name. |
| setAttributeNode( attr_node) | Adds the new attribute node to the element. If an attribute with the same name exists, it is replaced and the old attribute node is returned. |
| transformNode( stylesheet) | Processes this node and its children using an XSL style sheet specified in the stylesheet argument, and returns the resulting transformation. The style sheet must be either a Document node object, in which case the document is assumed to be an XSL style sheet, or a Node object in the xsl namespace, in which case this node is treated as a standalone style sheet fragment. |

# Attribute or Attr — IXMLDOMAttribute Object

This object represents an `Attribute` of an `Element` object. In the W3C DOM recommendations, the object name is `Attr` rather than `Attribute`, to avoid clashing with existing interface definition languages. An `Attribute` node has a `name` and a `value`, and attributes are normally manipulated through a `NamedNodeMap` object. In the following tables, •indicates properties and methods that are extensions to the base W3C object model. Microsoft implement the unextended object as `IDOMAttribute`).

## Attribute Properties

| Name | Description |
| --- | --- |
| attributes | Returns a collection of the `Attribute` (or `Attr`) objects for this node as a `NamedNodeMap` object. |
| • baseName | Returns the node name with any namespace removed. For example, in a node declared as `<nspace:elemname>` it returns the "`elemname`" part. |
| childNodes | Returns a `NodeList` containing all the child nodes of this node, for nodes that can have child nodes. |
| • dataType | Sets or returns the data type for this node. |
| • definition | For `EntityReference` nodes, returns the entry in the DTD or schema containing the definition for the entity, i.e. "`<!ENTITY entityname 'entity value'>`". For other nodes, returns `null`. |
| firstChild | Returns a reference to the first child node of this node. |
| lastChild | Returns a reference to the last child node of this node. |
| name | Sets or returns the name of the attribute. |
| • namespaceURI | Returns the URI for the namespace as a string. For example, in the namespace declaration `xmlns:name="uri"` it returns the "`uri`" part. |
| nextSibling | Returns a reference to the next sibling node of this node, i.e. the next node in the source data file at the same level of the hierarchy. |
| nodeName | Returns the name of the node, which will depend on the node type. See the list of Node Types at the end of this appendix for more details. |
| • nodeTypeString | Returns the node type as a string, depending on the node type. See the list of Node Types at the end of this appendix for more details. |
| nodeType | Returns the node type as a number. See the list of Node Types at the end of this appendix for more details. |
| • nodeTypedValue | Sets or returns the strongly typed value of the node, expressed in its defined data type. If no data type has been defined for the node, its `nodeValue` is returned. |
| nodeValue | Sets or returns the value of the node as plain text. |
| ownerDocument | Returns the root node of the document that contains the node. |

| Name | Description |
|------|-------------|
| parentNode | Returns the parent node of this node, for nodes that can have parents. |
| prefix | Returns the element namespace prefix as a string. For example, in a node declared as &lt;nspace:elemname&gt; it returns the "nspace" part. |
| previous Sibling | Returns a reference to the previous sibling node of this node, i.e. the previous node in the source file at the same level of the hierarchy. |
| specified | Indicates whether the node value is explicitly specified or derived from a default value in the DTD or schema. Normally only used with attribute nodes. |
| tagName | Returns the name of the element that contains this attribute. |
| text | Sets or returns the entire text content of this node and all its descendent nodes. |
| xml | Returns the entire XML content of this node and all its descendent nodes. |
| value | Sets or returns the value of the attribute. |

## Attribute Methods

| Name | Description |
|------|-------------|
| appendChild(new_node) | Appends the node object new_node to the end of the list of child nodes for this node. |
| cloneNode( recurse_children) | Creates a new node object that is an exact clone of this node, including all descendent nodes of this node if recurse_children is set to true. |
| hasChildNodes() | Returns true if this node has any child nodes. |
| insertBefore(new_node, this_node) | Inserts a new node object new_node into the list of child nodes for this node, to the left of the node object this_node or at the end of the list if this_node is omitted. |
| removeChild(this_node) | Removes the child node this_node from the list of child nodes for this node, and returns it. |
| replaceChild(new_node, old_node) | Replaces the child node old_node with the new child node object new_node, and returns the old child node. |
| selectNodes(pattern) | Applies a specified pattern to this node's context and returns a node list object containing matching nodes. The string pattern specifies the XSL pattern-matching operation to be used. |
| selectSingleNode( pattern) | Applies a specified pattern to this node's context and returns just the first node object that matches. The string pattern specifies the XSL pattern-matching operation to be used. |

*Table Continued on Following Page*

| Name | Description |
|------|-------------|
| • transformNode(<br>stylesheet) | Processes this node and its children using an XSL style sheet specified in the stylesheet argument, and returns the resulting transformation. The style sheet must be either a Document node object, in which case the document is assumed to be an XSL style sheet, or a Node object in the xsl namespace, in which case this node is treated as a standalone style sheet fragment. |

# Entity — the IXMLDOMEntity Object

This object represents a parsed or unparsed entity as declared with an <!ENTITY...> element in the DTD. However, it does not provide a reference to the entity declaration. The W3C DOM recommendation does not define an object in version 1.0 that models the declaration of entities. In the following tables, • indicates properties and methods that are extensions to the base W3C object model. In IE5 the unextended object is implemented by the IDOMEntity object.

## Entity Properties

| Name | Description |
|------|-------------|
| attributes | Returns a collection of the Attribute (or Attr) objects for this node as a NamedNodeMap object. |
| • baseName | Returns the node name with any namespace removed. For example, in a node declared as <nspace:elemname> it returns the "elemname" part. |
| childNodes | Returns a NodeList containing all the child nodes of this node, for nodes that can have child nodes. |
| • dataType | Sets or returns the data type for this node. |
| • definition | For EntityReference nodes, returns the entry in the DTD or schema containing the definition for the entity, i.e. "<!ENTITY entityname 'entity value'>". For other nodes, returns null. |
| firstChild | Returns a reference to the first child node of this node. |
| lastChild | Returns a reference to the last child node of this node. |
| • namespaceURI | Returns the URI for the namespace as a string. For example, in the namespace declaration xmlns:name="uri" it returns the "uri" part. |
| nextSibling | Returns a reference to the next sibling node of this node, i.e. the next node in the source data file at the same level of the hierarchy. |
| nodeName | Returns the name of the node, which will depend on the node type. See the list of Node Types at the end of this appendix for more details. |
| • nodeTypeString | Returns the node type as a string, depending on the node type. See the list of Node Types at the end of this appendix for more details. |

| Name | Description |
|------|-------------|
| nodeType | Returns the node type as a number. See the list of Node Types at the end of this appendix for more details. |
| nodeTypedValue | Sets or returns the strongly typed value of the node, expressed in its defined data type. If no data type has been defined for the node, its nodeValue is returned. |
| nodeValue | Sets or returns the value of the node as plain text. |
| notationName | Returns the name of the notation linked to the entity. |
| ownerDocument | Returns the root node of the document that contains the node. |
| parentNode | Returns the parent node of this node, for nodes that can have parents. |
| parsed | Returns true if this node and all its descendants have been parsed and instantiated. |
| prefix | Returns the element namespace prefix as a string. For example, in a node declared as <nspace:elemname> it returns the "nspace" part. |
| previous Sibling | Returns a reference to the previous sibling node of this node, i.e. the previous node in the source file at the same level of the hierarchy. |
| publicId | Sets or returns the PUBLIC identifier value for this entity node. |
| specified | Indicates whether the node value is explicitly specified or derived from a default value in the DTD or schema. Normally only used with attribute nodes. |
| systemId | Sets or returns the SYSTEM identifier value for this entity node. |
| text | Sets or returns the entire text content of this node and all its descendent nodes. |
| xml | Returns the entire XML content of this node and all its descendent nodes. |

## Entity Methods

| Name | Description |
|------|-------------|
| appendChild(new_node) | Appends the node object new_node to the end of the list of child nodes for this node. |
| cloneNode( recurse_children) | Creates a new node object that is an exact clone of this node, including all descendent nodes of this node if recurse_children is set to true. |
| hasChildNodes() | Returns true if this node has any child nodes. |

*Table Continued on Following Page*

| Name | Description |
|---|---|
| insertBefore(new_node, this_node) | Inserts a new node object new_node into the list of child nodes for this node, to the left of the node object this_node or at the end of the list if this_node is omitted. |
| removeChild(this_node) | Removes the child node this_node from the list of child nodes for this node, and returns it. |
| replaceChild(new_node, old_node) | Replaces the child node old_node with the new child node object new_node, and returns the old child node. |
| • selectNodes(pattern) | Applies a specified pattern to this node's context and returns a node list object containing matching nodes. The string pattern specifies the XSL pattern-matching operation to be used. |
| • selectSingleNode(pattern) | Applies a specified pattern to this node's context and returns just the first node object that matches. The string pattern specifies the XSL pattern-matching operation to be used. |
| • transformNode(stylesheet) | Processes this node and its children using an XSL style sheet specified in the stylesheet argument, and returns the resulting transformation. The style sheet must be either a Document node object, in which case the document is assumed to be an XSL style sheet, or a Node object in the xsl namespace, in which case this node is treated as a standalone style sheet fragment. |

# EntityReference — the IXMLDOMEntityReference Object

This object represents an entity reference node within the XML document. If the XML processor expands entity references while building the structure model, it's possible that no entity reference objects will appear in the tree, being replaced by the **replacement text** of the entity. In the following tables, •indicates properties and methods that are extensions to the base W3C object model. The object is implemented without extensions by Microsoft as the IDOMEntityReference object.

## EntityReference Properties

| Name | Description |
|---|---|
| attributes | Returns a collection of the Attribute (or Attr) objects for this node as a NamedNodeMap object. |
| • baseName | Returns the node name with any namespace removed. For example, in a node declared as <nspace:elemname> it returns the "elemname" part. |
| childNodes | Returns a NodeList containing all the child nodes of this node, for nodes that can have child nodes. |
| • dataType | Sets or returns the data type for this node. |

| Name | Description |
|------|-------------|
| definition | For `EntityReference` nodes, returns the entry in the DTD or schema containing the definition for the entity, i.e. `"<!ENTITY entityname 'entity value'>"`. For other nodes, returns `null`. |
| firstChild | Returns a reference to the first child node of this node. |
| lastChild | Returns a reference to the last child node of this node. |
| namespaceURI | Returns the URI for the namespace as a string. For example, in the namespace declaration `xmlns:name="uri"` it returns the `"uri"` part. |
| nextSibling | Returns a reference to the next sibling node of this node, i.e. the next node in the source data file at the same level of the hierarchy. |
| nodeName | Returns the name of the node, which will depend on the node type. See the list of Node Types at the end of this appendix for more details. |
| nodeTypeString | Returns the node type as a string, depending on the node type. See the list of Node Types at the end of this appendix for more details. |
| nodeType | Returns the node type as a number. See the list of Node Types at the end of this appendix for more details. |
| nodeTypedValue | Sets or returns the strongly typed value of the node, expressed in its defined data type. If no data type has been defined for the node, its `nodeValue` is returned. |
| nodeValue | Sets or returns the value of the node as plain text. |
| ownerDocument | Returns the root node of the document that contains the node. |
| parentNode | Returns the parent node of this node, for nodes that can have parents. |
| parsed | Returns `true` if this node and all its descendants have been parsed and instantiated. |
| prefix | Returns the element namespace prefix as a string. For example, in a node declared as `<nspace:elemname>` it returns the `"nspace"` part. |
| previousSibling | Returns a reference to the previous sibling node of this node, i.e. the previous node in the source file at the same level of the hierarchy. |
| specified | Indicates whether the node value is explicitly specified or derived from a default value in the DTD or schema. Normally only used with attribute nodes. |
| text | Sets or returns the entire text content of this node and all its descendent nodes. |
| xml | Returns the entire XML content of this node and all its descendent nodes. |

## EntityReference Methods

| Name | Description |
|------|-------------|
| appendChild(new_node) | Appends the node object new_node to the end of the list of child nodes for this node. |
| cloneNode( recurse_children) | Creates a new node object that is an exact clone of this node, including all descendent nodes of this node if recurse_children is set to true. |
| hasChildNodes() | Returns true if this node has any child nodes. |
| insertBefore(new_node, this_node) | Inserts a new node object new_node into the list of child nodes for this node, to the left of the node object this_node or at the end of the list if this_node is omitted. |
| removeChild(this_node) | Removes the child node this_node from the list of child nodes for this node, and returns it. |
| replaceChild(new_node, old_node) | Replaces the child node old_node with the new child node object new_node, and returns the old child node. |
| • selectNodes(pattern) | Applies a specified pattern to this node's context and returns a node list object containing matching nodes. The string pattern specifies the XSL pattern-matching operation to be used. |
| • selectSingleNode( pattern) | Applies a specified pattern to this node's context and returns just the first node object that matches. The string pattern specifies the XSL pattern-matching operation to be used. |
| • transformNode( stylesheet) | Processes this node and its children using an XSL style sheet specified in the stylesheet argument, and returns the resulting transformation. The style sheet must be either a Document node object, in which case the document is assumed to be an XSL style sheet, or a Node object in the xsl namespace, in which case this node is treated as a standalone style sheet fragment. |

# Notation — the IXMLDOMNotation Object

This object represents a notation declared in the DTD or schema with a <!NOTATION...> element. In the following tables, •indicates properties and methods that are extensions to the base W3C object model. The unextended object is implemented as the IDOMNotation object in IE5.

## Notation Properties

| Name | Description |
|------|-------------|
| attributes | Returns a collection of the Attribute (or Attr) objects for this node as a NamedNodeMap object. |
| • baseName | Returns the node name with any namespace removed. For example, in a node declared as <nspace:elemname> it returns the "elemname" part. |

| Name | Description |
|------|-------------|
| childNodes | Returns a NodeList containing all the child nodes of this node, for nodes that can have child nodes. |
| dataType | Sets or returns the data type for this node. |
| definition | For EntityReference nodes, returns the entry in the DTD or schema containing the definition for the entity, i.e. "<!ENTITY entityname 'entity value'>". For other nodes, returns null. |
| firstChild | Returns a reference to the first child node of this node. |
| lastChild | Returns a reference to the last child node of this node. |
| namespace URI | Returns the URI for the namespace as a string. For example, in the namespace declaration xmlns:name="uri" it returns the "uri" part. |
| next Sibling | Returns a reference to the next sibling node of this node, i.e. the next node in the source data file at the same level of the hierarchy. |
| nodeName | Returns the name of the node, which will depend on the node type. See the list of Node Types at the end of this appendix for more details. |
| nodeType String | Returns the node type as a string, depending on the node type. See the list of Node Types at the end of this appendix for more details. |
| nodeType | Returns the node type as a number. See the list of Node Types at the end of this appendix for more details. |
| nodeTyped Value | Sets or returns the strongly typed value of the node, expressed in its defined data type. If no data type has been defined for the node, its nodeValue is returned. |
| nodeValue | Sets or returns the value of the node as plain text. |
| owner Document | Returns the root node of the document that contains the node. |
| parentNode | Returns the parent node of this node, for nodes that can have parents. |
| parsed | Returns true if this node and all its descendants have been parsed and instantiated. |
| prefix | Returns the element namespace prefix as a string. For example, in a node declared as <nspace:elemname> it returns the "nspace" part. |
| previous Sibling | Returns a reference to the previous sibling node of this node, i.e. the previous node in the source file at the same level of the hierarchy. |
| publicId | Sets or returns the PUBLIC identifier value for this entity node. |
| specified | Indicates whether the node value is explicitly specified or derived from a default value in the DTD or schema. Normally only used with attribute nodes. |
| systemId | Sets or returns the SYSTEM identifier value for this entity node. |

*Table Continued on Following Page*

| Name | Description |
|------|-------------|
| text | Sets or returns the entire text content of this node and all its descendent nodes. |
| xml | Returns the entire XML content of this node and all its descendent nodes. |

## Notation Methods

| Name | Description |
|------|-------------|
| appendChild(new_node) | Appends the node object new_node to the end of the list of child nodes for this node. |
| cloneNode( recurse_children) | Creates a new node object that is an exact clone of this node, including all descendent nodes of this node if recurse_children is set to true. |
| hasChildNodes() | Returns true if this node has any child nodes. |
| insertBefore(new_node, this_node) | Inserts a new node object new_node into the list of child nodes for this node, to the left of the node object this_node or at the end of the list if this_node is omitted. |
| removeChild(this_node) | Removes the child node this_node from the list of child nodes for this node, and returns it. |
| replaceChild(new_node, old_node) | Replaces the child node old_node with the new child node object new_node, and returns the old child node. |
| selectNodes(pattern) | Applies a specified pattern to this node's context and returns a node list object containing matching nodes. The string pattern specifies the XSL pattern-matching operation to be used. |
| selectSingleNode( pattern) | Applies a specified pattern to this node's context and returns just the first node object that matches. The string pattern specifies the XSL pattern-matching operation to be used. |
| transformNode( stylesheet) | Processes this node and its children using an XSL style sheet specified in the stylesheet argument, and returns the resulting transformation. The style sheet must be either a Document node object, in which case the document is assumed to be an XSL style sheet, or a Node object in the xsl namespace, in which case this node is treated as a standalone style sheet fragment. |

# CharacterData — the IXMLDOMCharacterData Object

This object is the base for several higher-level objects including `Text`, `CDATASection` (which is inherited from the `Text` object) and `Comment`. It provides text information properties like `length`, and a range of text manipulation methods like `substringData()` that are used by these objects. The IE5 implementation of `CharacterData` follows the W3C recommendations for character data manipulation in the appropriate elements with the exception of those properties and methods marked with •in the following tables. The unextended W3C `CharacterData` object is implemented in IE5 by the `IDOMCharacterData` object.

## CharacterData Properties

| | Name | Description |
|---|---|---|
| | attributes | Returns a collection of the `Attribute` (or `Attr`) objects for this node as a `NamedNodeMap` object. |
| • | baseName | Returns the node name with any namespace removed. For example, in a node declared as `<nspace:elemname>` it returns the "`elemname`" part. |
| | childNodes | Returns a `NodeList` containing all the child nodes of this node, for nodes that can have child nodes. |
| | data | Contains this node's value, which depends on the node type. |
| • | dataType | Sets or returns the data type for this node. |
| • | definition | For `EntityReference` nodes, returns the entry in the DTD or schema containing the definition for the entity, i.e. "`<!ENTITY entityname 'entity value'>`". For other nodes, returns `null`. |
| | firstChild | Returns a reference to the first child node of this node. |
| | lastChild | Returns a reference to the last child node of this node. |
| | length | Returns the number of characters for the data, i.e. the string length. |
| • | namespaceURI | Returns the URI for the namespace as a string. For example, in the namespace declaration `xmlns:name="uri"` it returns the "`uri`" part. |
| | nextSibling | Returns a reference to the next sibling node of this node, i.e. the next node in the source data file at the same level of the hierarchy. |
| | nodeName | Returns the name of the node, which will depend on the node type. See the list of Node Types at the end of this appendix for more details. |
| • | nodeTypeString | Returns the node type as a string. See the list of Node Types at the end of this appendix for more details. |
| | nodeType | Returns the node type as a number. See the list of Node Types at the end of this appendix for more details. |
| • | nodeTypedValue | Sets or returns the strongly typed value of the node, expressed in its defined data type. If no data type has been defined for the node, its `nodeValue` is returned. |

| Name | Description |
|------|-------------|
| nodeValue | Sets or returns the value of the node as plain text. |
| ownerDocument | Returns the root node of the document that contains the node. |
| parentNode | Returns the parent node of this node, for nodes that can have parents. |
| parsed | Returns true if this node and all its descendants have been parsed and instantiated. |
| prefix | Returns the element namespace prefix as a string. For example, in a node declared as <nspace:elemname> it returns the "nspace" part. |
| previousSibling | Returns a reference to the previous sibling node of this node, i.e. the previous node in the source file at the same level of the hierarchy. |
| specified | Indicates whether the node value is explicitly specified or derived from a default value in the DTD or schema. Normally only used with attribute nodes. |
| text | Sets or returns the entire text content of this node and all its descendent nodes. |
| xml | Returns the entire XML content of this node and all its descendent nodes. |

## CharacterData Methods

| Name | Description |
|------|-------------|
| appendChild(new_node) | Appends the node object new_node to the end of the list of child nodes for this node. |
| appendData(text) | Appends the string in the text argument to the existing string data. |
| cloneNode(recurse_children) | Creates a new node object that is an exact clone of this node, including all descendent nodes of this node if recurse_children is set to true. |
| deleteData(char_offset, num_chars) | Deletes a substring from the string data of the node, starting at char_offset and continuing for num_chars. |
| hasChildNodes() | Returns true if this node has any child nodes. |
| insertBefore(new_node, this_node) | Inserts a new node object new_node into the list of child nodes for this node, to the left of the node object this_node or at the end of the list if this_node is omitted. |
| insertData(char_offset, text) | Inserts the string in the text argument at the specified character offset within the data contained by the node. |
| removeChild(this_child) | Removes the child node this_node from the list of child nodes for this node, and returns it. |

| Name | Description |
|------|-------------|
| replaceChild(new_node, old_node) | Replaces the child node old_node with the new child node object new_node, and returns the old child node. |
| replaceData( char_offset, num_chars, text) | Replaces the specified number of characters in the existing string data of the node, starting at the specified character offset, with the string in the text argument. |
| • selectNodes(pattern) | Applies a specified pattern to this node's context and returns a node list object containing matching nodes. The string pattern specifies the XSL pattern-matching operation to be used. |
| • selectSingleNode( pattern) | Applies a specified pattern to this node's context and returns just the first node object that matches. The string pattern specifies the XSL pattern-matching operation to be used. |
| substringData( char_offset, num_chars) | Returns as a string the specified number of characters, starting at the specified character offset, from the data contained in the node. |
| • transformNode( stylesheet) | Processes this node and its children using an XSL style sheet specified in the stylesheet argument, and returns the resulting transformation. The style sheet must be either a Document node object, in which case the document is assumed to be an XSL style sheet, or a Node object in the xsl namespace, in which case this node is treated as a standalone style sheet fragment. |

# Text — the IXMLDOMText Object

This object represents the text content of an element node or an attribute node. It is derived from the CharacterData object, and the CDATASection object is in turn inherited from it. In the following tables, •indicates properties and methods that are extensions to the base W3C object model; the W3C CDATASection object is implemented in IE5 by the IDOMText object).

## Text Properties

| Name | Description |
|------|-------------|
| attributes | Returns a collection of the Attribute (or Attr) objects for this node as a NamedNodeMap object. |
| • baseName | Returns the node name with any namespace removed. For example, in a node declared as <nspace:elemname> it returns the "elemname" part. |
| childNodes | Returns a NodeList containing all the child nodes of this node, for nodes that can have child nodes. |
| data | Contains this node's value, which depends on the node type. |

*Table Continued on Following Page*

| Name | Description |
|------|-------------|
| dataType | Sets or returns the data type for this node. |
| definition | For `EntityReference` nodes, returns the entry in the DTD or schema containing the definition for the entity, i.e. "`<!ENTITY entityname 'entity value'>`". For other nodes, returns `null`. |
| firstChild | Returns a reference to the first child node of this node. |
| lastChild | Returns a reference to the last child node of this node. |
| length | Returns the number of characters for the data, i.e. the string length. |
| namespaceURI | Returns the URI for the namespace as a string. For example, in the namespace declaration `xmlns:name="uri"` it returns the "`uri`" part. |
| nextSibling | Returns a reference to the next sibling node of this node, i.e. the next node in the source data file at the same level of the hierarchy. |
| nodeName | Returns the name of the node, which will depend on the node type. See the list of Node Types at the end of this appendix for more details. |
| nodeTypeString | Returns the node type as a string, depending on the node type. See the list of Node Types at the end of this appendix for more details. |
| nodeType | Returns the node type as a number. See the list of Node Types at the end of this appendix for more details. |
| nodeTypedValue | Sets or returns the strongly typed value of the node, expressed in its defined data type. If no data type has been defined for the node, its `nodeValue` is returned. |
| nodeValue | Sets or returns the value of the node as plain text. |
| ownerDocument | Returns the root node of the document that contains the node. |
| parentNode | Returns the parent node of this node, for nodes that can have parents. |
| parsed | Returns `true` if this node and all its descendants have been parsed and instantiated. |
| prefix | Returns the element namespace prefix as a string. For example, in a node declared as `<nspace:elemname>` it returns the "`nspace`" part. |
| previousSibling | Returns a reference to the previous sibling node of this node, i.e. the previous node in the source file at the same level of the hierarchy. |
| specified | Indicates whether the node value is explicitly specified or derived from a default value in the DTD or schema. Normally only used with attribute nodes. |
| text | Sets or returns the entire text content of this node and all its descendent nodes. |
| xml | Returns the entire XML content of this node and all its descendent nodes. |

## Text Methods

| Name | Description |
| --- | --- |
| appendChild(new_node) | Appends the node object new_node to the end of the list of child nodes for this node. |
| appendData(text) | Appends the string in the text argument to the existing string data. |
| cloneNode(<br>  recurse_children) | Creates a new node object that is an exact clone of this node, including all descendent nodes of this node if recurse_children is set to true. |
| deleteData(char_offset,<br>  num_chars) | Deletes a substring from the string data of the node, starting at char_offset and continuing for num_chars. |
| hasChildNodes() | Returns true if this node has any child nodes. |
| insertBefore(new_node,<br>  this_node) | Inserts a new node object new_node into the list of child nodes for this node, to the left of the node object this_node or at the end of the list if this_node is omitted. |
| insertData(char_offset,<br>  text) | Inserts the string in the text argument at the specified character offset within the data contained by the node. |
| removeChild(<br>  this_child) | Removes the child node this_node from the list of child nodes for this node, and returns it. |
| replaceChild(new_node,<br>  old_node) | Replaces the child node old_node with the new child node object new_node, and returns the old child node. |
| replaceData(<br>  char_offset,<br>  num_chars, text) | Replaces the specified number of characters in the existing string data of the node, starting at the specified character offset, with the string in the text argument. |
| selectNodes(pattern) | Applies a specified pattern to this node's context and returns a node list object containing matching nodes. The string pattern specifies the XSL pattern-matching operation to be used. |
| selectSingleNode(<br>  pattern) | Applies a specified pattern to this node's context and returns just the first node object that matches. The string pattern specifies the XSL pattern-matching operation to be used. |
| splitText(char_offset) | Splits the node into two separate nodes at the specified character offset, then inserts the new node into the XML as a sibling that immediately follows this node. |
| substringData(<br>  char_offset,<br>  num_chars) | Returns as a string the specified number of characters, starting at the specified character offset, from the data contained in the node. |

*Table Continued on Following Page*

| Name | Description |
|---|---|
| • transformNode( stylesheet) | Processes this node and its children using an XSL style sheet specified in the stylesheet argument, and returns the resulting transformation. The style sheet must be either a Document node object, in which case the document is assumed to be an XSL style sheet, or a Node object in the xsl namespace, in which case this node is treated as a standalone style sheet fragment. |

# CDATASection — the IXMLDOMCDATASection Object

CDATA sections in a DTD or schema are used to 'escape' blocks of text that is not designed to be interpreted as markup. The are declared in the DTD using a <!CDATA...> element. The IXMLDOMCDATASection interface is inherited from the IXMLDOMText interface, and adds no extra methods or properties. In the following tables, •indicates properties and methods that are extensions to the base W3C object model. IE5 implements the unextended W3C object as the IDOMCDATASection object.

## CDATASection Properties

| Name | Description |
|---|---|
| attributes | Returns collection of the Attribute (or Attr) objects for this node as a NamedNodeMap object. |
| • baseName | Returns the node name with any namespace removed. For example, in a node declared as <nspace:elemname> it returns the "elemname" part. |
| childNodes | Returns a NodeList containing all the child nodes of this node, for nodes that can have child nodes. |
| data | Contains this node's value, which depends on the node type. |
| • dataType | Sets or returns the data type for this node. |
| • definition | For EntityReference nodes, returns the entry in the DTD or schema containing the definition for the entity, i.e. "<!ENTITY entityname 'entity value'>". For other nodes, returns null. |
| firstChild | Returns a reference to the first child node of this node. |
| lastChild | Returns a reference to the last child node of this node. |
| length | Returns the number of characters for the data, i.e. the string length. |
| • namespaceURI | Returns the URI for the namespace as a string. For example, in the namespace declaration xmlns:name="uri" it returns the "uri" part. |
| nextSibling | Returns a reference to the next sibling node of this node, i.e. the next node in the source data file at the same level of the hierarchy. |

| Name | Description |
|------|-------------|
| nodeName | Returns the name of the node, which will depend on the node type. See the list of Node Types at the end of this appendix for more details. |
| nodeTypeString | Returns the node type as a string, depending on the node type. See the list of Node Types at the end of this appendix for more details. |
| nodeType | Returns the node type as a number. See the list of Node Types at the end of this appendix for more details. |
| nodeTypedValue | Sets or returns the strongly typed value of the node, expressed in its defined data type. If no data type has been defined for the node, its nodeValue is returned. |
| nodeValue | Sets or returns the value of the node as plain text. |
| ownerDocument | Returns the root node of the document that contains the node. |
| parentNode | Returns the parent node of this node, for nodes that can have parents. |
| parsed | Returns true if this node and all its descendants have been parsed and instantiated. |
| prefix | Returns the element namespace prefix as a string. For example, in a node declared as \<nspace:elemname\> it returns the "nspace" part. |
| previous Sibling | Returns a reference to the previous sibling node of this node, i.e. the previous node in the source file at the same level of the hierarchy. |
| specified | Indicates whether the node value is explicitly specified or derived from a default value in the DTD or schema. Normally only used with attribute nodes. |
| text | Sets or returns the entire text content of this node and all its descendent nodes. |
| xml | Returns the entire XML content of this node and all its descendent nodes. |

## CDATASection Methods

| Name | Description |
|------|-------------|
| appendChild( new_node) | Appends the node object new_node to the end of the list of child nodes for this node. |
| appendData(text) | Appends the string in the text argument to the existing string data. |
| cloneNode( recurse_children) | Creates a new node object that is an exact clone of this node, including all descendent nodes of this node if recurse_children is set to true. |

*Table Continued on Following Page*

| Name | Description |
|------|-------------|
| deleteData( char_offset, num_chars) | Deletes a substring from the string data of the node, starting at char_offset and continuing for num_chars. |
| hasChildNodes() | Returns true if this node has any child nodes. |
| insertBefore( new_node, this_node) | Inserts a new node object new_node into the list of child nodes for this node, to the left of the node object this_node or at the end of the list if this_node is omitted. |
| insertData( char_offset, text) | Inserts the string in the text argument at the specified character offset within the data contained by the node. |
| removeChild( this_child) | Removes the child node this_node from the list of child nodes for this node, and returns it. |
| replaceChild( new_node, old_node) | Replaces the child node old_node with the new child node object new_node, and returns the old child node. |
| replaceData( char_offset, num_chars, text) | Replaces the specified number of characters in the existing string data of the node, starting at the specified character offset, with the string in the text argument. |
| selectNodes (pattern) | Applies a specified pattern to this node's context and returns a node list object containing matching nodes. The string pattern specifies the XSL pattern-matching operation to be used. |
| selectSingleNode( pattern) | Applies a specified pattern to this node's context and returns just the first node object that matches. The string pattern specifies the XSL pattern-matching operation to be used. |
| splitText( char_offset) | Splits the node into two separate nodes at the specified character offset, then inserts the new node into the XML as a sibling that immediately follows this node. |
| substringData( char_offset, num_chars) | Returns as a string the specified number of characters, starting at the specified character offset, from the data contained in the node. |
| transformNode( stylesheet) | Processes this node and its children using an XSL style sheet specified in the stylesheet argument, and returns the resulting transformation. The style sheet must be either a Document node object, in which case the document is assumed to be an XSL style sheet, or a Node object in the xsl namespace, in which case this node is treated as a standalone style sheet fragment. |

# Comment — the IXMLDOMComment Object

Represents the content of an XML comment element. This object is derived from the
`IXMLDOMCharacterData` object. In the following tables, •indicates properties and methods that are
extensions to the base W3C object model. The unextended W3C `Comment` object is implemented in IE5
by the `IDOMComment` interface.

## Comment Properties

| Name | Description |
|------|-------------|
| attributes | Returns a collection of the `Attribute` (or `Attr`) objects for this node as a `NamedNodeMap` object. |
| • baseName | Returns the node name with any namespace removed. For example, in a node declared as `<nspace:elemname>` it returns the `"elemname"` part. |
| childNodes | Returns a `NodeList` containing all the child nodes of this node, for nodes that can have child nodes. |
| data | Contains this node's value, which depends on the node type. |
| • dataType | Sets or returns the data type for this node. |
| • definition | For `EntityReference` nodes, returns the entry in the DTD or schema containing the definition for the entity, i.e. `"<!ENTITY entityname 'entity value'>"`. For other nodes, returns `null`. |
| firstChild | Returns a reference to the first child node of this node. |
| lastChild | Returns a reference to the last child node of this node. |
| length | Returns the number of characters for the data, i.e. the string length. |
| • namespaceURI | Returns the URI for the namespace as a string. For example, in the namespace declaration `xmlns:name="uri"` it returns the `"uri"` part. |
| nextSibling | Returns a reference to the next sibling node of this node, i.e. the next node in the source data file at the same level of the hierarchy. |
| nodeName | Returns the name of the node, which will depend on the node type. See the list of Node Types at the end of this appendix for more details. |
| • nodeTypeString | Returns the node type as a string, depending on the node type. See the list of Node Types at the end of this appendix for more details. |
| nodeType | Returns the node type as a number. See the list of Node Types at the end of this appendix for more details. |
| • nodeTypedValue | Sets or returns the strongly typed value of the node, expressed in its defined data type. If no data type has been defined for the node, its `nodeValue` is returned. |
| nodeValue | Sets or returns the value of the node as plain text. |
| ownerDocument | Returns the root node of the document that contains the node. |

*Table Continued on Following Page*

| Name | Description |
|---|---|
| parentNode | Returns the parent node of this node, for nodes that can have parents. |
| • parsed | Returns true if this node and all its descendants have been parsed and instantiated. |
| • prefix | Returns the element namespace prefix as a string. For example, in a node declared as <nspace:elemname> it returns the "nspace" part. |
| previousSibling | Returns a reference to the previous sibling node of this node, i.e. the previous node in the source file at the same level of the hierarchy. |
| • specified | Indicates whether the node value is explicitly specified or derived from a default value in the DTD or schema. Normally only used with attribute nodes. |
| • text | Sets or returns the entire text content of this node and all its descendent nodes. |
| • xml | Returns the entire XML content of this node and all its descendent nodes. |

## Comment Methods

| Name | Description |
|---|---|
| appendChild(new_node) | Appends the node object new_node to the end of the list of child nodes for this node. |
| appendData(text) | Appends the string in the text argument to the existing string data. |
| cloneNode(recurse_children) | Creates a new node object that is an exact clone of this node, including all descendent nodes of this node if recurse_children is set to true. |
| deleteData(char_offset, num_chars) | Deletes a substring from the string data of the node, starting at char_offset and continuing for num_chars. |
| hasChildNodes() | Returns true if this node has any child nodes. |
| insertBefore(new_node, this_node) | Inserts a new node object new_node into the list of child nodes for this node, to the left of the node object this_node or at the end of the list if this_node is omitted. |
| insertData(char_offset, text) | Inserts the string in the text argument at the specified character offset within the data contained by the node. |
| removeChild(this_child) | Removes the child node this_node from the list of child nodes for this node, and returns it. |
| replaceChild(new_node, old_node) | Replaces the child node old_node with the new child node object new_node, and returns the old child node. |

| Name | Description |
|------|-------------|
| replaceData(<br>  char_offset,<br>  num_chars, text) | Replaces the specified number of characters in the existing string data of the node, starting at the specified character offset, with the string in the text argument. |
| • selectNodes(pattern) | Applies a specified pattern to this node's context and returns a node list object containing matching nodes. The string pattern specifies the XSL pattern-matching operation to be used. |
| • selectSingleNode(<br>  pattern) | Applies a specified pattern to this node's context and returns just the first node object that matches. The string pattern specifies the XSL pattern-matching operation to be used. |
| substringData(<br>  char_offset,<br>  num_chars) | Returns as a string the specified number of characters, starting at the specified character offset, from the data contained in the node. |
| • transformNode(<br>  stylesheet) | Processes this node and its children using an XSL style sheet specified in the stylesheet argument, and returns the resulting transformation. The style sheet must be either a Document node object, in which case the document is assumed to be an XSL style sheet, or a Node object in the xsl namespace, in which case this node is treated as a standalone style sheet fragment. |

# ProcessingInstruction — the IXMLDOMProcessingInstruction Object

This element represents an instruction embedded in the XML within the '<?' and '?>' delimiters. It provides a way of storing processor-specific information within an XML document. The text content of the node is usually subdivided into the target (the text after the '<?' and up to the first white-space character) and the data content (the remainder up to the closing '?>'. In the following tables, •indicates properties and methods that are extensions to the base W3C object model. The W3C Recommendation for this object is implemented in IE5 by the IDOMProcessingInstruction object.

## ProcessingInstruction Properties

| Name | Description |
|------|-------------|
| attributes | Returns a collection of the Attribute (or Attr) objects for this node as a NamedNodeMap object. |
| • baseName | Returns the node name with any namespace removed. For example, in a node declared as <nspace:elemname> it returns the "elemname" part. |
| childNodes | Returns a NodeList containing all the child nodes of this node, for nodes that can have child nodes. |
| data | Contains this node's value, which depends on the node type. |

*Table Continued on Following Page*

| Name | Description |
|------|-------------|
| dataType | Sets or returns the data type for this node. |
| definition | For EntityReference nodes, returns the entry in the DTD or schema containing the definition for the entity, i.e. "<!ENTITY entityname 'entity value'>". For other nodes, returns null. |
| firstChild | Returns a reference to the first child node of this node. |
| lastChild | Returns a reference to the last child node of this node. |
| length | Returns the number of characters for the data, i.e. the string length. |
| namespaceURI | Returns the URI for the namespace as a string. For example, in the namespace declaration xmlns:name="uri" it returns the "uri" part. |
| nextSibling | Returns a reference to the next sibling node of this node, i.e. the next node in the source data file at the same level of the hierarchy. |
| nodeName | Returns the name of the node, which will depend on the node type. See the list of Node Types at the end of this appendix for more details. |
| nodeTypeString | Returns the node type as a string, depending on the node type. See the list of Node Types at the end of this appendix for more details. |
| nodeType | Returns the node type as a number. See the list of Node Types at the end of this appendix for more details. |
| nodeTypedValue | Sets or returns the strongly typed value of the node, expressed in its defined data type. If no data type has been defined for the node, its nodeValue is returned. |
| nodeValue | Sets or returns the value of the node as plain text. |
| ownerDocument | Returns the root node of the document that contains the node. |
| parentNode | Returns the parent node of this node, for nodes that can have parents. |
| parsed | Returns true if this node and all its descendants have been parsed and instantiated. |
| prefix | Returns the element namespace prefix as a string. For example, in a node declared as <nspace:elemname> it returns the "nspace" part. |
| previousSibling | Returns a reference to the previous sibling node of this node, i.e. the previous node in the source file at the same level of the hierarchy. |
| specified | Indicates whether the node value is explicitly specified or derived from a default value in the DTD or schema. Normally only used with attribute nodes. |
| target | Specifies the application to which this processing instruction is directed. This is the text up to the first white-space character in the node content. |

| Name | Description |
|------|-------------|
| text | Sets or returns the entire text content of this node and all its descendent nodes. |
| xml | Returns the entire XML content of this node and all its descendent nodes. |

## ProcessingInstruction Methods

| Name | Description |
|------|-------------|
| appendChild(new_node) | Appends the node object new_node to the end of the list of child nodes for this node. |
| cloneNode( recurse_children) | Creates a new node object that is an exact clone of this node, including all descendent nodes of this node if recurse_children is set to true. |
| hasChildNodes() | Returns true if this node has any child nodes. |
| insertBefore(new_node, this_node) | Inserts a new node object new_node into the list of child nodes for this node, to the left of the node object this_node or at the end of the list if this_node is omitted. |
| removeChild( this_child) | Removes the child node this_node from the list of child nodes for this node, and returns it. |
| replaceChild(new_node, old_node) | Replaces the child node old_node with the new child node object new_node, and returns the old child node. |
| selectNodes(pattern) | Applies a specified pattern to this node's context and returns a node list object containing matching nodes. The string pattern specifies the XSL pattern-matching operation to be used. |
| selectSingleNode( pattern) | Applies a specified pattern to this node's context and returns just the first node object that matches. The string pattern specifies the XSL pattern-matching operation to be used. |
| transformNode( stylesheet) | Processes this node and its children using an XSL style sheet specified in the stylesheet argument, and returns the resulting transformation. The style sheet must be either a Document node object, in which case the document is assumed to be an XSL style sheet, or a Node object in the xsl namespace, in which case this node is treated as a standalone style sheet fragment. |

# Implementation — the IXMLDOMImplementation Object

This object provides access to methods that are application-specific and independent of any particular instance of the document object model. It is a child of the Document object.

## Implementation Method

| Name | Description |
|------|-------------|
| hasFeature( feature, version) | Returns true if the specified version of the implementation supports the specified feature. |

# IE5-Specific XML Parser Objects

While the document object is quite tightly standardized as far as the structure of the document is concerned, there are other peripheral activities that any XML application must handle. This includes managing and reporting errors, originating and handling HTTP requests, and interfacing with style sheets. These are all application-specific tasks, and in IE5 are managed by three subsidiary objects:

- ❑ ParseError (the IDOMParseError object)
- ❑ HttpRequest (the IXMLHttpRequest Object)
- ❑ Runtime (the IXTLRuntime object)

# ParseError — the IDOMParseError Object

The properties of this object return detailed information about the last error that occurred while loading and parsing a document. This includes the line number, character position, and a text description. In the following table, all are marked •to indicate that the W3C recommendations do not cover this area of the DOM.

## ParseError Properties

| | Name | Description |
|---|------|-------------|
| • | errorCode | Returns the error number or error code as a decimal integer. |
| • | filepos | Returns the absolute character position in the file where the error occurred. |
| • | line | Returns the number of the line in the document that contains the error. |
| • | linepos | Returns the character position of the error within the line in which it occurred. |
| • | reason | Returns a text description of the source and reason for the error, and can also include the URL of the DTD or schema and the node within it that corresponds to the error. |
| • | srcText | Returns the full text of the line that contains the error or an empty string if the error cannot be assigned to a specific line. |
| • | url | Returns the URL of the most recent XML document that contained an error. |

# HttpRequest — the IXMLHttpRequest Object

This object provides client-side protocol support for communication with HTTP servers. A client can use the HttpRequest object to send an arbitrary HTTP request, receive the response, and have the IE5 DOM parse that response. In the following table, all are marked •to indicate that the W3C recommendations do not cover this area of the DOM.

## HttpRequest Properties

| | Name | Description |
|---|---|---|
| • | readyState | Indicates the current state of the XML document being loaded: |
| | | 0 ("UNINITIALIZED") — the object has been created but the load has not yet been executed. |
| | | 1 ("LOADING") — the load method is executing. |
| | | 2 ("LOADED") — loading is complete and parsing is taking place. |
| | | 3 ("INTERACTIVE") — some data has been read and parsed and the object model is now available. The data set is only partially retrieved and is read-only. |
| | | 4 ("COMPLETED") — document has been completely loaded. If successful the data is available read/write, if not the error information is available. |
| • | responseBody | Returns the response as an array of unsigned bytes. |
| • | responseStream | Returns the response as an IStream object. |
| • | responseText | Returns the response as an ordinary text string. |
| • | responseXML | Returns the response as an XML document. For security reasons, validation is turned off during this process to prevent the parser from attempting to download a linked DTD or other definition file. |
| • | status | Returns the status code sent back from the server as a long integer. |
| • | statusText | Returns the status text sent back from the server as a string. |

## HttpRequest Methods

| | Name | Description |
|---|---|---|
| • | abort() | Cancels a current HTTP request. |
| • | getAllResponseHeaders( ) | Returns all the HTTP headers as name/value pairs delimited by the carriage return-linefeed combination. |
| • | getResponseHeader( header_name) | Returns the value of an individual HTTP header from the response body as specified by the header name. |

*Table Continued on Following Page*

| Name | Description |
|------|-------------|
| • open(method, url, async, userid, password) | Initializes a request, specifying the HTTP method, the URL, whether the response is to be asynchronous, and authentication information for the request. |
| • send() | Sends an HTTP request to the server and waits to receive a response. |
| • setRequestHeader( header_name, value) | Specifies an HTTP header to send to the server. |

# Runtime — the IXTLRuntime Object

This object implements a series of properties and methods that are available within XSL style sheets. In the following table, all are marked •to indicate that the W3C recommendations do not cover this area of the DOM.

## Runtime Properties

| Name | Description |
|------|-------------|
| • attributes | Returns a collection of the Attribute (or Attr) objects for this node as a NamedNodeMap object. |
| • baseName | Returns the node name with any namespace removed. For example, in a node declared as <nspace:elemname> it returns the "elemname" part. |
| • childNodes | Returns a NodeList containing all the child nodes of this node, for nodes that can have child nodes. |
| • dataType | Sets or returns the data type for this node. |
| • definition | For EntityReference nodes, returns the entry in the DTD or schema containing the definition for the entity, i.e. "<!ENTITY entityname 'entity value'>". For other nodes, returns null. |
| • firstChild | Returns a reference to the first child node of this node. |
| • lastChild | Returns a reference to the last child node of this node. |
| • namespaceURI | Returns the URI for the namespace as a string. For example, in the namespace declaration xmlns:name="uri" it returns the "uri" part. |
| • nextSibling | Returns a reference to the next sibling node of this node, i.e. the next node in the source data file at the same level of the hierarchy. |
| • nodeName | Returns the name of the node, which will depend on the node type. See the list of Node Types at the end of this appendix for more details. |
| • nodeTypeString | Returns the node type as a string. See the list of Node Types at the end of this appendix for more details. |

| Name | Description |
|---|---|
| • nodeType | Returns the node type as a number. See the list of Node Types at the end of this appendix for more details. |
| • nodeTypedValue | Sets or returns the strongly typed value of the node, expressed in its defined data type. If no data type has been defined for the node, its nodeValue is returned. |
| • nodeValue | Sets or returns the value of the node as plain text. |
| • ownerDocument | Returns the root node of the document that contains the node. |
| • parentNode | Returns the parent node of this node, for nodes that can have parents. |
| • parsed | Returns true if this node and all its descendants have been parsed and instantiated. |
| • prefix | Returns the element namespace prefix as a string. For example, in a node declared as <nspace:elemname> it returns the "nspace" part. |
| • previousSibling | Returns a reference to the previous sibling node of this node, i.e. the previous node in the source file at the same level of the hierarchy. |
| • specified | Indicates whether the node value is explicitly specified or derived from a default value in the DTD or schema. Normally only used with attribute nodes. |
| • text | Sets or returns the entire text content of this node and all its descendent nodes. |
| • xml | Returns the entire XML of this node and all descendent nodes of this node. |

## Runtime Methods

| Name | Description |
|---|---|
| • absoluteChildNumber( this_node) | Returns the index of a specified node within its parent's childNodes list. Values start from "1". |
| • ancestorChildNumber( node_name, this_node) | Finds the first ancestor node of a specified node that has the specified name, and returns the index of that node within its parent's childNodes list. Values start from "1". Returns null if there is no ancestor. |
| • appendChild( new_node) | Appends the node object new_node to the end of the list of child nodes for this node. |
| • childNumber( this_node) | Finds the first node with the same name as the specified node within the specified node's parent's childNodes list (i.e. its siblings). Returns the index of that node or null if not found. Values start from "1". |

*Table Continued on Following Page*

| Name | Description |
|------|-------------|
| • `cloneNode(`<br>`  recurse_children)` | Creates a new node object that is an exact clone of this node, including all descendent nodes of this node if `recurse_children` is set to `true`. |
| • `depth(start_node)` | Returns the depth or level within the document tree at which the specified node appears. The `documentElement` or root node is at level 0. |
| • `elementIndexList(`<br>`  this_node,`<br>`  node_name)` | Returns an array of node index numbers for the specified node and all its ancestors up to and including the document root node, indicating each node's position within their parent's `childNodes` list. The ordering of the array starts from the root document node. |
| | When the `node_name` parameter is not supplied, the method returns an array of integers that indicates the index of the specified node with respect to all of its siblings, the index of that node's parent with respect to all of its siblings, and so on until the document root is reached. |
| | When the `node_name` parameter is specified, the returned array contains entries only for nodes of the specified name, and the indices are evaluated relative to siblings with the specified name. Zero is supplied for levels in the tree that do not have children with the supplied name. |
| | *Although this method is included in the Microsoft documentation, it was not supported by IE5 at the time of writing.* |
| • `formatDate(date,`<br>`  format, locale)` | Formats the value in the date parameter using the specified formatting options. The following format codes are supported: |
| | m — Month (1-12 ) |
| | mm — Month (01-12 ) |
| | mmm — Month (Jan-Dec) |
| | mmmm — Month (January-December) |
| | mmmmm — Month as the first letter of the month |
| | d — Day (1-31) |
| | dd — Day (01-31) |
| | ddd — Day (Sun-Sat) |
| | dddd — Day (Sunday-Saturday) |
| | yy —Year (00-99) |
| | yyyy — Year (1900-9999) |
| | The locale to use in determining the correct sequence of values in the date. If omitted the sequence month-day-year is used. |

| Name | Description |
|---|---|
| formatIndex(<br>number, format) | Formats the integer number using the specified numerical system.<br><br>1 — Standard numbering system<br><br>01 — Standard numbering with leading zeroes<br><br>A — Uppercase letter sequence "A" to "Z" then "AA" to"ZZ".<br><br>a — Lowercase letter sequence "a" to "z" then "aa" to "zz".<br><br>I — Uppercase Roman numerals: "I", "II", "III", "IV", etc.<br><br>i — Lowercase Roman numerals: "i", "ii", "iii", "iv", etc. |
| formatNumber(<br>number, format) | Formats the value number using the specified format. Zero or more of the following values can be present in the format string:<br><br># (pound) — Display only significant digits and omit insignificant zeros.<br><br>0 (zero) — Display insignificant zeros in these positions.<br><br>? (question) — Adds spaces for insignificant zeros on either side of the decimal point, so that decimal points align with a fixed-point font. You can also use this symbol for fractions that have varying numbers of digits.<br><br>. (period) — Indicates the position of the decimal point.<br><br>, (comma) — Display a thousands separator or scale a number by a multiple of one thousand.<br><br>% (percent) — Display number as a percentage.<br><br>E or e — Display number in scientific (exponential) format. If format contains a zero or # (hash) to the right of an exponent code, display the number in scientific format and inserts an "E" or "e". The number of 0 or # characters to the right determines the number of digits in the exponent.<br><br>E- or e- Place a minus sign by negative exponents.<br><br>E+ or e+ Place a minus sign by negative exponents and a plus sign by positive exponents. |

*Table Continued on Following Page*

| Name | Description |
|------|-------------|
| • `formatTime(time, format, locale)` | Formats the value in the time parameter using the specified formatting options. The following format codes are supported:<br><br>`h` — Hours (0-23)<br><br>`hh` — Hours (00-23)<br><br>`m` — Minutes (0-59)<br><br>`mm` — Minutes (00-59)<br><br>`s` — Seconds (0-59)<br><br>`ss` — Seconds (00-59)<br><br>`AM/PM` — Add "`AM`" or "`PM`" and display in 12 hour format<br><br>`am/pm` — Add "`am`" or "`pm`" and display in 12 hour format<br><br>`A/P` — Add "`A`" or "`P`" and display in 12 hour format<br><br>`a/p` — Add "`a`" or "`p`" and display in 12 hour format<br><br>`[h]:mm` — Display elapsed time in hours, i.e. "`25.02`"<br><br>`[mm]:ss` — Display elapsed time in minutes, i.e. "`63:46`"<br><br>`[ss]` — Display elapsed time in seconds<br><br>`ss.00` — Display fractions of a second<br><br>The locale is used to determine the correct separator characters. |
| • `hasChildNodes()` | Returns `true` if this node has any child nodes. |
| • `insertBefore(new_node, this_node)` | Inserts a new node object `new_node` into the list of child nodes for this node, to the left of the node object `this_node` or at the end of the list if `this_node` is omitted. |
| • `removeChild(this_node)` | Removes the child node `this_node` from the list of child nodes for this node, and returns it. |
| • `replaceChild(new_node, old_node)` | Replaces the child node `old_node` with the new child node object `new_node`, and returns the old child node. |
| • `selectNodes(pattern)` | Applies a specified pattern to this node's context and returns a node list object containing matching nodes. The string `pattern` specifies the XSL pattern-matching operation to be used. |
| • `selectSingleNode(pattern)` | Applies a specified pattern to this node's context and returns just the first node object that matches. The string `pattern` specifies the XSL pattern-matching operation to be used. |

| Name | Description |
|---|---|
| transformNode( stylesheet) | Processes this node and its children using an XSL style sheet specified in the stylesheet argument, and returns the resulting transformation. The style sheet must be either a Document node object, in which case the document is assumed to be an XSL style sheet, or a Node object in the xsl namespace, in which case this node is treated as a standalone style sheet fragment. |
| uniqueID(this_node) | Returns the unique identifier for the specified node. |

# The DOM NodeTypes

Each node exposes its type through the nodeType property. In IE5, there is also a nodeTypeString property, which exposes the node type as a named string rather than an integer. This saves having to explicitly convert it each time. Each node type also has a named constant. These make up the IDOMNodeType enumeration.

# IDOMNodeType Enumeration

The IDOMNodeType enumeration specifies the valid settings for particular DOM node types. This includes the range and type of values that the node can contain, whether the node can have child nodes, etc. Note that default string and numeric entities (such as &amp;) are exposed as text nodes, rather than as entity nodes.

| Named Constant | nodeType | nodeName | nodeValue | nodeTypeString (IE5) |
|---|---|---|---|---|
| NODE_ELEMENT | 1 | tagName property | null | "element" |

Can be the child of a Document, DocumentFragment, EntityReference, Element node.
Can have child nodes of type Element, Text, Comment, ProcessingInstruction, CDATASection, EntityReference.

| | | | | |
|---|---|---|---|---|
| NODE_ATTRIBUTE | 2 | name property | value property | "attribute" |

Cannot be the child of any other node type. Only appears in other nodes' attributes node lists.
Can have child nodes of type Text, EntityReference.

| | | | | |
|---|---|---|---|---|
| NODE_TEXT | 3 | "#text" | content of node | "text" |

Can be the child of an Attribute, DocumentFragment, Element, EntityReference node.
Cannot have any child nodes.

| NODE_CDATA_<br>SECTION | 4 | "#cdata-<br>section" | content of<br>node | "cdata<br>section" |
|---|---|---|---|---|

Can be the child of a `DocumentFragment`, `EntityReference`, `Element` node.
Cannot have any child nodes.

| NODE_ENTITY_<br>REFERENCE | 5 | entity reference<br>name | null | "entity<br>reference" |
|---|---|---|---|---|

Can be the child of an `Attribute`, `DocumentFragment`, `Element`, `EntityReference` node.
Can have child nodes of type `Element`, `ProcessingInstruction`, `Comment`, `Text`, `CDATASection`, `EntityReference`.

| NODE_ENTITY | 6 | entity name | null | "entity" |
|---|---|---|---|---|

Can be the child of a `DocumentType` node.
Can have child nodes that represent the expanded entity, that is `Text`, `EntityReference`.

| NODE_PROCESSING_<br>INSTRUCTION | 7 | target<br>property | content of<br>node<br>excluding<br>target | "processing<br>instruction" |
|---|---|---|---|---|

Can be the child of a `Document`, `DocumentFragment`, `Element`, `EntityReference` node.
Cannot have any child nodes.

| NODE_COMMENT | 8 | "#comment" | comment<br>text | comment |
|---|---|---|---|---|

Can be the child of a `Document`, `DocumentFragment`, `Element`, `EntityReference` node.
Cannot have any child nodes.

| NODE_DOCUMENT | 9 | "#document" | null | "document" |
|---|---|---|---|---|

Represents the root of the document so cannot be a child node.
Can have a maximum of one `Element` child node, and other child nodes of type `Comment`, `DocumentType`, `ProcessingInstruction`.

| NODE_DOCUMENT_<br>TYPE | 10 | doctype name | null | "document<br>type" |
|---|---|---|---|---|

Can be the child of the `Document` node only.
Can have child nodes of type `Notation`, `Entity`.

| NODE_DOCUMENT_ FRAGMENT | 11 | "#document -fragment" | null | "document fragment" |
|---|---|---|---|---|

Represents an unconnected document fragment, so cannot be the child of any node type.
Can have child nodes of type `Element`, `ProcessingInstruction`, `Comment`, `Text`, `CDATASection`, `EntityReference`.

| NODE_NOTATION | 12 | notation name | null | "notation" |
|---|---|---|---|---|

Can be the child of a `DocumentType` node only.
Cannot have any child nodes.

# XML Schemas and Data Types

While XML documents can be successfully defined using a **Document Type Definition** (DTD), there is felt to be a requirement for a more flexible way of defining the structure of XML documents. It is also accepted that there needs to be a way for the data type to be indicated within the design of the XML document to make it easier for the handling of XML documents to be mechanized.

To this end, the W3C are – at the time of writing – working on a group of proposals that come under the general heading of **XML Schemas and Data Types**. This includes the proposed **Document Content Definition** (DCD) language. Internet Explorer 5.0 supports a reasonably standard implementation of XML Schemas and Data Types, as described in this reference section. This technology is still developing in IE5 and not all of the attributes listed here may work as described at the present time.

## XML Schemas

An **XML Schema** is a description or definition of the structure of an XML document. The schema is itself written in XML. This makes it easier for newcomers to understand when compared to the need to learn the SGML-like syntax of the Document Type Definition (DTD).

IE5 includes an implementation of XML Schemas that provides eight predefined elements for use in defining XML documents:

| Name | Description |
|------|-------------|
| Schema | The overall enclosing element of the schema, which defines the schema name. |
| ElementType | Defines a type of element that will be used within the schema. |
| element | Defines an instance of an element declared for use within an `<ElementType>` element. |

*Table Continued on Following Page*

| Name | Description |
|---|---|
| AttributeType | Defines a type of attribute that will be used within the schema. |
| attribute | Defines an instance of an element declared for use within an `<ElementType>` element. |
| datatype | Defines the type of data that an attribute or element can contain. |
| description | Used to provide information about an attribute or element. |
| group | Used to collect elements together to define specific sequences of elements. |

## IE5 XML Schema Elements

This section describes each of the XML Schema elements in alphabetical order, complete with their attributes.

### The attribute Element

The `<attribute>` element is used to define specific instances of an attribute that is used within an `<AttributeType>` or `<ElementType>` element.

| Attributes | Description |
|---|---|
| default | The default value for the attribute, used when `required` is `"no"`. If `required` is `"yes"` then the value provided in the document must be the same as the default value. |
| required | Specifies if a value for this attribute is required. Can be either `"yes"` or `"no"`. |
| type | Specifies the `<AttributeType>` of which the attribute is an instance. |

### The AttributeType Element

The `<AttributeType>` element is used to define a type of attribute that is used within elements in the schema. Specific instances of the attribute can be further specified using the `<attribute>` element.

| Attributes | Description |
|---|---|
| default | The default value for the attribute. If the attribute is an enumerated type, the value must appear in the list. |
| dt:type | The data type that the attribute will accept. |
| dt:values | A set of values that form an enumerated type, for example `"roses carnations daisies"` |
| name | A unique string that identifies the `<AttributeType>` element within the schema and provides the attribute name. |

| Attributes | Description |
|---|---|
| model | Defines whether the attribute can accept content that is not defined in the schema. The value `"open"` allows undefined content to appear, while the value `"closed"` allows only content defined in the schema to appear. |
| required | Specifies if a value for this attribute is required. Can be either `"yes"` or `"no"`. This and `default` are mutually exclusive when `required` is `"yes"`. |

The `dt:type` and `dt:values` are used in the same way as in the `<datatype>` element:

```
<AttributeType name="flowername"
               default="rose"
               dt:type="enumeration"
               dt:values="rose carnation daisy lilac" />
```

Note that, although `dt` is the usual namespace prefix for data types, we can replace it with a different prefix.

### The datatype Element

The `<datatype>` element is used to define the type of data that an attribute or element can contain. At the time of writing, support for this element was particularly limited.

| Attributes | Description |
|---|---|
| dt:max | The maximum (inclusive) value that the element or attribute can accept. |
| dt:maxExclusive | The maximum exclusive value that the element or attribute can accept, i.e. the value must be less than this value. |
| dt:maxlength | The maximum length of the element or attribute value. For strings this is the number of characters. For number and binary values this is the number of bytes required to store the value. |
| dt:min | The minimum (inclusive) value that the element or attribute can accept. |
| dt:minExclusive | The minimum exclusive value that the element or attribute can accept, i.e. the value must be more than this value. |
| dt:type | One of the specific or primitive data types listed at the end of this appendix. |
| dt:values | For an `enumeration`, the list of values in the enumeration. |

### The description Element

The `<description>` element is used to provide information about an attribute or element.

| Attributes | Description |
|---|---|
| *none* | The descriptive text for the element or attribute. |

### The element Element

The `<element>` element is used to define specific instances of an element that is used within an `<ElementType>` element.

| Attributes | Description |
|---|---|
| type | The name of an element type defined in this or another schema, and of which this element is an instance. |
| minOccurs | Defines whether the element is optional in documents based on the schema. `"0"` denotes that it is optional and does not need to appear, while `"1"` denotes that the element must appear at least once. The default if omitted is `"1"`. |
| maxOccurs | Defines the maximum number of times that the element can appear at this point within documents based on the schema. `"1"` means only once, while `"*"` means any number of times. The default if omitted is `"1"`. |

### The ElementType Element

The `<ElementType>` element is used to define a type of element that is used within the schema. Specific instances of the element can be further specified using the `<element>` element.

| Attributes | Description |
|---|---|
| content | Defines the type of content that the element can contain. `"empty"` means no content, `"textOnly"` means it can contain only text (unless the model is `"open"`), `"eltOnly"` means it can contain only other elements and no free text, and `"mixed"` means it can contain any mixture of content. |
| dt:type | One of the specific or primitive data types listed at the end of this appendix. |
| model | Defines whether the element can accept content that is not defined in the schema. The value `"open"` allows undefined content to appear, while the value `"closed"` allows only content defined in the schema to appear. |
| name | A unique string that identifies the `<ElementType>` element within the schema and provides the element name. |
| order | Defines how sequences of the element can appear. The value `"one"` means that only one of the set of enclosed `element` elements can appear, `"seq"` means that all the enclosed elements must appear in the order that they are specified, and `"many"` means that none, any or all of the enclosed elements can appear in any order. |

For examples of the `content` and `order` attributes, see the section on the `<group>` element next.

### The group Element

The `<group>` element is used to collect series of `<element>` and/or `<attribute>` elements together so that they can be assigned a specific sequence in the schema. This can precisely control the order that they can appear in documents that are based on this schema.

| Attributes | Description |
|---|---|
| minOccurs | Defines whether the group is optional in documents based on the schema. `"0"` denotes that it is optional and does not need to appear, while `"1"` denotes that the group must appear at least once. The default if omitted is `"1"`. |
| maxOccurs | Defines the maximum number of times that the group can appear at this point within documents based on the schema. `"1"` means only once, while `"*"` means any number of times. The default if omitted is `"1"`. |
| order | Defines how sequences of the groups and element types contained in this group can appear. `"one"` means that only one of the set of enclosed groups or element types can appear, `"seq"` means that all the enclosed groups or element types must appear in the order that they are specified, and `"many"` means that none, any or all of the enclosed groups or element types can appear in any order. |

This example shows some of the ways that groups and element types can be used to define the ordering and appearance of elements in a document:

```
<group minOccurs="0" order="seq">

   <ElementType content="empty" name="first" />

   <ElementType content="textOnly" dt:type="string" name="second" />

   <ElementType content="eltOnly" name="third" order="many">
      <element type="thirdEqual" />
   </ElementType>

   <group minOccurs="1" maxOccurs="1" order="one">
      <ElementType content="empty" name="fallen" />
      <ElementType content="empty" name="unplaced" />
      <ElementType content="empty" name="last" />
   </group>

</group>
```

Because the main (outer) `<group>` element has the attribute `minOccurs="0"`, the entire group of elements is optional in the document. However, if the group does appear, the following combinations are some of the legal and valid possibilities:

```
<first />
<second>too slow again</second>
<third />
<fallen />
```

```
<first />
<second />
<third>
   <thirdEqual />
</third>
<unplaced />
```

```
<first />
<second>still too slow </second>
<third>
   <thirdEqual />
   <thirdEqual />
   <thirdEqual />
</third>
<last />
```

### The Schema Element

The `<Schema>` element is the enclosing element of the schema. It defines the schema name and the namespaces that the schema uses.

| Attributes | Description |
|---|---|
| name | Defines a name by which the schema will be referred to. |
| xmlns | Specifies the default namespace URI for the elements and attributes in the schema. |
| xmlns:dt | Specifies the namespace URI for the `datatype` attributes in the schema. |

```
<schema name="myschema"
        xmlns="urn:schemas-microsoft-com:xml-data"
        xmlns:dt="urn:schemas-microsoft-com:datatypes"
```

As we noted above, the `datatype` namespace prefix does not have to be `dt`, but this is the usual value, and clearly indicates to a (human) reader that the attributes prefixed by it belong to the `datatype` namespace. However, the namespace definitions (the URN parts) *must* be as they appear here.

## The IE5 XML Schema Structure

The following code shows the overall structure of an IE5 XML Schema, with the type of value expected for each attribute. Where elements can appear in more than one place, the subsequent occurrences have the attribute list removed to avoid excessive duplication.

```
<Schema name="schema_name"
        xmlns="namespace_URI"
        xmlns:dt="namespace_URI" >

   <AttributeType default="default_value"
                  dt:type="xml_data_type"
                  dt:values="enumerated_value_list"
                  name="name_or_id"
                  model="open" | "closed"
                  required="yes" | "no">
```

```
        <datatype dt:max="maximum_value"
                 dt:maxExclusive="maximum_value_exclusive"
                 dt:maxlength="maximum_length"
                 dt:min="minimum_value"
                 dt:minExclusive="minimum_value_exclusive"
                 dt:type="xml_data_type" />
                 dt:values="enumerated_value_list" />

        <description>description_text</description>

    </AttributeType>

    <AttributeType>
        ... etc ...
    </AttributeType>

    <ElementType content="empty"|"textOnly"|"eltOnly"|"mixed"
                 dt:type="xml_data_type"
                 model="open|"closed"
                 name="name_or_id"
                 order="one"|"seq"|"many" >

        <description>description_text</description>

        <datatype ... etc ... />

        <element type="element_type"
                 minOccurs="0"|"1"
                 maxOccurs="1"|"*" />

        <attribute default="default_value"
                 required="yes"|"no" />

        <attribute ... etc ... />

        <group minOccurs="0"|"1"
               maxOccurs="1"|"*"
               order="one"|"seq"|"many" >

          <attribute ... etc ... />

          <element ... etc ... />

        </group>

    </ElementType>

</Schema>
```

# XML Datatypes

Data types are referenced from the data type namespace, which is declared within the XML `Schema` element of the schema using the `xmlns:`*datatypename* attribute, for example the usual namespace name is `dt:`

```
<Schema name="mySchema"
        xmlns="urn:schema-microsoft-com:xml-data"
        xmlns:dt="urn:schema-microsoft-com:datatypes" >
```

The data types that are proposed by W3C, and supported in IE5, are shown in the next table, which includes all highly popular types and all the built-in types of popular database and programming languages and systems such as SQL, Visual Basic, C, C++ and Java. This table is taken from the W3C note at

`http://www.w3.org/TR/1998/NOTE-XML-data/`

| Name | Parse type | Storage type | Examples |
|---|---|---|---|
| string | pcdata | string (Unicode) | Ομωνυμα λεγαται ων ονομα μονον κοινον, ο δε κατα τουνομα λ ογος της ουσιας ετερ ος, οιον ζυον ο τε αν θροπος και το γεγραμ μενον. |
| number | A number, with no limit on digits, may potentially have a leading sign, fractional digits, and optionally an exponent. Punctuation as in US English. | string | 15, 3.14, -123.456E+10 |
| int | A number, with optional sign, no fractions, no exponent. | 32-bit signed binary | 1, 58502, -13 |
| float | Same as for number | 64-bit IEEE 488 | .314159265358979E+1 |
| fixed.14.4 | Same as number but no more than 14 digits to the left of the decimal point, and no more than 4 to the right. | 64-bit signed binary | 12.0044 |
| boolean | "1" or "0" | bit | 0, 1 (1=="true") |
| dateTime.iso8601 | A date in ISO 8601 format, with optional time and no optional zone. Fractional seconds may be as precise as nanoseconds. | Structure or object containing year, month, hour, minute, second, nanosecond. | 19941105T08:15:00301 |
| dateTime.iso8601.tz | A date in ISO 8601 format, with optional time and optional zone. Fractional seconds may be as precise as nanoseconds. | Structure or object containing year, month, hour, minute, second, nanosecond, zone. | 19941105T08:15:5+03 |
| bin.hex | Hexadecimal digits representing octets | no specified size | |
| char | String | 1 Unicode character (16 bits) | |

| Name | Parse type | Storage type | Examples |
|------|-----------|--------------|----------|
| date.iso8601 | A date in ISO 8601 format. (no time) | Structure or object containing year, month, day. | 19541022 |
| float.IEEE. 754.32 | as above | IEEE 754 4-byte float | |
| float.IEEE. 754.64 | as above | IEEE 754 8-byte float | |
| i1 | A number, with optional sign, no fractions, no exponent. | 8-bit binary | 1, 255 |
| i2 | as above | 16-bit binary | 1, 703, -32768 |
| i4 | as above | 32-bit binary | |
| i8 | as above | 64-bit binary | |
| r4 | Same as number | IEEE 488 4-byte float | |
| r8 | as above | IEEE 488 8-byte float | |
| string.ansi | String containing only ASCII characters <= 0xFF. | Unicode or single-byte string. | This does not look Greek to me. |
| time. iso8601.tz | A time in ISO 8601 format, with no date but optional time zone. | Structure or object containing day, hour, minute, zone-hours, zoneminutes. | 08:15-05:00 |
| time.iso8601 | A time in ISO 8601 format, with no date and no time zone. | Structure or object exposing day, hour, minute | |
| ui1 | A number, unsigned, no fractions, no exponent. | 8-bit unsigned binary | 1, 255 |
| ui2 | as above | 16-bit unsigned binary | 1, 703, -32768 |
| ui4 | as above | 32-bit unsigned binary | |
| ui8 | as above | 64-bit unsigned binary | |

*Table Continued on Following Page*

| Name | Parse type | Storage type | Examples |
|------|-----------|--------------|----------|
| uri | Universal Resource Identifier | Per W3C spec | `http://www.ics.uci.edu/pub/ietf/uri/draft-fielding-uri-syntax-00.txt` |
| | | | `http://www.ics.uci.edu/pub/ietf/uri/` |
| | | | `http://www.ietf.org/html.charters/urn-charter.html` |
| uuid | Hexadecimal digits representing octets. Optional embedded hyphens should be ignored. | 128-bytes Unix UUID structure | F04DA480-65B9-11d1-A29F-00AA00C14882 |

The dates and times above reading `iso8601`*xxx* actually use a restricted subset of the formats defined by ISO 8601. Years, if specified, must have four digits. Ordinal dates are not used. Of formats employing week numbers, only those that truncate year and month are allowed.

# Primitive XML Data Types

The W3C also recommends tokenized data types for use in XML 1.0. These are sometimes referred to as **primitive types**. The primitive types supported in Internet Explorer 5 are:

| Name | Description |
|------|-------------|
| entity | The XML ENTITY type. |
| entities | The XML ENTITIES type. |
| enumeration | An enumerated type, i.e. a list of permissible values. |
| id | The XML ID type. |
| idref | The XML IDREF type. |
| idrefs | The XML IDREFS type. |
| nmtoken | The XML NMTOKEN type. |
| nmtokens | The XML NMTOKENS type. |
| notation | A NOTATION type. |
| string | Represents a generic String data type. |

# XMLHTTP

The MSXML component supports a useful interface, IXMLHTTP, for HTTP operations. This interface supplements the load() method of the XMLDOM parser by permitting script authors more control over HTTP requests from within their pages. This interface is introduced in Chapter 6, and used extensively in the sample applications built in Chapters 8 and 9.

## Creating the Object

In its present form, the IXMLHTTP interface can only be created on the client. This is because the component is based on the WinInet library. This library will not work within a Win32 service, which is how Microsoft Internet Information Server is implemented. You can create an instance of this component with the following call:

```
mycomponent = new ActiveXObject("Microsoft.XMLHTTP");
```

## Configuring the Server

If you will be sending XML documents to the client in response to requests, some configuration steps are required on the server. First, configure the MIME map to include the type text/xml with the file extension .xml. This may be done through the Microsoft Management Console by right clicking on the server or the Web site under the server and selecting Properties. From the Web Site property page, you select the HTTP Headers tab and click on the File Types... button within the MIME Map section. Click Add in the dialog box that appears and enter the new MIME type.

Within an ASP page intended to respond with an XML document, make the following call before sending anything back using the Response object:

```
Response.ContentType("text/xml");
```

If these two steps are used, XMLHTTP will be able to automatically load and parse the document you send back. In addition, the default stylesheet for XML supported by IE 5.0 will be enabled. This is sometimes useful for debugging.

# The Interface

The IXMLHTTP interface is a COM dual interface supporting a number of properties and methods. Script authors can use this interface to perform HTTP POST operations involving XML documents.

# Properties

The MSXML IXMLHTTP interface supports the following properties:

| Property | Meaning |
|---|---|
| readyState | Read-only; indicates the state of the request. The value of this four-byte integer is taken from the following enumeration:<br><br>UNINITIALIZED (0)    open has not been called<br><br>LOADING (1)    send has not been called<br><br>LOADED (2)    send has been called, the status and headers are available, but the response is not available<br><br>INTERACTIVE (3)    partial data has been received<br><br>COMPLETED (4)    all data has been received |
| responseBody | Read-only; the response as an array of unsigned bytes |
| responseStream | Read-only; the response as an IStream interface |
| responseText | Read-only; the response as a text string |
| responseXML | Read-only; the response as an XMLDOM parser instance |
| status | Read-only; the HTTP status code for the operation |
| statusText | Read-only; the HTTP status of the operation as a text string |
| onreadystatechange | Write-only; allows you to register a readyStateChange event handler |

The property responseText can be used following a successful request to check the type of the response. If the response carries a MIME type of text/xml, XMLHTTP will parse the response into a DOM tree owned by responseXML. If parsing is successful, the root of the tree will be the value of responseXML's documentElement property.

# Methods

The MSXML IXMLHTTP interface supports the following properties:

| Method | Meaning |
|---|---|
| abort | Terminates an asynchronous request |
| getAllResponseHeaders() | Retrieves all the HTTP headers and their values following a successful call to send. Each pair is delimited by a carriage return-linefeed character |
| getResponseHeader(sHeaderName) | Retrieves the string value of the HTTP header named by sHeaderName |
| open(method, URL, bAsync, UID, Pwd) | Initializes the request |
| | method HTTP method to use, e.g., POST |
| | URL absolute URL of the request |
| | bAsync optional; true for an asynchronous request (default value; open returns immediately) or false for a synchronous request (returns when response is completed) |
| | UID optional; user name for servers requiring login |
| | Pwd optional; user password for servers requiring login |
| send(vBody) | Sends the request and receives a response |
| | vBody the body of the request. May be one of four types: a string, an array of unsigned bytes, an XMLDOM object, or an IStream interface |
| setRequestHeader(sHeader, sValue) | Sets an HTTP request header |
| | sHeader the name of the HTTP header to set |
| | SValue string form of the value of the header |

In normal usage, you will create an instance of the object, call open to initialize the request, call setRequestHeader to set the value of Content-Type to application/x-www-form-urlencoded, then call send with the body of the request. If you are expecting an XML document in response, you may then access the document in DOM tree form through responseXML just as if you were working with MSXML's XMLDOM interface. You can find examples of this usage in the sample application constructed in Chapter 8.

# Deployment Opens for Scriptlets

## Trusted Intranet

I made the assumption in the text that our sample applications are deployed on a trusted intranet. This places a burden on the organization to ensure all clients have the scriptlet files locally deployed and registered. When that is done, you have greater control over the lifetime of the object. We bring it into being with a line like this:

```
var walker = new ActiveXObject("DirectoryWalker.Scriptlet");
```

You reclaim the object's resources with the following line:

```
walker = null;
```

The object is in memory only as long as we need it. The local file location of the scriptlet is read from the registry. This gives us a great deal of simplicity when we write scripts that use the components, but it makes it harder to deploy the applications. Besides registering the components, you also have to configure security properly. On a trust-worthy intranet, you can always lower the security requirements of the browser. Is there another way to deploy scriptlet components that makes the network administrator's life easier?

## Ease of Deployment

If we still need to execute components on the client but don't want to go through the registration steps, we can revert to the use of DHTML scriptlets. We are restricted in our object's lifetime, however. The object is created when the page is loaded and reclaimed when the page is replaced. Here's how to get an instance of the DirectoryWalker on a page using this approach:

```
<BODY>...
<OBJECT id=walker style="HEIGHT: 0px; LEFT: 0px; TOP: 0px; WIDTH: 0px"
```

```
type=text/x-scriptlet VIEWASTEXT><PARAM NAME="Scrollbar" VALUE="0"><PARAM
NAME="URL" VALUE="DirectoryWalker.html"></OBJECT>
. . .
</BODY>
```

This should be familiar to you from Chapter 4. We have embedded an object on an HTML page within the body and given it zero width and height. It has an `id` of `walker` so we can address it within our script as follows:

```
sLocation = walker.SearchHome("OrderCustomerQuery")
```

There is no need to do anything to reclaim the memory used by the object as Internet Explorer will do this automatically when the page is replaced. The great advantage to this approach is that there is very little to do to make the client work – Internet Explorer does it for you behind the scenes.

# Other Options

What we've shown so far are the two "pure" options. Our principles throughout have run to making clients and servers work cooperatively but independently of one another. That is to say, the XML exchange documents provided enough information to allow a client to get the job done without the server having to know anything about the client's implementation, and vice versa.

There are, however, many variations provided we compromise the five principles to some extent. It is possible to host all the components on the server provided we accept an intermediate level of pages that share some information. A local, application-dependent server might perform the scriptlet-based functions and feed processed XML or even HTML back to the client, thereby eliminating the need for client-side processing. The servers demonstrated in the text would remain application-neutral, but the new server pages would be application-specific.

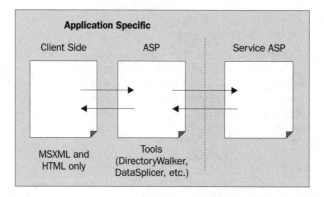

I still promote client-side components and application-neutral server pages as the ideal partitioning of distributed applications in general. You may find situations in your own work, however, where some compromise is necessary. I encourage you to experiment with the partitioning schemes I have presented in this book to find the mix that is right for your needs. The technologies presented and the five development principles are a robust set of tools. What you make with those tools is the expression of your expertise and creativity.

# Support and Errata

One of the most irritating things about any programming book can be when you find that bit of code you've just spent an hour typing in simply doesn't work. You check it a hundred times to see if you've set it up correctly and then you notice the spelling mistake in the variable name on the book page. Grrr! Of course, you can blame the authors for not taking enough care and testing the code, the editors for not doing their job properly, or the proofreaders for not being eagle-eyed enough, but this doesn't get around the fact that mistakes do happen.

We try hard to ensure no mistakes sneak out into the real world, but we can't promise that this book is 100% error free. What we can do is offer the next best thing by providing you with immediate support and feedback from experts who have worked on the book and try to ensure that future editions eliminate these gremlins. The following section will take you step by step through the process of posting errata to our web site to get that help. The sections that follow, therefore, are:

- ❑ Wrox Developers Membership
- ❑ Finding a list of existing errata on the web site
- ❑ Adding your own errata to the existing list
- ❑ What happens to your errata once you've posted it (why doesn't it appear immediately?)

There is also a section covering how to e-mail a question for technical support. This comprises:

- ❑ What your e-mail should include
- ❑ What happens to your e-mail once it has been received by us

So that you only need view information relevant to yourself, we ask that you register as a Wrox Developer Member. This is a quick and easy process, that will save you time in the long-run. If you are already a member, just update your membership to include this book.

# Wrox Developer's Membership

To get your FREE Wrox Developer's Membership click on Membership in the navigation bar of our home site

www.wrox.com.

This is shown in the opposite screen shot:

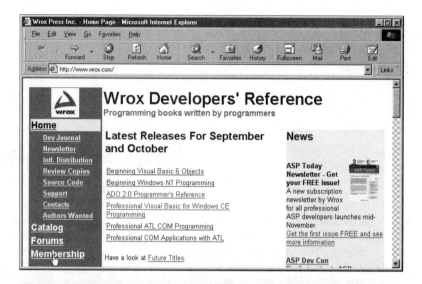

Then, on the next screen (not shown), click on New User. This will display a form. Fill in the details on the form and submit the details using the submit button at the bottom. Before you can say 'The best read books come in Wrox Red' you will get this screen:

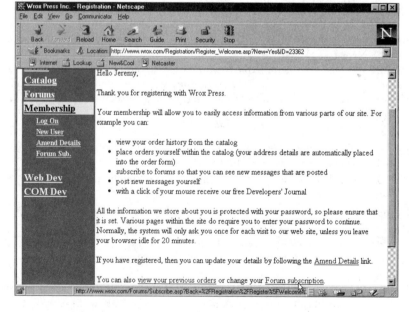

# Finding an Errata on the Web Site

Before you send in a query, you might be able to save time by finding the answer to your problem on our web site: **http:\\www.wrox.com**.

Each book we publish has its own page and its own errata sheet. You can get to any book's page by clicking on **support** from the left hand side navigation bar.

From this page you can locate any books errata page on our site. Select your book from the pop-up menu and click on it.

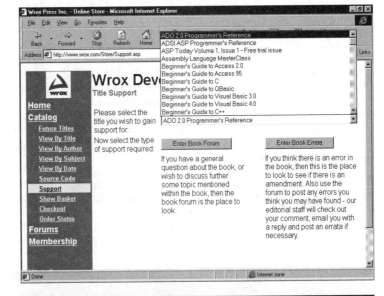

Then click on **Enter Book Errata**. This will take you to the errata page for the book. Select the criteria by which you want to view the errata, and click the **apply criteria** button. This will provide you with links to specific errata. For an initial search, you are advised to view the errata by page numbers. If you have looked for an error previously, then you may wish to limit your search using dates. We update these pages daily to ensure that you have the latest information on bugs and errors.

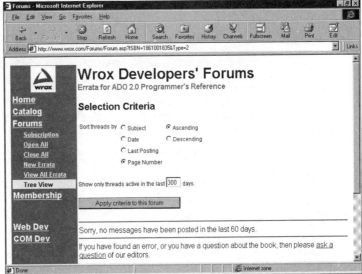

# Adding an Errata to the Sheet Yourself

It's always possible that you may find that your error is not listed, in which case you can enter details of the fault yourself. For example, it might be a faulty piece of code in the book. Sometimes you'll find useful hints that aren't really errors on the listing. By entering errata you may save another reader hours of frustration, and of course, you will be helping us provide even higher quality information. We're very grateful for this sort of advice and feedback. You can enter errata using the 'ask a question' of our editors link at the bottom of the errata page. Click on this link and you will get a form on which to post your message.

Fill in the subject box, and then type your message in the space provided on the form. Once you have done this, click on the Post Now button at the bottom of the page. The message will be forwarded to our editors. They'll then test your submission and check that the error exists, and that the suggestions you make are valid. Then your submission, together with a solution, is posted on the site for public consumption. Obviously this stage of the process can take a day or two, but we will endeavor to get a fix up sooner than that.

# E-mail Support

If you wish to query a problem directly related to the book with an expert who knows the book in detail then e-mail **support@wrox.com**, with the title of the book, the page you are having problems with and the last four numbers of the ISBN in the subject field of the e-mail. Your e-mail **MUST** include the title of the book the problem relates to, otherwise we won't be able to help you. The diagram below shows what else your e-mail should include:

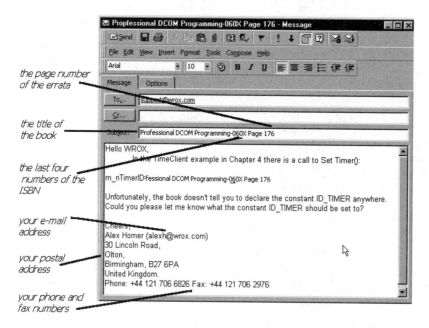

We won't send you junk mail. We need the details to save your time and ours. When you send an e-mail it will go through the following chain of support:

# Customer Support

Your message is delivered to one of our customer support staff who are the first people to read it. They have files on most frequently asked questions and will answer anything general immediately. They answer general questions about the book and the web site.

# Editorial

Deeper queries are forwarded to the technical editor responsible for that book. They have experience with the programming language or particular product and are able to answer detailed technical questions on the subject. Once an issue has been resolved, the editor can post the errata to the web site.

# The Authors

Finally, in the unlikely event that the editor can't answer your problem, s/he will forward the request to the author. We try to protect the author from any distractions from writing. However, we are quite happy to forward specific requests to them. All Wrox authors help with the support on their books. They'll mail the customer and the editor with their response, and again all readers should benefit.

# What We Can't Answer

Obviously with an ever-growing range of books and an ever-changing technology base, there is an increasing volume of data requiring support. While we endeavor to answer all questions about the book, we can't answer bugs in your own programs that you've adapted from our code. So, while you might have loved the help desk systems in our Active Server Pages book, don't expect too much sympathy if you cripple your company with a live adaptation you customized from Chapter 12. But do tell us if you're especially pleased with the routine you developed with our help.

# How to Tell Us Exactly What You Think

We understand that errors can destroy the enjoyment of a book and can cause many wasted and frustrated hours, so we seek to minimize the distress that they can cause.

You might just wish to tell us how much you liked or loathed the book in question. Or you might have ideas about how this whole process could be improved. In which case you should e-mail feedback@wrox.com. You'll always find a sympathetic ear, no matter what the problem is. Above all you should remember that we do care about what you have to say and we will do our utmost to act upon it.

# Index

# Index

# Index

# Index

# Index

# N

# Index

# Index

# Index

**456**

# XML books from WROX

### XML Design and Implementation

This is a relentlessly practical, and therefore unique, XML publication. It addresses how XML can help a group of small, specialist companies gain the market presence of large competitors. Whilst doing this Paul also explains how to ensure the application is accessible from browsers that are not XML-aware. Walking the reader through the implementation of a travel brokerage system in ASP, DHTML, and XML, it gives you enough background on XML to get you up to speed, then covers the design, construction and implementation of an e-commerce application in detail.

## XML IE5 Prog Ref

This book is about the support available in Microsoft Internet Explorer 5 for XML and its associated technologies, such as Extended Stylesheet Language (XSL) and the Document Object Model (DOM) that provides access to XML documents. Microsoft has undertaken to provide full support for XML and other associated standards in IE5. This early commitment to full standards-level support in IE5 may be the key that will give XML the chance to succeed where HTML failed in the compatibility stakes. Providing other browser manufacturers follow the published standards, we can hope to have a situation where a page works exactly the same in all browsers. However, Microsoft are also adding support for proposals that they themselves put forward to the W3C, and which are not yet ratified. This book covers these extensions to the standards.

### Style Sheets

This book is for the discerning and forward thinking web developer. One who recognises the limitations of plain HTML and wants to take full advantage of technological advancements such as CSS and XSL to create the most attractive, information packed and yet totally user friendly real world web pages. It assumes a basic understanding of HTML but requires no experience of XML. (Covers CCS1 + 2, however predates the XSL Working Draft 16th December 1999.)

## XML Applications

Provides a comprehensive introduction to XML, the language. It covers well-formed XML, DTDs (Document Type Definitions) XML schemas,...and much, much more. This is then followed up with a series of case studies demonstrating XML in action. The in-depth case studies from industry professionals make this book unique. Most books in this subject area give full coverage of the theory of XML and leave the reader asking - yes, but what can I actually use it for. This book covers the theory and provides practical examples that can be used as a guide for implementation of commercial XML-based data exchange systems.

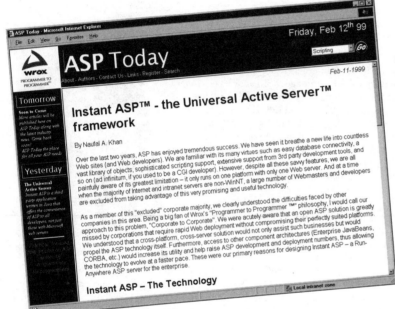

# ASP Today
### www.**asp**today.com

It's not easy keeping up to date with what's hot and what's not in the ever-changing world of internet development. Even if you stick to one narrow topic like ASP, trawling through the mailing lists each day and finding new and better code is still a twenty-four-seven job. Which is where we come in.

You already know Wrox Press from its series of titles on ASP and its associated technologies. We realise that we can't bring out a book everyday to keep you all up to date, so on March 1, we started a brand new website at www.asptoday.com which will do all the hard work for you. Every week you'll find new tips, tricks and techniques for you to try out and test in your development, covering ASP components, ADO, RDS, ADSI, CDO, Security, Site Design, BackOffice, XML and more. Look out also for bug alerts when they're found and fixes when they're available.

We hope that you won't be shy in telling us what you think of the site and the content we put on it either. If you like what you'll see, we'll carry on as we are, but if you think we're missing something, then we'll address it accordingly. If you've got something to write, then do so and we'll include it. We're hoping our site will become a global effort by and for the entire ASP community.

In anticipation,
Dan Maharry, ASPToday.com

**WROX**
PROGRAMMER TO PROGRAMMER™

Wrox writes books for you. Any suggestions, or ideas about how you want information given in your ideal book will be studied by our team. Your comments are always valued at Wrox.

Free phone in USA 800-USE-WROX
Fax (312) 397 8990

UK Tel. (0121) 687 4100          Fax (0121) 687 4101

---

**Designing Distributed Applications with ASP - Registration Card**

Name _____

Address _____

_____

_____

_____

City_____ State/Region_____

Country_____ Postcode/Zip_____

E-mail _____

Occupation _____

How did you hear about this book? _____

☐ Book review (name) _____

☐ Advertisement (name) _____

☐ Recommendation _____

☐ Catalog _____

☐ Other _____

Where did you buy this book? _____

☐ Bookstore (name)_____ City_____

☐ Computer Store (name)_____

☐ Mail Order _____

☐ Other _____

What influenced you in the purchase of this book?

☐ Cover Design

☐ Contents

☐ Other (please specify) _____

How did you rate the overall contents of this book?

☐ Excellent          ☐ Good

☐ Average           ☐ Poor

What did you find most useful about this book? _____

_____

What did you find least useful about this book? _____

Please add any additional comments. _____

_____

What other subjects will you buy a computer book on soon? _____

What is the best computer book you have used this year?

_____

*Note: This information will only be used to keep you updated about new Wrox Press titles and will not be used for any other purpose or passed to any other third party.*

*Check here if you DO NOT want to receive support for this book* ▮

**wrox**
PROGRAMMER TO PROGRAMMER™

**NB.** If you post the bounce back card below in the UK, please send it to:

Wrox Press Ltd., Arden House, 1102 Warwick Road,
Acocks Green, Birmingham B27 6BH. UK.

*Computer Book Publishers*